Digital Video Editing with Final Cut Express

Digital Video Editing with Final Cut Express
The Real-World Guide to Set Up and Workflow

Charles Roberts

AMSTERDAM • BOSTON • HEIDELBERG • LONDON
NEW YORK • OXFORD • PARIS • SAN DIEGO
SAN FRANCISCO • SINGAPORE • SYDNEY • TOKYO

Focal Press is an imprint of Elsevier

Focal Press is an imprint of Elsevier.

Kenneth Stone, technical editor
Jeffrey Warmouth and Ellen Warmouth, illustrations

Library of Congress Cataloging-in-Publication Data
Application submitted.

British Library Cataloguing-in-Publication Data
A catalogue record for this book is available from the British Library.

The publisher offers special discounts on bulk orders of this book. For information, please contact:

> Manager of Special Sales
> Focal Press
> 200 Wheeler Road, Sixth Floor
> Burlington, MA 01803
> Tel: 781-313-4700

For information on all Focal Press publications available, visit our Web site:
http://www.focalpress.com

10 9 8 7 6 5 4 3 2 1

Printed in the United States of America

Contents

Preface

The old cliche "What an age we live in . . ." is one I never thought I'd find myself muttering, and yet here I stand today looking around at the video editing possibilities on the market. Never before in the history of video have the tools been within reach for so many individuals. Cheap, high-resolution digital video (DV) cameras and desktop computers have removed the dollar sign from the list of practical reasons for not "makin' movies." The tools aren't free, but they aren't ruinously expensive anymore, either.

It used to be that you had to be in school or working in the industry to get your hands on video cameras and editing stations. To a large degree, that meant you got the perspective of two select, though admittedly broad, groups of people: the artists and the artisans—or some strange, delightful mixture of the two. That is not to say that video and film production in the past century has been lacking in quality—far from it. There's been lots of great stuff to watch, from the era of the Lumiere Brothers up to the present day. What there really hasn't ever been is a truly wide range of perspective and subject matter in video and film. The reasons are pretty simple: If only a small section of society can afford the time and money to acquire equipment and technical skills, then we are doomed to watch that small section of society's vision of the way things are.

We've had plenty of genre and documentary work about the Working Class and the Common Man, but not nearly enough Working Class- and Common Man-produced work. What a shame. And now it's more possible than ever to change that scenario. I believe it has been said, "the means of production in the hands of the people . . . ." We can stop letting the establishment make our entertainment for us and start making it for each other. We can stop waiting for people to address subject matter that is important to us; we can make it ourselves. That is the style and substance of a revolution; it's self-empowerment on a grand scale.

But with revolution and self-empowerment come responsibilities. If we intend to make our own video and film work, we owe it to ourselves, our viewers, and the medium to become skilled with the tools of the trade. Technically, digital video editing isn't really all that difficult a task, but there are some skills and habits that make it a lot easier to concentrate on the editing rather than fighting with a computer to make it do what you want. Most people in the past picked up these skills in school or in the field while working in the broadcast or film industries. For those who did not (and for a few who did, but are new to Final Cut Express), this book is for you.

The purpose of this book is to introduce new editors to digital video, the Macintosh platform, and the Final Cut Express application. Since it is assumed that the user is new and very green, the book covers capturing, editing, special effects, and output-to-tape techniques. The aim is to get the user from square one, which may be a blank slate, to square whatever, which means setting up a project correctly, learning some editing and compositing techniques, and then putting it all back out safely to tape.

How should you use this book? There are a few different ways to attack it. If you've just dropped a lot of money on a new Macintosh and you can't wait to get started, feel free to fly straight in with Chapter 1 and just work your way through the application. Periodically, you will be prompted to consult the appendixes at the back of the book for specialized information about particular topics. Don't be afraid of these advanced topics; the appendixes are free of jargon and are designed to teach you all the technical information culled from thousands of late nights of living inside this technology. There is valuable knowledge there, and you can save yourself a lot of gray hairs by taking advantage of it!

For those in film and video production programs and those looking to add digital video skills and the Macintosh platform to your repertoire, you are encouraged to sit down one fine Saturday morning and read the appendixes in total. One cannot exercise the true versatility of a medium like video without getting a good grounding in the nuts and bolts of the technology. And I also believe (as my preceding semi-Marxist rhetoric reveals) that the greatest benefit of the Final Cut DV system is that you *can* put it together yourself. You don't have to trust some middleman broker to make your editor work for you. Provided you do the homework, you can make a self-sustaining and self-sufficient editing station. Every penny you save by putting the thing together yourself is a penny you can add to funding the great video work you will no doubt produce. *Viva la revolución!*

No CD-ROM accompanies this book, because I want users to work with their own video materials from the get-go. If you do the exercises using your own video footage, you will be very confident after having completed all the chapters. Take the offered and suggested techniques as the hard-won wisdom of someone who has made most of the mistakes, some of them a few times. It's always better to learn from the painful mistakes of others, and DV editing is no exception.

This book, while comprehensive in some respects, is not the last word in DV editing. There are many different ways of approaching editing tasks, and it would be impossible to include them all in one volume. It is also not a "quick reference" guide that covers every single drop-down menu item in the application. It is not a silver bullet, promising that you'll be editing in Hollywood next week after you finish Chapter 2.

It is, however, a couple of things. It is honest, and intends to inform the reader as thoroughly as possible about the basic techniques of Final Cut Express and Firewire DV editing. It will establish a context for you to learn in, but it will not promise to learn for you. Like violin lessons, this book can't make you better without practice. It assumes that you know nothing about video beyond the On switch of your television. My mother is the litmus test here, and to her a "cold boot" is a heavy shoe in the freezer. By the end of the book, you should not only be able to navigate around the Final Cut Express editor, but you should have become familiar with video itself. It will enable the new user to move on to the next step, which is the act of editing unencumbered by confusion about what is happening under the hood of their editor. Once you master the tools, you can forget about them and *really* get to work.

Acknowledgments

Biggest thanks of all to Ken Stone. I don't know why you put up with the workload. Wait, yes I do; you are the best, man. And to Jeffu and Ellen Warmouth, for not going on a honeymoon this year. So, about that Studio Pro book . . .

Thanks to Dan "Big Dig" Berube of BossyPug, the Boston Final Cut Pro User Group, and Michael "Headcutter" Horton of Lafcpug, the Los Angeles Final Cut Pro User Group. What the heck am I saying? The whole danged FCPUGNet, Final Cut Pro User Group Network, kicked into gear by those two and Kevin "Telly" Monahan, and Sharon Franklin, and Gary Adcock, and Billy Sheahan, and Rick Young, and (I'm all out of breath) all those new user groups springing up across the face of the Earth. It is our grassroots organizations that helped make Final Cut Express and Final Cut Pro such excellent tools, and it is my honor to know and work with you all. See you all at NAB and CreativePro NY, and MacWorld SF, and . . .

Thanks to my colleagues in the Fitchburg State College Communications Media Department in Fitchburg, Massachusetts, for making our program so great to teach in. And, of course, the communications media students, who don't take it personally when I get on their case about doing their preferences.

Finally, thanks to Elinor Actipis, who has been along for the entire crazy ride. "Hey, Elinor, *new version!*" Gotcha . . .

1 The Initial Setup: Optimizing the Mac OS and Final Cut Express

Final Cut Express is a fully functional nonlinear digital video (DV) editing application. It stands alone as the most feature-rich application on the market in its price range. With this functionality comes a degree of user responsibility. The user still has to configure the application correctly and organize it for optimal performance and safety. Final Cut Express will function even if you configure it incorrectly. However, you will pay for such mistakes further down the road when you run across foul-ups that could have been easily avoided had you set up the application and project in an organized and safe fashion at the beginning.

What follows is a tried-and-true path for setting up Final Cut Express with a Firewire-based camera or deck. It is an especially effective method for multiuser editing stations in which more than one project or editor is working concurrently. If you follow these steps, you will experience few nasty surprises, and the few surprises you do encounter will be much less disastrous than if you simply plug in and begin editing.

The process for setting up your Final Cut Express station and project begins outside of Final Cut Express. The first thing we will do is to take a stroll through your Mac OS System settings and make sure they are optimized for Final Cut Express. Although you only see what is going on on the computer's Desktop, the Macintosh is constantly doing many things in the background, some of which can have a negative impact on Final Cut Express's performance. We will address the pre-critical system settings prior to moving on to Final Cut Express. For more in-depth information about the Macintosh hardware and operating software, read Appendix C of this book.

Macintosh OSX: The System Preferences

In Mac OSX, the System Preferences application (see Figure 1-2) replaces many of what were Control Panel settings in Mac OS 9. Like the old Control Panels, System Preferences is where you tell the Mac OS how to use many of its features. Access to System Preferences can be found in three different places. There will be an icon for the System Preferences on the Dock located on the Desktop. Alternately, the Apple Drop Down Menu in the top left-hand corner of the screen has a link to it. And finally, since the System Preferences window is actually an application, you can access it directly from the Applications folder inside the hard drive.

Licensed to:
charles roberts

Version:
Final Cut Express 1.0.1

B-123-FCP-555-CHA-000-WLA-456-ZZZ

Figure 1-1   Final Cut Express **Splash Screen**

Figure 1-2   System Preferences

The Energy Saver Preference

After opening System Preferences, locate the Energy Saver Preference icon and click to open. Click the Show Details button in the bottom right-hand corner to view all the possible options. You want to set System to Never and uncheck "Put Hard Disk to Sleep Whenever Possible." You can also set the Monitor Sleep to Never, although you may want to check it for a separate sleep setting—for instance, 15 minutes (see Figure 1-3)—to prolong its life and save on bills and CRT-generated heat, since monitor sleep should have no effect on Final Cut Express's performance. Once you have Energy Saver set, hit the Show All button in the top left corner of the window to return to the original System Preferences screen.

The Displays Preference

Next, from the System Preferences panel, click the Displays Preference icon. Here you can control not only how your monitors are set, but how multiple monitors are arranged with each other. On the right side of the panel, make sure to choose a refresh rate of 75 Hz or higher. If such a rate is not available, select a lower resolution on the left side of the window, and then see if 75 Hz is available. Make sure that Colors is set to Millions (see Figure 1-4).

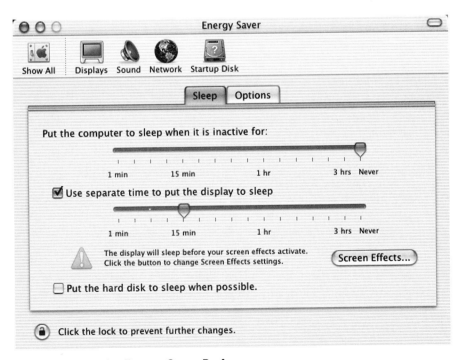

Figure 1-3 Setting the Energy Saver Preference

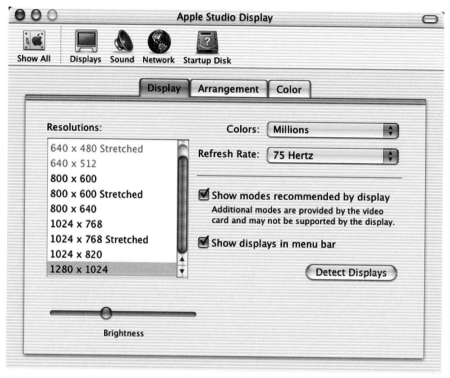

Figure 1-4   Setting the Displays Preference

If you have to select a smaller screen size than you feel comfortable working with, look into purchasing a new, more efficient monitor that can support higher screen resolutions at the refresh rate of 75 Hz. Although you can work in Final Cut Express with a screen refresh of 60 Hz, be aware that Final Cut Express's performance can suffer when the application is run at this lower refresh rate. In addition, you will soon find that 60 Hz can cause eyestrain because of the perceptible flicker that accompanies it. Editing usually involves a great deal of quickly focusing your eyes on the computer screen, and low refreshes like 60 Hz can lead to headaches and eye strain.

Note: *Never* deselect "Show Modes Recommended by Display." Although in rare cases you can get away with a better refresh rate that is unsupported by Apple and the monitor manufacturer, it is quite possible to accidentally select a refresh rate that your monitor cannot support but that the OS will not reject! If you do this, you may lose your display, which will be replaced with a message from the monitor that reads something on the order of "Scan Rate Out Of Range." Your computer is still working cheerfully away, waiting for you to respond, but it has no idea that you can't see the screen it thinks it is displaying.

If you choose a resolution that your monitor cannot display, give it at least 15 seconds before beginning the process of correcting this dreadful error. When you change the resolution of your monitor through the System Preferences panel, usually you will be given a dialog box asking you to confirm the change. This is precisely to avoid the situation in the previous paragraph. However, be warned that sometimes this message does not appear, and you will have to perform some interesting contortions to correct the problem. If you accidentally choose a scan rate the monitor cannot support, you'll have to reboot into Mac OS 9 to manually remove the System Preferences file and reset display. Since Mac OS 9 is not an option on newer Macintoshes, you need to be very careful with this.

Software Update

A final System Preference that should be visited is Software Update. When enabled, this feature automatically connects to the Internet periodically to check for updates to the system's software (see Figure 1-5). There are a few reasons to disable this automatic checking feature. First, if you are not on a WAN network or cable/DSL connection, Software Update will engage the modem and try to call your ISP. It is just doing its job, but remember that it is likely to do so when you are not at home as well! If you keep Software Update disabled, you can manually run the Updater at more suitable times.

Further, the capturing of video is a very system-intensive activity. Network activity, as we will see in the next section, can have serious negative impacts on system performance, and downloading and installing software from the Internet is a particularly demanding set of operations. Since the default Software Update checking time varies, your machine may try to look for updates at the worst possible moment. Disabling will avoid this problem.

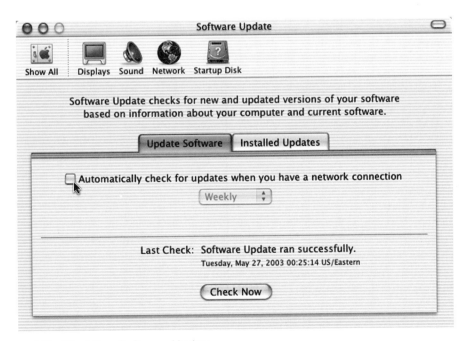

Figure 1-5 Disabling Software Update

Finally, disabling can eliminate a complication that has plagued video editors since the beginning of computer-based editing solutions. Although software updates generally deliver improved performance, it is an understood rule of thumb that you never want to make serious changes to your system's software in midproject. Nothing is more frustrating than allowing a system update to occur and then finding out that some small piece of it conflicts with your present third-party software. The time to upgrade your system is between projects or, at the very least, when you have some breathing space and the ability to patiently troubleshoot if you do run into problems.

Network Issues and AppleTalk

After setting the other System Preferences, click the Show All button in the upper left corner of the window and return to the System Preferences window. Find the Network Preference button and hit it. When the Network Preferences window loads, change the drop-down bar from Internal Modem to Built-in Ethernet, as shown in Figure 1-6. Select the AppleTalk tab. Uncheck Make AppleTalk Active, as shown in Figure 1-7.

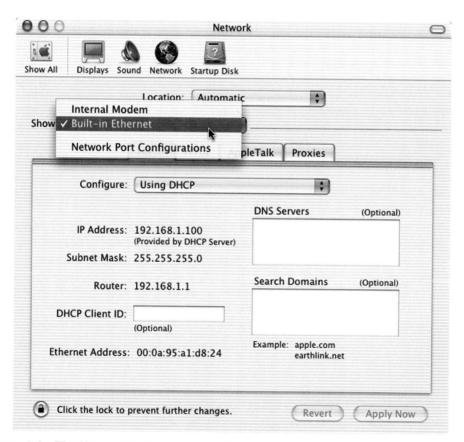

Figure 1-6   The Network Preferences panel

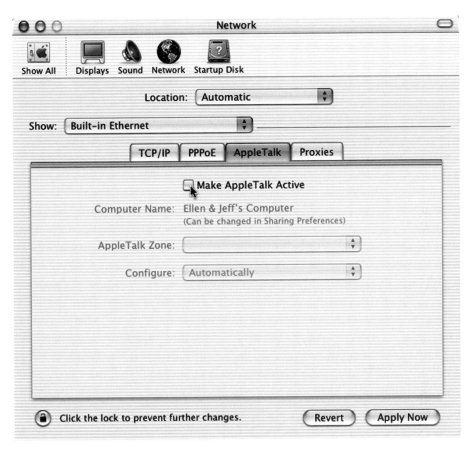

Figure 1-7 Making AppleTalk inactive

One of the nicer things about Mac OSX is its incredibly sophisticated network capabilities. The operating system really does do most of the work for you if you need to set up a network. Simply plug up your Mac to a hub/router/switch and plug your other systems in, and let the Mac OSX figure out and negotiate the protocols. Connecting with other computers and printers is effortless, even for a network novice.

Unfortunately, there are some situations where being on a network while running Final Cut Express could cause problems. These are rare situations, but you must take note and precautions. Whenever you are capturing or printing to tape, AppleTalk generally should be disabled. Some printers and networks must be accessed through AppleTalk, so you may want to keep it enabled most of the time. Just remember that when you are performing critical operations such as capture and print to tape, AppleTalk should be disabled, and you should remember to check it if you run into inexplicable bad behavior later on.

You should also always dismount any networked volumes before working in Final Cut Express. If you are accessing the drives of another computer through an Ethernet network, you should remove them from the Desktop of your Macintosh before running Final Cut

Express. It's easy to forget that you've mounted another machine's hard drive on your Desktop for a moment. But as you start working in Final Cut Express, any activity on the other computer that the mounted drive lives on could cause interruptions on your machine, leading to very annoying and unpredictable behavior.

A final note about networks and Final Cut Express is that being on a network is not necessarily anathematic to editing video. In fact, many editors have to rely on networks as an important part of their workflow. Clearly, the ability of your Macintosh to operate properly in a networked environment is important. The precautions about turning off AppleTalk and networked drives is simply a warning that networks, especially when utilized at critical moments, can cause lousy performance. Printing a giant file to a PostScript printer while capturing is not going to yield positive results! The injunction is not to isolate your editor from the rest of the world, but to realize that your Macintosh will likely have fits if asked to capture video and audio to a hard drive and parse out 5 MB per second to a printer or a network drive at the same time.

Multiuser and Administrator Issues

Mac OS X has fantastic administrative and multiuser functionality. It's possible to have many people using the same machine and allow each of them to contour the appearance and organization of their materials according to their own methods. It also protects individual users from their coworkers' tendency to accidentally wipe all their hard work away or steal their materials. As a final bonus, it allows a system administrator to retain total control over the workstation, keeping individual users from getting access to data they shouldn't or making changes to the hardware or software of the machine without permission.

In the past, keeping this running required additional software and some measure of professional expertise. But with Mac OS X, this level of administrative control is built into the system as a normal thing. When you get your Mac, or when you first install Mac OS X, you are installed as the Administrative User of the machine. The identity you create right then is the one that the Mac OS will regard from that point on as the user that can make changes to the system and install applications. After you configure your system the way you want, you can create new identities for each new user, and you can even allow administrative access for these new users if you choose. As the administrator, you set permissions for these users, allowing them access to different applications and files based on what you believe they will need to use while working (see Figure 1-8).

Sound like a great thing? Well it is, with a few caveats. The administrator has such control over the system that it really can't function optimally without relatively frequent oversight. Taking care of the periodic maintenance, and the rare emergencies that crop up, will usually require an administrative password. If anything needs to be changed or reinstalled, only the system administrator is allowed to perform these actions. If the administrator is difficult to track down, the system may be effectively out of service until they return! These maintenance situations can be anything from a lost password to the inability to access certain types of documents, folders, and hardware or software settings. Mac

Figure 1-8 Administering multiple users

OSX is incredibly secure, but keeping everybody locked out of everything may not always be such a great idea. For more information about setting up users in Mac OSX, consult the software manual and look into books and Web sites about Mac OSX. The more you know about the way multiuser functionality works, the more likely you'll set it up correctly and it will function efficiently and meet your laboratory needs.

Installing Final Cut Express Software

If you have now ascertained that the Mac OS is primed for editing, it is time to install the Final Cut Express software. Simply insert the CD, click the install icon, and let the installer go to work (see Figure 1-9).

Many new users are often frustrated by the process of registering their software with the provided serial number. If you try to enter the serial number that accompanies the Final Cut Express license, but the OK button remains grayed out, remember that Final Cut Express serial numbers are always a series of letters followed by numbers, followed by letters, etc. This will keep you from entering ones as Ls and so forth.

At the end of the installation process, Final Cut Express will ask you to give it some initial preset information about your equipment setup. After entering your serial number, you will be faced with a dialog box titled Choose Setup. This is simply Final Cut Express

Figure 1-9   Installing Final Cut Express

asking you to establish the initial parameters for a project. You will later be able to change anything you enter at this time. If you are unsure, simply choose either DV-NTSC (see Figure 1-10) or DV-PAL (whichever system your country uses) and pass on to the next window.

On choosing OK, you may be told that Final Cut Express is unable to locate a DV device. When Final Cut Express starts up, it will look for your DV camera or deck. The setup you just chose was telling the application which type of camera or deck it will be capturing video and audio from. If your camera or deck is not connected to the Mac, turned on, and (if applicable) switched to VTR rather than camera, Final Cut Express will ask where it is. The two choices given are Continue or Check Again (see Figure 1-11). If you will not be capturing video or printing video back out to tape, you can choose Continue

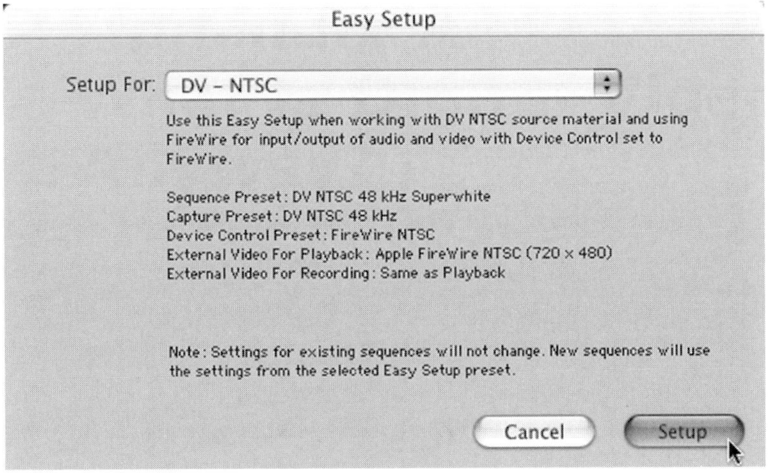

Figure 1-10 Choosing the initial setup parameters

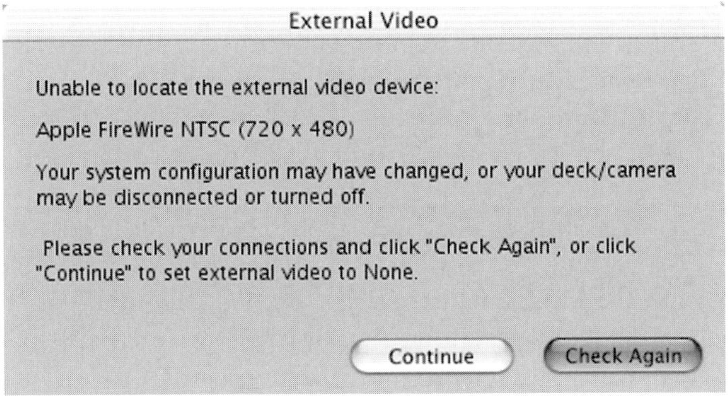

Figure 1-11 A camera or deck is not properly set up

and get to work. If you indeed need the camera or deck, make sure that it is properly connected, powered up, and set correctly; then hit Check Again. Beware that if you choose Continue when you meant Check Again, you will need to quit the application and start it again for it to see the device.

"Why bother with the camera if you aren't capturing from or recording finished productions out to tape?" you might ask. Because we can also watch our editing progress, the final video output, by using the DV deck or camera patched through to a television monitor for preview. You should also attach your external audio speakers to your camera or deck to monitor your Final Cut Express audio. This is always the preferable way to work, unless you are in a car or on an airplane, where such monitoring is impractical, or you are accessing the Real Time Effects that are only available with Firewire output disabled.

One of the greatest features of Final Cut Express is that your deck or camera will convert the DV coming out of the Firewire tube into real video that can be watched on a true video monitor. Although you can certainly edit using just the computer screen windows, you really can't get a sense of the impact of your edits until you see them play back in all their glory on an external video monitor. Colors will be different, playback on the computer screen may seem slightly stuttery, and in general what you see is not exactly what you get. However, what you see coming out of the Firewire connection and displayed on an external video monitor is what your final product will look like.

It is also very difficult to get a sense of audio and video sync when you are working only with the computer screen windows. Since audio follows video out through Firewire to the DV deck or camera, you can get timing down much tighter in your cutting when you base your editing decisions on what you see and hear in the external video monitor. Many new users are often confused by the fact that what happens on their computer screen window appears to be slightly out of sync with audio and video going out to the DV deck or camera and the external monitor. The best solution to this is to always monitor your editing progress by using your DV device hooked up to a video monitor with external audio speakers, as shown in Figure 1-12.

In addition, many users wonder initially why their text and graphics images look so bad on the computer monitor. The fact is that previewing these project elements in the Canvas and Viewer windows yields poor results. The Canvas and Viewer windows lower the quality level somewhat on the computer screen in order to salvage a little computer processing power. It is only on the true Firewire DV output to an NTSC or PAL monitor that you are able to make qualified judgments about the elements in your projects. You will also feel much better about your work when you see it the way it is supposed to look. Desktop previews in the Canvas and Viewer are exactly that—previews. They are meant only to get your project roughly in shape, not for critical judgment.

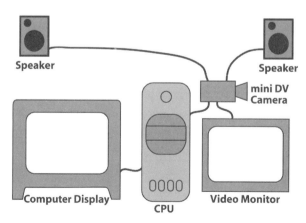

Figure 1-12   How to properly configure the components in your system

Project Setup: Do It Right the First Time and Every Time

So, you have completed the necessary installation steps and given the setup information. The next step is to set things up so that the application works properly. Then we want to create and save a new project. Finally, we want to institute an archival backup process that will keep us working even in the unlikely event that something happens to our original project file.

Starting Up Final Cut Express

To start up Final Cut Express, double-click the Final Cut Express icon, located in the Applications folder on your hard drive. You can create an alias, or application shortcut icon, by Control-clicking the Final Cut Express icon, selecting Make Alias, and then dragging the new alias to the Desktop of your Macintosh. You can also create a link to Final Cut Express by dragging the application directly from the Applications folder to the Dock. Whenever you want to start Final Cut Express, click the alias or the icon in the Dock.

    If you have just installed Final Cut Express, when you start it for the first time, it will open with a new Untitled Project. If, on the other hand, Final Cut Express was already installed and you have already created a project, it will open the project that was open when the application was last shut down. If you are looking at an Untitled Project in the Browser window, you should immediately name and save your new project (see Figure 1-13).

Figure 1-13 Never save a project as "Untitled"

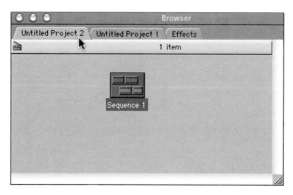

Figure 1-14   Multiple projects can be open in the browser simultaneously

Final Cut Express will actually let you name and save your project using "Untitled Project." But "Untitled" is never a suitable name for a project, especially since every new project created will initially carry this name. To work safely and effectively, you need to immediately give your project a unique name and save it, using the process described in the following section.

There is one exception to the rule that Final Cut Express always opens the last open project when starting up. If you start Final Cut Express up by double-clicking a project file you have previously saved rather than the Final Cut Express application icon, Final Cut Express will open that project. Once you have begun working with a Final Cut Express project, this will be the preferred method of starting the application, because only your intended project will open, rather than an untitled one or someone else's. But when beginning a new project from scratch, you must start from the Final Cut Express application icon and an Untitled Project.

Now it's time to save your project correctly and set up a solid system of archived backups. This process isn't complicated or time-consuming, but it is very necessary. Most editors unfortunately do not use such a system, and they are the ones who sweat the hardest when their project file corrupts or gets trashed accidentally. If you are careful and organized, you will find not only that you never lose a project, but that you can actually return to your project at any stage of its progress. And all it takes is a couple of seconds every hour or so and keeping your eye on the ball.

If someone else's project is open in the Browser window (more on this window momentarily), as shown in Figure 1-14, go to File>Close Project to return yourself to a pristine state with no open projects. When no project currently exists in the Browser window, go to the File drop-down menu and select New Project, as shown in Figure 1-15.

Saving Your Project Correctly

After you have a new Untitled Project in the Browser window, go to the File drop-down menu and choose Save Project As. In the dialog box that follows, simply click the Where

Figure 1-15 Create a new project

drop-down bar and choose Desktop, as shown in Figure 1-16. You could also save it in your Documents folder in your Home folder, which is located in the Users folder assigned to you by the administrator.

You also want to save this project in its own folder rather than simply as a lone file sitting on the Desktop. Before you name it and click the Save button, choose the New Folder button. In the dialog box that appears, type the name "first_project_folder" and hit Create, as shown in Figure 1-17.

On selecting Create, you will be returned to the Save Project As dialog box, but you should note that you are now inside the folder you just created, which will appear on the Desktop. Finally, type in the name "first_project" and hit Save (see Figure 1-18). You have now named and saved your project correctly. We want to save and run our project files from the start-up drive, where Final Cut Express and the Mac OS System live.

But we've only completed the first part of the naming and saving process. Although we have yet to actually do anything in our project, now is the time to start our archive of backups. You want to back up your project files to something safer and more permanent, such as a CD-R or an Iomega Zip drive. All new Macintoshes ship with either a CD or DVD/CD burner, and you should take advantage of this to make your project as secure as it can be. For the particular methods for doing this with Apple's included Disk Copy or the fantastically flexible and inexpensive Roxio Toast, see Appendix D of this book.

Now that your project is correctly named and saved, return to the application by bringing it up front (by clicking any Final Cut Express window). You can also simply

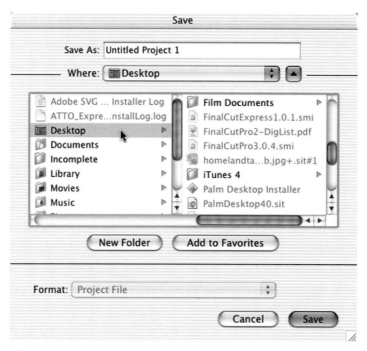

Figure 1-16 Save As

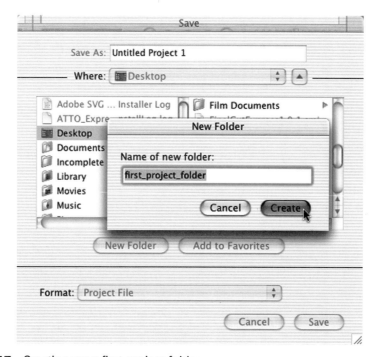

Figure 1-17 Creating your first project folder

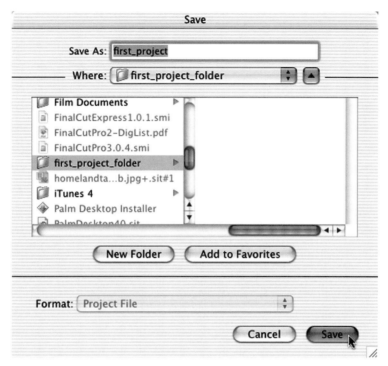

Figure 1-18 Saving your first project

click the Final Cut Express icon in the Dock, and all the windows will reappear on your Desktop.

The Structure of Final Cut Express

Now that the project has been named and saved correctly, let's take a look around and see what all those windows are for. When you created your new project, more than a few windows should have spontaneously opened up. These windows, in clockwise order from the top left (see Figure 1-19), are the Viewer, the Canvas, the Audio Meters, the Toolbar, the Timeline, and the Browser windows. The arrangement you see when you start the project is the default arrangement, which you can customize in any way you like.

If you ever get mixed up and are missing windows that have somehow gone offscreen, look under the Window drop-down menu, select the Arrange submenu, and then choose Standard, as shown in Figure 1-20. This will return your screen to the Final Cut Express default window setup. If any of your windows have closed and you need to access them, they are available from the Window drop-down menu as well.

Before we begin the discussion of Final Cut Express windows, it is important to note that most of the windows utilize what is referred to as *tab architecture*. A tab in Final Cut

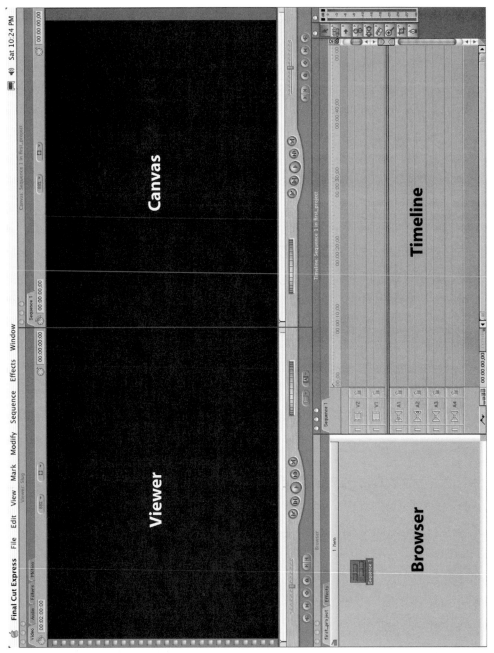

Figure 1-19 The default window arrangement in Final Cut Express

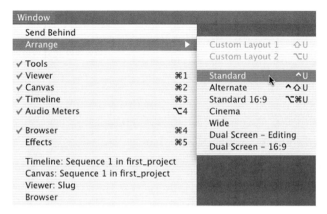

Figure 1-20 Returning to the standard window arrangement

Express is actually an individual page inside a window. This means that one Final Cut Express window may hold more than one tab, just as one filing cabinet can hold more than one folder. At the top of each window, you will see the tabs. To switch back and forth between the different tabs in a window, simply click the tab you want to bring up front.

Tabs can also be "torn away" from a window to create a new window occupied only by the "torn-away" tab. If you need to look at two tabs from the same window, simply grab one tab and drag it away from the window to create a new window, as shown in Figure 1-21. You can restore tabs to the windows from which they originated by clicking the tab and dragging it back into the window it came from. Simply let go of the tab when you see the heavy border appear around the tab you are inserting back into a window. You might want to take a moment and goof around with tearing away and returning tabs before

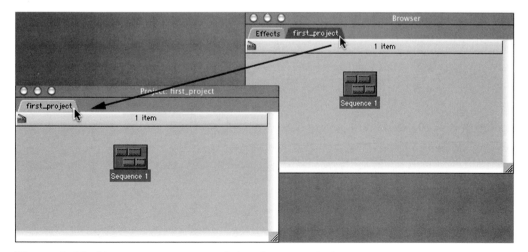

Figure 1-21 You can tear away a tab into its own window

moving on, to get familiar with this feature. It's one of the great innovative features of Final Cut Express that speeds up an editor's workflow, and being able to quickly tear a tab away and replace it can be useful when you start working out of several clip windows simultaneously.

The Browser Window

The Browser window is home to two separate tabs; the Project tab and the Effects tab. As in all windows we will explore, each tab has very specific uses and contents.

The Project Tab

The Browser window contains the Project tab, which represents your entire Final Cut Express project and all its contents (see Figure 1-22). The three objects used within the Project tab are the Clip; the Sequence, which is a linear timeline; and the Bin, which is an organizational folder. As you capture or import video, audio, and graphics clips, they will appear in this Project tab. When you create a new sequence to edit in the Timeline window, it will also appear in the Project tab. There should initially be one sequence in the Project tab, because all new projects are created with one sequence. Finally, anything that goes into the Project tab can be further organized inside bins, which are simply organizational folders that can be created in the Project tab of the Browser.

The two primary resources of a Final Cut Express project are the Sequence, the linear timeline into which we are editing the Clips, and the Clip, the individual icon that represents the media we edit into the Sequence. Both are available here in the Project tab. They are easily organized through the Bin, a folder that is used to store and organize Clips and Sequences according to your organizational needs.

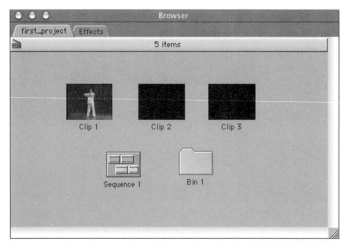

Figure 1-22 Clips, sequences, and bins in the Browser window

The Effects Tab

There is another tab in the Browser window that is always open, even when there are no open projects. This is the Effects tab (see Figure 1-23). It contains Final Cut Express's many different built-in effects, such as transitions, special effects filters, color bars, audio filters, and video and title generators. When you have clips available on the Timeline, you will be able to apply effects to them from this tab simply by dragging and dropping the effect filter you want to use on the clip. We will return to the Effects tab in Chapter 5.

The Viewer Window

The Viewer window (see Figure 1-24) is the window in which we directly work with individual clips. When you load a clip into the Viewer window by double-clicking it in the Browser or Timeline, you can manipulate it in many ways. You can play it back and review the footage. You can assign new In and Out, or edit, points, defining how much of the clip is to be used in the sequence. The tabs at the top of the Viewer window allow you to adjust features of the video and audio as well as apply special effects. These effects range from the motion-based suite on the Motion tab, which control the size, position, scale, and many other attributes of the clip, to the Filters tab and Controls tab, which offer an enormous choice of special effects plug-ins that you can apply to your work.

The general workflow in Final Cut Express is to capture clips from your DV tapes, which will appear in your Project tab. In the Project tab, you will organize these clips and sequences in bins. You will load clips into the Viewer window to trim them for use in your

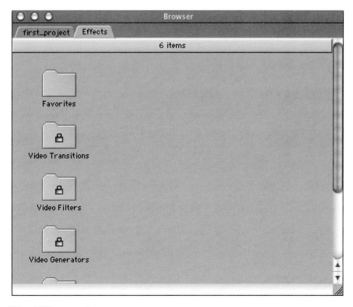

Figure 1-23 The Effects tab

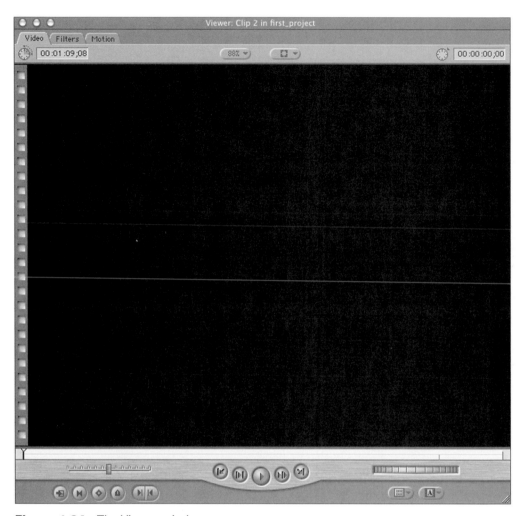

Figure 1-24   The Viewer window

edited sequence. When you are completely happy with your edit, you will play the sequence. As it plays, the video and audio will stream out the Firewire tube to your deck or camera, where you will record it on DV tape. That is your Final Cut, a term meaning the finished edited film. As you play your video from the Timeline, it will also appear in the Canvas window.

The Canvas Window

The next window is the Canvas window (see Figure 1-25), which displays a video preview of the Timeline. Whereas the Viewer window allows you to load, prepare, and preview clips

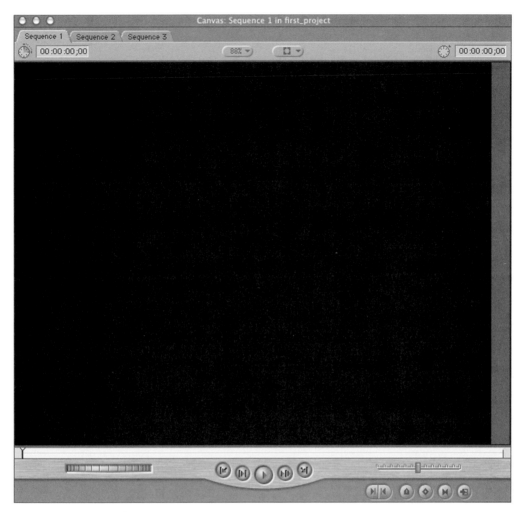

Figure 1-25 The Canvas window

for editing into a sequence, the Canvas window allows you to preview clips that have been placed into the sequence. Once again, there is a tab architecture to the Canvas, allowing you to switch back and forth between different sequences as you work, since it is quite normal to have many sequences in one project. One of the features of Final Cut Express that really shines is its ability to have more than one sequence in a project, which enables you to try many alternate edits of the same materials without having to undo your work each time.

Both the Viewer and the Canvas have video windows through which you view your progress as you edit. You can—and should—adjust these windows for optimum performance. Although some machines may have no trouble with other display settings, you

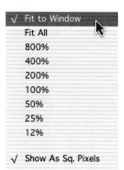

Figure 1-26 Fitting to Window

should generally set the window size to Fit to Window (see Figure 1-26) and have the window's frame size at the default size when playing back video. To get your windows back to the default size and arrangement, go to Window>Arrange>Standard. Having the video windows play at odd percentages can yield quirky performance, and 100% is usually too much to ask of the processor. Using the Window>Arrange>Standard selection along with choosing Fit to Window for the frame size will also keep you from getting the scroll bars in your video windows, which can cause severe performance problems. Scroll bars in these windows can even keep the application from outputting video to Firewire! If you have this problem, you might check your windows and set them for Fit to Window.

You should make sure that no objects or other windows ever overlap a video window when you are attempting to play back video (see Figure 1-27). Also make sure that the entire video window is visible and that there are no scroll bars along either the side or bottom of the window. If there is any cramping of the Viewer or Canvas window's style, you will get compromised performance or no performance at all. If you get Dropped Frames messages during playback, overlapping windows or scroll bars in the window are two of the first things you should check for.

Because you can have more than one project open at a time, it is easy to edit using resources from many different projects. Clips or sequences from one project can easily be edited into another one by simply dragging them into place from one open Project tab to another. Although this ability may seem minor at first glance, Final Cut Express is the only economically priced video editing application that offers this very handy timesaving feature. Rather than spending time shutting down and starting up new projects or exporting or importing huge files, you simply open whichever projects you want to access, move materials to or from them, and get right to work.

The Audio Meters

If we go clockwise, the next window is the Audio Meters. These meters show rising or falling bars in the left and right channels based on the level of audio. This allows you to keep an eye on the decibel (dB) level of your audio as well as troubleshoot your system's

Figure 1-27   Don't let anything overlap the Viewer or Canvas window

audio (see Figure 1-28). If you don't hear audio but you see audio levels in the meters, or if you hear nasty distortion but your Audio Meter levels are acceptable, it may be time to go in for a little system maintenance. Before suspecting problems in your system, though, make sure that you have your system put together correctly. If Firewire output is enabled (drop-down menu View>Video>Firewire) and you don't have external speakers attached to your camera or deck, you won't hear your audio. Audio always follows video out the Firewire tube; it is only available through your computer speakers when set to Realtime in the View>Video option.

Those with a background in analog audio should take special notice of these Audio Meters, which are based on digital audio. With digital audio, 0 dB is the highest possible audio level before clipping, or unacceptable noise artifacting, occurs. Unity, or the optimum reference level generally used by professionals, does not occur at zero as with common VU meters, but registers at −12 dB. Thus, we will use a −12 dB reference tone when mastering to tape in Chapter 7.

The Toolbar

The next window is the Toolbar. This strip contains all the useful tools that come into play when editing (see Figure 1-29). They are the same toolset found in Final Cut Express's big sibling, Final Cut Pro. Selecting an icon on the Toolbar changes the mouse pointer, making that tool available. Some of the tools have several different variations, or toolsets, which you can access by clicking a tool and holding the mouse button down for an extra moment. These tools will be covered in the sections on editing and compositing in Chapters 4 and 5.

The Timeline

Finally, the last window is the Timeline. The Timeline is not a sequence in and of itself; it is merely a container window that holds sequences. As with the Project, Viewer, and Canvas

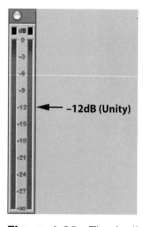

Figure 1-28 The Audio Meters

Figure 1-29 The Toolbar

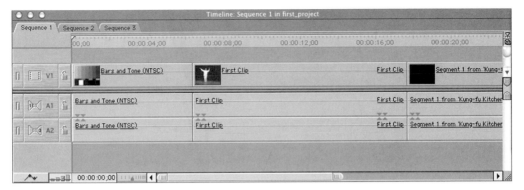

Figure 1-30 The Timeline

windows, the Timeline is based on a tab architecture so that you can have more than one sequence available in the Timeline window (see Figure 1-30). To switch from one sequence to another, simply click the tab. The Timeline window is linked to the Canvas through the sequence; whichever sequence is active in the Timeline window will be the sequence that is displayed in the Canvas window. The current location of the playhead in the sequence is displayed in the Canvas and down the Firewire tube to your monitor.

You will notice rather quickly that each of these windows is linked directly to the others. Adjustments made in one window will change the project *globally*, meaning that whenever you make a change in one window of the project, that change will automatically be reflected in the other windows. For instance, when you switch sequences in the Timeline window, the Canvas window tabs switch around to show that same sequence.

Moving a Clip Around the Windows

To see an example of this, and to exhibit the way the windows work, let's utilize a useful little video generator from the Effects tab that behaves like a clip, and pass it back and forth between the windows. Since we don't yet have any captured clips to work with, we'll use the Bars and Tone clip that comes preinstalled with Final Cut Express.

The Color Bars and Tone Generator Clip from the Effects Tab

Color bars and audio test tones are used with any video production to allow the viewer who receives edited video tapes to calibrate their equipment for the best possible playback. There is a standard audio tone, and a range of colors that you use to adjust your NTSC or PAL monitor. This Bars and Tone clip will come into play in the final chapter of the book, concerning output to tape. Since the preinstalled Bars and Tone clip acts just like a regular captured clip, we'll use it for example footage.

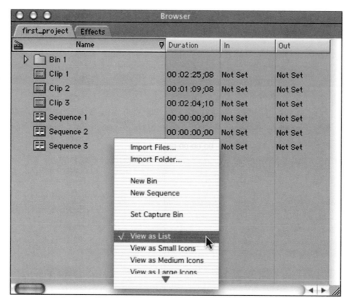

Figure 1-31   Control-click to access a contextual menu

First, make sure that the Project tab in the Browser is set to be viewed as a list, rather than as icons. To view it as a list, click the Browser window so that the Project tab is active, and then go to the View drop-down menu. Select the Browser Items submenu, and then choose As List. Alternatively, hold down the Control key and click (or Control-click) in the gray area of the Project tab and choose List view. Control-clicking will often reveal a contextual menu that offers shortcuts to common actions, such as changing the Browser view, as shown in Figure 1-31. As you get started editing in Final Cut Express, it's a good idea to Control-click periodically to find out what contextual menu shortcuts are available in each area and editing situation.

If any of your Project or Effects tab items appear as icons rather than a vertical list with information columns to the right, perform this View As List action for each separate tab or bin of the Browser. For this exercise, it is important to see the items as a list.

Moving the Clip from the Effects Tab to the Project Tab

Go to the Browser window and click the Effects tab. Grab the tab, drag it away from the Browser window, and drop it so that it becomes its own window. Locate the Video Generators bin and double-click it. The Video Generators bin will open up into yet another new window.

In the Video Generators bin, locate the Bars and Tone clip. There will be two Bars and Tone clips available—one for NTSC and one for PAL. Select the one that is correct for

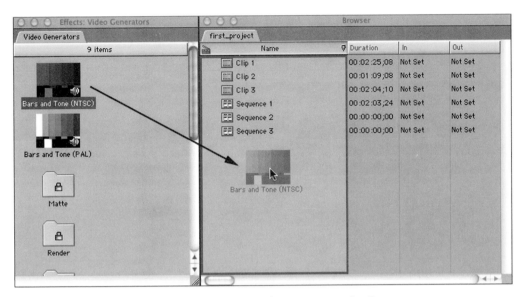

Figure 1-32 Dragging Bars and Tone from Generators to the Browser

your video standard and drag it from the Effects tab into your Project tab in the Browser window, as shown in Figure 1-32.

Creating a Bin and Using It as an Organizing Tool

With the Project tab active, go to the File drop-down menu and select New, followed by Bin in the submenu that appears, as shown in Figure 1-33. Alternatively again, you could have Control-clicked the gray area of the Project tab. A new bin will appear in the Project tab. When a new bin is created, the name of the bin will be highlighted. Immediately type in the name "First Bin." If the bin's name is not highlighted, single-click the default name "Bin 1" to highlight the name; then you can change it.

File		
New Project	⌘E	
New	▶	Sequence ⌘N
Open...	⌘O	Bin ⌘B
Close Window	⌘W	
Close Tab	^W	
Close Project		
Save Project	⌘S	
Save Project As...	⇧⌘S	
Save All	⌥⌘S	
Revert Project		
Restore Project...		

Figure 1-33 Creating a new bin

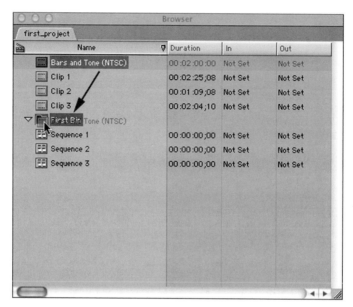

Figure 1-34   Dragging Bars and Tone to your bin

After renaming the bin, grab the Bars and Tone clip you just dragged from the Video Generators bin and drop it onto the First Bin icon (see Figure 1-34). It will disappear inside (hold the clip on the bin until you see that the bin is selected). If you double-click the First Bin, it will open into its own window, showing you the Bars and Tone clip inside. You've just completed your first act of project organization! You also could have opened up the bin first and dragged the Bars and Tone clip into the bin's window, although simply dropping the clip on the bin's icon is certainly faster and does exactly the same thing.

Moving the Clip from the Bin to the Viewer

Now let's open the Bars and Tone clip in the Viewer. This can be done in two ways. You can drag the clip physically from the First Bin into the Viewer window (see Figure 1-35), or simply double-click the clip in the bin. When you do either, the title at the top of the Viewer window will change, revealing that the clip loaded in the Viewer is the Bars and Tone clip from your project.

Clicking the play button in the Viewer window will begin playback of the clip. You will hear the 1 KHz audio test tone that accompanies the video color bars in the Bars and Tone clip. A quick glance at the Audio Meters window will show that the 1 KHz audio test tone registers at −12 dB, exactly as it should.

Although the color bars show no motion, the little yellow indicator (called the Playhead) near the play button at the bottom of the Viewer window moves along as the clip plays. You can click anywhere in the current time indicator bar and drag to move back and

Figure 1-35 Dragging Bars and Tone into the Viewer

forth in the clip. After we have captured a little video, you will see all the frames play back here, rather than the static color bars image.

Clicking the tabs at the top of the window reveals other aspects of the clip. The Audio tab (see Figure 1-36) shows a solid gray mass for levels, because the clip is a test tone with no variations in audio level. In other video clips you will work with, you will see a *waveform*, or a graphic representation of how loud or soft a clip's audio is. You will also be able to adjust those levels on this tab.

The Filters tab has no Effects filters listed, because we have not yet applied any. These will be covered later in Chapter 5, where we encounter compositing and special effects. The Motion tab presents many options, including the ability to change the size, position, rotation, and scale of the clip so that we can create professional-looking effects easily and naturally. We will also cover these in Chapter 5.

Moving the Clip from the Viewer Window to the Sequence

To move the clip to a sequence in the Timeline window, we can once again choose from a few different techniques, each of which will produce the same result. First, click anywhere in the video window of the Viewer that has the Bars and Tone clip loaded. Continuing to hold down the mouse button, drag the clip down into the beginning of the sequence on the Timeline window (see Figure 1-37). It will appear there as a long linear clip and stay positioned wherever you drop it. You have just edited your first clip into the Timeline.

Another method of moving the clip to the sequence is to grab the Bars and Tone clip in the Viewer as in the previous example, but this time drag it instead into the Canvas window and continue holding down the mouse button. Doing so will reveal a graphic overlay of boxes in the Canvas window proposing several different types of edits. Final Cut Express is asking how you wish to put the clip into the sequence. We will cover these in detail in Chapter 4, which covers editing techniques, but for now, drop the clip onto the red Overwrite box (see Figure 1-38). The clip will appear in the sequence in the Timeline window. It will be placed wherever the sequence playhead was positioned right before the edit took place.

Having completed either of these actions, you will find that there is now a Bars and Tone clip in the sequence in the Timeline window and that the Canvas window also now displays the Bars and Tone clip (see Figure 1-39). Clicking the play button in the Canvas window will show the current time indicator moving forward and, once again, we will hear the 1 KHz audio test tone.

These are not the limits of our ability to move clips around Final Cut Express, merely the basic methods meant to show how the windows work together in a project. For instance, we could have simply dragged a clip directly from the bin to the sequence or the Canvas if we had no need to work with it in the Viewer. There's really very little limit on how you can work with clips and sequences inside your project.

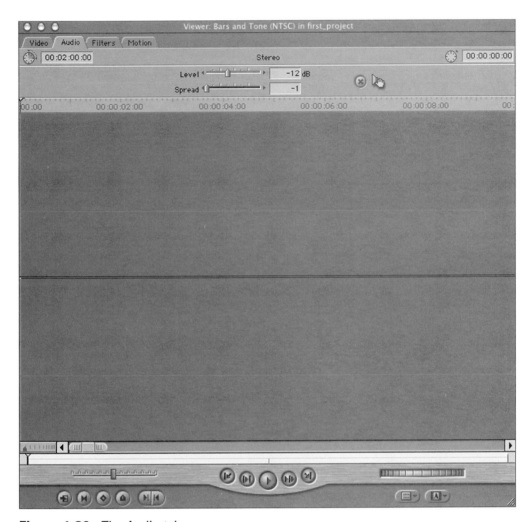

Figure 1-36   The Audio tab

Figure 1-37 Dragging Bars and Tone from the Viewer to the Timeline

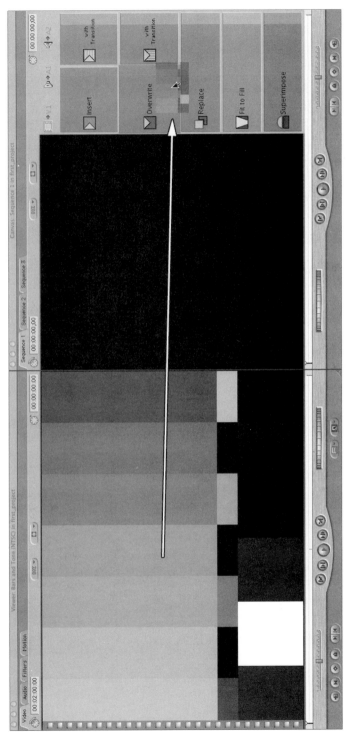

Figure 1-38 Dragging Bars and Tone to the Canvas will perform an overwrite

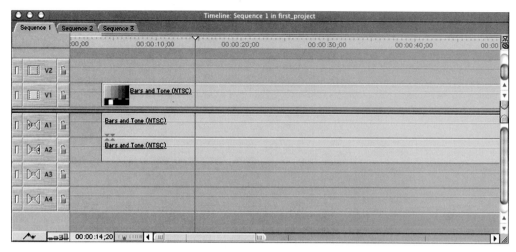

Figure 1-39   The Bars and Tone clip in the Timeline

But we get ahead of ourselves. The main thing to remember as you work through Final Cut Express is that there is always more than one way to get something done. The options are there to help you increase productivity and speed, based on the individual nature of your project and media. The more you work, the clearer this will become and the better judge you will be of which method is best for your needs.

2 Getting Your Footage into Final Cut Express

What Is Media and What Is Capturing?

In order to build a project, you need media to work with. Media is much more than just video or audio that you capture from Firewire. The term *media* refers to any content that you use in a project. This can range from video and audio captured from DV tape to audio imported from an audio CD. You can also use image files created in applications such as Adobe Photoshop or image sequences from compositing applications such as Adobe After Effects, Discreet Combustion, or Pinnacle Systems Commotion. You can even import special vector-based files such as the Macromedia Flash file format. In short, you can use nearly anything you can create elsewhere.

Anything that you bring into a Final Cut Express project to work with is media. This seemingly simple concept is an important one. There is a tendency among new users of nonlinear editing applications to think of the objects in the Browser window or Timeline as the actual media files themselves. This is an intuitive conclusion that unfortunately oversimplifies what is actually going on when you capture or import, and can lead to problems.

When you bring resources like video and audio into Final Cut Express, you are allowing Final Cut Express to access video, audio, or other such media files that exist somewhere on your hard drives. The clip that you see in the Viewer and in the sequence is not the actual media but is really just a reference or pointer to the real media; they are simply graphic icons that point to a media file. When you edit, you are telling Final Cut Express how much of the original media file to display.

The Clip icon, the pointer, is just computer code and is a part of your project file. Its code is used to determine how much of the captured media file is accessed and the way it is displayed. When you use an effect or you trim a clip for use in a sequence, you are not really affecting the media file on your hard drive. You are simply telling Final Cut Express how to display the media file in your project. The media icon in your Project tab can direct the media to appear shortened or lengthened and arranged in any order or repeated endlessly. It is said to be nonlinear, hence the name "nonlinear editor." This concept is also referred to as *nondestructive editing*, because you are making changes to the clip in your project file, not to the actual media. You are only changing the way that Final Cut Express displays the media when it plays back.

This is to be contrasted with the venerable system of linear tape editing, in which one edits with the original tape media and must assemble each piece in the order it is to occur in playback. The convenience of nonlinear editing should be obvious compared with this. In linear tape editing, if you aren't happy with an edit you have made, you must go back and re-record a new edit the way you want it using the original tapes. In addition, all the edits you have made following the edit you are changing generally must be reedited.

With a nonlinear editor, on the other hand, we can simply arrange our clips in the sequence in any order that we like. Not happy with an edit? Just rearrange the clips. Since the clip is just referring to a media file, it makes no difference where it is displayed in the sequence; it will play back every time in just the way you planned it.

The reason for belaboring this point is that the safe and secure capturing process depends on our understanding of what media is, the distinction between our project clips and our actual media files, and where those media files go when we capture or save them. In this chapter, we will investigate the proper procedure for getting media into our project. We will first set all the necessary Preferences and Easy Setup to make sure that our media comes into the project properly so as to avoid problems later on. Then we will walk through the process of capturing our media so that we can edit with it.

Setting the Preferences and the Easy Setup

The first step before capturing media is setting up Final Cut Express's Preferences and the Easy Setup. This step is an absolute necessity. Some other applications do not require the user to alter the default preferences at all. Many of the settings in Final Cut Express, however, directly affect the way it functions and interacts with the Mac OS, your camera or deck, and hard drives. Thus these settings must be checked and set correctly. Users who skip taking care of these settings usually pay for it in frustration later on down the line.

Preferences are mostly concerned with the toolset and functionality of Final Cut Express and, generally speaking, won't require changing until your working methods themselves change (the one important exception is that of Scratch Disk Preferences assignment). Preferences define the workflow of Final Cut Express and allow you to focus the way you approach editing. These settings are generally not application-critical; changing them in most cases would not cause Final Cut Express to malfunction.

The Easy Setup and the Scratch Disk Preferences located in the Preferences window, on the other hand, are directly related to how Final Cut Express deals with your particular hardware and software situation. These settings are critical to Final Cut Express's functioning correctly, and you must define them.

Unlike the Mac OS System settings you completed in Chapter 1 that must be set or checked only initially or when you encounter system misbehavior, the Easy Setup and the Scratch Disk Preferences should be checked and set properly whenever you work with Final Cut Express. Setting the preferences is a very quick process, and Apple has instituted some great preset tools for streamlining the preferences process. However, you should check them every time, especially if you are not the sole user of FCE or if there is more than one active Final Cut Express project per machine. Depending on how your editing station has been configured under Mac OSX, it is possible that no one else has reset your Preferences or Easy Setup; but even under these circumstances, it's always a good idea to check them every time to keep up with how your system is configured and where you are storing media and backup files. It only takes a second, but it could save you hours.

The reason for this is that Final Cut Express does not store or link your preference settings with your particular project file. Thus, when you start a Final Cut Express project, the preferences you encounter will be whatever they were set to the last time Final Cut Express was used. In a multiuser environment not configured with separate User Login Identities for each user, this can have disastrous effects if it is allowed to get out of control. Setting preferences is a user's responsibility; the awesome flexibility of Final Cut Express really depends on the individual users keeping their end of the bargain and doing their settings.

The Essential Preferences

Open the Preferences dialog box in the Final Cut Express drop-down menu. A dialog box with four tabs at the top will appear, as shown in Figure 2-1.

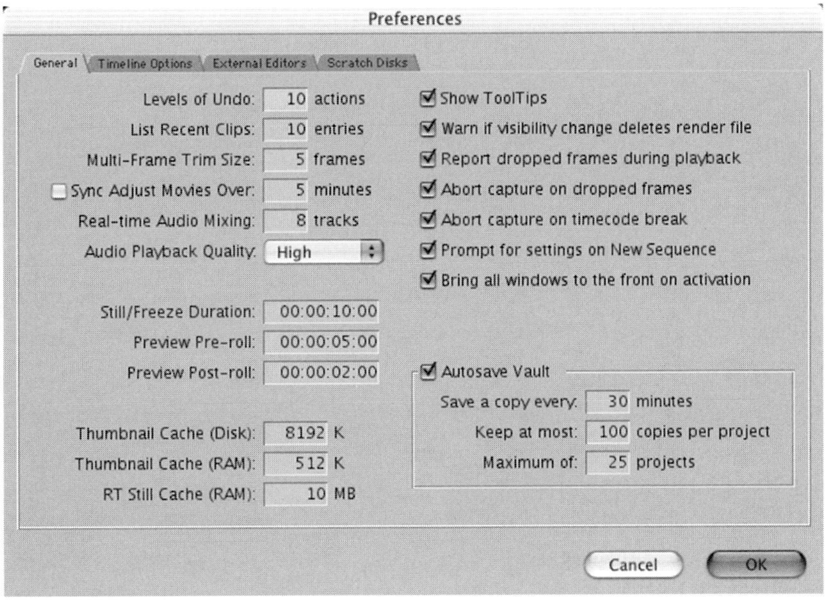

Figure 2-1 General Preferences

The General Preferences Tab

The first tab is General settings. Many of the items on this tab have important implications in the workflow of Final Cut Express and can ensure that the application warns you in the event of problematic behavior. Although some settings on this and other Preferences tabs do not directly affect Final Cut Express's performance, as we go through and set the crucial ones, we will also visit the other items and discuss their functionality.

Levels of Undo

The first item is the Levels of Undo. Levels of Undo are the number of actions that you can undo in sequential order should you make a mistake while editing or simply want to go back to where you were. Having a certain number of actions available for undoing is very handy if you want to try something in your editing that you're not sure you will want to keep, or if you make a mistake. If you don't like the results of any action, select Undo from the Edit drop-down menu or simply hit Command-Z, the keyboard shortcut. Final Cut Express will return your project to the way it was prior to initiating the last action. You can go backward in your actions as many times as you have specified in the Levels of Undo setting in the General tab of the Preferences (see Figure 2-2). Undoing also acts as a sort of "actions list" in that you can redo actions you have undone, by using the keyboard shortcut Command-Y.

The number of undoable actions can be set up to 99, although be warned that greater levels of Undo require more RAM. As you perform each action, it is stored in Final Cut Express's RAM allocation for instant removal should you choose to undo it. The more actions you store away, the more RAM you burn up. There are more effective ways of returning to earlier versions of your project, and it is recommended that you leave Levels of Undo set to the default value of 10.

List Recent Clips

The List Recent Clips box (see Figure 2-3) allows you to specify how many recently used clips are displayed in a certain pop-up menu of the Viewer window. This can be a handy way to access clips you want to work with without having to manually drag them across the Desktop. The default value here is 10, although you can set it for up to 20. However, 20 is too many to choose from in most situations and will create a giant drop-down bar if set that high. Leave this set at the default of 10 unless you find that you need more to speed up your working style.

Levels of Undo: [10] actions

Figure 2-2 Setting Levels of Undo

List Recent Clips: [10] entries

Figure 2-3 List Recent Clips

Multi-frame Trim Size

Multi-frame Trim Size is a setting for a specialized editing tool within Final Cut Express. Each editor has an opinion about how many frames should be available for quick trimming in the Trim Edit window, and until you have used it, leave this set for the default of five frames (see Figure 2-4). When you get to the editing stage and begin using the Trim window, you will find that this setting not only allows for a very precise adjustment of your edit but also helps you make very quick adjustments of the edit. This is not an application-critical setting but one that should be set according to your editing style.

Sync Adjust Movies Over

This setting (see Figure 2-5) is fraught with confusion in the community of Final Cut Express and Final Cut Pro users. To dispel that confusion, we need to understand what this feature is supposed to address and how it works. The Sync Adjust Movies (SAM) feature was designed to deal with the issue of nonstandard audio sample rates in prosumer DV cameras and decks, particularly the Canon XL1 DV cameras.

For the moment, use the following guideline for setting Sync Adjust Movies. If you are using footage recorded with the Canon XL1 camera and your clips are longer than 5 minutes, you should enable this feature. If you are using any other cameras or decks, you can safely disable it. Just remember that if you have even a hint of timecode breaks on your tape, or you are using a DV converter or any DV device that does not access timecode, you should disable it. For more detailed information about the nature of the problems that SAM fixes (and potentially causes), see Appendix A.

Real-time Audio Mixing

The Real-time Audio Mixing setting (see Figure 2-6) allows you to put a limit on the number of audio tracks in the sequence that Final Cut Express will attempt to play back without rendering. You can have up to 99 tracks of audio in any sequence, but your system hardware determines how many of these can be played back simultaneously without having to be mixed together in a rendering process.

The default value of eight tracks is the maximum for Firewire configurations of Final Cut Express, provided there are few or no audio filters. Eight tracks of real-time mixed audio should perform fine in a system that has the recommended amount of RAM and is using a hard drive configuration that isn't below par or overly fragmented. If you use more

Figure 2-4 Multi-frame Trim Size

Figure 2-5 Sync Adjust Movies Over

Figure 2-6 Real-time Audio Mixing

than eight tracks of audio at a time, you will likely hear the beeping alarm warning you that you have exceeded the possible number of tracks. In most cases, simply rendering the audio sections in question by using Mixdown Audio (from the Sequence drop-down menu) will allow them to be played back correctly. Audio rendering is incredibly fast. If you hear this beeping and you only have a couple of audio tracks, you should check your Easy Setup, as well as the sample rates of your clips, to determine whether you have other problems, such as seriously nonstandard sample rates.

Audio Playback Quality

The exact function of the Audio Playback Quality drop-down bar (see Figure 2-7) is a little different from what it probably sounds like. We all want the best in audio quality, right? What Audio Playback Quality really does is determine the quality of the playback of audio resampled on the fly. This could be audio resampled during playback for the reasons described in the section on Sync Adjust Movies in Appendix A. It could also be resampling of audio tracks with other sample rates, such as audio CD tracks that have not been converted using the import process, to be described in the next chapter.

High means that the best quality resampling is taking place, and the processor takes a correspondingly large performance hit, potentially causing Final Cut Express to beep and ask for an Audio Mixdown. Low means that Final Cut Express is doing a sloppier job of resampling the audio on the fly. The audio quality will be lower (unacceptably lower for most purposes other than quick preview), but the processor is taxed less, and Final Cut Express will allow more real-time audio tracks to be mixed.

Later, in Chapter 3, you will be shown the method for converting sample rates manually to avoid the need for resampling on the fly. Typically, the only time this resampling will occur is when Sync Adjust Movies kicks in, when you have gotten the Easy Setup incorrect, or if you bring in audio CD tracks without properly prepping the sample rate of the files. These are situations you should avoid by setting things up correctly, rather than using Audio Playback Quality to patch things up after the fact. Set this drop-down bar to High and forget about it. It should never come into play if you do things correctly. If you get beeping because you need more tracks of audio than the High setting will allow, either use Mixdown Audio or set this preference to Medium, which doesn't sound too bad, but is more relaxed in regard to processor demand.

Show ToolTips

Let's return to the top of the General tab, where the ToolTips setting should be enabled (see Figure 2-8), particularly for new users and those unfamiliar with the Macintosh

Figure 2-7 Audio Playback Quality drop-down menu

Figure 2-8 Show ToolTips

platform's keystroke conventions. When ToolTips is enabled, Final Cut tells you the function of any on-screen item. Simply leave the mouse pointer over the item for a couple of seconds without clicking, and a small text box will appear, telling you what the item does. The bonus is that many ToolTips boxes include the keyboard shortcut for the item as well. As we will see, keyboard shortcuts are something all users of Final Cut Express should master to speed up their workflow and reduce strain on their wrists.

Warn If Visibility Change Deletes Render File

As with all "alarm" switches, this preference should be left enabled (see Figure 2-9). It refers to a situation in Final Cut Express in which clips can become unrendered simply by turning off track visibility, a Timeline feature that is discussed in Chapter 4. Doing so can accidentally eliminate hours and hours of rendering with the push of one button. This preset simply forces you to go through a dialog box before committing to that action. Leave it enabled.

Report Dropped Frames During Playback

This setting is an alarm switch to let you know if, for some reason, playback performance was impaired and Final Cut Express was unable to play back at the required frame rate. Dropped Frames is a situation in which, for whatever reason, Final Cut Express was not able to process the video and/or audio data quickly enough to provide the 29.97 or 25 frames per second demanded by NTSC or PAL. Many different things can cause Dropped Frames; this is the primary reason for doing your Preferences and Easy Setup! Sometimes the problems are hardware-related (e.g., fragmented drives), but most often they are the result of not having your settings in order.

Dropped Frames are not acceptable. Final Cut Express is fully capable of playing back NTSC and PAL video at the proper frame rate, given that your hardware and settings are in order. If you are receiving reports of Dropped Frames, go through your settings first and make sure that you haven't missed something. You should keep the Report Dropped Frames During Playback switch enabled (see Figure 2-10) so that you become aware the instant that Final Cut Express is not performing properly. Disabling the Dropped Frames report is like trying to put out a fire by removing the batteries from a smoke alarm. If you receive a Dropped Frames warning while playing back, eliminate the problem, not the alarm.

Abort Capture on Dropped Frames

This alarm setting is similar to the preceding one. The application will halt what it is doing if it encounters impaired performance and Dropped Frames. The only difference here is that it is occurring during capture, not during playback. That distinction is unimportant.

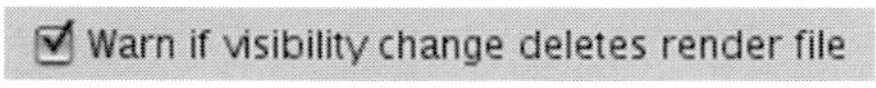

☑ Warn if visibility change deletes render file

Figure 2-9 Warn If Visibility Change Deletes Render File

☑ Report dropped frames during playback

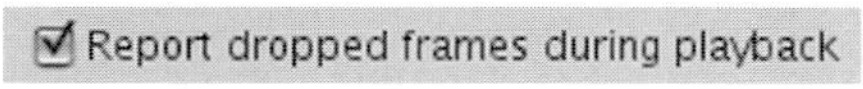

Figure 2-10 Report Dropped Frames During Playback

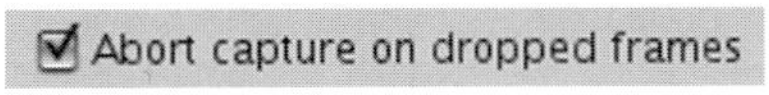

☑ Abort capture on dropped frames

Figure 2-11 Abort Capture on
Dropped Frames

☑ Abort capture on timecode break

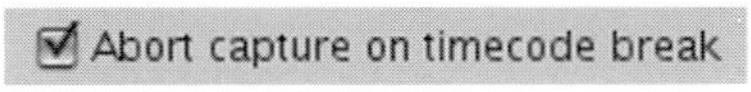

Figure 2-12 Abort Capture on
Timecode Break

Dropped Frames are unacceptable in either situation. This setting should be enabled (see Figure 2-11). If you are not capturing and playing back at the full frame rate, then you are not exercising the true value and potential of the Final Cut Express editing software.

Abort Capture on Timecode Break

Once again, this alarm switch should be enabled (see Figure 2-12). It will stop a capture if Final Cut Express encounters a break in the timecode of your DV tape. Although time-code isn't always necessary to capture DV footage, you will find that you don't ever want to work without it. Not having clips with timecode means that if something happens to your captured media files, you will have to start over from scratch.

Timecode is a system that videotapes use to identify individual frames of video. Each frame of video on the DV tape has a unique number that never changes, unlike the time counter you may have seen on consumer VCRs. This number is much like a digital clock—i.e., 01:29:15;18—where the fourth number is the frame number. For much more detail about timecode, see Appendix A.

In addition to allowing you to automate your capturing and editing process, timecode allows you to easily and effortlessly reconstruct your project from the original tapes. Unfor-tunately, if you have timecode breaks on your tapes, recapturing them becomes difficult and in some cases may be impossible. Either way, if you originally capture a clip that has broken timecode, you will not be able to automatically recapture that clip. There are ways to get around the problem of DV tape footage with timecode breaks, but the main thing to remember here is that you need timecode, you need to know when it is flawed or broken, and you should not disable the alarm that does this for you.

Prompt for Settings on New Sequence

This preset is another setting that should be enabled for safety (see Figure 2-13). When-ever you create a new sequence in the Timeline, Final Cut Express will ask you for its specifics, ensuring that you choose the right ones instead of simply using whichever sequence settings have been previously invoked. Sequence settings are some of the most critical ones, so having Final Cut Express put this reminder in front of you is a good way of making sure you never forget to do the settings correctly.

Bring All Windows to the Front on Activation

One very convenient option for users is to choose whether all of Final Cut Express's windows come up front when you switch to that application from another one (see Figure

Figure 2-13 Prompt for Settings on New Sequence

☑ Prompt for settings on New Sequence

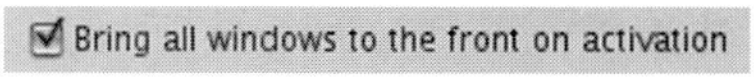

☑ Bring all windows to the front on activation

Figure 2-14 Bring All Windows
to the Front on Activation

Still/Freeze Duration: 00:00:10:00

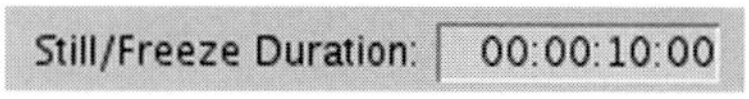

Figure 2-15 Still/Freeze Duration

2-14). Like most computers, the Macintosh can have more than one application open at a time. When you click on another application's window, it becomes the active application. Two applications cannot both be active at the same time. So it is often necessary to switch back and forth between applications.

The option offered here is that if "Bring all windows . . ." is disabled, clicking a Final Cut Express window will bring only that particular window to the front as active. If the option is enabled, clicking any Final Cut Express window will bring all of its windows up to the front of the Desktop. This feature will help you make the most of limited screen real estate, especially for those users with only one computer monitor. In general, keep this turned on so that all of Final Cut Express's windows will come up when you switch. But if you begin to work frequently with several other applications open at the same time, you may want to experiment with it disabled.

Still/Freeze Duration

This setting allows the user to determine the duration of the clip that results from importing a still image generated by another application, such as Adobe Photoshop, into Final Cut Express. It also applies to the length of a freeze frame generated by Final Cut Express. Although you can easily change the lengths of either the imported image clip or a freeze frame, this setting allows you to specify its initial duration (see Figure 2-15). The default is 10 seconds.

Preview Pre-Roll and Preview Post-Roll

These two settings are preferences that relate to the way the Canvas, Viewer, and Trim Edit windows allow the user to quickly check an edit within a user-defined range of time. That functionality is described later. For now, it's best to leave these set at the defaults (see Figure 2-16).

Thumbnail Cache, Disk and RAM

These settings allow you flexibility in dedicating drive space and RAM for thumbnails of the clips you will be working with. Thumbnails are very small icons that represent your captured or imported clips in a project and contain a still image, called a "poster frame," representing the footage in the clip. You can always adjust these amounts (see Figure 2-17) later if you notice sluggish performance in previewing thumbnail clips.

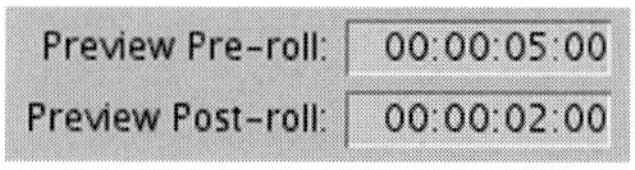

Preview Pre-roll: 00:00:05:00

Preview Post-roll: 00:00:02:00

Figure 2-16 Preview Pre-roll and Preview Post-roll

Thumbnail Cache (Disk):   8192 K
Thumbnail Cache (RAM):   512 K

Figure 2-17 Thumbnail Cache, Disk and RAM

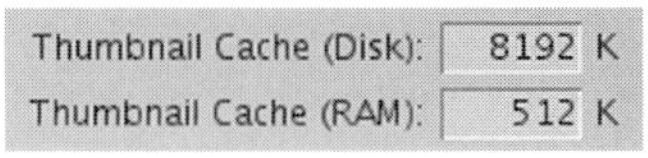

RT Still Cache (RAM)

In Final Cut Express, certain features can generate real-time effects that do not have to be rendered to be played back for preview on your desktop computer monitor. Although you cannot preview these features out through Firewire to an NTSC monitor, users who have access to a G4 desktop unit with processor speeds in excess of 500 MHz have access to real-time effects for preview on the desktop.

One of the real-time preview features available on such machines is the ability to play back still images without having to render them. Titles and other still images you create in Photoshop, or even freeze frames you make from a single frame in a Final Cut Express video clip, can be previewed in playback in the sequence. When you set the RT Still Cache (RAM), you tell Final Cut Express how much extra RAM it should use for storing these still images. This number should obviously factor in how much RAM your system has installed, and is another good reason to get more RAM if possible. Remember, this RAM will be in addition to any RAM in use by the Mac OS and Final Cut Express, so you'll soon be wanting more. We have to be careful to make sure that we are not forcing the system into using virtual memory because we have asked it to use too much RAM in the RT Still Cache. If you set the RT Still Cache too high for the amount of physical RAM you have installed, you could quite possibly choke your system by denying it the RAM it needs, causing virtual memory pageouts and Dropped Frames errors. See Appendix C about the Mac, its operating system, and how this relates to RAM and hard drive use.

Until this becomes a real burning issue for you as an editor, set it for 10 MB (see Figure 2-18) and forget about it. If and when you decide to use the real-time preview system with stills and Photoshop images, you may want to bump the number up, congruent with the amount of installed physical RAM in your system. Of course, if you have a G3 or a G4 Power Macintosh with a 450 or slower processor, you will not have access to real-time effects and previews, and this option will be missing in your General Preferences tab.

Autosave Vault

Autosave Vault has two parts; there is a check box for enabling it, and three boxes for entering some specifics about how you want to configure the automatic backups of your project. The Autosave Vault is a pretty nice functional short-term backup system that you should enable. Although it should not replace the backing up of your project files to CD-R, as described in Appendix D, Autosave Vault is another method of making your project bulletproof from accidental loss in the event of a crash.

RT Still Cache (RAM):   10 MB

Figure 2-18 RT Still Cache

There are two important things to remember with the Autosave function. First, Autosave is an automatically timed function that does not wait until you have completed a task before beginning a timed save. It begins its saving operation whether you are in the middle of a complex series of edits or simply staring at the screen. Thus, it can be a very interruptive function, particularly since a highly complicated project file can take up to 30 seconds to completely save. If you are concentrating on your editing, having the whole application lock up every 5 minutes to save itself can ruin your concentration.

The way Autosave works is that every so often, at the predetermined intervals that you specify in the Preferences, the application saves a copy of your project file into a special backup archive folder called the Vault. This Autosave file is an exact copy of your project as it is at that moment, and is named with the date and the time of the autosave. If you ever need to return to your project as it was at the time it was saved, you have only to use Restore Project from the File menu, which will show you a list of all the autosaved copies of the project it sees in the Vault. Autosave never actually saves your original project file; it merely creates copies in a separate folder for safety. You need to manually save (drop-down menu File > Save Project) to your real project file to save it.

Since this feature can only help, the only reason you would consider disabling Autosave Vault would be to eliminate its interruptive behavior. But when doing so, you must be very careful to develop excellent project backup behavior. Most people aren't so diligent and have to learn the hard way that regular saving, whether through Autosave, manual backup, or both, is a must.

What should your settings be? Although they will be different for each user, a good place to start is with Autosave enabled; "Save a copy every" set for 30 minutes; "Keep at most: *X* copies per project" set for 100; and "Maximum of: *X* projects" set for 25 (see Figure 2-19).

"Keep at most: *X* copies per project" defines when Final Cut Express begins removing the oldest copy and replacing it with a newer one. Even so, Final Cut Express never actually deletes any copies; it simply moves the oldest one out of the Vault folder and into the Trash, intending for you to save it to a another disk before deleting it.

The Timeline Options Tab

The second tab in the Preferences is used to set the Timeline Options (see Figure 2-20). In general, you will set these once and not alter them again until your editing needs change.

Figure 2-19 Autosave Vault

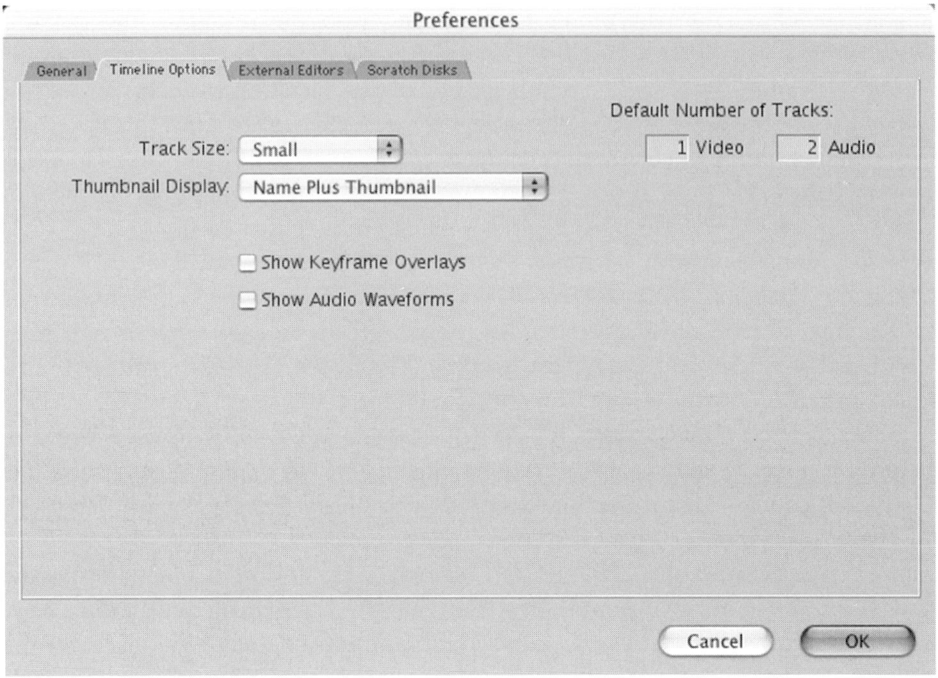

Figure 2-20 Timeline Options Tab

Although they are mostly noncritical, they deserve mention. Since Final Cut Express contains many separate windows, and Desktop real estate is at a premium, the way you set your Timeline Options can optimize your workflow, prioritizing the way you see things in the Timeline as well as its defaults. The Timeline is the only truly linear part of Final Cut Express. It is a beginning-to-end cutting window that can be customized according to your needs.

Track Size

The first setting is for Track Size. The default track size of a new sequence can be preset using this option (see Figure 2-21). Small, the default setting, represents the most efficient trade-off between convenience and accessibility, although you can adjust this according to your needs and available workspace. Like many options in the Preferences, this setting affects only the default settings for new sequences. To change the appearance or features of

Figure 2-21 Track Size

an existing sequence, you will have to make the change in the Sequence Settings, found in the Sequence drop down menu. This Timeline option can also be adjusted directly from the Timeline.

Thumbnail Display

Thumbnail Display is an option that displays a thumbnail of the clip as it sits on the Timeline. This can be a very handy way of remembering which clip you are looking at on the Timeline. The options in this field are Name, which displays only the name of the clip; Name Plus Thumbnail, which displays the name of the clip plus one thumbnail image from the clip; and Filmstrip, which displays as many thumbnail images as can be fitted within the clip, depending on the current time scale and range of the Timeline itself. The default is Name Plus Thumbnail (see Figure 2-22).

It is worth noting that generating a thumbnail in a clip on the Timeline actually steals some processor power. Although in small doses this is negligible, when you have constructed a sequence with 500 clips, it can take Final Cut Express a few seconds to call up and generate them all, during which time you may be stuck looking at a "Preparing Video For Display" progress bar. On another tab, you will be shown how to adjust a setting to improve this performance. If you are getting repeated and long "Preparing" messages, you may want to set the preference to Name instead of Name Plus Thumbnail and see if the processor is simply overburdened by the display of thumbnails in your Timeline clips.

Show Keyframe Overlays

Show Keyframe Overlays (see Figure 2-23) enables a special tool for each clip on the Timeline. This functionality is commonly known as *rubberbanding*. When Show Keyframe Overlays is enabled, you can adjust the opacity, or transparency, of a video clip or the volume level of an audio clip simply by grabbing the line that appears in the clip on the Timeline and dragging it up or down. This is a very easy way to create fades or quickly control audio levels without having to go into a clip's window to apply an effect.

The keyframing of these lines is also possible, allowing you to change the level of opacity or volume over time. The term *rubberbanding* comes from the fact that the straight line created from keyframe to keyframe when rubberbanding resembles a rubber band stretched from nail to nail on a flat surface (see Figure 2-24). Keyframing is thoroughly covered in Chapter 5. Setting this preference isn't critical, since the feature can be enabled directly from the Timeline window.

Show Audio Waveforms

When this preference is enabled (see Figure 2-25), clips on the Timeline will display their audio levels as a waveform. Audio level, or the clip's loudness, is displayed as a long

Figure 2-22 Thumbnail Display    **Figure 2-23** Show Keyframe Overlays

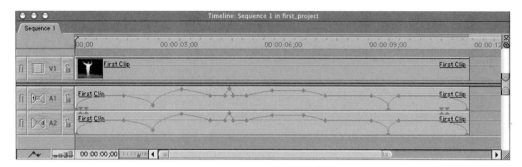

Figure 2-24   Keyframes, or rubberbanding, on an audio track

Figure 2-25   Show Audio Waveforms

continuous series of waves. The higher the peak and the lower the trough of each wave, the higher the level of audio.

Sometimes, the easiest way of finding footage in a clip on the Timeline is to have the Timeline display the Audio Waveform and to look for the waveform spike that identifies your footage (see Figure 2-26). You'd be surprised how easy it is to see the relationship between volume levels and different types of footage. Audio Waveforms can also be a very convenient marker for finding footage or for resyncing tracks that have accidentally been unlinked. Unlike other Timeline preferences, this setting cannot be enabled by a button in the Timeline window itself, but can be turned on and off using the keyboard shortcut Command-Option-W.

One might wonder why such a useful tool should not be enabled all the time. The simple answer is that Final Cut Express must draw many thousands of separate tiny Audio Waveforms on the clips in the sequence when the feature is enabled (remember the 48 in 48K audio is 48,000 times per second!). Each time you make a change, it must redraw all of these thousands of waves. The delay caused by redrawing can take forever, even when using the latest and fastest processors of the Macintosh line. In general, you should keep this feature disabled unless you have a specific need for it; then use the keyboard shortcut to toggle it on and off.

Default Number of Tracks
The final setting for the Timeline Options is for the Default Number of Tracks. This will determine how many new tracks of video and audio are included in the Timeline when you create a new sequence. The default is set at 1 video track and 2 audio tracks (see Figure 2-27), although you can set either for up to 99. In general, you should leave the default setting. As you will see, creating new tracks on a Final Cut Express Timeline is as easy as dropping a clip where you want the new track to be. There is no reason to start out with extra tracks; simply create them as they become necessary.

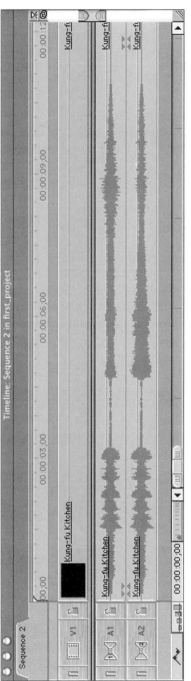

Figure 2-26 Audio Waveforms of an audio track

Figure 2-27   Default Number of Tracks

The External Editors Tab

The third tab in the General Preferences is called External Editors tab. This tab allows you to assign specific applications to work on individual pieces of your project (see Figure 2-28). You could, for instance, set Photoshop as the external application to work on Still Image files that you are currently using in your project. Likewise, you could set Adobe After Effects as the external editor for working with video clips, and Protools or Peak DV to work with audio clips.

While editing in Final Cut Express, you could quickly jump over to another application to tweak some aspect of an item in a sequence or the Project tab without bothering with the import/export process of taking the item outside of Final Cut Express. This can be a very valuable timesaving operation if you use other applications in your media generation process. There are special rules that apply to using external editors for items in your project, though, so make sure to investigate the specifics before engaging in the heavy use of the External Editors tab. For basic work inside Final Cut Express, there is no need to adjust or set this tab.

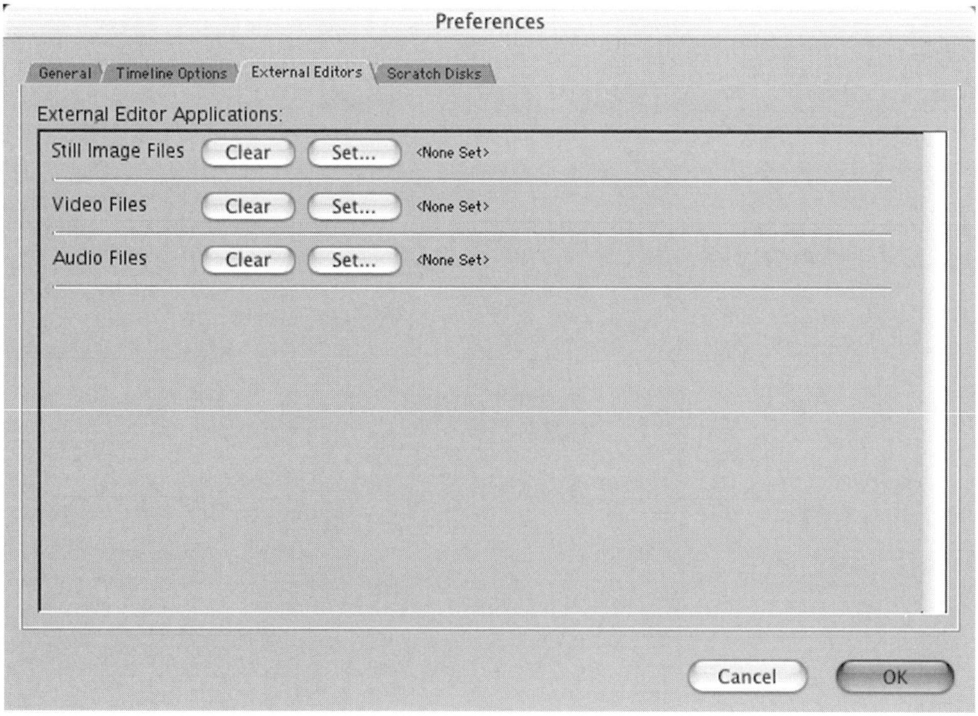

Figure 2-28   External Editors

The Scratch Disk Preferences Tab: The Issues for Scratch Disk Assignment

The fourth and final tab of the Preferences is perhaps the most critical setting in Final Cut Express. It is called Scratch Disk Preferences, and its name does not belie its importance. It is in the Scratch Disk Preferences that you assign the media drive to which all the captured video, audio, and render files are written (see Figure 2-29). It is imperative that this setting be done correctly. There is no getting around the need to visit this setting each time you start to work.

Before we describe the proper procedure for setting up the Scratch Disks tab, it is important to take a moment and examine the physical issues at play here, and make sure that you have arranged your system in the best possible configuration. The footage we want to capture from the DV tape is already digital video. It was digitized as it was recorded in the camera. Digital video contains a certain amount of data, or digital information, in every frame. For high-quality video like DV, this yields a relatively high "data rate," or amount of data per frame per second. There are 29.97 frames per second in NTSC video, and the data rate of DV NTSC is just over 3.6 MB per second. For more detailed information about the processes of analog (pre-digital) and digital video, please refer to Appendix A.

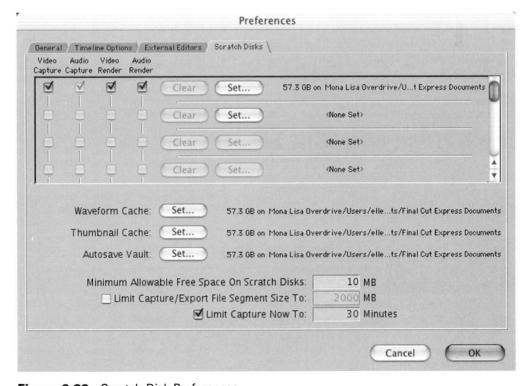

Figure 2-29 Scratch Disk Preferences

What all this means is that as the camera or deck is playing the footage, it is also sending the video data down the Firewire tube to the Macintosh. When it reaches the Macintosh, Final Cut Express writes that data to the hard drive you have set here as the Scratch Disk location. For the data to be written to or played from the Scratch Disk drive correctly, the hard drives installed in our Macintosh will need to be able meet or exceed this 3.6 MB per second data rate when writing the digital video data to the Scratch Disk.

In practice, this is relatively easy. The standard hard drives and buses on today's Macintosh far exceed the 3.6 MB per second data rates required. There's no need to spend lots of money on extremely fast drives to work with broadcast-quality video anymore. However, the inexpensive drives we are talking about must be configured correctly, and you must access and assign them appropriately in Final Cut Express if you expect them to deliver satisfactory performance. Like anything else, the devil is in the details, and if you pay attention to the details, you will find that you never run into data rate-related issues.

The first issue to be addressed is that it is highly recommended that you use at least two separate physical hard drives with Final Cut Express. One of these hard drives is your start-up drive. This is the drive that contains your Mac OS System, Users folder, the Applications folder, Final Cut Express, and any other software you want to install on your system, such as image or audio editing apps. This hard drive is dedicated to software only.

The rest of the drives on your system will be dedicated as media drives (see Figure 2-30). These media drives will be used only to capture and play back the digital files you bring in from the deck or the camera. You will also use these media drives for the render files, which are generated whenever you render an effect in Final Cut Express.

Keeping your start-up and media drives separate will keep Final Cut Express from fighting itself to maintain an acceptable data rate; consequently, it will play back your video files correctly. Although 3.6 MB per second is not an astonishingly high data rate, it does require

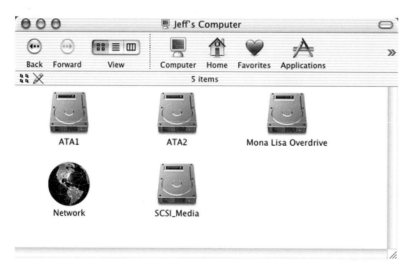

Figure 2-30 Maintain separate physical start-up and media drives

that Final Cut Express have unfettered access to the media files on the drive. That access can be compromised if a drive is busy accessing system files or application files at the same time it is trying to access media files. Any interruption in the steady data rate of 3.6 MB per second can result in unacceptable performance, Dropped Frames, and an interruption of capture or playback.

Another problem with using a start-up drive as a media drive is that it may result in fragmentation of the drive and thus poor performance. A start-up drive containing the system and applications contains many thousands of small files that are used constantly by the system. As you work, you will also be saving files all the time that relate to your work. Since files are constantly being created, saved, thrown away, and so forth, the hard drive can quickly become littered with files scattered across a large, relatively empty disk.

A frequent result of mixing a lot of these small files and large files on a single hard drive is that sometimes the larger files must be broken up into smaller pieces to fit on the drive. Although there is plenty of free space on the drive, it may not be contiguous (i.e., unbroken) space. For example, if you have 2 GB of space left on a drive, but that drive has small files written randomly around its area, you may have only a few much smaller contiguous spaces left on the drive. The space left may equal 2 GB, but it is actually 1 GB plus 250 MB plus 500 MB plus 250 MB.

In order to write or read at the highest level of efficiency, you want to be able to write large files as contiguous files that are not broken up into smaller pieces to fit the available drive space. Fragmentation is not merely a malady for start-up drives. It occurs anytime you begin to approach the limits of capacity for a hard drive. Fragmentation can also occur on a dedicated media drive, even though there are few small files there. Whenever you are constantly writing and throwing away files, especially as you approach a drive's capacity, fragmentation can occur.

Consider this analogy. You are a parking lot attendant, and you have a certain number of parking spaces to use. At the beginning of the day, there are a lot of free parking spaces for you to choose from to park the incoming cars. It takes you almost no time to find a place to park a car. But as the lot fills up, the empty spaces get farther and farther apart and harder to find, until it takes you several minutes to find a free space. The cars leaving the lot do not leave in an orderly fashion, but just free up spaces based on where they were originally parked. As the cars back up, waiting to be parked in your lot, your performance as an attendant decreases.

As the drive fills up from capturing, the free spaces get harder and harder to piece together so that large video files can be written to them. As the drive reaches full capacity, it takes longer and longer to write or read the file. As a result, our data rate dips down below the necessary 3.6 MB per second. Correct playback and capture become impossible, and you start to get Dropped Frames warning messages.

One method that some people use to try to wring more drive space from their Macintosh is to partition their single hard drive into smaller partitions. Partitioning involves creating two apparent logical drives from a single physical hard drive. The single physical hard drive is formatted into two distinct sections that are treated by the system as two completely different hard drives. If you had an 80 GB start-up drive, this might seem like a clever way to reclaim much of the wasted start-up drive space for media purposes, since any given start-up drive uses at the most 20 GB.

The problem is that this method does not really increase data rate performance, since you are still dealing with a single physical hard drive, however dissected. While you may eliminate fragmentation as an issue, you will encounter spotty performance as your start-up partition and the media partition fight for dominance. Using two separate physical hard drives, on the other hand, ensures that if the system or application files need to be accessed while media files are in use, there will be no competition between the two, and there will be a lower probability of fragmentation resulting from the mixture of system or application and media files. There's nothing wrong with partitioning your start-up drive or partitioning your media drive either, as long as you don't use the same physical drive for your start-up drive and for your Scratch Disk media drive.

Learning to manage your media drives through the Scratch Disk Preferences will keep this from happening to you. You must learn to organize your media and not simply blindly accept the default media locations that appear when you start up Final Cut Express. Although you may not experience problems initially when you begin working or even after many edit sessions, the time will come when sloppiness in maintaining your media will come back to haunt you. Those situations can be avoided if you begin work with your media resources organized and under control. Before you scream about Final Cut Express being buggy and causing Dropped Frames messages, consider whether your drive configuration is the culprit!

Can you get away with using your system drive for your Scratch Disk location? Sure, Final Cut Express will let you set any drive location as a Scratch Disk location. It will even let you specify that an Iomega Zip disk is your Capture Scratch! Obviously, that would never do. Unfortunately, this makes it your responsibility to use a separate hard drive. You can work for a while without a dedicated media hard drive for your video, but eventually it will cause performance problems, and probably at the worst possible moment. If you don't have a separate physical hard drive that you can dedicate to capturing video, start saving and looking for one so that you can rectify the situation. For help on figuring out hard drive solutions, refer to Appendix C.

A Look at the Scratch Disks Preferences Tab

To properly set your Scratch Disk Preferences, take a look at the top of the Scratch Disk Preferences tab (see Figure 2-31). Starting at the left of the tab, you will see four check boxes, two buttons, and a bit of text. The four check boxes are labeled Video Capture, Audio Capture, Video Render, and Audio Render. The two buttons are labeled Clear and Set. The information to the right of these items is a number describing the amount of free space that currently exists on the presently set Scratch Disk drive, followed by the directory path to that drive. The default drive assignment when you install Final Cut Express is the start-up drive, and it should be changed before you begin work if you have a second drive specifically for capturing media (the recommended configuration). You will see that

Figure 2-31 Scratch Disk Preferences

there are a total of 12 lines of check boxes and buttons, which means that you can assign up to 12 different media drives or partitions (you'll have to use the scroll bar there to get to them all).

When you capture or render media, the check boxes on the left indicate the drive location where Final Cut Express will send the designated media files. If you are using Firewire and DV, you should always have all four enabled for each Scratch Disk location you assign. You should be using the same drive and folder for not only the video and audio files you capture through Firewire, but also the video and audio files that you generate when rendering footage in Final Cut Express. If you assign more than one drive or folder for your media, make sure to enable each check box for each assigned location.

The Clear and Set buttons allow you to navigate to and change the media locations when necessary. Clicking Clear will remove the current media location from the right and replace it with the message "⟨None Set⟩". The only exception to this is that there must always be at least one media location assigned, so if you have only one line assigned, the Clear button will be grayed out and unavailable.

Scratch Disk Assignment: Follow the Next Steps Precisely

1. Click the Set button of the first Scratch Disk assignment line. You will be immediately be confronted by a dialog box named Choose a Folder, asking you to select the appropriate location for designation as the Scratch Disk. Drag the bottom scroll bar all the way to the left so that you are looking at all the drives available on your system (see Figure 2-32).
2. Single-click the drive you want to set as your media drive. When you do, the pane to the right should show you what, if anything, already exists there. Hit the New Folder button below the directory panes. In the New Folder dialog box, name the folder "1stProject_Media_Folder" or something equally project-specific and

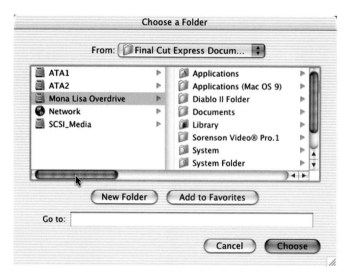

Figure 2-32   Choose a folder

distinctive. Be careful not to include any forward slash characters ("/") in the name of this folder, which can cause problems in the file naming method of the Mac OS. Click the Create button (see Figure 2-33).

3.   After clicking the Create button, you will see that the folder has been created and that it is selected in the dialog box. If you accidentally click something else and deselect it, simply single-click it again to reselect it. With the folder selected, hit the Choose button at the bottom right of the dialog box (see Figure 2-34). Immediately after hitting this button, you will be returned to the Scratch Disk Preferences.

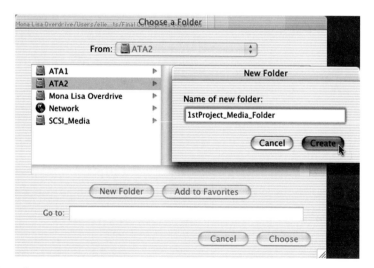

Figure 2-33   Create a new folder

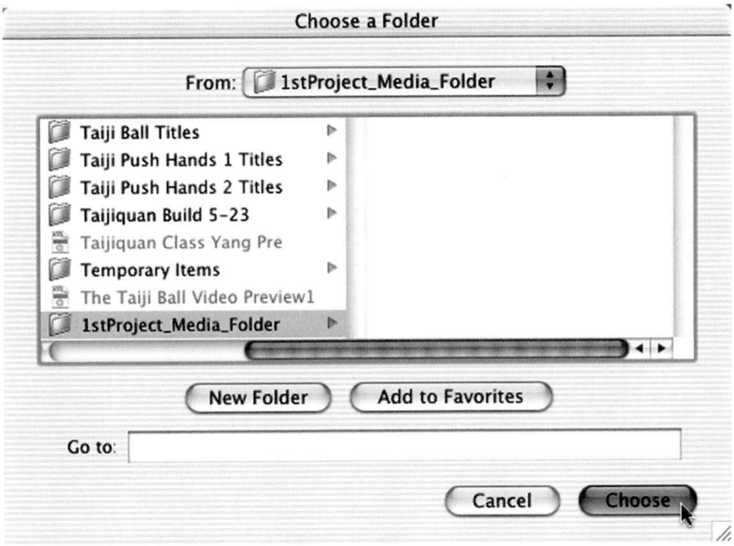

Figure 2-34 Hit Choose with the folder selected

You've just set your first Scratch Disk, and you've done it correctly! Take a look at the information next to the Set button, and you should see the amount of free space on your media drive displayed in gigabytes (GB), followed by the exact directory path to the place in which you saved the folder (see Figure 2-35).

When you name your media drive and your project's media folder, make sure to give them distinctive names. Final Cut Express can miss the difference between "Media1" and "Media2," for example. A better system is to actually number the drives, using a number at the beginning of the drive's name (e.g., "1Media" and "2Media"). If you have more than

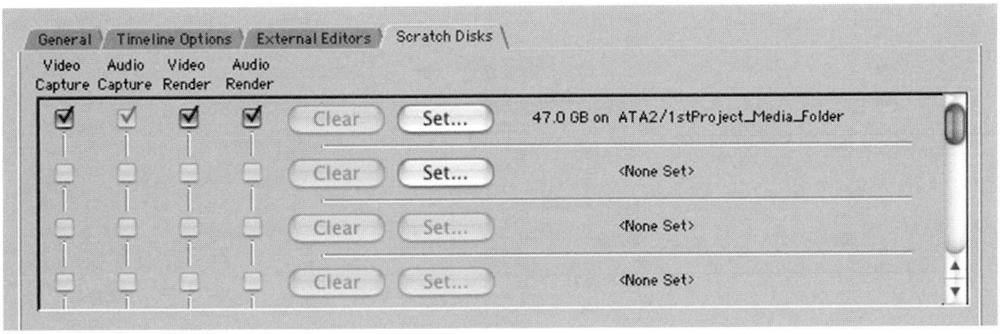

Figure 2-35 A correctly chosen Scratch Disk

one type of drive on your system, such as both ATA and SCSI drives, you may want to include such information in the drive name (e.g., "1_SCSI_30GB"), where 1 is the drive name, SCSI is the drive type, and 30 GB is the capacity. The name might look a little ungainly, but after you've got four or five drives in your system, it can be a little difficult to remember whether "Fred" is an ATA or a SCSI and how big it is.

To rename a drive or partition, simply single-click its present name. When the name becomes highlighted, type in the new name, up to 31 characters. You should take similar care when you name the Capture Scratch folder you will be selecting in the Scratch Disk Preferences tab. "1stProject_Media_Folder" may be a good idea for the folder you establish on your first media drive, but you should name the next one something distinctly different.

Another thing to remember is not to include the forward slash character ("/") in any Scratch Disk name or directory. Since Mac OSX is a Unix-based operating system, the forward slash has a unique meaning to the system itself. Using it for a folder, file, or drive name can cause huge problems. Restrict naming conventions to alphanumeric characters.

Every location that you have dedicated as a Scratch Disk will have one such media folder on it. It may seem a little strange to create a folder on the media drive, but understanding how Final Cut Express organizes its captured media resources will demonstrate how quickly media can get out of control and clarify how important it is to have media folders set up uniformly and consistently.

Take a look at the project media folders you just created on your media drive (see Figure 2-36). When you assign a drive or folder as the Scratch Disk, Final Cut Express creates three folders inside of it: a Capture folder (for video and audio, which Firewire captures together and considers as one file), a Render folder (for rendered video from the project),

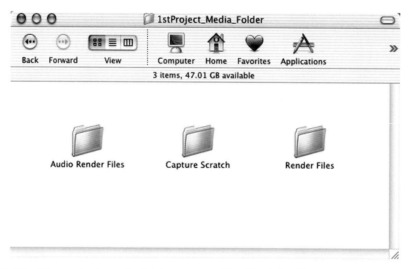

Figure 2-36 The project media folders created by Final Cut Express

and an Audio Render folder. These Final Cut Express-generated folders cannot be renamed without unlinking everything in your project, so don't rename or even move them, especially while Final Cut Express is running.

When you go to capture video or audio, Final Cut Express looks in the Capture folder in the Scratch Disk folder you assigned. If it does not find a folder whose name matches the name of the current project, it creates a new folder for this purpose. Every time media is captured using a new project, Final Cut Express will create yet another project media folder in the Capture folder of the folder you have assigned as the Scratch Disk.

It is easy for this process to get out of hand, particularly if you are sharing your editing station with other users. The problem can be compounded by the fact that, when started up from the application alias, Final Cut Express always opens the last project that was open and always retains the Scratch Disk settings that were used the last time Final Cut Express was run (with the exception that logging in as individual users keeps these settings separate). This means that unwary users can start up another person's project, capture a lot of media to the wrong drive or folder, and then walk away without realizing the damage they have done to both themselves and their colleague.

These issues highlight the care that must be taken in the proper setup and maintenance of media resources in a Final Cut Express editing station. Setting up the Scratch Disk is not difficult, and if you follow the preceding method for setting it up, you may never have to find out why the process is so necessary. After you have set up a Scratch Disk folder for each media drive you want to use, you can get to work. As you return to Final Cut Express to continue editing your project, simply select the media folder you created the first time for your Scratch Disk again rather than setting up a new media folder each time you edit. Make sure you do so, though.

To wrap up the settings on the Scratch Disks tab, look underneath the Scratch Disk assignment columns. You will find six items that need to be addressed (see Figure 2-37).

Waveform and Thumbnail Cache

Waveform and Thumbnail Cache locations are set on this tab. Thumbnail and Waveform caches store the thumbnail and waveform data for faster screen redraw. Final Cut Express will function quite well with these caches defaulted to the start-up drive, although choosing a very fast media disk can dramatically improve the rubberbanding and thumbnail

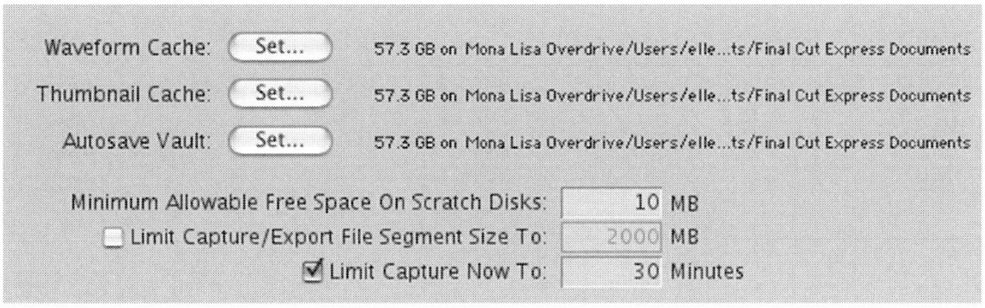

Figure 2-37 Additional Scratch Disk settings

display performance described earlier in the chapter. Some users have reported performance boosts through using high-speed disk solutions for these caches. If you are getting a lot of "Preparing Video for Display" dialogs and long hangs before a sequence loads, consider reassigning these caches to your media drive.

Autosave Vault

Once again, we encounter the Autosave function, this time in determining the location that Final Cut Express will use to save the autosave archive files. Click the Set button and locate the Documents folder within the Users directory on your start-up drive. Simply pull the bottom scroll bar all the way to the left of the dialog box, and then select the Mac OSX start-up drive. In the next pane, select the Users folder, and in the next pane select the appropriate user (if more than one exists on that station). Finally, choose the Final Cut Express Documents folder (see Figure 2-38). Within this folder, Final Cut Express will create a folder called Autosave Vault. It will further create a folder for each project inside the Autosave folder. In this final folder, Final Cut Express will automatically save each copy it makes of your project.

Don't worry; you will rarely, if ever, have to search in that folder for anything. One of the coolest features of Final Cut Express is that if you ever have to return your project to the way it was when it was autosaved at any time, there is a command in the File drop-down menu to allow you to choose the correct backup project file from inside Final Cut Express itself (see Figure 2-39)!

Minimum Allowable Free Space on Scratch Disks

Adjust the Minimum Allowable Free Space on Scratch Disks setting to at least 10% of your smallest media drive capacity. Minimum Allowable Free Space on Scratch Disks is a setting that helps to eliminate the problem of disk fragmentation mentioned earlier in the chapter. The field next to it allows you to enter an amount in megabytes (see Figure 2-40). When a Scratch Disk fills up and has only the assigned value of remaining storage space, Final Cut Express either switches to your next assigned Scratch Disk, or, if another Scratch Disk has not been assigned, aborts the capture. We can set a healthy buffer here to avoid reaching a situation in which an overcrowded drive might deliver compromised drive performance.

The default setting for this field is 10 MB, but this is far too low to provide any measure of security. There is much room for argument regarding the best Minimum Allowable setting, and it really depends on the size of the media drives in question. A good rule of thumb is that the Minimum Allowable should be set to at least 10% of the drive's capacity. This means a setting of 2 GB (or 2,000 MB) for a 20 GB drive. Such a buffer space is generally large enough to protect a drive from fragmentation but doesn't waste much drive space.

Limit Capture/Export File Segment Size To

This setting contains a couple of options, a couple of implications, and a bit of history. The options of the setting are to disable it completely or to enable it with a specified limitation

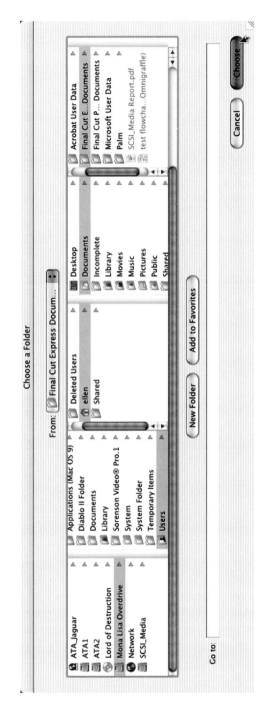

Figure 2-38 Autosave Vault settings

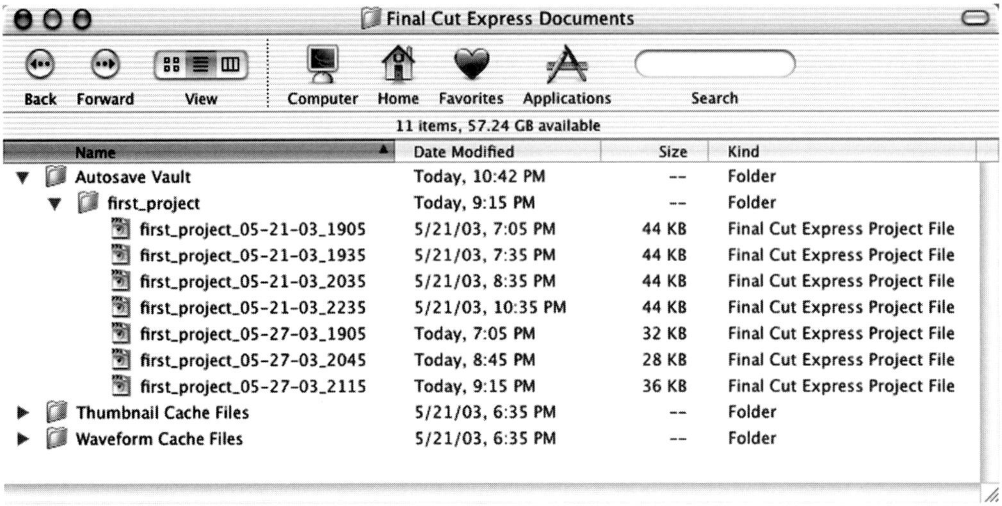

Figure 2-39   Autosave Vault folders

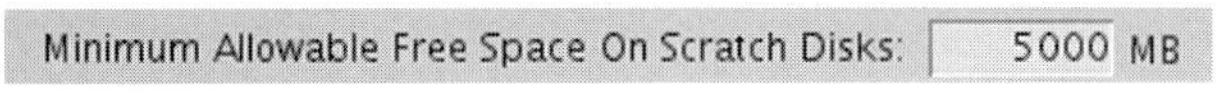

Figure 2-40   Adjust the Minimum Allowable Free Space

to the size of the file either captured or exported using Final Cut Express. If the setting is enabled, the default file size limitation is set for 2,000 MB, or 2 GB (see Figure 2-41).

Several years ago, in the old days of Mac OS version 8 disk formatting, file sizes larger than 2 GB would result in a file error. In order to capture DV clips that were longer than about 10 minutes (about 5 minutes to the gigabyte for DV compressed material), the solution was to segment the capture files so that no individual file size reached this 2 GB file size limit. The segments were linked together for correct playback, but they were individual files on their own. All video editing applications had to deal with the file size limit of 2 GB in some proprietary way.

With the arrival of Mac OS 9.1, the 2 GB file size limitation was eliminated, allowing the capture or export of file sizes up to 2 TB (terabytes)! File segmentation is no longer necessary, and this option may be safely disabled, with an important rare exception: Files larger than 2 GB—or ">2 gig," as they are sometimes referred to—require the drive to which they are written to be formatted with the Mac OS Extended Format. If you have a disk in your system that is formatted using the original Mac OS Standard Format, or that is PC-formatted (quite possible if you purchased the drive bare from a company that sells both

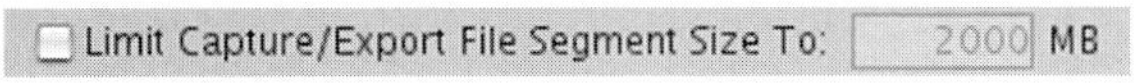

Figure 2-41   Limit Capture/Export File Segment Size

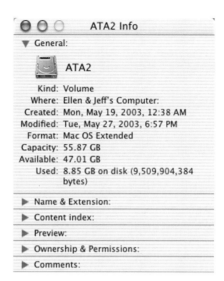

Figure 2-42 Get information about your media disk

Macs and PCs), you cannot write files larger than 2 GB to it. If you are receiving file errors whenever you capture or attempt to export files or clips longer than 10 minutes, this may be the cause.

If you are not sure about the type of format of a disk, select the disk at the Desktop level, go to the File drop-down menu and select Get Info, or hit Command-I for the shortcut. The General Information will describe the format type as either Standard or Extended (see Figure 2-42). If the drive shows Standard, you should reformat at your earliest convenience to Extended using Mac OSX's Disk Utility tool. Be aware that this reformatting will wipe the drive and irrevocably delete any data on it.

Limit Capture Now To

The setting Limit Capture Now To can be disabled or set to limit the length of the capture to a specified number of minutes (see Figure 2-43). You can use this setting to capture long clips without having to sit and watch your machine go through the process. Since there are issues with capturing clips that have timecode breaks, you can avoid the problem by starting a Capture Now process and setting a limit to the length of the capture such that the capture process ends before the footage on the tape. This eliminates the necessity of your being present to stop the capture.

Another issue of relevance is that this avoids long hang-ups between the time you hit the Capture Now button and the time the capturing process actually begins. When Final Cut Express captures a clip, it has to prepare a space for the clip on the Scratch Disk drive. If you are using the Capture Clip process, this is quick and simple. Final Cut Express knows

Figure 2-43 Limit Capture Now To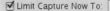

exactly how much drive space will be necessary for the clip to be captured, since it knows both the data rate of the capture and the length of the capture (for instance: 10-second clip ×3.6 MB per second = 36 MB capture file).

If you are using Capture Now, Final Cut Express has not been informed of the ultimate length of the capture and assumes that the resultant clip will use up all the available disk space on the Scratch Disk! It can take time to arrange this, which can lead to a rather long hang-up as you wait for Final Cut Express to actually begin capturing. If you have very large Scratch Disks in excess of 120 GB, you might have to wait for as long as several minutes, all the while watching your footage pass by with Final Cut Express still not beginning the capture. Timing the beginning of the capture so that it begins where you want it to begin can be frustrating as well.

If you cannot log your clips and must rely on Capture Now, the Limit Capture Now To setting can correct this problem. If you set it to, say, 5 minutes, Final Cut Express will know that the captured clip will need only so much Scratch Disk space, and the capture process will begin almost instantly. The default time, if the setting is enabled, is 30 minutes, but you can choose a limit that suits your purposes.

The Easy Setup

Having completed the Preferences for the application, we now move on to the Easy Setup necessary for correctly capturing video and audio footage. Many of these settings are critical, and you should visit them at each edit session and make sure that they are appropriate for your situation. As with the Preferences, these settings are not stored in the project file and will simply be the same as the last time they were used.

Although the hardware on your Final Cut Express station will not change much over time, you must inform Final Cut Express correctly about such things as the type of video and audio data it will be receiving, whether or not timecode will be present, etc. The beauty of Final Cut Express is that it is what we call *hardware agnostic*. This means that it will function more or less the same whether we have a camcorder, deck, or Firewire converter box.

Easy Setups are simply presets of all different possible arrangements that are to be used at a given edit session. The Final Cut Express software installs 18 presets that are a pretty good generic guess at what you will be using. Unfortunately, even within the closely standardized world of Final Cut Express Firewire DV editing, there are subtle variations in the Easy Setup that can have a major impact on the progress of your project. The presets that Final Cut Express installs may not be accurate for your DV source footage, camera, deck or converter box, timeline needs, or video and audio monitoring situation. Clearly you need to correctly configure based on your specific needs. The rule of thumb is "Your capture settings must match what's on your tape, and your sequence settings must match your capture settings."

Fortunately, this is an easy process. Upon launch, Final Cut Express is able to detect video and audio hardware such as camera and decks at each of the Macintosh's ports and buses. Before going through the process of choosing your Easy Setup, make sure that your camera, deck, or converter is plugged in, turned on, and connected to the Macintosh via Firewire. If you do this and still do not see the device as an option as you step through the settings, quit Final Cut Express, reboot your Macintosh, and then restart Final Cut Express. That should cause Final Cut Express to recognize and initialize the device.

In the section that follows, we will go through and come to understand the settings in the Easy Setup tabs that must be addressed specifically for correct capturing of video and audio. In working on your own materials, you will likely find that it is easiest to approach these settings by glancing through them at the beginning of each session with Final Cut Express (or whenever you need to change them!).

The Easy Setup Dialog Box

To access the Easy Setup choices, look under the Final Cut Express drop-down menu and choose Easy Setup, or hit Control-Q (see Figure 2-44). A window will pop up with a drop-down menu and some descriptive text (see Figure 2-45). The drop-down menu lets you pick the Easy Setup that's appropriate to your situation. The text gives you the particulars of that setup. Each bit of information in this text tells you which option in the Easy Setup tab is appropriate for your own system. No matter what camera, DV deck, or converter you have, Apple has an Easy Setup preset ready for you in the list. It's your job just to select the right one.

The default drop-down choice will be the one you selected after you first installed Final Cut Express, probably DV-NTSC or DV-PAL. Although everything you will be capturing and editing will be DV material, there are still some variations that have to be taken into account. When you capture video and audio, you create a link from a clip in your project file in the Browser to the digital video and audio data that is saved in the media folder of your Scratch Disk or media drive. Correct capture settings determine whether the media works correctly once it is in your system, whether the clip in your project accurately reflects

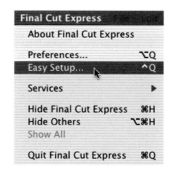

Figure 2-44 Accessing Easy Setup

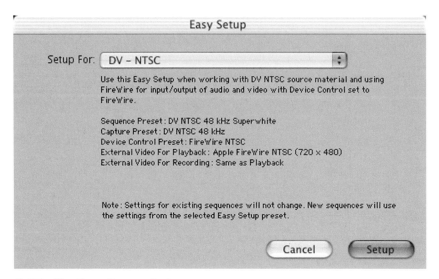

Figure 2-45   The Easy Setup window

the media that is on your drive. If they are not set correctly, the media in your projects will misbehave, causing you no end of grief. This is the most common cause of problems in beginner use. You have to tell Final Cut Express exactly what it is capturing. If you don't give it the correct information about the video and audio coming in, it will misbehave later on.

There are many different presets for generic DV Firewire capture with audio sample rate settings for 48K and 32K, for anamorphic 16×9, and Basic Firewire or Normal Firewire for both NTSC and PAL. In addition, there is a DV Converter variation. Each of these possible arrangements of audio sample rates, aspect ratio (normal 4×3 and widescreen 16×9), basic or more specialized Firewire protocols, and DV Converter is available. In the next section, we will sort out the correct Easy Setup for your project.

Audio Sample Rates

When we capture from DV tape, we need to tell Final Cut Express which audio sample rate the tape was originally recorded (see Figure 2-46). In DV cameras, the sample rate is usually referred to as 12 bit or 16 bit rather than 32K or 48K. If you are not sure about the correct rate, play the tape back in the camera or deck. In most devices, you will see an on-screen display telling you the sample rate of the footage. When you see the 12 bit or 16 bit rate displayed, you will know which to use in your Easy Setup—12 bit means 32K and 16 bit means 48K. Determine which sample rate the footage you intend to capture is recorded at and keep this in mind as we look at the other variations. For a great deal more information about sample rates, see Appendix A.

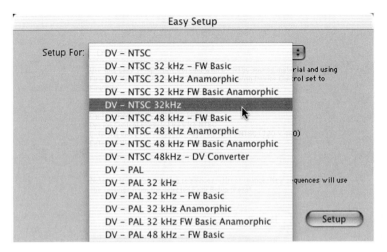

Figure 2-46 Audio sample rates

Anamorphic Video

The next variation is called *anamorphic* (see Figure 2-47). This is a more technical term for what we usually call widescreen or 16×9. With DV, it is possible to shoot with a far wider angle, and thus differently shaped video frame, than normal, or 4×3, video. The two different possible shapes of the film and video screen are referred to as *aspect ratios*. If you've ever watched a Hollywood film on television and wondered why there are black bars at the top and bottom of the video frame, known as *letterboxing*, it is because the wider angle of widescreen and the different shape of the 16×9 aspect ratio mean the whole frame must be shrunk to fit in the regular television 4×3 frame.

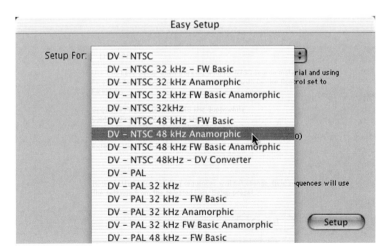

Figure 2-47 Anamorphic video

Now to explain what *anamorphic* really means, we have to go into how cameras and decks do this magic of widescreen. When you change the camera into widescreen, or 16×9 mode, the camera stretches the image it is recording so that the subjects in the frame look too thin. When the time comes for playback, the image will be squeezed back into the correct ratio. When it is squeezed down to display correctly, the video frame will have black bars at the top and bottom, which is the area left blank when the originally stretched footage is compensated for.

Why use anamorphic instead of normal 4×3 aspect ratios? There are a few reasons. Many people consider it to be particularly cinematic, since the short, wide shape of the frame is very close to the elongated shape of a movie theater projection screen (this is why Hollywood movie releases for home viewing are usually letterboxed). Another reason that it is useful is that the high definition television standards approaching on the horizon will use 16×9 as the normal aspect ratio. This is why the High Definition Televisions (HDTVs) you see in stores and advertisements appear so wide. Many content producers are now generating material in 16×9 so that it can be repurposed when HDTV becomes a reality in most homes.

When Final Cut Express encounters DV footage that was shot with the widescreen setting in the camera's menus, it is smart enough to recognize that the material is anamorphic and to mark the captured clip as such. Unfortunately, many DV shooters are increasingly using "widescreen adapters," relatively expensive special lens adapters that optically stretch the image out rather than letting the camera do it digitally from a menu setting. The reason is that the camera's menu option doesn't yield as high quality an image as does the lens adapter, because the camera's digital method doesn't actually use the entire camera imaging chip. The problem is that when one uses the lens adapter, Final Cut Express will be unable to see that the footage needs to be squeezed. Thus, for the material to be handled correctly, you need to tell it that the footage is stretched, or it will appear skinny and weird. Thus, if you have used a widescreen setting in the camera or have used a lens adapter, you want to make sure that you have this set correctly in Final Cut Express.

Device Control

This option is concerned with Final Cut Express's ability (or inability) to remotely control the deck or camera you are capturing from. DV Firewire carries timecode and Device Control data along with the video and audio. Correctly configuring the Device Control presets allows you to take advantage of this feature, adding both security and convenience to your working process (see Figure 2-48).

Final Cut Express preinstalls three variations on the Device Control concept that work with most DV editing setups. The options are Firewire, Basic, and DV Converter. The difference between Firewire and Basic are that Firewire contains some special tweaks that may improve performance with devices that can access them. Essentially, Basic is a stripped-down version of Firewire that only includes the most basic device controller. The Firewire preset will work with most DV cameras or decks that are approved for use with Final Cut

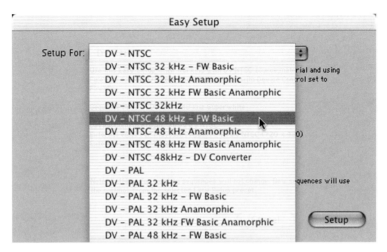

Figure 2-48 FW Basic

Express (and quite a few that aren't). That said, there are a few cameras and decks that deliver much more stable performance when set to Basic. You can find this information about your particular camera or deck on the compatibility charts at Apple's Web site.

DV Converter

DV Converter is an option for working with a DV device that does not generate timecode, or is used in situations in which timecode could hamper your capture operations. DV converter boxes convert analog video and audio, such as Betacam or VHS/SVHS source tape into DV data that can be captured using the Firewire connection and Final Cut Express. However, most converter boxes do not generate DV timecode or Device Control data along with that DV data stream when capturing. Final Cut Express always looks for timecode and Device Control data in the Firewire data stream prior to a capture unless you tell it not to by selecting the DV Converter option in the Easy Setup (see Figure 2-49). In order to capture video through Firewire from a source that does not generate timecode and Device Control data, you must tell Final Cut Express to stop looking for it. If you experience a long delay when you start to capture, and the Capture window says, "Waiting for Timecode," chances are you have this set incorrectly.

There is another situation where this Device Control setting can be useful. Suppose you are working with a deck or camera that does in fact generate timecode and Device Control data but has lots of timecode breaks on the tape. When there is a space between two recorded segments on a tape in which nothing is recorded, we say that there is a timecode break on the tape. Timecode breaks are the bane of editors and can cause tons of problems in capture.

Timecode breaks are usually easy to identify on most consumer and prosumer DV cameras and decks, because when the device begins recording on a tape where there is no

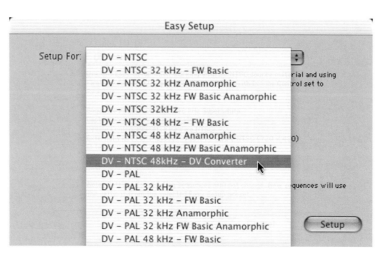

Figure 2-49   DV Converter

timecode already present, the deck or camera sets the timecode of the first frame recorded to 00:00:00:00. If recording is begun where timecode already exists, the device will pick up the timecode number that is present and continue from that number, a process called *regenerating timecode.*

You can therefore easily determine whether your timecode is clean (i.e., has no breaks) by watching the numbers as the tape plays. As long as the displayed timecode number never resets to 00:00:00:00 (or skips a large number of frames), you can be reasonably sure that your tape has no timecode breaks.

If you have timecode breaks that keep you from being able to capture specific areas of your material, setting Easy Setup to DV Converter, and thereby ignoring timecode entirely, may provide some flexibility in overcoming the problem. In general, though, the best medicine is always prevention. Avoid timecode breaks, and always work with a preset other than DV Converter whenever possible. Taking advantage of timecode will make your editing experience much safer and more efficient. Remember that capturing footage with timecode breaks can have a consequence with the audio sample rate and the Sync Adjust Movies feature of the Preferences as well. Timecode breaks are just no good.

Making the Easy Setup Choice

Knowing what we know of the options now, we can correctly set up based on what we are going to capture and edit with. Look at the tapes you are capturing, take note of the video standard in use in your area (NTSC or PAL), the audio sample rate (32K or 48K), the aspect ratio (anamorphic or normal) and Device Control (Firewire Basic or normal). After you have selected the appropriate combination, select the one you need, hit Setup, and the application will be ready to go.

Capture

Now that we have Final Cut Express perfectly set up to capture our video and audio from DV, let's get right to it. There are three basic techniques to bring media in: capturing logged clips, capturing "Now," and Project (see Figure 2-50). These three methods have different requirements and come into play based on differing situations. Capturing logged clips requires not only that you use a deck or camera that Final Cut Express can control, but also that you use timecode. Capture Now, on the other hand, simply captures whatever is currently streaming through the Firewire connection, regardless of the presence or lack of timecode data or Device Control. Finally, Project allows you to recapture your entire project if something goes wrong, such as accidental deletion or a failed hard drive.

What Is Capture?

Capturing is the actual method of finding the footage on the DV tapes you want to edit and bringing them onto the computer's hard drives so that you can access the material in your project. There are two different ways to capture your footage in Final Cut Express: Capture Now and Capture Clip. Each involves a different approach to the initial stages of our edit session, so we will go through both. But first, we will look at a few things you can do to make the most out of your hard drive storage resources.

Efficient Capture Techniques: The Paper Log

Before we discuss the capture process, it is important to mention that there are a couple of different strategies you can use to make the most of your hard drive resources. The first is referred to as a *paper log*. This old but reliable system involves simply watching your tapes and writing down the timecode numbers of the clips you want to use when editing.

Most shooters produce source tapes that include far more material than will be used by the editor. The amount of material shot on tape compared with the amount of material used in the final edited project is called a *shooting ratio*. Because tape is so incredibly cheap, many shooters are inclined to let the tape run rather than stop and start it for the important parts. Common shooting ratios for video production are often higher than 6×1 and produce tons of material that will only waste space on your drives if captured en masse.

Captured video files are huge, even when using DV, which has a relatively low data rate of 3.6 MB per second. Five minutes of footage takes up over a gigabyte of hard drive storage space. If you were shooting at roughly a 6×1 ratio and you just captured an entire tape, this would mean that you stored 60 minutes, or 12 GB of video on your drive, when you only needed to store 2 GB at most.

Clearly, this is not the most efficient way to work, even with today's enormous and inexpensive hard drive solutions. You will find that you still run out of drive space far too quickly. There is no such thing as too much hard drive space. Previewing your tapes and

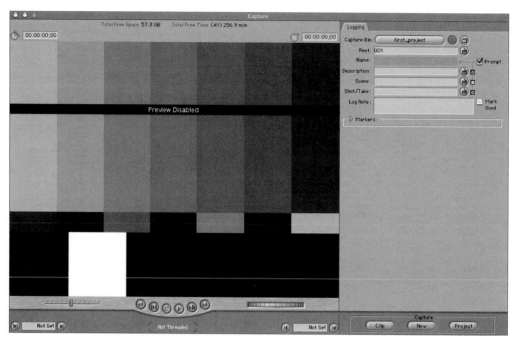

Figure 2-50 Capture window

taking loose notes can easily eliminate the problem. Simply jot down the beginning and ending timecode numbers for each section of footage you know you need to capture and edit (see Figure 2-51). Never fear that you might need something you forgot; if you ever need more footage, simply go back in and get that as well.

What if you are collaborating with someone in a project and you both need access to the tapes to create paper logs? You have only one set of source tapes, and moving them around makes you a little nervous, not to mention the fact that constantly playing back and shuttling around on the source tapes increases the likelihood of damage to the tapes themselves.

The solution is another time-tested one. Create what is referred to as a Timecode Window Burn Dub. Most DV cameras will allow you to output the video and audio to analog VCRs. Indeed, your Final Cut Express editing station will be based on this ability so that you can preview the editing on an NTSC or PAL video monitor. Many DV decks and cameras will also let you display the timecode numbers of the footage on-screen in the bottom corner as the video plays.

To create a Timecode Window Burn Dub, simply record a copy of your source tapes to VHS tape with the timecode display turned on in the deck or camera (see Figure 2-52). Then you can use this VHS dub to get the numbers you want by pulling them right off

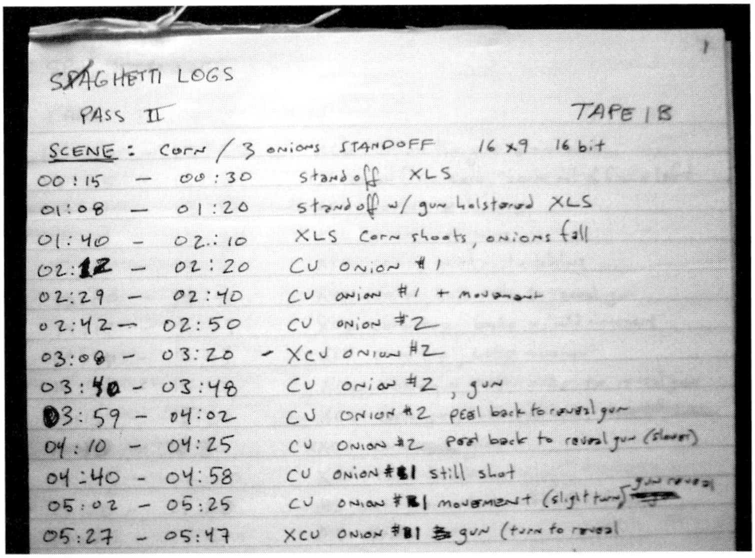

Figure 2-51   Paper log

the television screen without having to jeopardize your precious source DV tapes. Since the displayed timecode numbers will exactly match the timecode numbers on the DV source tape, you will have an accurate log display of timecode on your VHS tapes. This will eliminate excess playing of the original DV source tapes.

Figure 2-52   Timecode Window Burn Dub

Do you have to use paper logs to capture, though? Not at all. You can easily manually log and capture your clips from right inside Final Cut Express (albeit one at a time). Either system is good, although you will find that, once again, your particular source material decides which method is most appropriate. Paper logs are most useful when the shooting ratio is very high and when your necessary footage is spread over many source tapes. Manually logging your tapes from inside of Final Cut Express is more useful when very precise and instant logging and capturing is necessary over a limited amount of source material and, of course, when paper logs do not exist for whatever reason.

Manual logging is a very simple act. Simply shuttle back and forth around your footage in the Capture window, locating the footage that you want, setting In and Out points, and naming each of the clips you intend to create. After setting an In and Out point for a clip, you simply hit the Capture button, and Final Cut Express will roll up and capture exactly what you want, right down to the frame.

Let's go through and log a clip. As you might expect, there is a recommended process for this. Although Final Cut Express will allow you to log clips in a sloppy, haphazard manner, doing so really negates the safety, security, and reliability you are gaining through the process of capturing with timecode. Setting up and organizing your project will save headaches later on.

Create a Capture Bin

First we will create a Capture Bin, which is simply a bin in your project, but is the specific bin that all clips will be placed in as they are captured. If you have not established a Capture Bin yet, Final Cut Express assumes that the Project tab itself is the Capture Bin. This might be OK for the first few clips you create, but very quickly, you will have masses and masses of clips cluttering your Project tab, making it difficult to find anything at all.

Don't make that mistake. Start out with good organizational habits. Final Cut Express offers really strong tools for organizing your project, so take advantage of them. Start by creating and naming a separate Capture Bin for each source tape you capture from. As you get the hang of logging, you will find that certain types of projects need different organizational techniques, and you will find that Final Cut Express is flexible enough to accommodate them.

1. Go to the File drop-down menu, and select New and then Bin in the submenu. When the bin appears in your Project tab, change the name of the bin to "#1 Tape_Logging_Bin" and hit Enter (see Figure 2-53). If you Control-click the Project tab, you will find options for both creating a new bin and setting the Capture Bin.
2. After changing the name of the Bin, make sure it is still highlighted, then Control-click the bin, and select Set Capture Bin (see Figure 2-54). When you do this, a little film-slate clapper icon should appear next to the bin's icon in the Project tab.

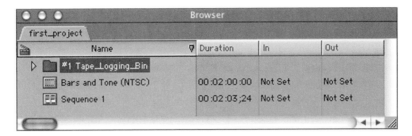

Figure 2-53 Creating a new bin

This clapper icon identifies the bin as the current Capture Bin. Once you change that status, any clips that you capture will be automatically sent to that bin for storage, rather than just dumped into the Project tab.

Opening the Capture Window

Make sure that your deck or camera is connected through Firewire to the Macintosh, is powered on, and the camera set to the VTR mode. Make sure that there is no DV tape inserted in the deck or camera just yet. Although it is not technically necessary to remove the tape before going through the next few steps, in a moment you will see the rationale for doing so.

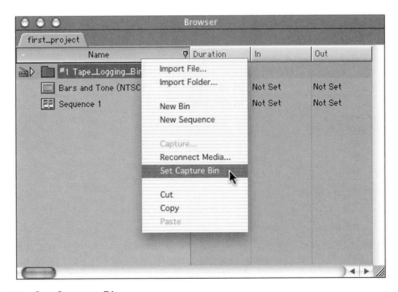

Figure 2-54 Set Capture Bin

Go back to the File drop-down menu and select Capture, as shown in Figure 2-55. A window will appear that bears the name Capture. From this window, you will capture your clips, either by running through your tapes and manually finding the footage you want or by using previously organized paper logs.

You may notice that when the Capture window appears, the video signal from your deck or camera jumps a little and switches from whatever was showing before to a blank screen. This is because, despite Firewire's amazing flexibility, it can still send data in only one direction at a time. When you initialize the Capture window, Final Cut Express reverses the direction of this data from going out of the Macintosh and into the DV device, to going out of the DV device and into the Macintosh. For this reason, you have to remember to close the Capture window when you are finished working in it. Otherwise, you will not be able to switch back to Firewire output from the Macintosh.

The Capture window is divided into halves. On the left is the Video Preview window, which initially displays color bars when not being fed a video source. Ignore the "Preview Disabled" message. The preview will be enabled as soon as you feed it some video. More important, below the preview window and underneath the Play transport button, you should see the message "Not Threaded," which means that the DV device is present, but

Figure 2-55 Opening the Capture window

no tape is inserted (see Figure 2-56). If you see "VTR OK," this means that a deck or camera is connected, it currently has a tape loaded, and Final Cut Express sees it. Either of these messages indicates that Final Cut Express is in fact communicating with the deck or camera.

Any other messages in this location when you open the Capture window could be an indication of misconfigured settings or even hardware problems. Setting your Easy Setup to DV Converter, for example, will yield a "No Communication" message, as if you had a Firewire device connected but turned off. Of course, if you are using a converter box without timecode or Device Control, you will have to get used to the "No Communication" message.

In addition, do not be concerned that the video quality in this window is rather low. DV Firewire capture is simply a data transfer, and your footage will look exactly the same in Final Cut Express as it does on the tape. The low quality in this window is simply a result of Final Cut Express's saving a little processing power for the capture process. If you need to see higher quality as you scan your tapes, you can watch the footage on a video monitor coming from the video outputs on your DV device. The frames you choose will be the same ones whether you select them by viewing the monitor outputs from the DV device or from the Capture window.

The right half of the Capture window is the Logging tab (see Figure 2-57). The Logging tab contains information fields that we need to fill out for each clip as we log it. The information you include in this tab when you log a clip will stick with it even after you have captured it. While most of the information you enter here is basically gratuitous and is necessary only for your own organizational purposes, some is critical to your ability to later recapture the media you associate with the clip.

You can never have too much information about a clip. Be as thorough as possible when filling out the fields. You might not think some items are important, but keep in mind that you will be able to organize or perform searches for clips based on the information you put in these fields. For instance, you could stratify a bin based on which clips are marked Good, or alphabetically by name, description, date, or Reel Name. The more information, the better. Because most of this sort of logging work is often repetitive, Final Cut Express will automatically repeat information in some fields, such as the Reel Name and the Clip Name, from one clip into the next as you go.

Figure 2-56 "Not Threaded" message

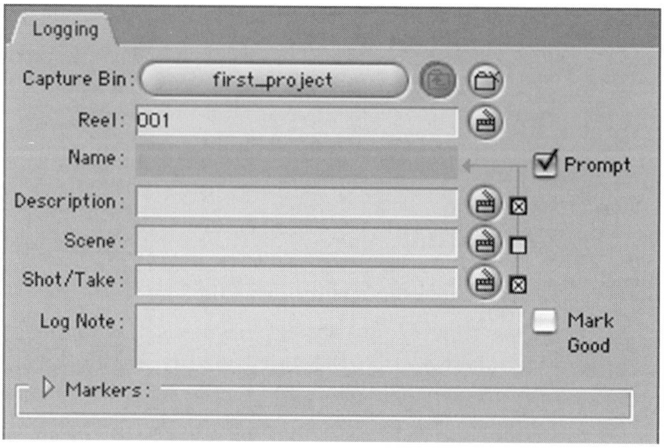

Figure 2-57   The Logging tab

The Reel Name

The most critical field for you to address here is the Reel Name. The Reel Name refers to the particular tape that relates to the timecode numbers you assign with the clip you are logging. The Reel Name is the special link between the real-world DV tape and the Final Cut Express clips you are capturing. Different source tapes can and will have the exact same timecode numbers you are associating with this clip (because almost all DV cameras start their timecodes at 00:00:00:00). The only way to differentiate one clip's timecode numbers from another clip's identical timecode numbers is to give them different Reel Names based on the different tapes they were captured from. If you wanted to recapture a project's clips based on their timecode numbers and then were unable to remember which particular tapes all those clips were originally captured from, you'd be in a lot of trouble very quickly.

It is imperative, therefore, that you develop a system of individually naming your tapes and labeling them in a durable and easily recognizable fashion. Then you must consistently change the Reel Names as you log and capture clips from different named tapes. You will find that if ever the time comes to recapture all the clips you have logged, Final Cut Express will go through and ask you for each tape by Reel Name as it needs them.

We initialized the Capture window without a tape inserted in the DV device for a reason. We want to get into the habit of giving each separate DV tape a distinct Reel Name, as described earlier. Although Final Cut Express will happily allow you to go to the Log window with a tape already queued up in the deck or camera, doing so causes a default Reel Name of 001 to be inserted in the Reel Name field of the Logging tab. Unless you make a point of changing the Reel Name before you begin logging clips, each clip will be assigned the Reel Name 001.

This obviously will not do. However, if you get into the habit of inserting tapes only after initializing the Log window, you will find that each time, Final Cut Express will greet you with this message, as shown in Figure 2-58: "A new tape has been inserted in the VTR. You may wish to change the Reel setting." Although Final Cut Express will not change the Reel Name for you, you will find that you never forget to stop and change it as necessary if you are alerted by this message. The message will reappear anytime you insert a new tape in the deck or camera with the Capture window open.

If you found that you accidentally set the wrong Reel Name for your clips, you do have a way to correct this. If your Browser window is set to display in List view with columns, scroll the window all the way to the right until you find the Reel Name category for the clip(s). You can always select the clip's Reel Name and change it here (see Figure 2-59). Final Cut Express will wisely ask you if you are sure you want to do that, since the Reel Name is so critical. When you go to recapture, Final Cut Express will ask for the correct Reel Name, based on the current information in the Reel Name field of the clip in the Browser window.

In the Logging tab, look above the Reel box, and you will see a broad button labeled Capture Bin. Inside the button should be the name "#1 Tape_Logging_Bin," which you assigned as the Capture Bin earlier in the chapter. Although you cannot directly change the Capture Bin to another preexisting bin from the Capture window, you can create a totally fresh Capture Bin by clicking the New Bin button to the right. You can also open the current Capture Bin into a new window by clicking the Capture Bin button. You can have only one Capture Bin set at a time, no matter how many projects you have open at one time, so you have to be a little careful about where you are sending your logged clips.

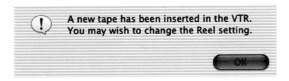

Figure 2-58 Prompt when inserting a new tape

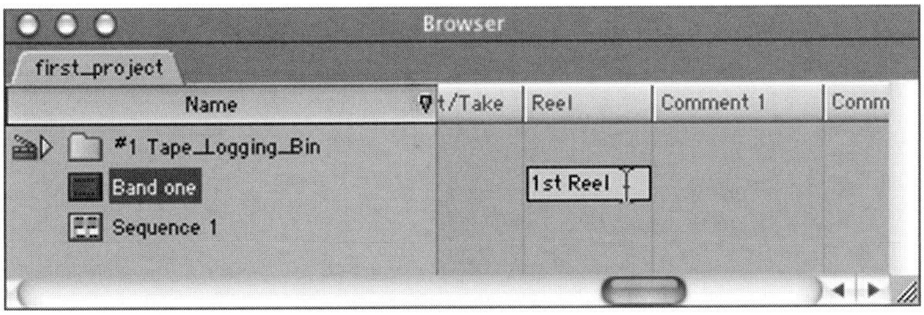

Figure 2-59 Changing the Reel Name

Keeping your eye on the ball will keep your clips in order and your project free of clutter and lost work.

The Name, Description, and Marker Fields

Below the Reel field is the Name field. You have two choices here, since for some reason you cannot type directly into the Name field. You can type the name into the Description field, and when you hit Enter, you will see the information appear as well in the Name field. The other method is to wait until you have selected your Timecode In and Out Points and are ready to actually capture the clip to name it. Next to the Name field is a small check box labeled Prompt. If you check this box, on starting the capture of a clip you will be greeted by a dialog box that asks you to name it. The box will provide fields to describe it with logging notes and to mark it as Good or Not Good (see Figure 2-60). Although this method does not give you the option of giving the clip Scene or Shot/Take designations or Markers, you may find it more useful because it forces you to make choices about the naming of your clip, rather than letting Final Cut Express simply add a number onto the end of the name of the last Clip Name you logged. Always take responsibility and make choices that are right for your project.

In the Logging tab, click the sideways triangle to reveal the area labeled Markers (see Figure 2-61). As you log each clip, you can leave special Markers at various points in the clip to help you remember where specific sections are. The Markers are associated only with the timecode of the clip and do not affect your footage at all. But they can make it very easy to divide larger clips into smaller ones, as well as remind you where important parts of the clip are once you bring the media into Final Cut Express.

As you log the clip, just hit the Set Marker button when the playhead is parked on a frame you want to mark, making sure that you enter both the first frame and the last frame of the marked sections. If you want to mark only a single frame, make that frame's timecode value both the beginning and end timecode value for the Marker. If you want to mark a range of frames, add a Mark In point, then move to the end of the range of frames you want to mark and add a Mark Out point. Add as many Markers or ranges of marked frames

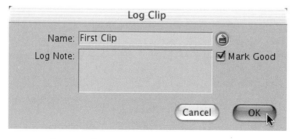

Figure 2-60   The prompt for naming new logged clips

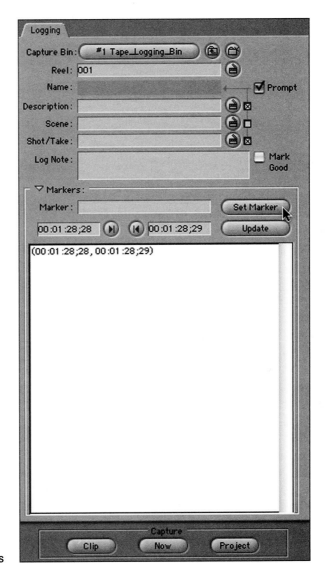

Figure 2-61 Markers

as you want. Name each Marker; you'll be able to go in and change any information in the Marker after the clip is captured.

The Capture Buttons

Finally, at the very bottom of the Logging tab, you will find three buttons of great importance. The three buttons are enclosed in a box labeled Capture (see Figure 2-62). They refer

Figure 2-62 The capture buttons

to the different methods by which Final Cut Express can capture media. The three buttons are named Clip, Now, and Project, and when pushed, they initiate the kind of capture that they refer to. Each one has a different value in the production process. There are instances where Capture Now will be the smartest option, whereas in other situations, Clip will be the most effective. And in case of disasters such as failed hard drives and the like, Final Cut Express will allow you to recapture the entire project from your original tapes, provided you have been careful to use Reel Names and avoid timecode breaks.

Capture Clip

The first method, Capture Clip, functions by capturing one clip at a time, based on the present values in the Timecode In and Out Points in the Capture window. You can get only one clip at a time this way, although you must still log your footage to get the timecode values you need to capture with. This option will be most useful if you have paper logs with the timecode right in front of you.

Capture Now

The second method, Capture Now, is probably the most frequently used method of capturing clips into Final Cut Express, because to the new user it often appears more intuitive. Push the button and the capture starts. Capture Now begins capturing whatever happens to be streaming down the Firewire tube when you press the button. It will continue capturing from the Firewire tube until you hit the Escape key on your keyboard, or until it reaches the time limit you specified in the Scratch Disk Preferences.

The most important feature of Capture Now is that, unlike Capture Clip, it does not require timecode data for capturing clips. Although when capturing without timecode, you must specify that no timecode is present by choosing DV Converter in the Easy Setup, Capture Now will capture anything coming down the Firewire tube, including a blank blue video screen from a deck with no tape inserted!

Of course, if you are capturing from a DV device that does have timecode, Capture Now will capture and use the timecode that is there. But if you are using any of a number of solutions that do not pass timecode data through the Firewire tube—such as DV converter boxes, Digital 8 camcorders that are playing back video originally recorded on a Hi8 camera, or DV tapes that have extremely spotty timecode data—Capture Now will be the only way that you can capture directly into Final Cut Express.

The Process of Capturing

Let's log and capture a single clip, using the Capture window to the left of the tabs. We will go through both methods for capturing, first using Capture Clip and then using Capture Now.

Incidentally, if the Capture window is too large and takes up too much of the window, close it and reduce the size of your Canvas and Viewer windows. The size of the Log window is based on the size of those two windows. Keep the Viewer and the Canvas set at 50%, and then tighten up the window dimensions using the pull tab in the bottom right-hand corner of each window (or the green Aqua Minimize Window button that is found in the top left-hand corner of all Mac OSX windows). You want the video window to fit the Viewer and Canvas without resulting in scroll bars on either the side or the bottom. You should adjust the window so that there is almost no gray area surrounding the video window itself. Then reopen the Capture window, and you will see that its size is minimized as well.

The Capture Window

The Capture window is dominated by the Capture screen on the left. Unless Final Cut Express is currently receiving video data through the Firewire tube, the Log preview window will simply show color bars. Insert a DV tape. As soon as you do so, you will receive a message recommending that you assign a Reel Name to the new tape that has been inserted. Do so, using the Reel Name "Tape_#1," which corresponds to your Capture Bin name (see Figure 2-63).

Scratch Disk Info

After you name the reel, take a look back at the Capture window. At the very top of the window you will see two phrases: Total Free Space and Total Free Time (see Figure 2-64). The values for these designations are the amount of free disk space on the current Scratch Disk-assigned drive and the amount of footage that free drive space can accommodate. This is merely another warning for you regarding your Scratch Disk Preferences. If you see anything unusual here, such as a drive space figure that is too high or low, or a capture limit that is too short, you may have committed an error in assigning the Scratch Disk

Figure 2-63 Assigning a Reel Name "Tape_#1"

Figure 2-64   Total Free Space and Time

location. Final Cut Express can't fix this for you, but it can help you catch your own errors.

Current Frame Timecode Field

Moving to the top right-hand corner of the window, you will see a small watch dial followed by a field containing a timecode value. This field is the timecode for the video frame on which the DV tape is currently parked (i.e., paused). If you have a tape in your deck that contains timecode and Final Cut Express is configured correctly, this window will always report the exact timecode number of the frame on which the tape head is currently parked.

You can also use this field to shuttle around the tape. Because the Capture window actually controls the deck as well as receiving video from it, this field works both ways; it tells you which frame is queued up on the tape head, and you can tell it to go to a certain frame by entering the timecode number into the box and hitting Enter. This is but one of many ways to navigate to locations on your tape.

The Tape Transport Controls and J-K-L Support

Moving below the video window, you will see the playback buttons, otherwise referred to as transport controls. Using these controls, you can shuttle back and forth, remotely controlling the deck from inside Final Cut Express. There are six buttons for controlling playback as well as two knob-wheel-type controllers that mimic physical deck controls.

The most important buttons on the transport controls on any deck are obviously the rewind, pause, play, and fast-forward controls. Final Cut Express makes using this window—and other windows—easier by using a keyboard shortcut convention called J-K-L support. What J-K-L means is that the J key initiates rewind, the L key initiates play, and the K key simply pauses the playhead where it is (see Figure 2-65). Beyond this, J-K-L has the flexibility of variable-speed playback. If you hit either the J key or the L key repeatedly, you will find that the playback speed increases, while K always stops the playback entirely.

Using J-K-L means that you can leave the mouse alone and forget about looking at the keyboard to find the right combination. Resting your hand on the keyboard with your

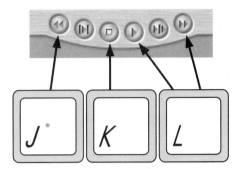

Figure 2-65 The transport controls and J-K-L keys

middle three fingers spread over the J-K-L keys is very natural, which is why it has become very popular. Practice using it to move back and forth to find frames you want, and you'll quickly get addicted to using it.

The other two buttons on the transport are Play Around Current and Play In to Out. Play Around Current simply plays a certain number of frames before and after the frame on which the tape is currently paused. Where does this certain number of frames originate? It is determined by the settings in the General tab of the Preferences, where it is referred to as Preview Pre-roll and Preview Post-roll. Whatever values you entered in that preference correspond to the number of frames that will be played before and after the current frame on which the playhead is parked. Play In to Out is simply a preview of the In point to the Out point based on what is currently entered in the In and Out point fields.

The Jog and Shuttle Wheels

The other two controllers hark back to the world of physical decks. They are referred to as Jog and Shuttle controls. The control on the left-hand side is the Shuttle controller. If you click the Shuttle knob and drag it in either direction, you will find that the deck responds by moving in that direction. The speed of playback corresponds directly to how far in either direction you tug the knob. Shuttling is a great variable-speed method of moving around. The J-K-L controls we just described are referred to as Shuttle controls, because we can determine how fast or slow the playback is by the number of times we strike the same key repeatedly.

The controller on the right-hand side is called a Jog controller. The difference between Jog and Shuttle is that with Jog, a complete turn of the knob results in a limited number of frames playing on the tape, no matter how much force you use to tug the controller. Unlike the Shuttle controller, which can be pulled only so far in either direction, the Jog controller turns a complete 360 degrees, after which a number of individual frames have been advanced. There is also a keyboard frame advance and retreat that corresponds to the

Jog controller's frame-by-frame navigation. These are the Left and Right Arrow keys, which will advance or retreat one frame at a time. Hold the Shift key down when doing so, and it advances or retreats one second.

You will find that Jog and Shuttle have their places and are meant to be used together. Shuttle is useful for moving quickly over large sections of tape, while Jog finds the exact frame you need to edit with. Use Shuttle to get into the neighborhood and then Jog to get the perfect edit frame. But master the J-K-L and Left Arrow–Right Arrow shortcuts rather than dragging the mouse around. Apple will not compensate you for damages caused by carpal tunnel syndrome, so you'd better start protecting your wrist from harm with the keyboard shortcut conventions.

Set the In and Out Points for a Clip

Once you have decided on the In and Out points (i.e., the frames you want to use for the beginning and end of your clip), look below the transport controls to find two timecode data fields, each of which is accompanied by two buttons (see Figure 2-66). These are the In and Out points you will establish for your clip. Before you set any In or Out points, these fields will read, "Not Set."

Remember that you have to leave enough room for the deck to pre-roll, or get the tape rolling at the right speed, before the capturing starts. The recommended Pre-roll setting is 5 seconds, so you need to make sure that there are 5 full seconds for the deck to roll into before you begin the capture. Otherwise, you will receive an "Unable to lock deck servo" error message when you initiate the actual capture. That means that you can't really set your first In point for your clips before 00:00:00:06 on your tape! This issue is usually only related to the first clip on each reel number, although it may also apply if you are dealing with a broken timecode, where your timecode resets to 00:00:00:00 in the middle of the tape.

When you have selected a suitable frame for an In point, locate the timecode field on the bottom left-hand side of the window. Click the button to the right of this timecode field, and you will see the timecode number appear there. This button is the Mark In point. The button to the left of the In point field is the Go To In point button, which will simply return the tape to the currently established In point should you need to get there quickly.

Now shuttle a little farther into your tape. When you have found a good location for the end of the clip, look over to the timecode data field on the bottom right-hand side of the window. You will find an Out point button on the left side of this field. Clicking the Out point button inserts a value into the Out point field. As with the In point field, the button on the right of the Out point field is Go To Out point and will quickly roll the

Figure 2-66 Setting In and Out points

tape to that frame if engaged. With the establishment of an In and an Out point, you now have a valid, if not yet captured, clip in the Capture window. If you don't like the In or Out points you created, simply go to a new frame and hit In or Out again.

As always, there is a much faster way to insert In and Out points using convenient keyboard shortcuts. The I key and the O key will insert In and Out points into these fields. The convenience is reinforced by the fact that these keys are directly above the J-K-L keys that you use for shuttling (see Figure 2-67). You rarely need look at keyboard again. Simply keep your hand poised on the J-K-L keys, and when you find either an In or an Out point, move your fingers a half inch up and strike the key. There's no faster way to log clips, or one that is less stressful on the wrist. A little practice is all it takes, and you'll be able to log clips without thinking about the process at all. Being able to focus on your editing without thinking about which on-screen button you need to mouse your way to is the key to becoming a good editor.

The Clip Duration Timecode Field

Now that you have entered a valid In and Out point for the clip, look in the top left-hand corner of the window, where you will find another timecode data field (see Figure 2-68). This is the Clip Duration field, which calculates the duration of the current clip, based on the In and Out points. You should see a value here now that you have entered an Out point that follows an In point.

Of course, as with the Current Frame field on the upper right-hand corner of the window, this field can affect the other fields. If, for example, you have already set the In point and you know that you need to log 10 seconds following that In point, there is no need to shuttle forward and find the frame number or even to calculate the Out point in your head. Simply type 1000—which is a shorthand for the timecode value of 00:00:10:00, or 10 seconds—into the Clip Duration field, and it will automatically update the Out point based on the In point and the Duration timecode value.

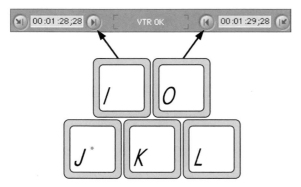

Figure 2-67 Using I and O keys to set In and Out points

Figure 2-68 Clip Duration field

Capture Using Capture Clip

Now that you have entered the required information for the clip, you are ready to capture. Click the Clip button in the Capture box on the Logging tab side of the window, and Final Cut Express will begin the capture process. If you selected the Prompt check box on the Logging tab, you will be presented with a box asking you to name the clip. Do so, click OK, and Final Cut Express will wake up the deck and begin searching for the In point. You will see a black screen with a message at the bottom telling you what Final Cut Express is doing at the moment. When it finds the In point on the tape, it will begin capturing and continue to do so until your clip is completely captured. It is now located in your Capture Bin and available for editing (see Figure 2-69).

If you take a moment and look back into the Capture window, you will see that it has set a new In point that is one frame later than the Out point of the clip you have just finished capturing. The new Out point is one frame later than the new In point because you will need to log a new Out point, no matter what the new In point is. This means that Final Cut Express is now ready for you to log the next clip you want to capture.

Capture Now

Logging your clips with timecode for immediate capture strategies is definitely the safest and most efficient method of capturing media. But some Firewire configurations do not

Figure 2-69 Using Capture Clip

have access to timecode. And in some situations, capturing a quick clip will be more productive than logging a clip manually as described in the previous section. In these instances, Capture Now will be more effective.

Capture Now and the Relationship with DV Timecode

First, you need to determine whether you are sending timecode data from the DV device through the Firewire tube to Final Cut Express. Remember that just because video and audio are getting captured doesn't mean that timecode data is being captured as well.

If you are using a Digital 8 camera, only footage that was shot using the Digital 8 camera has valid DV timecode written into the data of the footage. If you are using a tape that was recorded in a standard Hi8 or 8 mm video camera, the footage will not have DV timecode. Although you can still easily capture this footage using Capture Now, you cannot do so using the normal Easy Setup and will have to use the DV Converter preset; thus you will not be able to get timecode data for the clip when you capture it. If you are using a DV converter box, no DV timecode will accompany the DV data stream through Firewire.

Also, remember that this refers to any device that offers pass-through (also known as EE-In-Out) operation. Many DV decks and cameras will allow you to connect an analog device to the inputs of the DV deck or camera, which will convert the analog signal to DV on the fly and pass it directly to Final Cut Express through the Firewire connection. Such pass-through connections also do not carry DV timecode and act precisely like a DV converter box.

If you are using Capture Now with one of the aforementioned devices and do not have DV timecode, you may use Capture Now to capture your clips, but you must switch your Easy Setup to DV Converter. This preset will keep Final Cut Express from looking for DV timecode that does not exist. If you do not switch this preset, the attempt to Capture Now will result in a long system hang followed by an error message complaining about "No Communication."

On disabling Device Control, you will see that the Clip and Project buttons have gone gray and become unavailable. This is because they require Device Control and timecode to operate. Because you have no access to timecode, Final Cut Express will not be able to control the device. This means that you will have to queue up the footage that you want to capture on the deck by hand. This is a slightly awkward way of working in which you hit Play on the device, hit Now in Final Cut Express, and hope that it begins capturing before the first frame you wanted to work with passes by. Although it may work in a pinch, it becomes frustrating rather quickly in larger jobs.

On the other hand, if your device has DV timecode, you can use Capture Now with complete Device Control and timecode. In this case, make sure that the Device Control preset is still set correctly for the configuration you want to use and not to DV Converter.

The Capture Now Process

If you have Device Control and DV timecode, make sure that you fill out the Logging tab information to the right, as if you were performing a logged capture. In particular, make sure to enter a Reel Name and Clip Name, since your clip will carry valid timecode data and should be associated with a specific tape. Of course, if you have no DV timecode, such logging data will not be stored with the clip anyway.

If you have Device Control, start the tape rolling using the J-K-L keys, as described in the section on Log. They will perform the same way. If you have no Device Control, simply hit Play on the DV deck or camera. You will need to queue up your tape a few seconds ahead of the place you want to start capturing, because it takes a moment for Final Cut Express to prepare the Scratch Disk for your media. Think of this as a pre-roll and add at least 5 seconds so that you are sure you get the In point you wanted plus a little extra. If you have rather large media drives, be warned that you will need to start the tape rolling much earlier than you think. Setting the Limit Capture Now To field in the Scratch Disk Preferences to a reasonable number will help speed the beginning of the Capture a great deal.

As the tape is rolling, hit the Now button in the Capture options. When you do so, the Currently Capturing window will pop up, and you will watch what is being captured stream in (see Figure 2-70). When you are ready to stop the capture, simply hit the Escape key. The Escape key is the only way to stop Capture Now, with the exception of reaching the Capture Now limit that you set in the Scratch Disk Preferences tab in the Preferences.

Figure 2-70 Using Capture Now

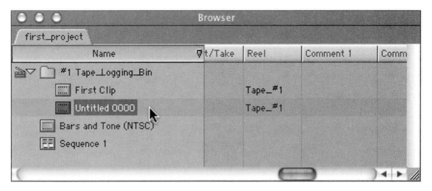

Figure 2-71 Untitled 0000

When the Currently Capturing window disappears, you will see that a new clip has appeared in the Capture Bin (see Figure 2-71). If you did not name the clip in the Description field of the Capture window, the clip will carry the name Untitled 0000 (or 0001, 0002, and so on as you accumulate clips). Now your clip is available for editing, just as is the clip we logged earlier.

When was the last time you saved and backed up your project? After you have completed your capturing is the right time to save the project you have created the clips in. Although the actual media files have been properly saved to the media drive, the clip, which is now associated with the project, has not yet been saved as part of the project file. If your system had crashed for any reason, the clip would not be there when you reopened the project, and you would need to find the media files in your Capture Scratch folder and manually import them.

Using DV Start/Stop Detection

In the preceding description of Capture Now, it was stated that Capture Now is a very inefficient system for getting lots of different clips into a project. Although that is generally accurate, there is one example in which it can be even more efficient than capturing logged clips. Final Cut Express includes a feature called DV Start/Stop Detection, which can easily and automatically break up your camera's DV footage from a one huge captured clip into individual clips. Although it won't work in all situations, it bears mentioning since for some it may dramatically decrease the amount of time they have to sit in front of the screen scrolling through their footage.

When you are shooting with your camera, it includes data based on the time and date of the recording taking place. When you hit Pause and then start recording again later, the camera records data about the date and time, even if you have Date and Time display turned off in the controls. Although there is no timecode break between these pause and record actions, the fact that the recording action started a little later than previous material on the tape is retained by the video frames as a "scene break" on the tape.

If you bring in a clip that has a series of takes or pauses (for instance, if you shot with the camera, getting this shot and then pausing, that shot and then pausing, etc.) and you have no timecode breaks on the tape, use Capture Now to capture the entire section of tape, pauses and all. After the capture is complete and the clip is loaded into the Viewer (or selected in the Project tab), you can go to the Mark drop-down menu and choose DV Start/Stop Detection (see Figure 2-72). It is not necessary that you use Capture Now for DV Start/Stop Detection; clips captured from the log process will work just as well, since the tool is only concerned with the clip, no matter how it got into Final Cut Express. It is mentioned here because the workflow of DV Start/Stop Detection is extremely useful for those with long camera-recorded tapes that must be captured completely from beginning to end and that may be more easily captured and chopped up in this way rather than through laborious logging.

When you choose this option, Final Cut Express will examine the clip and automatically insert special markers everywhere that it sees evidence that the camera was paused while in the midst of shooting. The great news is that the markers it inserts are treated like clips themselves, independently manipulated from the master clip they were captured as a part of (we will explore subclips in greater detail in Chapter 4). If you keep good shot logs while acquiring your footage, you can save yourself the hassle of shuttling through your footage to organize your clips, and let Final Cut Express break it up into scenes for you.

As an example, find a clip you have just captured (or capture another such clip) that has scene breaks as described earlier. This time, double-click the clip to load it into the Viewer window. After it is loaded into the Viewer, go to the Mark drop-down menu and select DV Start/Stop Detection. After a short progress bar appears, you will see a series of yellow markers in the Viewer window's timeline (see Figure 2-73). Each of these markers indicates a scene break.

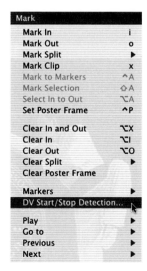

Figure 2-72 DV Start/Stop Detection

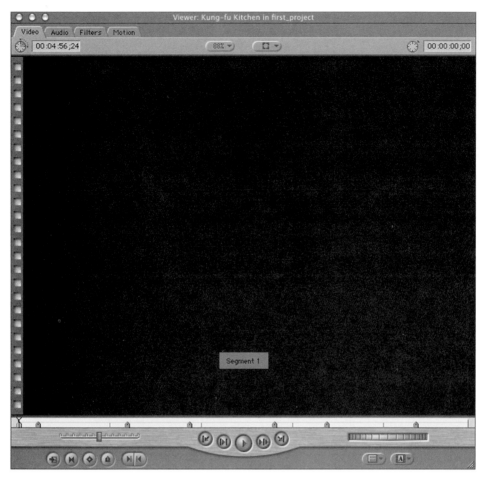

Figure 2-73 Markers that indicate scene breaks

Even better, look back at the original clip in the Project tab, and you will see a small widget next to its icon (make sure you are in List view mode). If you click this widget, you will see it drop down to reveal a number of these same markers (see Figure 2-74). Double-click any of the markers, and you will see that only the section delimited by that particular marker loads into the Viewer, not the entire original clip.

Capture Project

Disaster often strikes without warning. One day you are working on a project that has taken you a month to construct. The next day you start up the machine and the drive holding all your footage is no longer on the Desktop. All the clips in the Project window now have

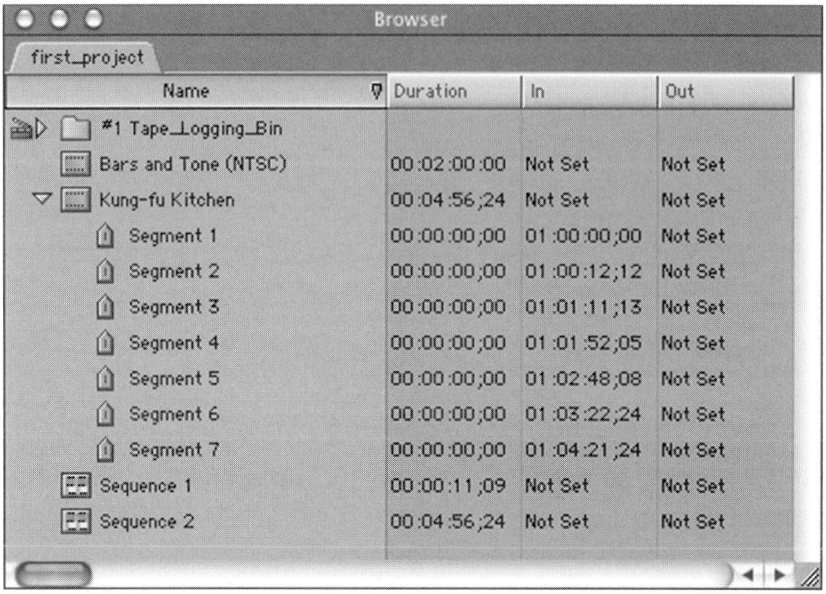

Figure 2-74 Markers revealed in List view mode

red slashes running through them telling you that the clips are now offline. A cold chill runs down your spine. You reboot, you run maintenance, you pray, and still nothing. The drive is dead.

Without timecode and proper reel names, you would really be in trouble. There would be no way to reconstruct your project short of having an expensive computer repair facility try to repair the drive (a shaky proposition at best). Now it may be a little more obvious why the precautions are necessary. Every editor has a story like this to tell, and it is usually followed by the warnings you are hearing here. These are mistakes you tend to make only once!

It doesn't take much time or effort to do things right, and if you stick to the rules, you can completely reconstruct your project by simply popping your original tapes in the deck and hitting a few buttons. What follows is the method for recapturing a project when the originally captured media has disappeared for whatever reason.

Getting Your Project Back Online

When you want to get everything back on the drives again, all you have to do is go to the Capture window as if you were going to bring more media in, but this time choose Project instead. You can also use the Control-C keyboard shortcut without even having to pull up the Capture window. When you do this, you will get the Capture Project window (see

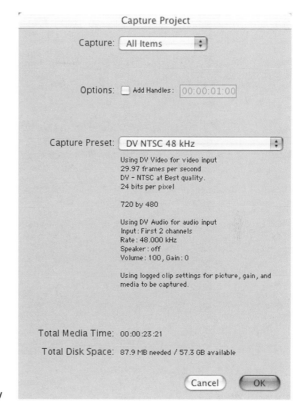

Figure 2-75   Capture Project window

Figure 2-75). If there is nothing in the sequence yet, you will also be given a message that the project cannot be recaptured because it is empty; simply hit Continue in that instance.

In the Capture Project window, you need to look at a few options before proceeding.

Capture Drop-Down Bar
It appears that there are never any options for this bar.

Options Check Box: Handles
The Options check box contains a timecode field for entering handles. "Handles" simply means having Final Cut Express grab a specified extra number of video frames during the capture in addition to the number you asked for when you logged In and Out timecode numbers for the clip. If you set a value for handles of 15 frames, Final Cut Express will capture an extra 15 frames at the beginning and end of every clip you capture (see Figure 2-76). This will not affect the In and Out points of your captured clip. The frame handles

Figure 2-76   A clip with handles

will stay safely out of view until you need to bring them into play. Your In and Out points will always reflect the way that you logged them for the clip.

You can, of course, override the option to get handles on your captured clips by disabling the check box, but doing so is a pretty bad idea. Once you've captured the clip and you begin editing, you will usually find at least one clip for which you need a little more material than you originally thought while logging, especially when an edit between one clip and the next requires a transition such as a fade or a dissolve, a subject we will work with in Chapter 4. It's hard to predict exactly how much video you'll need for these purposes, but a good solid 15-frame handle is usually about right. In addition, this will protect you from a rare occurrence in which the capture process accidentally duplicates the first frame it captures. Inserting handles will completely eliminate this as a potential threat.

Capture Preset Choice Bar

The next item is a drop-down bar that allows you at the last minute to switch the Capture Preset you want to use for the Batch Capture (see Figure 2-77). Although it is not likely that you will have to change this, you at least have the option. This would be the right time to make sure that you have selected the proper audio sample rate and to switch it if you

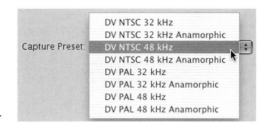

Figure 2-77 Capture Preset choice bar

have chosen an incorrect one. Below the Capture Preset drop-down bar, you will find a summary of the settings for the current Capture Preset.

Batch Capture Idiot Check Summary

Underneath the Capture Preset bar, you will see your last "idiot check" summary information. The first item, labeled Total Media Time, refers to the total amount of time to be captured in the entire Batch Capture. It is the total of all the clips' durations combined. If you see a particularly odd number here, such as 12 hours, you should probably abort the capture and check your clips.

The second item is labeled Total Disk Space and will contain two numbers. The first number is a calculation of the total amount of drive space necessary to capture the amount of Total Media Time based on the data rate of the codec in your Capture Preset. Since Firewire DV editors will be using the DV codec, which we know has a data rate of roughly 3.6 MB per second, this number should be easy to calculate mentally. The second number is the amount of drive space currently available on the assigned Scratch Disk drive.

If you see a problem, hit the Cancel button and rectify the issue. If everything is set and checks out, click OK and begin the Capture Project process. You will be greeted with a box confirming which tapes are necessary for the capture and how many clips are to be

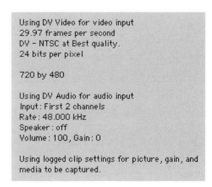

Figure 2-78 Batch Capture idiot check summary

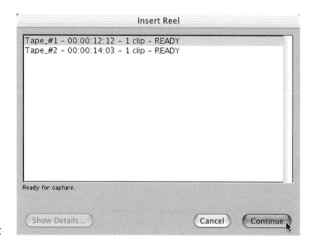

Figure 2-79 Using Capture Project

captured from the tapes (see Figure 2-79). When you hit Continue, Final Cut Express will proceed to capture all the clips. When it has finished capturing, you will receive a similar box showing that the capture is complete. Hit Done, save your project, look in the Logging Bin in the Project tab, and you will find that the offline clips have lost their red lines. Having associated media files, they will now appear as online clips.

3 Importing Media

Capturing footage from DV tape is not the only way of getting media to work with in Final Cut Express. This chapter is concerned with the process of importing the large range of file formats that Final Cut Express is capable of accepting and using as media. A very common misconception for beginners is that opening a file is the same thing as importing. This eventually leads to confusion over what needs to be backed up, what applications can deal with which sorts of files, etc. This misconception is totally unnecessary.

This chapter's aim is to give the reader a clear understanding of the import process. Although we will only be working through two of the most common examples, importing CD audio tracks and Photoshop image files, the import process in theory is universal. Master these import techniques and you will be able to apply what you do here to every other file format Final Cut Express is capable of working with.

What Importing Is and What It Is Not

Frequently, when we try to describe what we are doing with digital applications, we get a little fast and loose with our terminology. But sometimes, splitting hairs is important in describing what you need to do to avoid problems. Importing and exporting from an application is one such instance.

In the video editing world, there are two types of files: project files and media files A project file is a file that is opened by Final Cut Express. It contains all the code that describes what happens with the media files in use by the project. The project file itself is not video or audio footage; it is a sort of director for all the footage you use in the project, like a blueprint. You open it, and then you work inside it.

A media file, on the other hand, is your footage or other elements such as graphics from Photoshop or CD audio—things you use inside your project. It is what is controlled by the project file. Although you can watch or listen to your media files in various other applications, you cannot edit or arrange them unless they are inside a Final Cut Express project. The video footage you captured in Chapter 2, for instance, is media. Likewise, files that we import into the project will be media files.

So you can see that these two types of files are very different, though very dependent on each other when you edit. A project file is something you open with an application, while a media file is something you bring into that project by either capturing while in the application or by importing.

Final Cut Express can easily import the following file formats, arranged by file type: Still Image

- BMP
- Flashpix
- GIF
- JPEG/JFIF
- MacPaint
- Photoshop
- PICS
- PICT
- PING
- QuickTime Image File (QTIF)
- SGI
- Targa
- TIFF

Video

- AVI
- QuickTime Movie (MOV)
- Image Sequences
- Flash (Video only)
- MPEG1 (Video only)

Audio

- AIFF
- Audio CD Data (Macintosh)
- System 7 Sound
- Wave (WAV)

Some of these formats may seem obscure, but they all have one thing in common: Final Cut Express can import them into your project and use them as clips for editing. Such importing is very common. By using audio tracks from an audio CD or using Photoshop files to create graphics, you can easily add professionalism and class to your finished production. Although Final Cut Express is an advanced editing solution, there are some things that other applications can do much better.

Graphics applications such as Photoshop have tools that are much more suited to developing beautiful text and other visual elements. Audio applications such as Digidesign Protools and Bias Peak DV are often used to texture, mix, and clean up audio tracks that initially don't sound their best. Further, if you deal with clients who provide you with standard graphics or sound elements, you'll have to deal with importing their materials.

CD Import: The Right Way

To import CD audio tracks, we have to take a couple of things into account. First, we can't simply put the CD in the Macintosh and select Import from the File menu. That is a rookie mistake that will backfire on the user in 10 minutes. Getting your CD audio tracks into Final Cut Express isn't complicated, but you have to take care of a few things along the way.

If you put the CD in and selected Import, your project would link itself to the CD. The problem is that as soon as you removed the CD from the Macintosh, the audio track would become unavailable to your project! Second, even if the CD were still inside the player, if you tried to play the clip in the Timeline, you would likely end up receiving a Dropped Frames warning. CD-ROMs, though reasonably fast, are generally not fast enough to keep up with the demands that Final Cut Express places on playback. As a result, the CD-ROM drive would spin at top speed, but not fast enough, thus yielding Dropped Frames warnings.

Importing by saving your music tracks as files to your hard drive is very important. But there is still one complication for importing audio CD tracks to Final Cut Express. Our audio recorded in camera—and therefore the appropriate audio sample rate for our Easy Setup—is either 48 K or 32 K. The standard sample rate for audio CDs is 44.1 K. But we are aware that we should never mix audio sample rates in our sequences. So how can we get the sample rate of the 44.1 K audio CD track up to the 48 K or down to the 32 K that will be required by our sequence?

Using iTunes to Import and Convert Sample Rates

The answer is simple: When we import the audio track, we will use another application, such as iTunes, to convert it to 48 K from its original 44.1 K. To do so, we need to do a little setup work in iTunes. Start up the iTunes application. When it is opened, go to the iTunes menu and choose Preferences. In the Preferences window, click the Importing button at the top. First, change the encoder setting from the default MP3 Encoder to AIFF Encoder (see Figure 3-1).

You will see that the default settings for AIFF encoding are the standard 44.1 K that we are trying to avoid. We need to change this by clicking the Configuration bar and selecting Custom. When we do, we will get a window that allows us to specify exactly what we want to change (see Figure 3-2). Set the Sample Rate for 48 K, the Channels to Stereo, and the Sample Size to 16 bit. Now, when we import CD tracks to iTunes, the tracks will be automatically converted to 48 K.

One last step remains; we want iTunes to save its imported 48 K audio tracks into an easily accessible place. Now you have to be careful, because if you have been using iTunes for your personal music collection, you will need to set a different location for saving to keep your AIFF imports at 48 K separate from your MP3s and such in normal use. You'll only want to change the next setting when you create AIFFs; then you'll change it back.

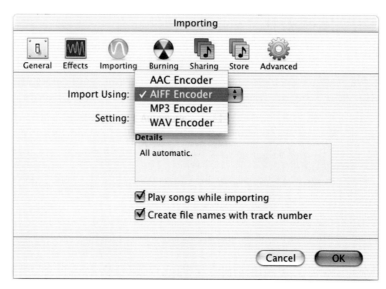

Figure 3-1 Set the import encoder in iTunes to AIFF Encoder

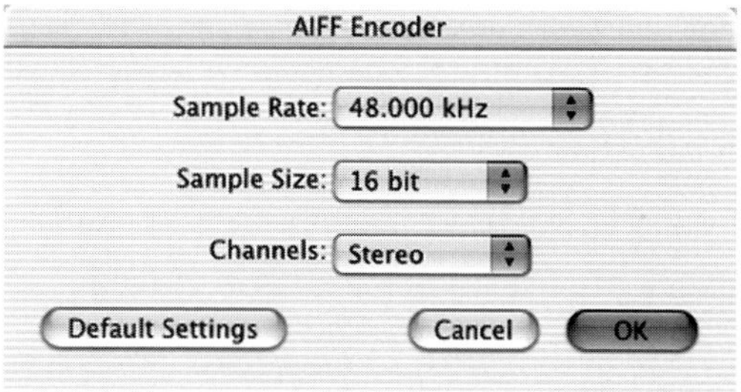

Figure 3-2 Customizing the AIFF Encoder

Click the Advanced button. You will see the iTunes Music Folder Location. Hit the Change button. Choose Desktop from the from drop-down and then navigate to your Scratch Disk folder location. In the Scratch Disk folder, click the New Folder button and create a folder called "CD audio," and then hit Choose. The location you chose will appear in the iTunes Music Folder Location (see Figure 3-3). Hit OK, and you'll return to the main window.

Now that you have set up the location, pop the audio CD in. It will appear in the left-hand side of the iTunes window. Select it and you will see all the tracks on the CD. Instead of hitting Import immediately, uncheck all the tracks you don't want so that the ones you want to use are still selected. Then hit the Import button in the upper right-hand corner of the window. iTunes will start importing the selected tracks (see Figure 3-4), in the process converting the sample rate to 48 K as AIFF and saving them into your Capture Scratch location.

Figure 3-3 Set the iTunes Music Folder Location

Figure 3-4 Import CD tracks in iTunes

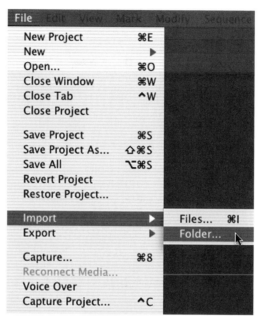

Figure 3-5 Importing into Final Cut Express

Once the import and conversion is complete, be sure to reset your iTunes Music Folder Location and the AIFF Encoder in the Preferences if you use iTunes regularly for encoding MP3s and such.

Next we have to get the converted tracks into Final Cut Express. From here the process is very simple. Click the Browser window Project tab. Go to the File menu and choose Import>Folder (see Figure 3-5). From the dialog box that follows, navigate to the folder you just used for the iTunes import in your Scratch Disk. Select it and hit Import. Of course, if you had brought only one CD track into the Scratch Disk you could have selected Import>File and selected the single CD track.

When you have completed this folder import, a new bin will appear in the Project tab. In that bin will be the audio tracks from the CD. They will be identified with a small speaker icon, which means that the clip contains no video content (see Figure 3-6). It is now available for use in your project.

Using QuickTime Pro to Import and Convert Sample Rates

One of the nice things about OSX is the degree to which Apple's own applications are designed to work with each other and augment each other's functionalities. Another useful application that Apple distributes is QuickTime Pro. QuickTime Player is a QuickTime viewer application that Apple distributes for free so that people on both PCs and Macs can access various QuickTime files and formats. QuickTime Player is very limited in its func-

Figure 3-6 A bin containing audio tracks properly imported from a CD

tionality, mostly giving the ability to play back QuickTime files that already exist, say, as downloaded from the Web or distributed via CD-ROM.

For a small price (currently around $30), you can upgrade Player to QuickTime Pro. Using QuickTime Pro, you can open almost any file format and then export it in a Quick-Time format at the drop of a hat. After you purchase the Pro upgrade (from The Apple Store), you need to unlock your Player application to Pro functionality. To unlock Quick-Time Pro, go to your Applications folder and start the QuickTime Player application. When QuickTime Player has finished loading, go to QuickTime Player>Preferences and select Registration. In the window that follows (see Figure 3-7), be careful to enter your serial number correctly (ones aren't Ls, and Os aren't zeroes).

Using QuickTime Pro to import audio from a CD is a little more streamlined than doing so with iTunes, and it is also faster at converting the audio. QuickTime Pro opens

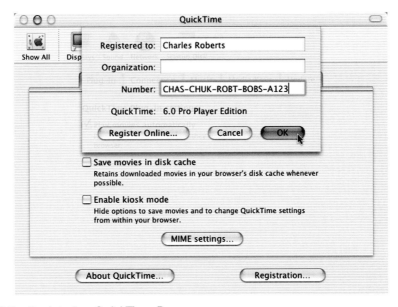

Figure 3-7 Registering QuickTime Pro

CD audio tracks directly and then allows you to save them in another format, such as 48 K AIFF. With your CD mounted on the Desktop, in QuickTime Pro go to the File drop-down menu and select Import. In the following dialog box, pick the track you want and hit Open (see Figure 3-8).

A moment later, your track will open up in a Player window. Because it is only a stereo audio track, there will be no video window. In the Player window, you will find the usual transport controls: play, rewind, fast forward, beginning of track, and end of track (see Figure 3-9). In the Timeline, you will see a playhead triangle on the top and two smaller triangle shapes underneath.

The two triangle shapes underneath the track are a very useful reason for going through QuickTime Pro instead of iTunes for the import/sample rate conversion. Here you can set an In and an Out point for the audio track you are about to convert. Thus, if you only wanted about 10 seconds of the song, you can specify that instead of converting and importing the entire song, only to have to trim it down later in Final Cut Express.

To set the In and Out points, click the right triangle and drag it to the right. You will see that it is repositioned wherever you drop it; this is your Out point (see Figure 3-10). Go back and click and drag the In point to a new position. To listen to only the selection

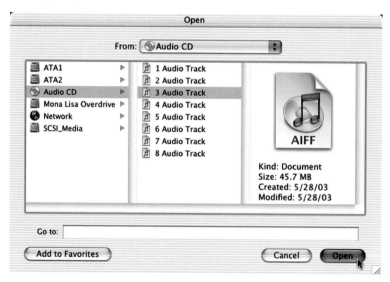

Figure 3-8   Importing a CD track in QuickTime Pro

Figure 3-9   QuickTime Pro Audio Timeline

Figure 3-10 Setting In and Out points in QuickTime Pro's Timeline

you have created with the In and Out points, go to the Movie drop-down menu, and toggle Play Selection Only. If you have made a very short selection and you need to hear it repeatedly, toggle Loop from the same menu. When you have set your In and Out points, from the Edit menu select Trim.

After you are satisfied with your selection, the time has come to convert the sample rate and make the audio track available to Final Cut Express. Go to the File drop-down menu and select Export (see Figure 3-11).

First, address the sample rate conversion settings. Click the Export bar and select Sound to AIFF. Then click the Options button. In the next box, make sure the setting is for no compression, and switch the sample rate to 48 K (unless you will be using 32 K sequences in your project, in which case you should convert to 32 K instead). Choose 16 bit and Stereo, hit OK, and return to the dialog box (see Figure 3-12).

Finally, you need to name the file and choose the correct folder on your media drive to save it to. Just as with the iTunes import process, you want to save this file in a dedicated "imported audio files" folder in your project's Scratch Disk folder (see Figure 3-13). After completing this task, hit OK to begin the conversion process.

Once that process is complete, all that remains is importing the correct audio files into your project. This can be done by importing from the File drop-down menu, as we have done before. If you did all your importing and exporting to a dedicated "audio imports"

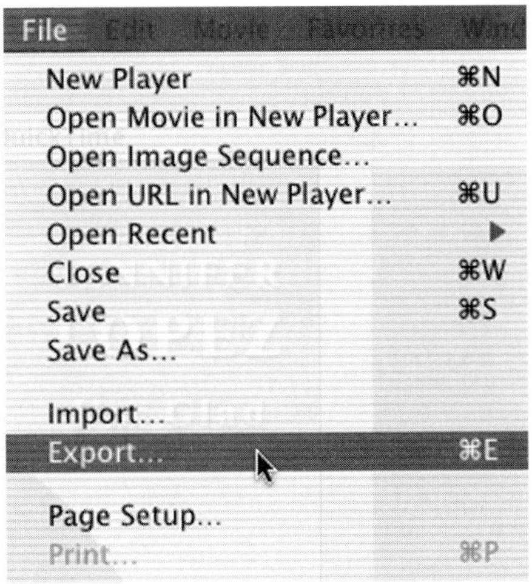

File	Edit	Movie	Favorites	Win
New Player				⌘N
Open Movie in New Player...				⌘O
Open Image Sequence...				
Open URL in New Player...				⌘U
Open Recent				▶
Close				⌘W
Save				⌘S
Save As...				
Import...				
Export...				⌘E
Page Setup...				
Print...				⌘P

Figure 3-11 Exporting from QuickTime Pro

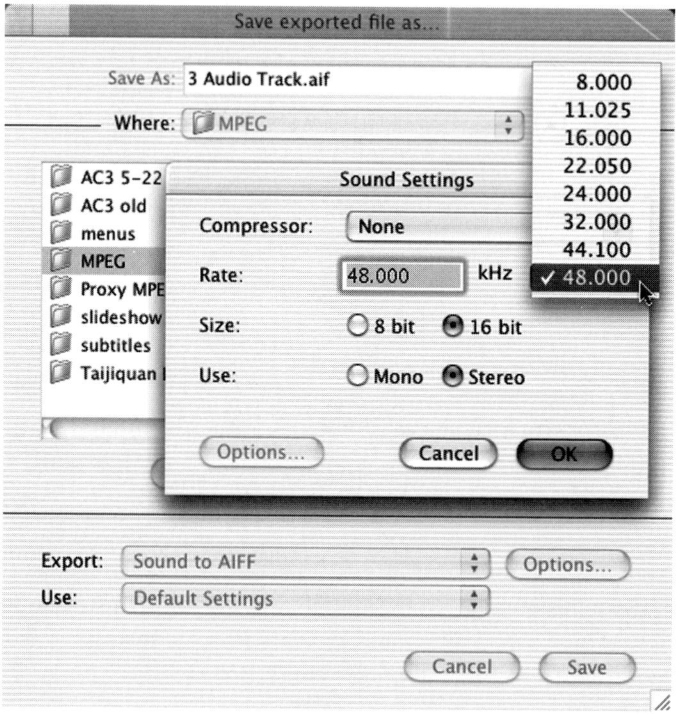

Figure 3-12   Setting compression and sample rate options for AIFF

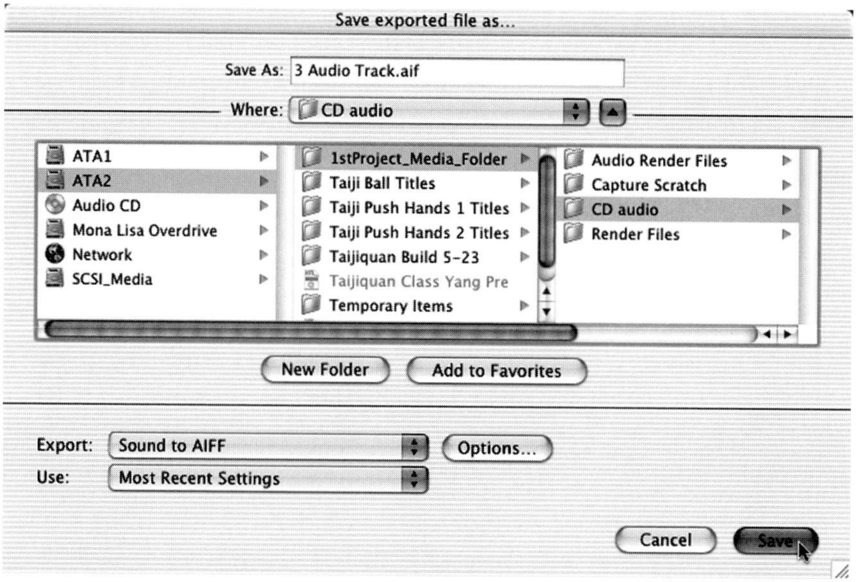

Figure 3-13   Saving your audio files in a dedicated folder in your project's Scratch Disk folder

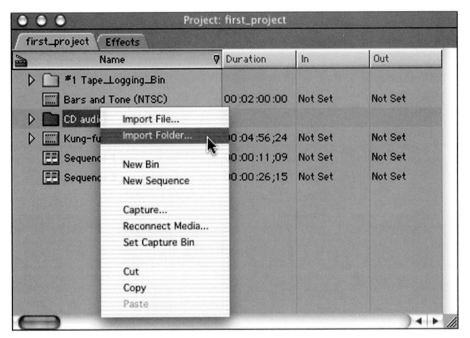

Figure 3-14 Import a folder using the Import contextual menu

folder, you can choose Folder from the Import contextual menu, rather than File, and get them all at once (see Figure 3-14). Beyond this you can grab the audio files from your Scratch Disk folder and drop them directly into your Project tab in the Browser window, which automatically imports them as audio-only clips.

Importing Photoshop Image Files

Graphics files created in Photoshop are easy to integrate into your Final Cut Express project. Why settle for the limitations of Final Cut Express's built-in Title Generator, when you can come up with well-designed graphics files that incorporate image content as well as stylistic text? Best of all, it's easy to get these into your project.

As with audio files, there are a couple of complications in the import process that must be taken into account. With image files from Photoshop, the two issues are square vs. nonsquare pixels and accessing Photoshop layer effects in Final Cut Express. Failure to take these into account will result in distorted images and/or missing features on completion of the import process.

Square vs. Nonsquare Pixels

The first issue, that of square vs. nonsquare pixels, calls for a little explanation about the way different systems display images. A digital image (see Figure 3-15) is broken down into

Figure 3-15   A digital image is made up of (square) pixels

individual dots of image detail called pixels, short for picture elements. It is an atomic model in which the pixel is the smallest indivisible section of an image. We measure all digital images using pixels (with the exception of vector-based images, which are addressed in the section that follows), whether that image is a still digital video frame or a scanned image.

If computer and video pixels were both square, this would make things very simple. And in fact, all computer-driven display systems use square pixels to interpret digital imagery. Most computer applications, like Photoshop, also use square pixels. Video that is to be viewed only on computer screens, such as Web and CD-ROM multimedia codecs, uses square pixels as well.

But the problem is that most professional DV editing systems, including Final Cut Express, use video codecs that require images to be processed using rectangular pixels (taller than wide), which are commonly referred to as nonsquare pixels. If your images are not prepared in advance to deal with the difference in the shape of the pixels, the images will be stretched vertically and will appear tall and thin. The square pixels of the image that were created in a square pixel graphics application such as Photoshop are interpreted into the nonsquare pixel shape of the DV codec Final Cut Express is using (see Figure 3-16).

There is a way around this problem. Create your images in your square pixel graphics application using a stretched frame size that Final Cut Express can stretch back to the proper pixel shape for mixing with nonsquare pixel video. The process involves prefiguring the dimensions of the DV frame in the graphics application slightly larger than it would normally be. Then, right before importing into Final Cut Express, you squeeze the image down in the equal and opposite direction that you know it will be stretched in when the square pixels get interpreted as nonsquare.

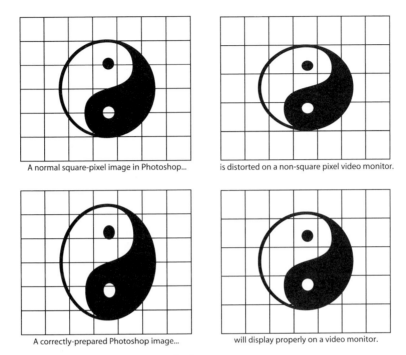

A normal square-pixel image in Photoshop...

is distorted on a non-square pixel video monitor.

A correctly-prepared Photoshop image...

will display properly on a video monitor.

Figure 3-16   Square vs. nonsquare pixels

Don't let the math or the process bother you. It's a simple series of steps that has been ingrained in every Final Cut editor's head since day one. DV NTSC, which has an actual nonsquare pixel size of 720×480, would be 720×534 if its pixels were perfectly square. DV PAL, which has an actual nonsquare pixel frame size of 720×546, would be 768×576 if its pixels were perfectly square.

In Photoshop, you will create graphics images using the prefigured 720×534 or 768×576 square pixel size of your DV video frame. Then the last step you will take before saving your graphics file will be to use the Image Size command in Photoshop (or the equivalent in whichever application you use) to squeeze the pixel dimensions of the graphics file down (to 720×480 for NTSC or 720×546 for PAL) for import into Final Cut Express (see Figure 3-17). When you import to Final Cut Express, the squeezed image will automatically be stretched back out as the square pixels are stretched into nonsquare pixel shapes. No detail or data is lost or gained. The pixels are just shaped a little differently. This process will be covered later in this chapter.

Getting Photoshop Layer Effects into Final Cut Express Intact

The other thing to understand about importing images is the way that Final Cut Express deals with Photoshop layers. Photoshop files can be flattened single-layer files or stacked multilayer files. When you create a Photoshop image, you can add imagery to it either on the initial image layer, rather like painting on a flat canvas, or on new layers that exist

Figure 3-17   A 720×534 image converted to 720×480 and then imported into DV NTSC

as discrete images stacked one on top of another. This adds a lot of functionality to the Photoshop image, allowing you to edit parts of an image without altering other parts of it and to create one file that contains many different image components, all separated and discrete.

The way this is organized in the Photoshop file is that each layer of a multilayer file is actually a distinct image layer. Each layer of the Photoshop multilayer file could be viewed as an individual still image, but they are composited together, one on top of the next so that you see them from the top down as a composite image (see Figure 3-18). This just means that you see the multiple layers of the file from the top down as if they were one image. Anything on the upper layers covers whatever is beneath on the lower layers.

Final Cut Express integrates with Photoshop in a special way. It accepts single-layer flattened Photoshop files as you would expect, simply translating the still image into video frames. But it can also import multilayer Photoshop images with the individual layers still separate, each layer being regarded as an individual still image, even maintaining transparent backgrounds. When a layered Photoshop file is imported into Final Cut Express, it comes in as a sequence with each layer of the Photoshop image acting as an individual clip in the sequence stacked one above the other, each in its own video layer (see Figure 3-19).

Figure 3-18   A Photoshop image may be composed of many layers

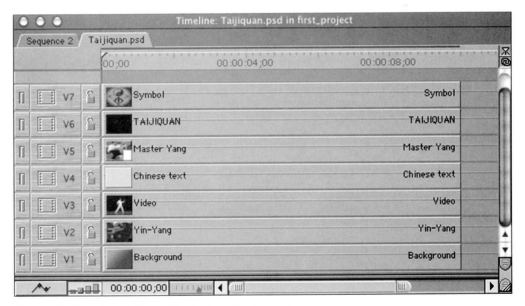

Figure 3-19   A multilayer Photoshop file imports as a sequence

This is a real bonus, because it allows you to apply Final Cut Express effects or motion to the individual layers of the graphics you've created, rather than having to apply all your effects to an entire image. This can speed up your workflow enormously, especially if you work with a lot of Photoshop-generated text and graphics that must be manipulated and adjusted on a case-by-case basis.

The problem with this is that many of the really excellent effects that can be applied to image layers in Photoshop cannot be directly accessed when a multilayer file is imported to Final Cut Express. Because many of these effects are Photoshop's proprietary vector-based effects, they are lost when the image is directly imported into Final Cut Express, which cannot understand them. On the other hand, if you convert the multiple layers to bitmapped layers while still in Photoshop, the layer effects cease to be vector-based and become a part of a rasterized bitmap, or raw pixel data. This means that they will still be present when you import the image into Final Cut Express. For much more on the difference between vector-based and bitmap-based systems, please refer to Appendix D.

The Process

The issue for our two applications here is that Photoshop performs some of its image editing effects using vector-based calculation and display methods. At present, video applications, with only a couple of fairly limited exceptions, use a bitmap format, in which every space in the image contains a colored pixel. A video frame is simply a still image composed of a certain number of pixels. The series of these still images creates video, and those still images are all bitmaps.

Photoshop has many applications and tools that were not created strictly to address creating images for video applications. For this reason, some of the more interesting visual effects, such as Drop Shadow or Bevel and Emboss, that you can create with text and image are vector-based and unavailable for direct use in Final Cut Express (see Figure 3-20).

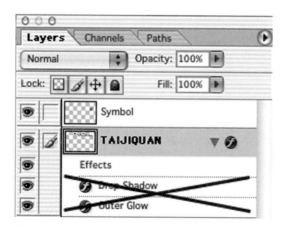

Figure 3-20 Layer effects are vector-based and will not import into Final Cut Express

This does not mean that we have no way of taking advantage of such vector-based effects. It just means that we have to, at some point, convert the vector-based effects into bitmapped image data. This is a process called *bitmapping*, or *rasterizing*. When you bitmap a layer that has vector effects, you take all the geometric vector shape information and turn it into raw pixel bitmaps that describe the shape of the original vector-based effects (see Figure 3-21).

We will create a Photoshop text graphics file, add some vector-based shading effects, then bitmap it and import it into Final Cut Express. Let's step through the process of importing a text image from Photoshop. In Photoshop, create a new image that has a resolution of 72 pixels per inch (the native resolution for DV video) and whose size is 720×534 for DV NTSC projects or 768×576 for DV PAL (see Figure 3-22). Since we will want to be able to use this text image over a video clip as a superimposed element, select Transparent for background. Photoshop will record transparency information in the empty areas

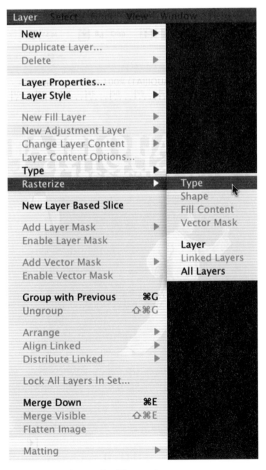

Figure 3-21   Rasterizing a type layer in Photoshop

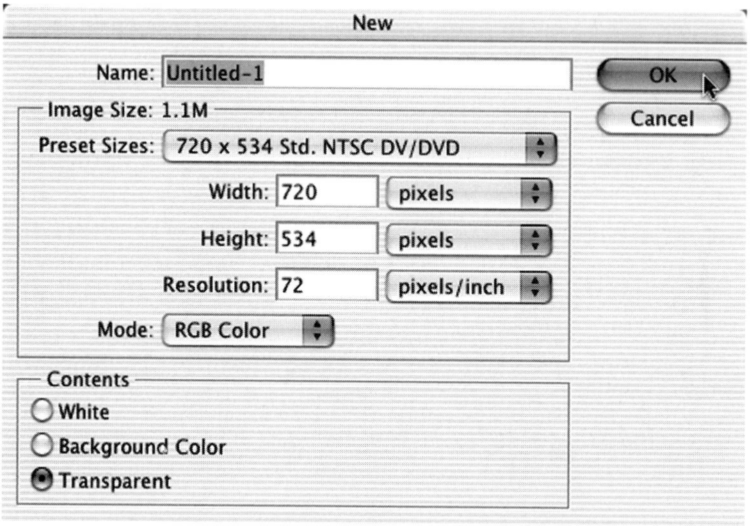

Figure 3-22   Create a new file in Photoshop

of the image that Final Cut Express will be able to interpret as transparent, thus allowing you to see through those spaces and view the video on the layer underneath.

The Title-Safe Zone and Overscan

Create some text using the Photoshop text tool. Be careful not to get your text too close to the edge of the image, or it will go out of what is called the *title-safe zone*. The title-safe zone is a rectangle slightly smaller than the actual frame size of the video standard you are using (see Figure 3-23). All video monitors and television have a frame running around the front edge of the screen, cropping what the cathode ray tube displays into a nice, tidy 4×3 rectangle. Unfortunately, this crop is not only slightly different on all video monitors and TVs, it is also a good deal smaller than what the television tube is capable of displaying. The area that is cropped from display is called the overscan.

When you are working in Photoshop, you have to imagine where this title-safe area rectangle should be and get your text inside of it. There is no law about the size of the title-safe zone any more than there is a law about the individual cropping of the television screens by television manufacturers. A safe bet is to use 10% of the screen height and width to determine the distance in pixels from each side. For DV NTSC, this would be a centered rectangle in the Photoshop image of 576 pixels wide and 384 pixels high. You can easily set up guides in the Photoshop image window to keep you in the safe area (see Figure 3-24).

Once you have the image set up, select the text tool. Click near the center of the image and type in the word "Text" (see Figure 3-25). If the text is very small, you can select it and increase the font size on the Character palette. You could also switch to the selection

Figure 3-23 Be aware of the title-safe zone.

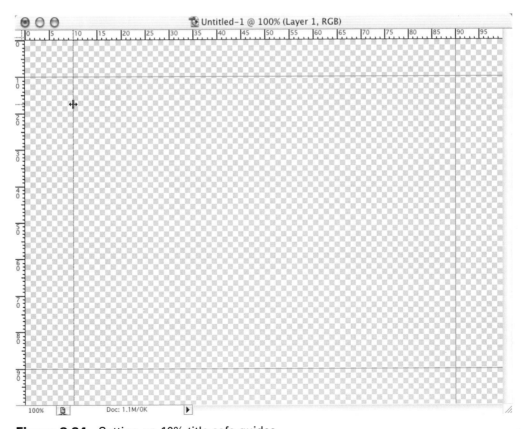

Figure 3-24 Setting up 10% title-safe guides

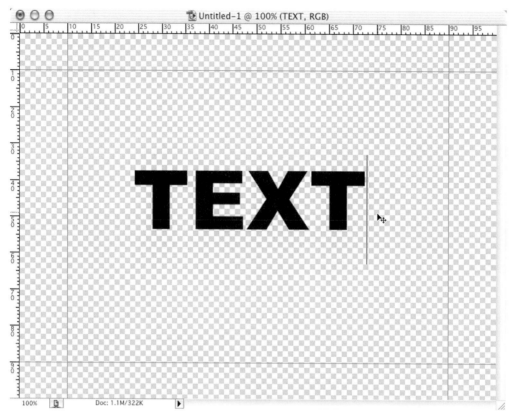

Figure 3-25   Create a text layer in your Photoshop image

tool and then choose Edit>Transform>Scale. Until we commit the step of rasterizing, any reshaping or resizing of the text will not harm its quality. When you are happy with the size of the text, move on to the next step.

Select the text layer in the Layer palette, go to the Layer drop-down menu, select the Layer Style, and then in the submenu that follows, select Bevel and Emboss. Tweak the settings to your amusement and hit the OK button (see Figure 3-26). This will add a nice 3-D rounded edge and some shading to give the text a little depth.

Now is the time to save a copy of the image. The next two steps will perform actions that make it impossible to change the content, such as the spelling of words or the size of the text. If you need to go back in and change something, you can always open the file you have saved at this point, make the change, and perform the following steps to get it ready. That's a lot faster than starting from scratch every time you need to make a little change. Simply save the file as a Photoshop document and include some indicator in the name that it is a production image, not the image you are going to actually use in Final Cut Express.

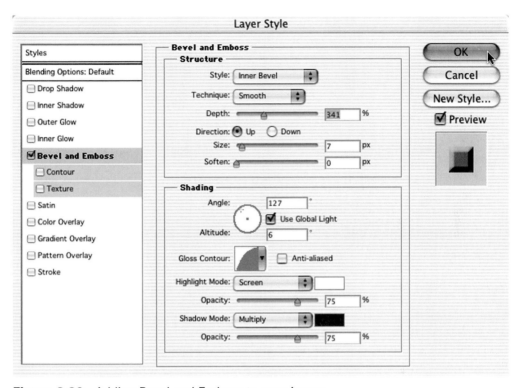

Figure 3-26   Adding Bevel and Emboss to your image

Prepping the Image for Final Cut Express

We now have some nice looking text to take into Final Cut Express. But there are two steps left that are necessary if we want the image to look this good once it gets there. First we have to resize it to account for the nonsquare pixel issue we described earlier in this chapter. Then we have to convert the vector-based effects to rasterized bitmap so that we get the Bevel and Emboss effect on import. Although it is not necessary to complete these steps in the following order, you should maintain the highest quality, since the resizing might degrade the image if committed after rasterizing.

First, we want to do the image squeeze that we described earlier, to prepare the image for import to Final Cut Express. Go to the Image drop-down menu and select Image Size. Immediately uncheck Constrain Proportions, since we need to squeeze the image vertically and not horizontally. For DV NTSC projects, leave 720 for the width and type in 480 for the height (see Figure 3-27). For DV PAL projects, enter 720 for the width and 546 for the height. Hit OK. The image should resize itself, gently squishing the text slightly out of shape. It is now ready to be interpreted by Final Cut Express as a correctly nonsquare pixel image.

Unfortunately, the Bevel and Emboss shading effects, being vector-based layer effects, will disappear if we import this Photoshop file as is into Final Cut Express. Since we want

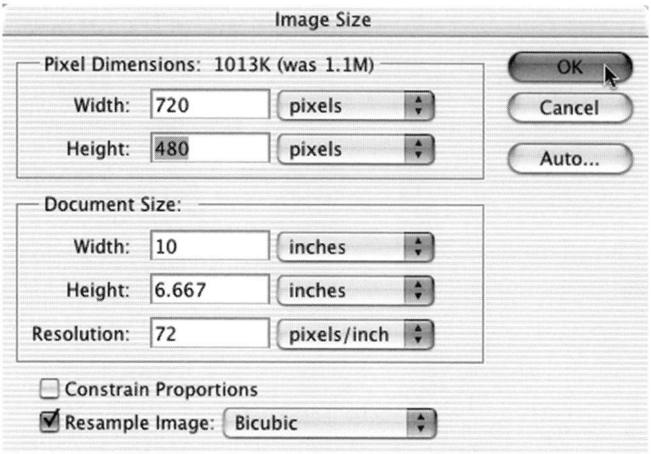

Figure 3-27   Using Image Size to squeeze the image for nonsquare pixels

to retain the special layer effects we just added, we will have to bitmap this layer such that its vector-based effects are retained in Final Cut Express.

The easiest way to change vector-based effects into bitmapped information is to merge two layers into one. When two Photoshop layers are merged, all the separate layer information (e.g., vector-based effects) is bitmapped into the one layer. It becomes a flat group of pixels, rather than a range of vector data.

We could do this by merging down or flattening from the Layer drop-down menu right now. But there's a complication. If we flatten this text layer, we will lose the transparency of the areas surrounding our text and be left with a white background. The easiest way to get around this problem is to create an empty layer just beneath the text layer and merge down. That way, the text layer gets bitmapped with an empty layer, and the transparency areas stay intact.

Go to the Layer drop-down menu, and select New and then Layer from the submenu. Click OK in the Layer dialog box that follows. Go to the Layer palette, grab the text layer, and drag it up above the new empty layer in the palette. Make sure the text layer is selected. Go back to the Layer drop-down menu and choose Merge Down (see Figure 3-28). When you choose Merge Down, the text layer will merge with the empty layer directly underneath it, converting the nice shading effects of the text to bitmapped image data.

Now we need to save the Photoshop image for import. Go to the File drop-down menu and select Save As. In the Save As dialog box, navigate to the Desktop and select New Folder. Name the folder "Production Graphics folder," and click Create. Name the file "Text.psd," making sure that it is followed by the .psd suffix (see Figure 3-29). Click Save. Quit Photoshop and start up Final Cut Express.

Importing Photoshop files into Final Cut Express is simple. You can go through the File drop-down menu process of importing the individual file, but it is much easier to

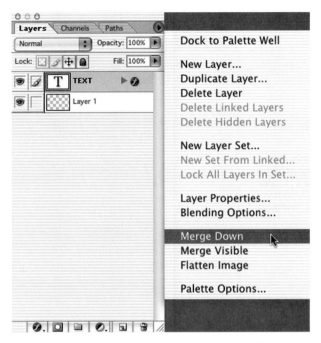

Figure 3-28   Merging down to rasterize vector-based layer effects

simply pick up the folder your Photoshop files are in and drag it directly into the Project tab or individual bin of the Browser window, as shown in Figure 3-30. The folder you drop into your project becomes a bin, and Final Cut Express automatically imports all the files it contains. With no fuss, Final Cut Express instantly recognizes the files and creates icons for them. The actual Photoshop files do not move from the Production Graphics folder; Final Cut Express merely creates a link to them from the icons representing them in the Project tab.

Unlike the audio file we imported and the video clips we captured, still images need not be saved to a special media drive. This is because the image file will not come into play when the clip referencing it is played. Instead, imported still image files must be rendered to play back correctly. The render files that will be created during the render process will be played back from the Scratch Disk location. Thus the original graphics file will not be directly accessed during playback. Still, if it helps you to keep your graphics folder in a unique location, such as your Scratch Disk folder, to maintain order and organization, then by all means do it. Just remember not to move the image file's location after importing it to the project, or you will break the link between the graphics files themselves and the clip in the project.

If your Macintosh is a G4 with a 500 MHz or faster processor, this Photoshop still image can be played back without rendering by virtue of the RT Cache (RAM) setting mentioned in Chapter 2 section on Preferences. Although Firewire output of the video

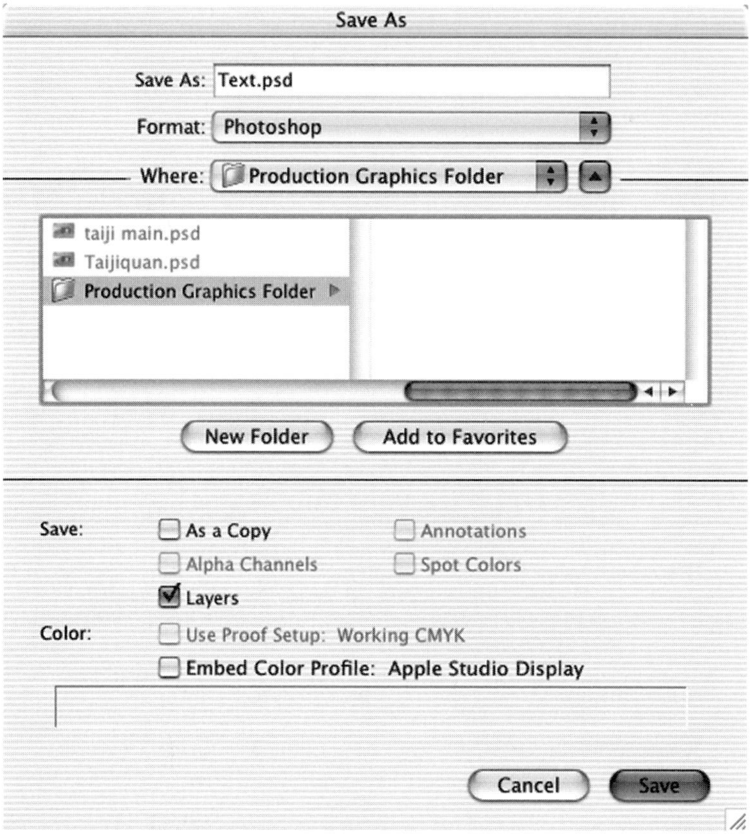

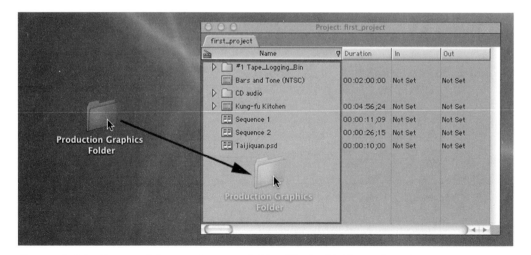

Save As

Save As: Text.psd

Format: Photoshop

Where: Production Graphics Folder

- taiji main.psd
- Taijiquan.psd
- Production Graphics Folder ▷

New Folder   Add to Favorites

Save: ☐ As a Copy   ☐ Annotations
        ☐ Alpha Channels   ☐ Spot Colors
        ☑ Layers

Color: ☐ Use Proof Setup: Working CMYK
        ☐ Embed Color Profile: Apple Studio Display

Cancel   Save

Figure 3-29   Saving the Photoshop image for import

Figure 3-30   Drag and drop to import a folder filled with Photoshop files

preview needs to be disabled, you can watch these stills played back without rendering on your computer monitor. To disable Firewire output briefly, hit Command-F12 or go to the View drop-down menu and select Video>Real-Time (see Figure 3-31). For Firewire output, the stills must be rendered, though.

Open the new "Production Graphics" bin. Take a look at the icon used for the "Text.psd" Photoshop image file. Immediately you will notice something interesting. Instead of your Photoshop image file being imported as a normal clip, it is imported as a sequence. When Final Cut Express encounters a Photoshop image that contains layers (is not flattened), it interprets it as a nested sequence, a concept we will discuss in Chapter 5. For now, take a look at what is in this sequence.

Double-click "Text.psd" in the Project tab so that it opens as a sequence in the Timeline window. You will see that there is one video layer; it contains the text image. If you had created more layers of text in Photoshop, each would be on its own video track in this special sequence (see Figure 3-32). This is the best part about importing Photoshop multilayer images. Because the Photoshop layers are still discrete, you can manipulate them as individual clips. This sequence can be used just like a clip. To see its transparency, you'll need to superimpose it on a video layer above another clip, one of the subjects of the upcoming chapters.

Figure 3-31 Set Video to preview in real time

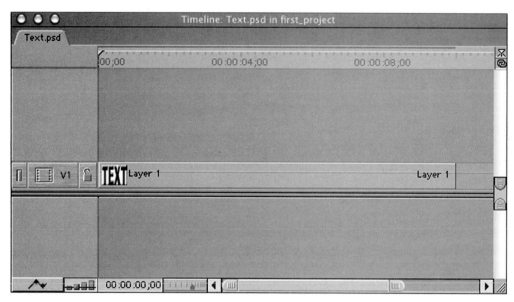

Figure 3-32 A Photoshop image imports as a sequence, and each layer becomes a track

Organizing and Backing Up Your Project's Imported Media

Much was said in the preceding chapter about ways of organizing the various media in your projects, and for good reason. The Project tab is an open slate at the beginning of a project, but it quickly gets confusing as the many different forms of media crowd in (see Figure 3-33).

Simply employing unique naming conventions is not enough. It is important to use the many tools Final Cut Express offers for keeping your project clean. Make sure to establish bins early, separating not only different types of media, such as imported audio and graphics files, but also the different Reel Names and tapes utilized in your projects.

A more important issue for any media you import rather than capture is that such media will most likely not have timecode data the way that a captured DV clip does. Although there are exceptions to this rule, any file that does not carry timecode should be backed up to an archive format, such as CD-R or removable disk. If anything happens to your drives, you can use timecode to recapture your video clips. But without timecode, your production graphics and CD audio tracks would have to be prepared all over again from scratch.

Most audio files and production graphics files are relatively small in comparison to video files, and since they cannot be recaptured the way that video can, backing up copies is good insurance against accidental loss. This is especially easy in view of the fact that all

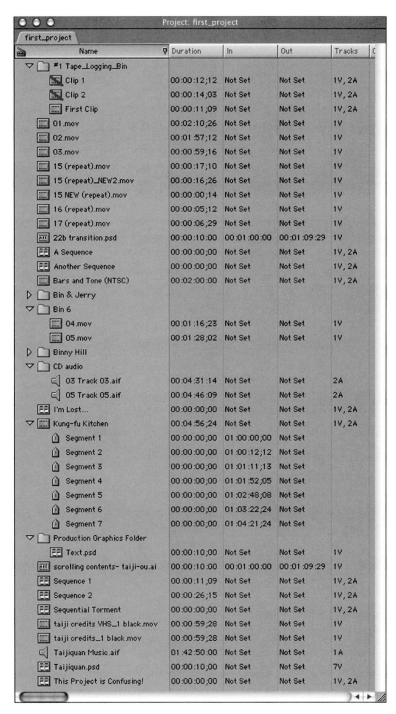

Figure 3-33 A complex project can become confusing if bins are not managed adequately

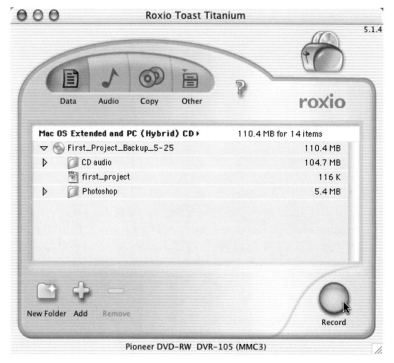

Figure 3-34   Back up your imported media files to prevent disaster

new Macintosh models ship with CD and DVD burners as the stock CD-ROM drive. A good idea at the end of each workday would be to pop in a CD-ROM disk and, using the Apple Disc Burner application or Roxio's great, ubiquitous Toast, burn a copy of all new or changed graphics, audio tracks, and project files (see Figure 3-34). You don't need to do this with captured video and audio since you can simply use timecode to restore them. But a burned CD-ROM containing all your nontimecode media and project files is the best sort of insurance against disaster.

4 What Is Editing?

Now that you have media clips gathered in the Project tab of your Browser window, what do you do with them? Edit, of course. But what is editing? Most good editors will tell you that it is telling a story with a series of images and sounds. This is certainly correct. Editing means being able to take isolated pieces of media and arrange them to communicate an idea. That is the gratifying and artistic part of the process.

But there is a technical aspect to editing that has more to do with the tools and less to do with your message. *Video editing* is the process of modifying and arranging video and audio resources so that they play back in the linear order you desire. The flexibility and functionality of the tool you use to accomplish this defines how easy it is to achieve that goal. And there are some fairly standard tools among nonlinear editors for accomplishing this.

Final Cut Express is a very flexible editing application. It is open-ended enough to allow for many different editing styles. Your own working style will ultimately develop as you get used to the different tools available to you within the interface. Unlike the project setup process, which is very rigid and defined by your DV camera and Macintosh configuration, your editing style depends on how you feel most comfortable working and the types of projects you work on.

As we saw earlier, the various windows in Final Cut Express are linked together based on the clips and sequences passing through them. We load clips into the Viewer window to trim them with In and Out points prior to editing them into a sequence. The Canvas window displays what is currently active in the sequence in the Timeline window. And the Timeline is the linear window, displaying the order of clips as they are played back in the sequence. But this is only one way to view the usefulness of these windows.

The Timeline window is not only useful for arranging the horizontal linear order of clips; it can also be used to stack many vertical layers of video. We can thus control exactly which layer is seen and how much of each layer is seen, much as with the Photoshop layers discussed in the preceding chapter, but over time rather than as a still image. Clips can be loaded into the Viewer window for further manipulation directly from the sequence in the Timeline instead of being loaded from the Project tab in the Browser window. You can trim or cut the length of a clip directly from where it sits in the sequence rather than trimming it in the Viewer. The Viewer can do more than simply load and manipulate clips from the Project tab and the sequence. You can load up whole sequences as if they were individual clips and manipulate them in the Viewer as well. It will be up to the individual editor to become adept at fully utilizing the many possible methods of completing an edit.

Working in the Viewer Window

Editing is a process of arranging clips so that they can be replayed in a particular order. To perform such an action, each media clip must be prepared based on two editing factors: the clip duration (how short or long each clip will be in the sequence) and the edit type (how the incoming clip will meet the clip occurring before it and after it in the sequence).

Determining the duration of a clip is initially performed in the Viewer by setting In and Out points. When you originally captured the clip, you gave it In and Out points, but they were probably rough decisions. You will want to trim frames away and adjust the clip's duration before you put it into the sequence. The beauty of a nonlinear editor is that such actions are very simple. Since we are dealing with a clip, we can put In and Out points wherever we want, or change them later if they don't suit us.

Double-click one of your captured clips in the Project tab to load it into the Viewer. You will be happy to find that the playback controls of the Viewer utilize exactly the same conventions as the Capture window (see Figure 4-1). The Viewer window, and all other windows in the Final Cut Express interface, use the same keyboard navigation conventions (J-K-L for playing, and I and O for In and Out points). In addition, you use the Right and Left Arrow keys for advancing and retreating a single frame on the Timeline (holding the Shift key down while using the Arrow keys advances or retreats for a full second as an option).

As with the Capture window, the top left timecode field displays the duration of the clip loaded into the Viewer. The top right-hand field displays the frame the playhead is currently parked on in the clip. Below the Viewer's video window, you will see that there are no timecode fields for In and Out points, which have been replaced by a few buttons, as

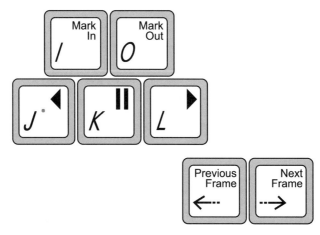

Figure 4-1 Playback controls while editing

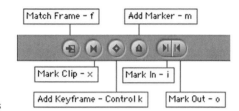

Figure 4-2 Viewer window buttons

described next. Take a look at the buttons on the very bottom of the Viewer window (see Figure 4-2).

Match Frame Button

The first button on the left is the Match Frame button. If a clip loaded into the Viewer window is already being used somewhere in a sequence in the Timeline window, the Match Frame button will call up the sequence in the Canvas and Timeline windows, and it will place the sequence playhead on the same frame of the clip in the sequence that the playhead is parked on in the clip in the Viewer window. It is used for quickly finding exactly the same frame that is being used elsewhere in a project. This is an invaluable tool if you want to make sure you are not accidentally reusing footage. It also works in the other direction from the Canvas window. If you park the playhead on a frame in the Timeline and hit the Match Frame button in the Canvas window, Final Cut Express will load the master clip that the clip in the sequence originated from into the Viewer!

Mark Clip Button

The next button, the Mark Clip button, is like a quick reset button for In and Out points for a clip loaded in the Viewer window. Clicking it immediately places In and Out points at the beginning and end of the clip. If you want to quickly clear the In and Out points you have already placed in the clip, or if you know that you want them to encompass the entire clip, click this button. You will see two sideways triangles appear in the clip's timeline area, defining the duration of the portion of the clip to be used in an edit.

Of course, these points are totally malleable, and setting them is as temporary as you want it to be. You can grab the points themselves and move them manually, set them using the In and Out point commands to be described in a moment, or simply use Mark Clip to set them back to the beginning and end limits of the media file associated with the clip. Mark Clip has more usefulness in the sequence, as we shall see presently.

Add Keyframe Button

Add Keyframe, the next button, allows you to manipulate the clip's physical attributes over time. These attributes are located in the Motion tab of the Viewer window. Keyframing will be addressed in more detail in Chapter 5, Compositing and Special Effects.

Add Marker Button

Add Marker applies a Marker to the frame on which the Viewer playhead is currently parked. Markers are very useful tools for editors. Although they do not affect playback at all and are visible only to the editor of the clip in the Viewer, Canvas, or Timeline windows, Markers allow you to insert detailed information about a frame or entire sections of your clip. Do not confuse the Markers with the Mark Clip button. Mark Clip addresses In and Out editing points for the clip, while Markers are just accessory information about the clip that is linked to a frame or range of frames.

Look under the View drop-down menu and make sure that Overlays is enabled. The Marker is an overlay element that you will see in the Viewer window (see Figure 4-3), rather than seeing it on the output to Firewire and your NTSC or PAL monitor. Click the Add Marker button to add a Marker to the clip loaded in the Viewer window. If you do not see "Marker 1" in the Viewer's video window, make sure you see a little yellow triangle in the

Figure 4-3 Viewing a Marker in the Viewer window

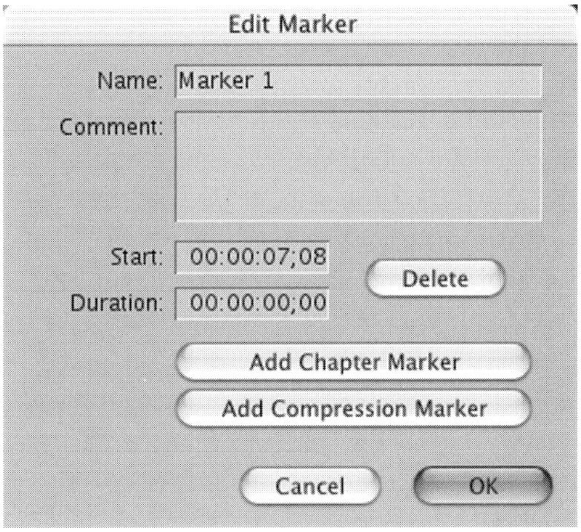

Figure 4-4 The Edit Marker dialog box

Viewer window's timeline. If you do, move the playhead around the Marker point in the Viewer playhead timeline until you see "Marker 1" appear in the Viewer window.

When you see "Marker 1" in the video window, press the M key. This brings up the Edit Marker dialog box (see Figure 4-4). The usual method for adding a marker to a frame or group of frames is to hit the M key twice in rapid succession. The first M keystroke creates the Marker, then the second brings up this dialog box for renaming, etc. Here in the Edit Marker dialog box, you can rename the Marker anything you want, give it a duration so that the information you include in the Marker can be viewed on more than one frame, and type a message about the area covered by the Marker. All this information will be displayed in the Viewer window whenever the Viewer playhead is in the area of the clip containing the Marker. Best of all, the Marker does not affect your edit at all. It only provides another means of adding information about the clip so that you can be better organized.

Adding Markers to clips is especially useful when two or more editors collaborate on a project. Since they may not be working at the same time, it's often critical to leave notes about specific footage that cannot be missed as the editing process moves forward. As discussed in the last chapter, Markers can also be set in the clip during the capture process. Those Markers will still exist within the clip after capture, being available to the editor long after the process of logging tapes is completed. This is an excellent way for producers to communicate their desires for a clip's manipulation to the editor, who may start working on a project long after the producer has become unavailable for questioning.

Another important use for Markers involves exporting video for use in DVD production. We will be discussing such exports in Chapter 7, but for now it is important to note the buttons for Compression Marker and Chapter Marker (see Figure 4-4). Once again, inserting these markers will not affect playback in Final Cut Express, but if you are exporting video for use in iDVD or DVD Studio Pro, a professional DVD authoring solution for the Macintosh, such Markers will be invaluable.

In and Out Point Buttons

The remaining two buttons here are the In and Out points for the clips. The In and Out points will determine the first and last frame from this original, or master, clip to be used when the clip is edited into the sequence. The idea of a master clip and subclips is important here. The clip you load into the Viewer window from the Project tab is referred to as a master clip. The master clip is the original clip captured into the project. It likely contains extra footage and can be trimmed down using In and Out points before it is moved to the sequence.

A funny thing happens, though, once this master clip is dragged from the Viewer window to a sequence. Instead of the master clip itself moving to the sequence, a new subclip—an edited and shortened version of the master clip—is created in the sequence. This subclip is exactly like the master clip in the Viewer it was created from, with one exception. When you load the master clip into the Viewer window, you see all the frames of the clip, regardless of where the In and Out points are positioned. But the new subclip in the sequence utilizes the In and Out points you applied in the Viewer to determine the beginning and end of the clip in the sequence. Thus, playing a master clip from beginning to end will show all the captured frames (even the handles). On the other hand, playing the subclip edited into the sequence will only play what is included between the In and Out points of the newly created subclip.

The master clips and subclips used here should not be confused with the Final Cut Express Subclip command, which is a special command to be discussed later. The use of master and subclip here is standard usage for describing the way that nonlinear editing systems relate an initially captured clip to subsequently edited versions of that clip. The reason for belaboring the point is to make the reader aware that the clip edited into the sequence is not the same clip as the one in the Project tab, although they relate back to the same media file on the media drive. You can create as many subclips from a master clip as you wish, and indeed you do so each time you drag a master clip from the Viewer window into a sequence. Applying changes to the subclip in the sequence will not affect the original master clip in the Project tab!

Remember that the capture keyboard conventions apply in the Viewer window as well, so use the I and O keys to set the clip's In and Out points, and the J-K-L keys to shuttle around the clip quickly. Hitting an In or Out point clears and replaces the previously selected In or Out point, so you can constantly reset them to your heart's desire. You really want to avoid having to search out the little buttons on the Viewer and Canvas windows with the mouse; learn to use the keyboard shortcuts early and often.

Drag and Drop to the Sequence: Insert/Overwrite

Once you have set an In and Out point for the clip in the Viewer window, it's time to edit it into your sequence. There are a couple of ways to do this, and the best way depends

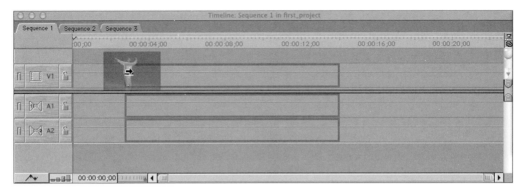

Figure 4-5 Dragging a clip to the Timeline

not only on how you like to edit but what sort of project you are working on. Once you master the two main methods, you'll be able to judge which is best suited to any particular situation.

The first and most basic method is to simply drag the clip from the Viewer video window into the sequence in the Timeline window (see Figure 4-5). Click in the video window of the Viewer and drag the clip down to the sequence without releasing the mouse button. Keep the mouse button pressed as you move the clip around the sequence, and watch the mouse pointer change direction (down or to the right) as the sequence prepares to receive the clip.

As you drag the clip around the sequence, a ghost of the clip's video and audio tracks appears there, showing you which sequence tracks the clip will be dropped into if you let go. Notice that the ghost clip may also appear to sit outside the visible tracks in the sequence. This is because Final Cut Express will allow you to drop a clip in the blank area outside the existing tracks, creating a new track automatically to accommodate it.

Continue to hold the ghost clip so that it appears to sit in Video 1 and its audio tracks sit in Audio 1 and 2. Move the mouse pointer up and down the base line of the tracks in the sequence, and pay close attention as the arrow cursor changes direction. Notice that depending on where in the sequence track you hold the ghost clip, the mouse pointer sometimes appears as a white arrow pointing either down or to the right. This indicates whether the edit you accomplish here will be an Overwrite edit with the arrow pointing down or an Insert edit with the arrow pointing to the right. Insert and Overwrite are the two most basic edit actions in a nonlinear system.

An Insert edit, represented by the "right arrow" mouse pointer, neatly slips your clip into a sequence. If the sequence already contains clips occurring after the position where you are placing your new clip, an Insert edit will move or ripple all those clips over to the right to make room for the incoming clip. If the sequence playhead was parked on a frame in the middle of a clip, that clip will be split into two sections at the position of the playhead, and the section of the clip after the playhead position will be moved to the right to make space for the incoming inserted clip. If the Insert edit is placed between two existing contiguous clips in the sequence, then the clip(s) following the Insert edit will move or ripple to the right to make room for the incoming clip. No frames or clips are removed from the sequence; clips occurring after the edit In point are merely moved farther down the Timeline.

An Overwrite edit, represented by the "down arrow" mouse pointer, lays the clip down wherever you drop it in the sequence regardless of what is currently sitting on the Timeline. If any clips occupy an area of the sequence where the incoming clip will sit, it overwrites them. Unlike the Insert edit, which maintained the same clips in the sequence by moving them out of the way, the Overwrite edit deletes any frames of any clips in the sequence that it encounters.

The fundamental difference is that Insert editing changes the duration of the sequence. Since the new clip moves everything over to the right and adds its duration to the sequence's total duration, the result is more footage in the sequence. Overwrite, on the other hand, keeps the duration of the sequence exactly the same, since it is replacing whatever clip it overwrites with itself. No clips are moved over to compensate, and the duration stays the same unless the overwrite clip extends beyond the clips it is overwriting. These two types of editing require more than one clip to highlight the difference between them.

Using either the Insert or the Overwrite arrow, drop the clip you dragged from the Viewer window onto the first frame at the beginning of the sequence so that there is only one clip in the sequence. If the clip is long and you can't see all of it, press Shift-Z, the keyboard shortcut to resize all the clips to fit everything in the Timeline window. Although the duration is no different, the scale of time you are looking at in the Timeline is shorter, so you can see more clips at once.

If there are no clips present in the sequence, the effect of Insert and Overwrite is exactly the same, since there is no clip to overwrite or insert into. Notice that the clip, once dropped in the sequence Timeline, appears in the Canvas window. Wherever the playhead is moved in the sequence Timeline, the playhead in the Canvas moves there as well; conversely, when you click and drag the playhead in the Canvas timeline (just below the video preview window, as in the Viewer), the playhead in the sequence Timeline moves in concert, mirroring the action in the other window. We say that the Canvas window is a video preview of the sequence in the Timeline window.

For this example, we will edit in the same clip already loaded into the Viewer window, although you could load another clip and set In and Out points for it just as easily. Until you load another clip into the Viewer window, the previous clip you loaded will still be sitting there.

Play through the clip in the sequence, and park the playhead on a frame somewhere halfway through the clip. The position of the playhead in the sequence sets the location, or In point, for the new incoming clip. Return to the Viewer window where your previous clip is still loaded. Once again, click and drag the clip from the video window and move it down to the sequence without releasing the mouse button.

When you bring the ghost clip down to the area where you previously parked the playhead in the first clip, the mouse pointer will snap to the playhead in the sequence (if the clip does not snap to the playhead in the sequence window, hit the N key to enable

Snapping, which may have been disabled. The Snapping feature will be more thoroughly described further on in the chapter.)

Continue to hold the mouse button down, and as you move the mouse pointer around this area, you will see the Insert-right/Overwrite-down arrows appear. When the arrow is pointing to the right, indicating an Insert edit, let go of the mouse button to perform the edit. You will see that the first clip is split in two and that the second incoming clip is inserted between the first and second half of the initial clip (see Figure 4-6). No footage was removed from the sequence; footage after the playhead was moved down the Timeline to create the space necessary for the incoming video clip.

Hit Command-Z (the shortcut for Undo) to undo the Insert edit from the last step so that you are once again looking at a single clip on the sequence. You can always quickly undo the last action performed by hitting the Command-Z shortcut. Once again, play through the clip in the sequence, and park the playhead on a frame somewhere halfway through the clip.

Return to the Viewer window where the previous clip is still loaded. Click and drag the clip from the video window, and move it down to the sequence without releasing the mouse button. When you bring the ghost clip down and it snaps to the playhead on the sequence Timeline, you will see the Insert/Overwrite arrows appear again. When the arrow is pointing directly down, let go of the mouse button to perform an Overwrite edit (see Figure 4-7).

Instead of splitting the clip in half, moving the remaining footage over and inserting the incoming clip, Final Cut Express simply lays down the second clip in the place of the material that comes after the playhead position. It overwrites any footage that lies in the path of the incoming video clip.

Drag and Drop to the Canvas: Insert/Overwrite with a Transition

There is another way to perform Insert and Overwrite edits, this time with the option of adding another important element, the *transition*. Instead of dragging the clip from the Viewer window directly to the sequence, we will use the Canvas window. As we perform the edit using the Canvas, we will also address the second important issue in the process of editing: how we get from one clip to the next clip in our finished edit.

We use the venerable old tape-editing terms *straight-cut editing* and *transition editing* to describe the two primarily different ways of getting from one clip to the next in a sequence. *Straight-cut editing* means that when the playhead reaches the end of the first clip, it immediately moves to the second clip. There is no transitional area in which both clips are simultaneously in view on the screen, and clips do not overlap or fade into one another. One clip stops on one frame, and another one starts on the very next frame.

Transition editing allows for a different sort of cut between clips, called a transition. A *transition* is a juncture between two clips. But unlike the straight-cut juncture, which has

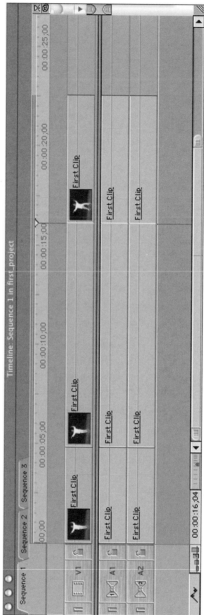
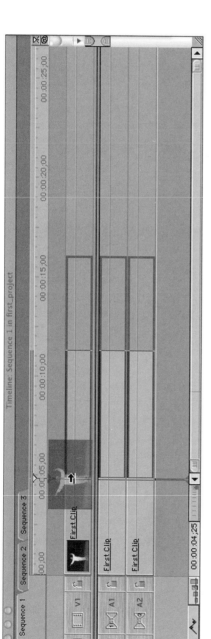

Figure 4-6 Performing an Insert edit

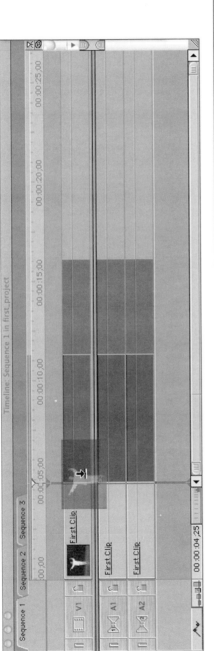

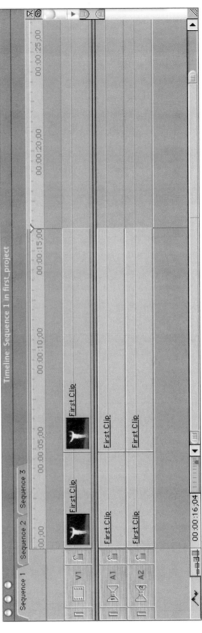

Figure 4-7 Performing an Overwrite edit

no overlapping, the transition lets us see a portion of both the outgoing and the incoming clip simultaneously. This can be a common dissolve, in which the outgoing clip fades out and the incoming clip fades in. A transition can be a wipe, in which a line crosses the screen, covering the outgoing clip and revealing the incoming clip. It can be any number of stylistic effects, but the main point is that the two clips are both seen simultaneously for the duration of the transition.

The frames of video where we are able to see both clips at once is the transition that we apply to the cut where the two clips abut. Here we encounter the most important component of the transition, the *handle*. An overlap is required between the two clips to allow us to see the two clips simultaneously. This overlap, called a handle, will be provided by the extra, unused footage that lies beyond the In and Out points of the clips we edited into the sequence. Each clip needs handles in order to create a transition. Since the transition requires overlap area between the two clips, you need to make sure there is footage that the transition can access from outside the In and Out points of each clip. This extra footage on either side of the In and Out points of the clip is referred to as its handles (see Figure 4-8).

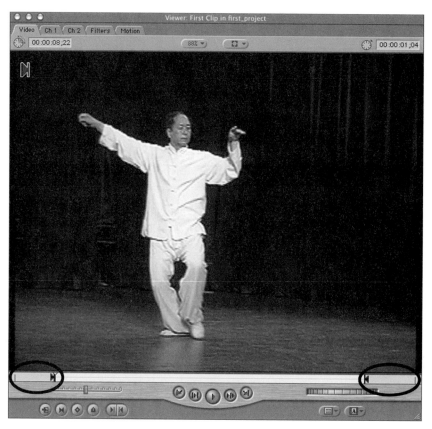

Figure 4-8   The handles of a clip

Once again, we will take advantage of Final Cut Express's drag-and-drop technique to create this transition. On the sequence, move the playhead a little farther down to an area where there are presently no clips. Now go back to the Viewer window where your clip is still loaded. This time, create new In and Out points, making sure that there are at least 30 frames before the In point, meaning between the first frame of the originally captured master clip and the In point you apply to it. Likewise, with the first or outgoing clip, make sure that there are at least 30 frames after the Out point.

These 30-frame handles on either side of the In and Out points will provide plenty of overlap frames for our transition. Click the clip in the Viewer video window and this time drag it into the video window of the Canvas without releasing the mouse button. As you hold it over the Canvas, you will see that the overlay windows appear, offering the choice of Insert, Overwrite, Replace, Fit to Fill, and Superimpose (see Figure 4-9). In addition, the Insert and Overwrite areas will have an optional extra window for including a transition.

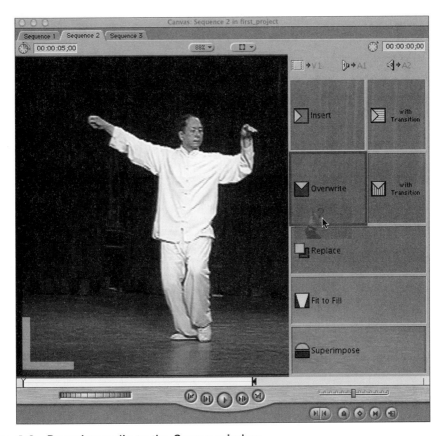

Figure 4-9 Dragging a clip to the Canvas window

Because there is currently no video clip in the sequence, we could choose either Insert or Overwrite with equal results. You will perform exactly the same edit as you did when dragging directly to the sequence earlier. This time, however, instead of determining the frame to edit into the sequence by dragging the clip, you will edit to the place in the sequence where the playhead is currently parked. When you are using the Canvas window to add clips to the sequence, the position of the playhead in the Timeline will always determine where the new clip will be placed.

Hold the clip over either Insert or Overwrite (do not choose the transition option just yet), and you will see the choice highlighted. Release the mouse button, and you will see the clip appear on the sequence exactly where the playhead is parked.

To add a second clip, with a transition, first make sure that the playhead is parked at the end of the clip you just inserted into the sequence. When you edit a clip into a sequence, the playhead immediately moves to the last frame of the edited-in clip, since it assumes your next edit will follow that clip. If the playhead has been moved, drag it back over to the end of the clip you just added to the sequence, making sure that it is on, not following, the last frame of the clip.

Transitions, such as the default Cross Dissolve that we are about to use, are difficult to see if the clip being transitioned to is very similar to the clip being transitioned from. Since the Cross Dissolve fades from one clip to the next, you might not even be able to see the transition. For this reason, pick a new clip from your Project tab that looks substantially different from the clip you have just edited into the sequence.

Double-click a new clip in the Project tab to load it into the Viewer window. Once again, set In and Out points, making sure that you leave at least 30 frames on either side of the In point and the Out point to provide adequate overlap space for the transition. Pick up the clip in the Viewer window and drag it into the Canvas window, this time releasing it as it hovers over the Overwrite with Transition area (see Figure 4-10). Instantly, the clip appears on the sequence following the first clip, but this time there is a small gray bar connecting the two.

The small gray bar between the two clips is the Transition. It is an area in which footage from both clips is present, although it is actually composed of footage that exists beyond the previously established In or Out points of the clips. In this nonlinear system, Final Cut Express can reach back into the media file associated with your clip when it needs more footage as long as there are handles, or more footage in the clip to access. The benefit of adding frame handles in the capture process of the last chapter becomes more obvious now that footage beyond our In and Out points becomes valuable as transition overlap footage.

If you receive a message stating "Insufficient Content for Edit," it means that you do not have enough footage beyond the In or Out point of either one or both of the clips for Final Cut Express to create the transition. Remember that an overlap of footage means that both clips must have at least some footage outside the In and Out points. Although the number of frames outside the In and Out points does not have to be equal, it does have to exist and be at least as long as the transition you are applying.

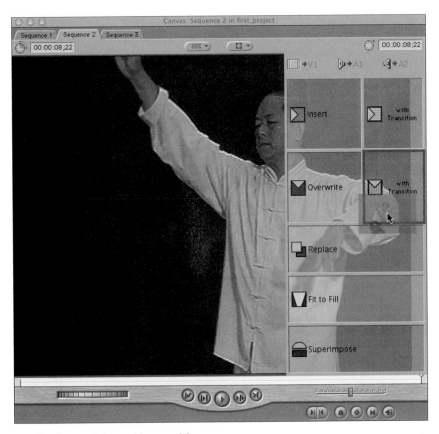

Figure 4-10   Overwriting with transition

By default, this transition is a Cross Dissolve, which will fade one clip out and the other in over the length of the transition. You can choose any other transition available to replace the Cross Dissolve after it has been applied. After applying the transition, place the sequence playhead directly in the center of the transition. You will be able to see both the first and second clips at half their opacity or visual strength, since one is fading out and the other is fading in (see Figure 4-11).

A Few Words About Real-time and Rendering Effects

Depending on your system setup and its processor power, you will have a couple of different viewing experiences here. If you are using a DV device for output to a true video monitor, you will likely see a red line above the transition. When you try to play this short sequence back, you will notice that when the playhead crosses the transition, the footage

Figure 4-11   The resulting Cross Dissolve applied to your clips

disappears and the word "Unrendered" appears, as shown in Figure 4-12. Once the play-head is past the transition, the video footage appears again. This is because to be played back correctly, transitions must be rendered when you are sending out to Firewire.

If, on the other hand, your system has the specifications for Real-time Previews and you are not sending video out to Firewire, you will see a green line above the transition, meaning that the transition can be played back and previewed on your computer screen

Figure 4-12   Unrendered footage

without rendering! There is a Command key shortcut to toggle back and forth between sending output to the Firewire DV device and previewing Real-time transitions on the computer screen. Command-F12, or Command combined with the 12th function key, will toggle ouput to Firewire. Also, you can look under the View drop-down menu and select Video, then Real-time or Firewire. Of course, if your Macintosh is not fast enough for Real-time features, you will not have such an option and will need to render.

If you are not using Real-time features, it bears a moment of discussion to look into that issue, since the relationship between clips and media is so paramount for the serious editor. The reason that normal captured footage can be played back without rendering is that the footage already exists on your hard drive as captured media. This is the media that the clip is pointing to. When the playhead encounters the clip, the media is accessed and the video plays back. But a transition is different. There is no media clip yet that corresponds to the dissolve between the two clips. Final Cut Express knows that the transition footage needs to be created or rendered to be played back correctly, so it warns you that the material is unrendered.

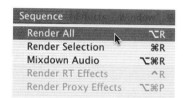

Figure 4-13   Render All

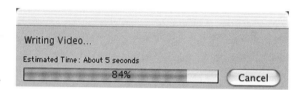

Figure 4-14   Render progress bar

Any footage in a sequence that must be rendered will have a red bar over it in the Time-line window. The red bar indicates that render files have not yet been created for the clip and that it will not be displayed properly upon playback. Anytime you see this red bar, it means that there is an effect of some sort—a Motion tab effect, an effects filter, or a transition—that must be rendered.

Rendering the transition is simple. Make sure the Timeline window is active, then go to the Sequence drop-down menu and select Render All (see Figure 4-13). There are other choices available for rendering in this drop-down menu. What choices are available depends on what clips, if any, are selected on the sequence. If an individual clip or transition is selected, you can choose Render Selection to avoid rendering all clips or transitions you may not be presently concerned with. If no clips or transitions are selected, then Render Selection will render all clips in the sequence.

A render progress bar will appear, showing you the time remaining until the render process is complete (see Figure 4-14). After the render is complete, the red bar will be replaced by a barely perceptible light gray bar, indicating that the material has been rendered. Go back to the sequence and play through the transition. You will now see the dissolve properly played back out to Firewire.

Refining the Transition

Of course, you are not limited to the way this dissolve performs. You are looking at the default settings for the Cross Dissolve transition. You can easily change the parameters of the transition itself, being limited only by the number of overlap frames, or handles, available past the In or Out points of either the outgoing or the incoming clip.

To change the parameters of the transition, go to the Timeline window and double-click the gray transition itself. Make sure that you click the gray transition and not the cut, or edit point, between the two clips (if a Trim Edit double video window appears, close it

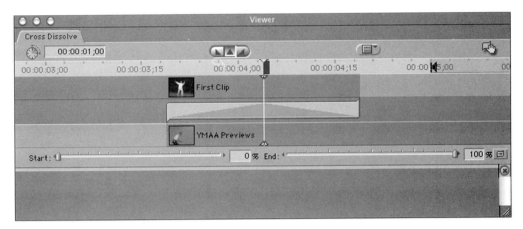

Figure 4-15 A transition loaded into the Viewer window

and try again; you may need to change the scale of the Timeline window so that you can more accurately click the transition). When you successfully double-click the transition, it will load into the Viewer window as if the transition were a clip, but as a single tab for the transition parameters (see Figure 4-15).

When the transition is loaded into the Viewer window, you can adjust how long the transition lasts, where the middle point of transition occurs, and many other factors that depend on the type of transition you have created. You will see that as you adjust the parameters in the Viewer window, the transition in the sequence is updated. You will also see that the Canvas window shows you two windows as you adjust where the transition occurs, displaying where the beginning and end frames of the transitions are relative to your change.

You may also see that the red render bar has returned, because the render files you created no longer reflect what the transition does. To view the new transition parameters, you may need to render again. The Real-time playback possibilities become valuable when you are doing a lot of this sort of editing, since you only have to render the transition when you have it just the way you want it rather than having to render it each time just to see it in action.

More About Transitions

Drag-and-Drop Transitions

The method discussed in the preceding text is not the only way to apply a transition to two abutting clips. There is yet another simple drag-and-drop technique for applying transitions. Clear off the sequence by activating the Timeline window, clicking the dark gray area of the sequence Timeline, and clicking and dragging through the clips with the mouse button pressed (see Figure 4-16).

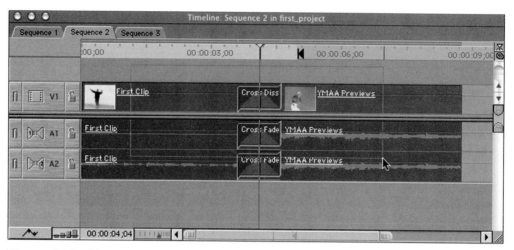

Figure 4-16 Marquee selection

This action is called a *marquee selection.* You will notice that each clip marqueed this way turns brown, indicating that the clip was selected. You can also quickly select more than one clip by clicking clips with the Shift key depressed (i.e., Shift-clicking). As you Shift-click more clips, they all stay selected, whereas if you were not Shift-clicking, selecting one clip would deselect the previously selected clip(s). Shift-clicking changes the selection status of a single clip without changing the selection status of other clips. To deselect an individual clip while Shift-clicking clips, simply Shift-click the clip again to remove it from the group of selected clips.

Once all the clips in the sequence have been selected, hit the Delete key to remove them from the sequence. When the sequence is again empty, quickly perform two Overwrite edits into the sequence so that two clips are abutted with no transition but have the previously described overlap frames or handles on either side of their In and Out points.

Go to the Browser window and select the Effects tab. Double-click the bin named Video Transitions. Inside the Video Transitions bin that opens up, double-click the Dissolve bin. Inside the Dissolve bin, click the Cross Dissolve icon and drag it onto the cut between the two clips you just edited into the sequence (see Figure 4-17). When released onto the edit point between the two clips, the transition will pop right in, just as if you had applied it from the Canvas.

Double-click the gray transition you just dropped onto the edit point between the clips so that it loads into the Viewer window. Once again, adjust the various parameters of the transition until you are satisfied with the results. Click the Timeline window again, hit Command-R if you are not using RT Preview (the keyboard shortcut for Render), and after the brief render process, play the transition back.

Using the drag-and-drop method of applying transitions to edit points between clips, you can select any of the available transitions in the Video Transitions bin of the Effects

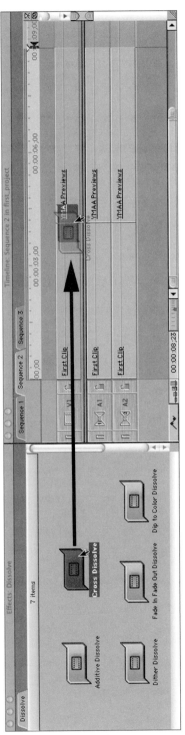

Figure 4-17 Dragging and dropping to apply a Cross Dissolve

tab. It should be noted that not all transitions or effects filters are available as Real-time Preview effects. Whenever you see a transition or effects filter, the name of which is in bold letters, you know that it is one of the Real-time-enabled Real-time effects. Also, remember as you work that the processor of your machine largely determines how many Real-time effects you can use without requiring a render, if any at all. The faster your machine, the more Real-time effects you can include. Obviously, some machines that can run Final Cut Express will not have access to any Real-time effects, as was stated earlier in this book.

Creating Customized Transition Favorites

Once you have adjusted the parameters of a transition the way you want them, you can save a new version of the transition that retains the parameters you have changed for quick access in the future. Instead of having to change the parameters for a transition every time you use it, you will make a copy of the transition you have customized and apply that instead of the default one you started with. This is called creating a Favorite. As an example, let's say that you prefer for your Cross Dissolves to last for 15 frames instead of the full 1 second that the default Cross Dissolve transition is set to last.

In the sequence, double-click the transition so that it loads into the Viewer window. In the timecode field to the upper left of the window, change the value from 00:00:01:00, or 1 second (29.97 frames for NTSC and 25 for PAL), to 00:00:00;15, or 15 frames (see Figure 4-18). The transition will automatically shrink both in the Viewer and in the sequence.

Now that the transition in the sequence has a new customized parameter that differs from the one in the Video Transitions bin, we will create a Favorite of it. Double-click the Favorites bin in the Effects tab of the Browser window so that it opens up. Go back to the sequence, grab the gray transition, and drag it to the opened Favorites bin, as shown in Figure 4-19.

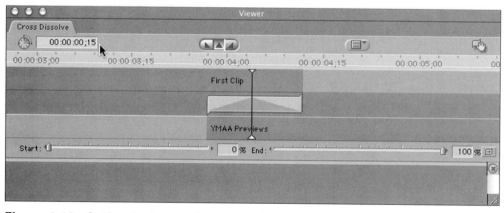

Figure 4-18 Setting the length of your transition

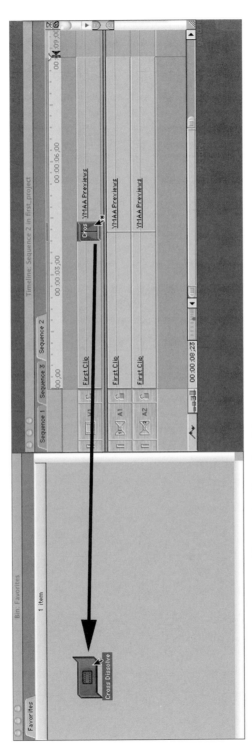

Figure 4-19 Dragging a transition to the Favorites bin

A new Cross Dissolve transition bearing the parameters you changed is now in the Favorites bin. Although it is still named Cross Dissolve, it actually has a different length than the Cross Dissolve you originally pulled from the Video Transitions bin. Before you can confuse one Cross Dissolve with the other, click the name of the Cross Dissolve transition in the Favorites bin to highlight it. Type in the new name "CD15frames" to distinguish it from the original Cross Dissolve or any further variations of the Cross Dissolve transition you may create as Favorites (see Figure 4-20).

Now whenever you wish to apply a 15-frame Cross Dissolve, you can simply drag this transition from the Favorites bin and apply it. The transition will also be available from the Effects drop-down menu under the heading Favorites. You could also have placed the transition on the edit point by moving the playhead in the sequence to the edit point between the two clips and going to the Effects drop-down menu. There, under the Video Transitions submenu, you will find all the Final Cut Express transitions available to you (see Figure 4-21). The Effects drop-down menu is your access menu for many other effects, to be described later in Chapter 5.

If it seems arbitrary to have waited until this point to describe the drop-down menu items for performing transitions and effects, there is a reason. Your speed and agility within Final Cut Express, as well as other production applications, greatly depends on your ability to use the interface of the application directly rather than hunting through menu items one

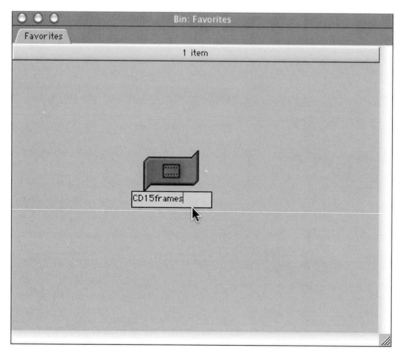

Figure 4-20 Customizing the name of your effect

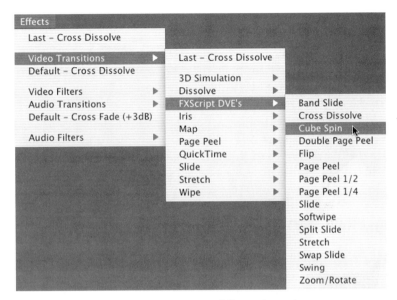

Figure 4-21 Setting a transition by using the Effects drop-down menu

by one to find what you are looking for. The risk of carpal tunnel syndrome is another reason for avoiding the repetitive action of pulling down drop-down menus. Learning the keyboard shortcuts for actions and using the mouse only for things like dragging clips around will save your wrist a lot of work and speed up your process into the bargain.

A Super Quick Transition Sequence

One of my favorite quick tricks is taking a huge group of clips or images and quickly applying an identical transition type between each of them. Rather than having to drag the same transition to each edit point between each clip, as usual there's a way to leverage Final Cut Express's powerful interface to do the whole thing for you instantly.

Clear off your sequence again, this time using the Select All method. Make sure the Timeline window is active, then hit Command-A, the shortcut for Select All. When you do so, all clips on the sequence are selected. Hit the Delete key and they disappear. After they are gone, edit a series of clips into the Timeline, making sure that each one has plenty of frame handles such that a transition can be performed. (You may need to go back to your tapes and capture a few more clips; if that is not possible, it's OK for demonstration to simply reuse the same clip repetitively in your sequence; just make sure you have adequate handles.)

After you have five or more clips edited in, hit the Home key, which is the keyboard shortcut to return the playhead to the beginning of the sequence. Also, hit the Shift-Z combination to make sure that all your clips are in view. Once the playhead is at the first frame of the sequence, hit Command-A to select all the clips, pick them up, and drag them into the Canvas window.

Once there, you will see the overlay options again. This time, drop the selected range of clips on the Overwrite with Transition area (see Figure 4-22). Instantly, your sequence will change as the original clips in the sequence are overwritten with the selection of them that you dragged into the Canvas. However, this time, there is a transition inserted between each one! Using this method, you can very quickly arrange a slideshow of still images into the order you want them to appear in, and then instantly insert a nice soft dissolve between them all. After the transitions are all in place, you can go back in and tweak the timing of when those edits occur. That is the subject of the next section of this chapter.

Trimming Those Edits

At this point, you can bring clips into Final Cut Express, select In and Out points for them, and get them to the sequence in the Timeline window with or without a transition. That is enough to edit with. But it implies that we don't want to change things once they make it to the sequence.

What we have done up to this point isn't that far removed from the process of tape editing. With tape editing, cuts follow cuts. You lay down an edit onto the edit deck, and then you lay down the next edit, possibly with a transition. You continue doing so until you complete the piece.

But that is linear editing. If you discovered that you've made a clip a little too long before editing it in, you have to go back through and reedit the whole thing from the offending clip on. But we are using a nonlinear editor here, and we should take full advantage of its unique ability to alter clips from within the sequence itself, instead of simply adding edit to edit in a linear fashion.

Of course, we've already seen a little nonlinear action with the Insert edit. With the Insert edit, we put a clip exactly where we wanted it to occur without overwriting what was already there. But we can do much more with our nonlinear editor. We can trim our clips with great precision in the sequence itself, using tools that are dedicated to helping us arrive at the most appropriate cut between any two clips that adjoin.

There are a few ways of trimming clips on the Timeline. These include directly grabbing the edge of the clip and moving its In or Out point, using the dedicated Trim Edit window, or using certain dedicated tools that live on the Toolbar. These different methods offer differing conveniences. One is less precise but easily accessible, one is more precise but must be accessed in a separate window, and another is a unique mixture of both.

The key is to master them all so that you can automatically reach for the most suitable trimming method without thinking about it. Only experience can instill the quick, appropriate use of each method, so try them all until you get the hang of them, and then access them frequently. Trim functions often confuse new users because the relationship between clips and other clips or between clips and their media is unclear.

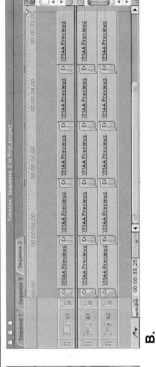

Figure 4-22 Overwriting multiple clips with transition

Trimming is not difficult, however, as long as you remember that each clip on the sequence is only a small carved-out section of a larger master clip that you originally captured or imported into the Project tab. Because the clip is only a section of the master clip, Final Cut can easily change the In and Out points for that section on the fly without the need to revisit the Viewer window's edit tools. As you change the In and Out points for the clip, you are only defining which section of the master clip the smaller section in the sequence refers to. Trimming a clip that exists in a sequence does not affect the master clip in the Project tab. You are only tweaking the subclip you made from the master clip in your initial edit into the sequence.

Mastery of the various trim functions will turn your Final Cut Express station from a nice editing package into a real professional editor. It will give you control over every aspect of the sequence and enable you to make quick changes that dramatically alter the nature of your production without having to rebuild entire edited sequences from scratch. Trim is the secret weapon of all good editors and is an essential tool to grasp.

The Easiest Trimming Technique

The simplest trim function you can perform involves trimming the In or Out point of a clip directly on the edges of the clip itself in the sequence. This trim is so basic, it does not require more than one clip. You are simply changing the In or Out point for the clip in the sequence.

Start with a fresh, clean sequence in the Timeline by selecting and deleting all the clips there. Perform an Overwrite edit to edit a clip onto the sequence. Move the mouse pointer near either the beginning or the end of the clip until you see it change from the generic Selection arrow to two vertical lines with an arrow pointing left and right (see Figure 4-23). When the mouse pointer is shaped like this, it has assumed a trim function.

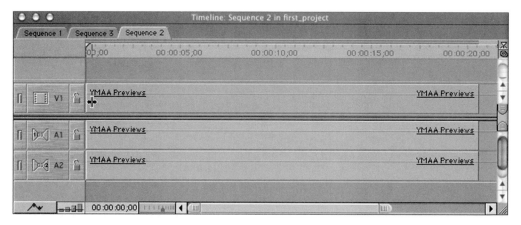

Figure 4-23   The trim function of the mouse cursor

Click the end of the clip and drag in either direction. You will see that the length of the clip adjusts following this tool. When you let go of the mouse button, the new In or Out point for the clip will stick, and you will have changed the duration of the clip. Also notice that as you adjust the trim, a small text box appears next to the clip, indicating the number of frames you have added to or subtracted from the clip in the trim operation and the new total length of the clip measured in duration (see Figure 4-24). In addition, the Canvas window will change as you trim the clip, showing the current last frame as the window changes.

Click the clip edge again and perform the same drag motion, dragging as far to the left or the right as the tool will allow. At some point, you will reach the limit of the actual media file that the master clip refers back to. Obviously, you cannot extend a clip beyond the limits of the media file that the master clip refers to, so this is the limit of the trim for the clip.

Although easy to grasp, this tool can be very limiting for a couple of reasons. When you trim a clip, you are usually doing so to refine an edit point, something that you want to approach with precision that may require removal or addition of only a single frame. Unfortunately, this direct trimming action can be very unwieldy for precise editing. Much of the time, you will be looking at your Timeline scaled out so that you can see several seconds or even minutes at a time. In such situations, trimming a single frame using the direct method is practically impossible, like using your entire fist to dial a number on a touch-tone telephone. Although it can be done, the edit may take several hair-raising and frustrating moments, during which all your creative juices leak away.

Another problem with using the direct trimming tool is that you can trim only one end of one clip at a time. This may not seem limiting at first glance. But what if you have two clips abutted as a straight cut in a sequence, and you want to take one frame away from the first and add one frame to the second? Using the direct trim method described earlier would require clicking both clips, probably more than one time. And if you weren't

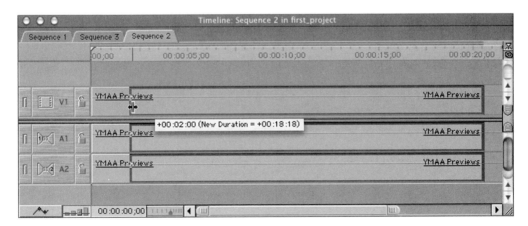

Figure 4-24 Trimming directly on the timeline with the mouse cursor

sure that's what you wanted, you'd have to go back through the same motions to change it back.

More Trimming Precision: The Trim Edit Window

Final Cut Express has a solution for such issues. It's called the Trim Edit window, and it is a dedicated window for allowing extreme precision in selecting the exact point at which two adjoining clips meet each other. Using the dedicated Trim Edit window, you will be able to quickly add or remove frames from the Out point of the first clip and the In point of the second clip. You will also be able to easily preview the trimmed edit from inside the window so that you can adjust it again before committing to it. And best of all, you can choose to adjust the first, the second, or both clips simultaneously. It is very flexible.

Calling Up the Trim Edit Window

To use the Trim Edit window effectively, you need to have two abutting clips. Clear off the sequence of clips using Select All and Delete so that you start with a fresh sequence. Perform two edits so that you have two clips with generous handles abutting on the sequence in a straight cut with no transition. Go to the sequence and double-click the edit point between the two clips. Doing so will immediately open a large double video window called the Trim Edit window (see Figure 4-25).

In similar fashion to the Capture window, there are two sizes for the Trim Edit window. If it appears too large or too small, you can adjust this by making the Canvas window 50% or smaller, since the Trim Edit window's size is determined by the size of the Canvas window.

The two video windows of the Trim Edit window each correspond to one of the video clips; the left window is for the first, or outgoing, clip, and the right window is for the second, or incoming, clip. Inside the Trim Edit window are all the tools you need to prepare a frame-specific edit between any two adjoining clips.

Some of the navigation tools will appear familiar, but make no mistake—this window functions according to its own rules. What you do here updates the sequence it was opened from, as one would expect. Until you are familiar with the functioning of the Trim Edit window, make sure to keep the Timeline window in view so that you can monitor the effect the Trim Edit window has on the sequence it originated from.

On the top left-hand corner of each video window in the Trim Edit window, you will find the familiar Clip Duration fields. These give the present duration of their respective clips, based on the current In and Out points of the clips in the sequence. The duration will change as you trim the clips.

Figure 4-25 The Trim Edit window

The Track Drop-Down bar

In the center of the top of the window is a Track drop-down bar that lets you select which video or audio tracks you are basing your trim adjustments on (see Figure 4-26). You can apply the same trim action to more than one track at the same time, which can be a big help in keeping two or more clips on different video tracks equal in duration or alignment.

There are many reasons for trimming multiple edit points at once. Chances are that you will encounter situations in which you need to extend or retract the edit points for more than one clip to keep a group of clips aligned with each other. By Command-clicking the additional edit points between two abutting clips on different video tracks in the sequence, you add those edit points to the choices in the Track drop-down bar at the top of the Trim Edit window.

The only two restrictions on this activity are that there can be only one edit point selected per video or audio track (you can only trim one edit point per video track at a time) and that the trim applied in the Trim Edit window is applied equally to all selected edit points, regardless of which edit point is selected in the Track drop-down bar. This lets you base the trim effect of many different edit points across all the video and audio tracks on how you trim one critical edit point in any one of the video or audio tracks.

Leave the abutting video clips in the Video 1 track. Next, edit in a new clip from the Viewer window, but this time, drag it from the Viewer and drop it into the sequence in the space above the Video 1 track so that it creates a new Video 2 track (see Figure 4-27). Make sure that this new clip's edge is not vertically lined up with the edit point of the two clips you have abutted on the Video 1 track.

Single-click an edge of the new clip in the Video 2 track, and then Command-click the original edit point division between the other two clips in Video 1. You will see that each edit point becomes brown as it is selected. Now, double-click one of the two selected edit points to open up the Trim Edit window. Go to the Trim Edit window that opens, and click the Track drop-down bar at the top and center of the Trim Edit window (see Figure 4-28).

You will see that you now have an option between using the Video 2 or Video 1 track or any of the four accompanying audio tracks as the basis for the trim. Any trimming that takes place will be applied to all the clips that are selected. And since any trim is applied to all these edit points, this also means that any clip with media limits will shorten the

Figure 4-26 The Track drop-down bar

Figure 4-27 Editing a new clip onto a new Video 2 track

amount of trimming that can be applied to any of the clips. If you had more tracks and you wanted to add additional edit points to the group already selected and present in the Track drop-down bar, you would just Command-click in the sequence to add them to the selection. Just remember that you can have only one edit point selected per track.

You will also notice that as you switch between the choices in the Track drop-down bar, the timecode value just below it changes and the playhead moves from edit point to edit point in the sequence. This center value always reflects the sequence frame number that the edit point currently selected in the Track drop-down bar is positioned on. As you trim the edits, this number will likely change as you move the In and Out points back and forth.

Figure 4-28   Selecting multiple edit points to trim

Make sure that the Track drop-down bar is set on Video 1, so that there is both an outgoing (left) clip and an incoming (right) clip. Look directly below the two video windows in the Trim Edit window to find a little timeline track containing a couple of items (see Figure 4-29). The playhead of the track is a little vertical line topped with a yellow triangle. Accompanying this in the track will be an In or Out point marker, depending on the video window in question. There will be an Out point marker on the clip in the left, outgoing window and an In point marker on the right, incoming window.

Move the playhead around in this little timeline, and you will see that it is previewing the media available for use by the clip, giving you the opportunity to quickly scan through it for the optimal new edit point. Make sure that as you move the playhead around, the mouse pointer is shaped like an arrow; otherwise, you are probably adjusting the trim. Do not touch the In or Out points just yet. Use Command-Z or Undo to quickly negate an accidental trim action.

Figure 4-29 The little timeline track in the Trim Edit window

The range of frames you can preview for the new edit point is equal to the limits of the master clip and the media file associated with the clip. The lighter area of the little timeline is the range of frames that are already in the clip in the sequence. The darker area is the range of frames that exist in the master clip but are not yet included in the clip in the sequence.

Navigating the Clips in the Trim Edit Window

Underneath this track bar are the familiar tools for navigating around a clip. There is a Jog and a Shuttle for moving around. Predictably enough, there is J-K-L support for each separate window, although the response will not be nearly as rapid as in the Viewer or the Canvas. There is also a Play button and a button for advancing or retreating one frame.

Beneath each of these video windows is an Out Shift or an In Shift button for the outgoing or incoming video windows. This button will move the Out or In point to where the playhead is parked in the Trim Edit's little timeline. It is accompanied by a timecode value that displays how many frames the new Out or In point is from the original edit point position when the Trim Edit window was first opened. Of course, this In Shift and Out Shift uses the I and O keys as keyboard shortcuts, moving the In or Out point to wherever the playhead is parked in the little timeline of the Trim Edit window, just as with the In and Out functions in the Viewer and the Capture windows.

Trimming edits using this window can be done in two ways. As is usual for Final Cut Express, there is a direct click-and-drag method and a more precise numerical entry. Care must be taken when performing the trim, though, because you have to tell Final Cut Express which of the incoming or outgoing clips you want to trim, or if you want to simultaneously trim both.

It is easy to identify which clip is to be affected by the trim action you initiate. The Trim Edit window will show a long green bar at the top of the window for the clip that is active. If the bar is present above a video window, trimming actions will affect the clip in that window. You can choose to have one, the other, or both clips enabled. To enable the green bar and trim actions for a clip, simply click in its video window (see Figure 4-30). You will notice that clicking in one video window enables it while disabling the other. To enable both video windows so that trim actions are applied to both clips, either Shift-click in the second video window or click in the thin space between the two video windows.

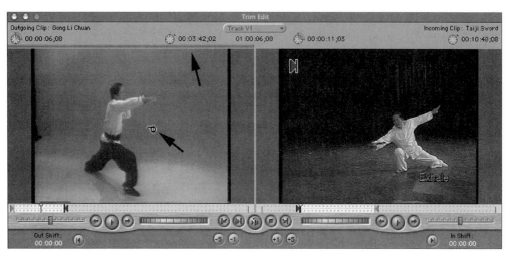

Figure 4-30   Clicking to select one clip in the Trim Edit window

When you move the mouse pointer over the video windows, you'll notice that its shape changes again. This time it appears in one of three shapes, depending on where in the Trim Edit window you have it. If it lies in the left, outgoing clip window, it appears as a little filmstrip roll with the tongue hanging out to the left (see Figure 4-30). This shape, referred to as a Ripple Edit, is a metaphor for a film take-up reel. It's called a Ripple Edit because as you trim using it, the change in duration ripples back through the rest of the sequence the trim applies to, shortening or lengthening it and eliminating the possibility of creating a gap between any of the clips. When a clip is ripple trimmed, as it is shortened or lengthened, all other clips in its track are moved over either to give it more room or to cover any gaps the trim might have created.

If the mouse pointer is lying in the right video window, the mouse pointer becomes a Ripple Edit take-up reel for the incoming video clip. It performs exactly the same function as the other Ripple Edit tool, except that it applies to the incoming clip. Once again, the tongue is hanging in the direction of the clip that will be trimmed by the tool (see Figure 4-31).

The third possible shape is just a combination of the two and is called a Roll Edit. If you place the pointer between the two video windows, you will see a combination of the two Ripple Edit spools and tongues, symbolizing that the trim function will now be applied to both the outgoing and incoming clips (see Figure 4-32). Do not be confused, though, because the Roll Edit is just moving the edit point relatively for each clip. Rather than taking away a frame from or adding a frame to each clip separately, the Roll Edit takes away from one clip and adds to the other at the same time. The net effect of this action is that the new edit point occurs earlier or later in both clips. The clips themselves are not moved, and the total duration is not changed; only the edit point at which one of them stops and the other starts is changed.

Figure 4-31 The Ripple Edit cursor

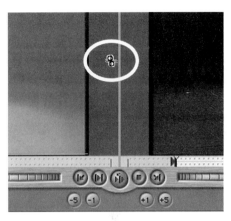

Figure 4-32 The Roll Edit cursor

The gist of this is as follows. If you only want to trim frames on the outgoing (left) clip, you click on the left video window to select the outgoing Ripple Edit. If you want to trim frames on the incoming (right) clip, click on the right video window to select the incoming Ripple Edit. If you want to trim from one clip and add to the other so that you move the edit point between the clips without changing the duration of the two clips together, click in between the video windows and select the Roll Edit. You can always easily tell which window is enabled for trimming by seeing which window, if not both, has the green bar on top.

There are two ways to perform the trim, one of which is imprecise but fast, the other of which is frame-specific but slower. After you have chosen the Roll Editor or either of the Ripple Edits, you will notice that clicking in the video window has no effect other than enabling that window for trimming.

Click in the left video window to enable the outgoing Ripple Edit. Position the mouse pointer over the Out point in the little timeline track of the left video window. Clicking the Out point and dragging it will trim the outgoing clip and ripple all the subsequent clips in the track to keep from creating gaps between any clips. Continue to drag the Ripple tool in either direction and watch the sequence update as you adjust the trim (see Figure 4-33).

Click in the right video window to enable the incoming Ripple Edit. Position the mouse pointer over the In point in the little timeline track of the right video window. Clicking the In point and dragging it will trim the incoming clip and ripple all the subsequent clips in the track to keep from creating gaps between any clips. Continue to drag the Ripple tool in either direction and watch the sequence update as you adjust the trim.

Click in between the two video windows to select the Roll Edit. Position the mouse pointer over the In or the Out point in either of the two little timeline tracks. Clicking the edit point for either the outgoing or incoming clip and dragging it will trim both clips.

Figure 4-33 Trimming by dragging in the Trim Edit timeline

Continue to drag the Roll tool in either direction and watch the sequence Timeline update as you adjust the trim.

As you trim using these tools, watch the Out Shift and In Shift numbers in the bottom left- and right-hand corners, respectively, to see how far you have adjusted in either direction as you drag. As you will notice, this sort of click-and-drag trimming is a bit imprecise. Once you've moved the edit point for either clip, it's difficult to get the Out Shift and In Shift numbers back to zero such that the points are in exactly the same position as they were when the Trim Edit window was opened. If you made a change to the edit points and then decided you didn't like it, it could take you all day to get the original edit points back.

For this purpose, Final Cut Express has a much more precise method. At the very bottom and center of the Trim Edit window, you will find four buttons with the values −5, −1, +1, and +5 (see Figure 4-34). These buttons simply perform the same trimming action described previously, but for the value of the button. The −1 button, for example,

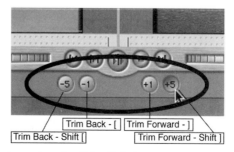

Figure 4-34 Trimming by using the Trim Edit buttons

will move the edit point one frame to the left for either or both clips, depending on whether a Ripple or a Roll is enabled. The +1 button will move the edit point one frame in the opposite direction. The −5 and +5 buttons move the edit point even more quickly.

You will in all likelihood find that using the precise buttons is easier and faster than the click-and-drag technique. Since it's easy to count as you mouse-click, you can always quickly click in corrections without having to struggle. To make things even easier, there is a keyboard shortcut for these precise trim buttons. The bracket keys, "[" and "]", correspond to the −1 and +1 buttons, respectively. The key combinations Shift-[and Shift-] correspond to the −5 and +5 buttons. You can customize the number of frames that appear in the −5 and +5 buttons by setting a value higher or lower up to a maximum of 9 in the Multi-Frame Trim Size field in the General tab in the Final Cut Express Preferences.

Previewing the Trim Before Leaving the Trim Edit Window

Finally, there are a few buttons for previewing your edit before leaving the Trim Edit window. Remember that when you close this window, the Out Shift and In Shift values will be set in the sequence. Once the In or Out Shift value in the Trim Edit window has been applied to the sequence and the Trim Edit window has been closed, it can be difficult to get your edit point back to where it was before you changed it. If you catch a mistake before leaving the window, it's easy to make the adjustment based on the number of frames that the new edit points have shifted from what they were when the window opened. Previewing the edit to make sure it is what you want is a good way to avoid having to go back and piece together your previous edit points.

There is a tool specifically for this purpose. Just below and between the two video windows are a few play buttons (see Figure 4-35). The one in the center is called Play Around Edit Loop. When you press this button, Final Cut Express previews the edit by playing from a few seconds before the edit to a few seconds after it. You customize the amount of Play Around either before or after the edit by changing the values for Preview Pre-roll and Preview Post-roll in the General tab of the Final Cut Express Preferences (see Figure 4-36).

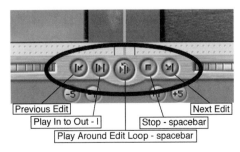

Figure 4-35 The play buttons in the Trim Edit window

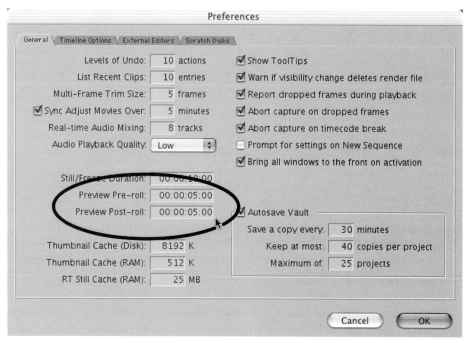

Figure 4-36   Using Preview Pre- and Post-roll settings to customize Play Around Edit Loop

   The farthest left of the five buttons, Previous Edit, is for moving from the current edit point loaded into the Trim Edit window to the previous edit. Be careful, though, because it refers to the previous edit point that occupies the same track as the current edit point. If you were looking for the previous edit point on another track, you might end up quite far from where you expected to be. The farthest right button of the five, Next Edit, performs the same function, except that it moves forward in the track rather than going in reverse. This is useful if you need to trim a whole series of edit points on the same track. Instead of trimming and editing, and then going out of the Trim window to select a new edit point, just hit either of these buttons to directly move to the next or previous edit.

   The button just to the left of the Play Around Edit Loop is the Play In to Out. This will preview from the beginning of the outgoing (left) clip to the end of the incoming (right) clip, regardless of how your Preview Pre- and Post-roll Preferences have been set. The preview playback is a loop, so to stop the loop, there is a button to the right of the Play Around Edit Loop. You can also hit the Spacebar to start or stop it.

   Trimming is fast and easy using the Trim Edit window. Just double-click the edit point you want to trim in the sequence. When the Trim Edit window pops up, select which clip you want to Ripple Edit, or choose to perform a Roll Edit of both clips. Click the plus or minus frame buttons or the "[" and the "]" bracket keys to define the points the way you want them. Preview the cut to make sure it performs the way you want it to. Then close the window (with a quick Command-W), and you're done.

An even faster method is to start up the loop preview immediately on entering the Trim Edit window and trim as it plays back. You get to use both the In and Out point keystrokes (I and O keys) and the Trim Frames keystrokes ([and]) on the fly as the preview plays back. The I and O keystrokes perform as In and Out commands and will reset the trim to whatever frame you are on at that moment; and the bracket keys ([and]) will trim single frames from the current edit point. The difference is that you do this *while* the preview is playing so that you instantly see the results rather than start, stop, start, stop, etc. Typically, I might have to view an edit point previewed up to 10 times before deciding on the proper frame to cut on, so this "trim during preview" method saves a lot of keystrokes and time.

The Timeline and the Toolbar, a Deadly Duo

A lot of the material that has been discussed previously has been about how Final Cut Express allows you to edit in the Timeline from other areas of the application. We created In and Out points in the Viewer window to edit clips into the sequence Timeline. We saw Insert and Overwrite editing from the Canvas window. We learned to trim our sequence's edit points from inside the Trim Edit window. We'll even see later on how to load up a sequence in the Viewer as if it were just another clip.

But don't get me wrong. The sequence and the Timeline window it lives in are powerful tools. Many of the preceding trimming actions can be accomplished directly on clips within the sequence itself. It's necessary to include the Toolbar in this discussion as well, because, with only a few exceptions, the Toolbar tools work directly within the Timeline window. Although editing on the Timeline can sometimes feel a little sloppy and imprecise, there are times when quickly grabbing a clip and nudging it into place will do the trick. It's the editor's job to figure out the fastest, most efficient way of working so that more thought process goes into the "why" of editing and less into the "how."

Let's quickly go through the Timeline window and take a closer look at its features and controls. From the top left-hand corner of the window, the tabs for the open sequences are displayed, as shown in Figure 4-37. If you have more than one open sequence, you can switch between them by clicking their tabs. You will notice that when you switch tabs, the tab in the Canvas window switches to match. Every sequence in the Timeline has a sister tab in the Canvas window. The Canvas will always reflect what is taking place in the sequence. It is an exact mirror, and until we address how compositing and effects work, it should simply be regarded as a video preview monitor for the sequence.

The Timeline Tracks

Moving down into the Timeline itself, we find tracks. The default number of tracks when you create a new sequence was set back in the Timeline Options tab of the Preferences.

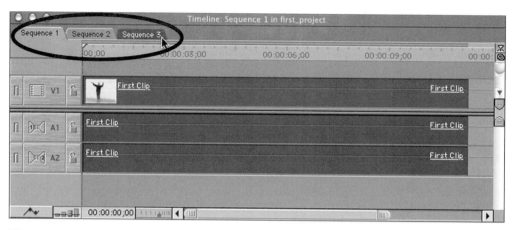

Figure 4-37 Tabs in the Timeline

Unless you changed that preference, the default for a newly created sequence will still be one video and two audio tracks.

The video track area is separated from the audio track area by a thick gray double line. You can adjust how much of the window is dedicated to the video tracks vs. the audio tracks by clicking this line and dragging it up or down (see Figure 4-38). If you have only

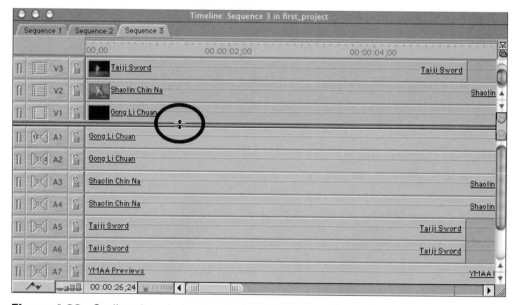

Figure 4-38 Scaling the window to display video or audio tracks

a few tracks currently in a sequence, you won't see much difference from moving it around. But when you have 10 tracks of video and audio, you'll see that being able to scale the window for video or audio tracks will make a big difference.

As we saw in the previous section on trimming, it's easy to create a new video or audio track in the sequence by simply dropping a clip into the space where the next video or audio track should be (see Figure 4-39). When you let go of the clip, the track will be automatically created. You can also create new tracks or remove tracks you don't want by selecting Insert Tracks or Delete Tracks from the Sequence drop-down menu (or by Control-clicking next to the track name). You can have up to 99 tracks of video and 99 tracks of audio in any sequence.

The only serious limitation to the number of possible tracks in your project is the number of audio tracks that Final Cut Express and your Macintosh hardware can play at once, or what is referred to as real-time audio mixing. We know, for example, that when video must be displayed that does not exist yet (e.g., a dissolve or a wipe), it must be rendered. The render is a mixdown or merging of all the video elements into one composite video clip that can be played out to Firewire.

Video has a much higher data rate than audio, and the processing to show a real-time playback of such unrendered material out to a video monitor requires a great deal of processing power. Audio, on the other hand, can be mixed and output to Firewire without rendering, up to a certain point. The rule of thumb is that eight tracks of audio that have no effects applied to them can be mixed together down to two channels and sent out to Firewire along with video. This is referred to as real-time audio mixing.

So what do you do if you need more than eight tracks? You can simply perform a quick mixdown using Mixdown Audio from the Sequence drop-down menu for the sequence (see Figure 4-40). The ensuing render is quite fast; it's much faster than video rendering. At the

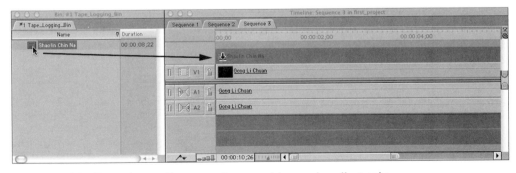

Figure 4-39 Dropping a clip to create new video and audio tracks

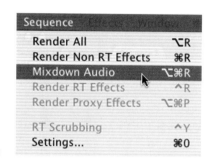

Figure 4-40 Mixing down audio

end of the render process, the audio tracks in the sequence will still be discrete and editable, but they will be linked to a render file so that everything above eight tracks can be mixed together and played correctly. If you have too many audio tracks to play back without Mixdown Audio, you will hear a pulsing beep as you play back.

Sometimes, your system may not have the wherewithal to mix all the eight tracks of audio that it is generally capable of doing. This can yield Dropped Frames errors and can be the result of disk fragmentation or sluggish system performance. In these instances, a quick mixdown using Mixdown Audio will usually take the stress off of your processor or drives and allow your system to do what you want. Remember that the number of tracks you assigned in the Real-time Audio Mixing field of the General tab in the Preferences is the number of tracks you are limiting Final Cut Express to attempting to mix in real time in the sequence. Setting this number higher than 8 will not make your system perform better; it will just try to real-time Real-time mix more tracks than most Macs are generally capable of doing. Keep this preference set to 8 tracks or less for best results (see Figure 4-41).

The track portion of the sequence is divided into two parts: the target track selection area to the left (see Figure 4-42) and the actual Timeline area to the right. The target track selection area is of crucial importance for editing because of the flexibility it allows you when editing into the sequence. There's more than one way to skin a cat, but some ways are quicker than others. Properly controlling the target track selection area can save you lots of time.

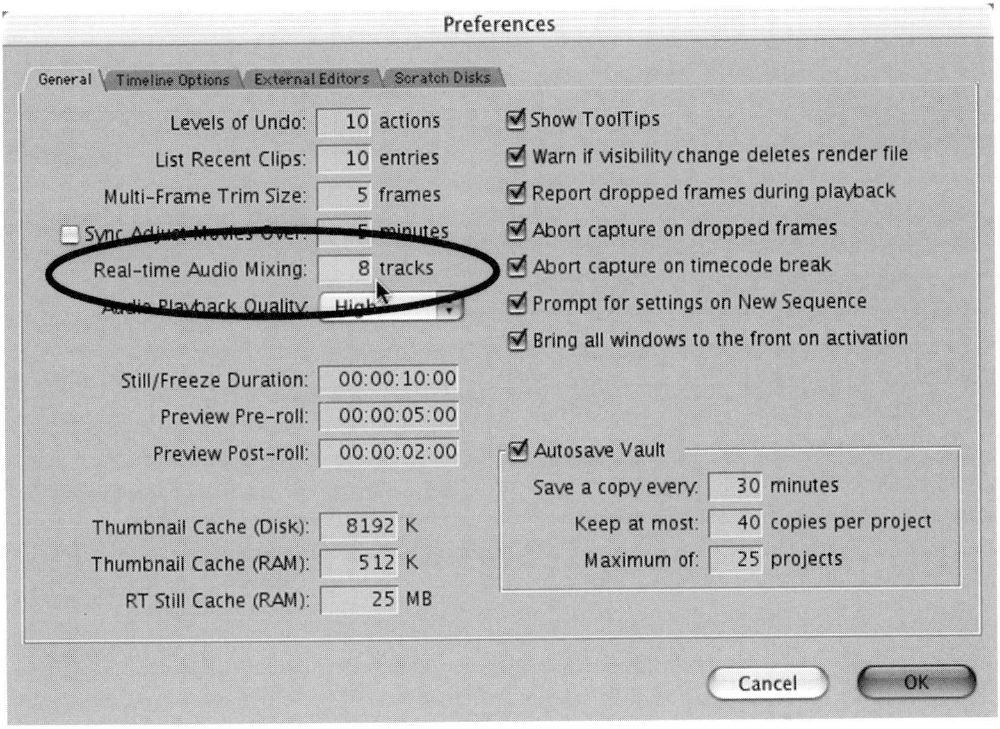

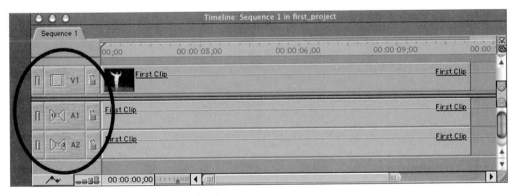

Figure 4-41   Setting the number of real-time audio tracks

Figure 4-42   The target track selection area

The Target Track Selection Area

To the far left of the target track selection area, there is a green light for each track. This is called the Track Visibility switch. Clicking off this green light grays out the track and makes it invisible in the Canvas (see Figure 4-43). It's basically a way to hide a track's contents temporarily. Any audio in the track would not be heard, and any video in the track would not be seen. Some care must be taken with this; turning tracks off irrevocably breaks the link between a clip and its render files. If you have rendered a clip, you want to avoid turning its track off.

The middle item in the target track selection area is the target track assignment. For video tracks, this is displayed as a small film frame next to the track's name. For audio tracks, this is displayed as two little speakers pointed in opposite directions. In either case, the track whose icon is displayed in yellow is a current target track. A target track is the track into which clips will be accepted when they are brought into a sequence. When you perform an Insert or Overwrite edit from the Canvas, the clip is automatically routed into whichever track is set as the target track.

In our earlier examples of Insert and Overwrite, there were only an initial video and two audio tracks in the sequence. This was sufficient for the requirements of our standard, DV-captured clips that are composed of one video and two audio tracks. But in some instances, particularly when we get into compositing, you will need to create more tracks than this. To make sure that your edits get sent to the proper tracks, you must make sure that they are targeted.

Clicking a target track icon turns it yellow and sets it as the target track. While there can be only one target video track at a time, there can be two target tracks for audio, since the Firewire connection with our DV device supports two audio channels. The target track allows for a designation of a left channel and a right channel, or stereo pair, in the target track box, since most clips will have two channels of audio. Only one video track can be targeted at a time, since an individual clip will have only one associated layer of video.

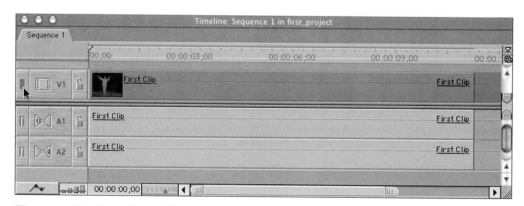

Figure 4-43 Switching off Track Visibility to temporarily hide a track's contents

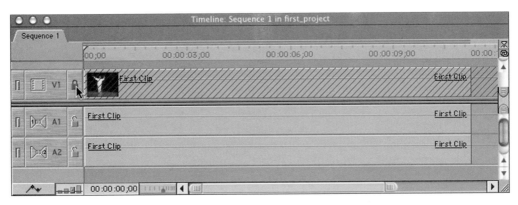

Figure 4-44 Locking a track

Setting the target track is critical for editing when using more than one video and more than two audio tracks. Target track assignments do not change until you change them. If you are using the Drag to Canvas method of editing, the target tracks are the only way Final Cut Express knows where to send the incoming clips. As you speed up your editing process by accessing keyboard shortcuts and automated features such as Drag to Canvas editing, you can easily confuse things by not defining things such as target tracks.

Finally, there is a track locking feature to the right of the target track selection area, symbolized by a padlock (see Figure 4-44). Normally, this is in the unlocked position, given that you want to be able to work in the tracks, which locking them would disallow. But track locking can be very useful. No matter how experienced you are with Final Cut Express, it can sometimes be tricky to see all the consequences of a single action. One false move could undo hours of precise cutting through an accidental series of edits. Locking tracks in these instances is a good way of making sure that nothing happens to a track or tracks when you are sure they are complete. It's also a good way to lock two tracks that have been manually synced so that they cannot be accidentally shifted by subsequent edits.

Timeline Customization Controls

Below the tracks are various controls for adjusting the Timeline so that you can customize its appearance and how much of the sequence's contents are visible at a time. There are tools for changing the time scale of the Timeline so that it displays larger or smaller increments of time, a timecode field that indicates where the playhead is parked at the moment, and, finally, buttons that provide additional control and display of the tracks themselves.

The time scale of the Timeline defines the increments of time used to display your sequence contents. Because your clips may range in length from several seconds to many minutes, it can sometimes be difficult to view all the contents of the sequence at once. Similarly, you may need to edit your clips on a very large scale so that you can distinguish between the individual frames in a clip. You need to be able to adjust the time scale of the Timeline so that you can alternate between looking at all the contents of your sequence and focusing on a smaller section of it. The Shift-Z shortcut, which we used earlier, defined as "Fit to Window," is used to adjust the scale of this window as well.

The Time Scale Bar

At the bottom of the Timeline window, there are two controls that adjust the time scale of the Timeline: the Zoom Slider and the Zoom Control meter. The Zoom Slider is a manual scrolling bar control with a handle on either end. The Zoom Slider bar only works when there is a clip on the Timelime. If you grab either one of the handles and drag it, you will see that the increments above the tracks become larger or smaller. Drag the bar out longer, and you will be looking at seconds—even minutes, depending on the length of the clips in the sequence. Drag either of the handles in to make the bar shorter, and you will be looking at smaller increments, down to single frames of video. This can be especially helpful when you need to make very specific adjustments to positioning of clips or if you need to select many different clips at once. Adjusting the time scale allows you to put as little or as much of your sequence contents into the viewing area as you need (see Figure 4-45).

This bar can move the viewing area of the Timeline as well (see Figure 4-46). Grabbing the bar anywhere between the handles and dragging moves the whole viewing area forward and back along a sequence's length, allowing you to move to areas quickly without having to get there by moving the playhead. Remember that this movement does not move the position of the playhead itself and that you will need to move it up to the window by clicking within the view area.

Navigating on the Timeline efficiently is a skill in itself. There is no correct time scale. The appropriate time scale depends as much on the relative lengths of your clips as it does on the type of editing you need to do at the moment. Your ability to quickly change the

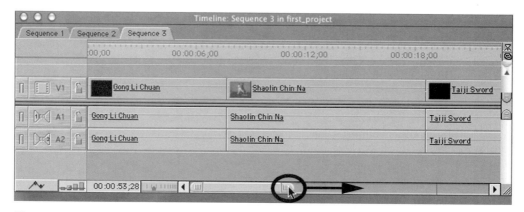

Figure 4-45 Adjusting the time scale

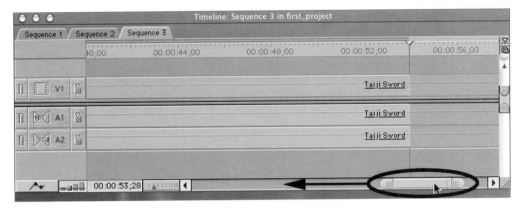

Figure 4-46   Adjusting the viewing area of the Timeline

scale and move to the next area of the sequence takes time and practice, but to work efficiently you really need to master it.

The Zoom Control Meter

Because Timeline navigation is so important, Final Cut Express provides a couple of other tools for quick and precise Timeline redefinition. The next tool to the left of the navigation bar is the Zoom Control. It is shaped like a meter and redefines the time scale based on where the marker is in the Zoom Control box (see Figure 4-47). When the marker is farther to the right, the time increments will be larger, meaning that you will be looking at whole minutes and can see more of the sequence at a time. Moving the marker to the left makes the increments smaller and more precise. Move the marker to the extreme left and you will see each frame; move it to the extreme right and you will be looking at a much

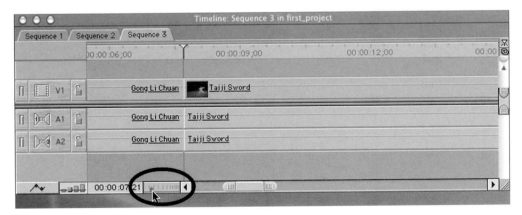

Figure 4-47   The Zoom Control meter

larger scale that allows you to see every clip that sits in the sequence. In between these two positions are jumps in scale that you can access based on your needs.

Playhead Timecode Field

To the left of this meter is the sequence Playhead Timecode Field (see Figure 4-48). This field has two major functions. The first is to display the frame that the playhead is currently parked on. Since this is a timecode value for the sequence and not for the clips within it, the first frame of the sequence will be the timecode value 00:00:00:00.

The second function of the field is to manually move the playhead at a specific timecode location. Navigating to a specific frame to make an edit can be crucial. Entering values into this box is simple; you don't even have to click on the box to do so. Because this box is only one of two places you can enter numeric information into the Timeline window, simply typing numbers when the Timeline window is active with nothing selected will enter them there.

That said, you do need to make sure that nothing *is* selected when you begin typing numbers. If a clip is selected when you begin entering numbers, the Move functionality is enabled. Instead of changing the position of the playhead, the selected clip will be moved the number of frames you enter. Before typing numbers in the Timeline window, always either click in the window to deselect any clips, or hit Command-D for De-select All.

Final Cut Express makes things easy for entering timecode values. Although timecode values require colons or semicolons to delineate hours, minutes, seconds, and frames, Final Cut Express can insert these for you. All you need to do is type in the numbers (see Figure 4-49) and make sure that you enter zeros where applicable—for example, type 300, and Final Cut Express will convert this to 00:00:03:00, or the third second of the Timeline. When you hit the Enter key, Final Cut Express will insert the colons and move the playhead to the new location. It can even tell that the earlier values should stay the same if you

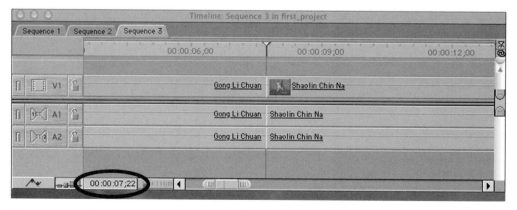

Figure 4-48   Timecode displayed in the Playhead Timecode Field

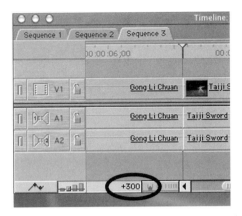

Figure 4-49 Moving the playhead by entering numbers on the keyboard

enter only a few. For example, typing in the previous value lands the playhead on 00:00:03:00. Then typing in 15 will move it up to 00:00:03:15. Typing in 215 will then move it to 00:00:02;15.

To make things even more convenient, you can type in a certain number of frames to retreat or advance. Instead of having to do the math to figure which frame to move to, simply type in + or − followed by a number, and the playhead advances or retreats that many frames, seconds, minutes, or even hours. For example, if you are at 00:00:02:00 and you want to move up to 00:00:03:00, simply type in +100, or plus 1 second and zero frames.

Using the numeric keypad for navigation is the easiest way to work. Rather than wear your wrist out using the mouse to drag a playhead around, move it exactly the distance you want. But what if you want to advance or retreat only one frame? The keyboard shortcut for advance or retreat one frame is the Left or Right Arrow key. Holding the Shift key and hitting the Left or Right Arrow key changes this to advance or retreat 1 second. Combine this with the Up and Down Arrow keys that move the playhead from the In point to the Out point, or edit points, of each clip in the sequence, and you have awesome tools for flying around the timeline without ever touching the mouse.

Using each of these three tools, you can quickly jump around your sequence and hone in on the areas you need to work with at the time scale you need to work with. While general and imprecise, the Zoom bar is a quick-and-dirty method of getting your sequence in roughly the area and scale you want. The Zoom Control meter provides a more precise method of choosing the time scale. Using the timecode field is the most precise way of moving your playhead around to new locations. Mastering all three techniques of Timeline navigation will enormously speed up your operations.

Looking to the left of the time scale and playhead location controls, you will see three buttons that allow further customization.

Track Height Switch

The first is called Track Height (see Figure 4-50). Track Height simply gives you four options for the vertical size of each track within a sequence. If you are working with 12 layers of video, then you'll probably want to keep the track height low so that you can see most of them simultaneously. If, on the other hand, you are working with straight-cut editing on a single video track and you've got a lot of screen real estate to burn, expanding the track height may make things a little easier on the eyes, particularly if you are looking at the audio waveforms. This setting can be switched on the fly and has no effect on your sequence or clips other than making them more or less visible in the Timeline.

The Clip Overlays Button

The next button on the lower left-hand side of the Timeline window (see Figure 4-51) is incredibly useful. It's called the Clip Overlays button in Final Cut Express parlance, but it's popularly known as a *rubberband tool*. We first saw this mentioned in the section on Preferences in Chapter 2. The Clip Overlays button overrides that preference whenever it is clicked and enabled or disabled. Rubberbanding allows us to alter audio levels (loudness) and opacity (the amount of transparency) within a clip in the Timeline. In addition, when used with another tool (to be discussed with the Toolbar functions), rubberbanding allows us to *keyframe*, or change these audio and opacity levels over time. This is a quick, creative way to customize video and audio fades and to even out audio tracks that exhibit too much variation in audio levels.

Figure 4-50 Setting the track height

Figure 4-51 The Clip Overlays button, or the rubberband tool

When the Clip Overlays button is engaged, all clips within a sequence display a thin horizontal colored line—black for video tracks and purple for audio. These lines describe the level for audio or video opacity in a video clip. Open a sequence on the Timeline, edit a clip into it, and enable the Clip Overlays button so that horizontal lines appear in the clip. Move the mouse pointer over the Clip Overlays lines in the clip's audio tracks. The mouse pointer will change into two parallel horizontal lines with arrows pointing up and down. While the mouse pointer is shaped as such, click the line and drag it up and down without releasing the mouse button.

As you drag the line up and down, you will see a small box appear with a dB value that changes as you move the mouse position (see Figure 4-52). Release the mouse button when the dB box reads −12 dB. Now perform the same action for the other audio track in the same clip (if the audio tracks for a clip are stereo, changing the level of one track will change the other as well). If you go back and play this clip from the beginning, you will notice dramatically lower audio levels.

When you adjusted the levels, you probably noticed that the entire line for the clip adjusted evenly across the clip. This means that the level adjustment evenly affects the entire clip—i.e., the same level of boost or cut is being applied for the entire clip. When we cover the Toolbar later in this chapter, we will discover a way to vary the change in level within the clip itself through keyframing.

Video opacity can be affected the same way that audio levels are adjusted. This is easier to see when the adjusted video clip is *superimposed,* or occupies the video track directly above another video clip. Using the Drag to Canvas editing method, we will perform a Superimpose edit of a new clip into a Video 2 track. Make sure you don't use the same or similar clips for both video tracks, or you will fail to see much of an opacity change after rubberbanding.

Position the sequence playhead at the beginning of a clip in the Video 1 track. Set the target track indicator for the Video 1 track. Load a new clip into the Viewer window that is longer than the clip already occupying the Video 1 track (or you will get an "Insufficient

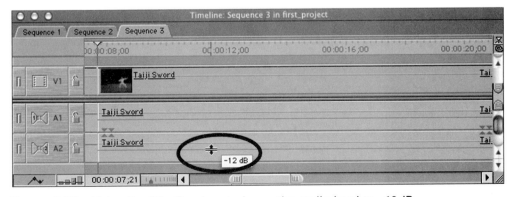

Figure 4-52 Using the Clip Overlays to lower the audio level to −12 dB

content for edit" message—we'll see why in a moment), and then drag it to the Canvas window and drop it into the overlay box named Superimpose (see Figure 4-53).

The Superimpose edit sends the video portion of the clip being edited into the track above the currently selected target track. The newly edited clip should be in the Video 2 track, so that it is positioned exactly above the original clip in the Video 1 track. The incoming superimposed video clip is also automatically trimmed down to the exact length of the clip it is being superimposed above. If there is no Video 2 track to superimpose the clip into, Final Cut Express automatically creates the track and then performs the edit. This is why you needed a longer clip than the one already present in Video 1; if it were shorter, it could not match the length of the clip on Video 1 exactly.

Move the mouse pointer over the line in the video portion of the superimposed clip in the Video 2 track. When the mouse pointer changes to the familiar parallel line/arrow shape, click the mouse button and drag the line down. The same box will appear next to the mouse pointer, this time giving a percentage value for the opacity of the clip (see Figure 4-54). A value of 100 means completely opaque, or visible. A value of 0 means completely transparent, such that anything on a layer underneath the video track is completely visible.

Drag the line to around the 50% point and release it. A glance back at the Canvas reveals that the clip in Video 2 track is half transparent, revealing the layer underneath (see Figure 4-55). Readjusting the position of this opacity line gives varying degrees of opacity.

You will probably notice that the red line has appeared over the clip that you applied the opacity change to. This is because once again there is no video file to associate with the visual mixture of the clips in the Video 1 and Video 2 tracks. The clip must be rendered to play back correctly. If you are performing this on a machine capable of Real-time effects and they are enabled as described earlier, you will see a green line instead, indicating that this effect can be previewed in Real-time on the desktop monitor without rendering. The audio level change should not require any rendering or mixdown, because Final Cut Express can process the level change and real-time mix the audio out to Firewire.

Toggle Snapping Button

In the top right-hand corner of the window is a button with a small yellow triangle (see Figure 4-56). This is the Toggle Snapping button. *Snapping* is a behavior that enables quick editing on the Timeline by accurately "snapping," like a magnet, the beginning or end edges of clips to the edges of other clips or the sequence playhead in the sequence Timeline. Its chief usefulness is as a tool for avoiding gaps between clips and accidental Overwrite and Insert edits from imprecise drag-and-drop operations. Snapping is disabled by default. Clicking the Toggle Snapping button or hitting the N key toggles it on and off.

When Snapping is disabled and clips are manually dragged to the sequence, they are placed exactly where the mouse pointer is when the mouse button is released. This is fine for Insert edits in which a large degree of exactitude is necessary. As you move the

Figure 4-53 Dragging a clip from the Viewer into the Canvas to perform a Superimpose edit

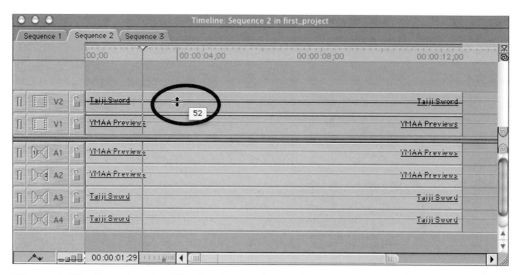

Figure 4-54 Dragging the Clip Overlays to lower the opacity value of a video clip

incoming clip around in the area of the sequence you want to put it in, the Canvas window will show the frames it is currently over, allowing you to find the exact point you want to drop the new clip in.

As an example, open a sequence that already contains at least one clip. Go to the Toggle Snapping button and make sure it is disabled and light gray in color. Grab a clip from the Viewer and drag it into the Timeline; without releasing the mouse button, ease it through another clip already in the sequence. Watch the Canvas window update as you move through the clip. When you locate a frame that would make an acceptable edit, confirm that the mouse pointer will perform an Insert (arrow pointing right) and drop the clip. The clip will drop right where you released the mouse button, as you would expect it to.

But there are some instances where such exactitude can be a hindrance. If you are moving a clip around on the sequence and you simply want to place it immediately following a preceding clip, dragging and dropping it against the last frame of the previous clip can be tricky. It's easy to accidentally drop the clip a few frames over the end and overwrite or insert into the first clip rather than at the exact end of it.

Snapping automates this process for you. If Snapping is enabled, when the playhead or the In or Out point of a clip comes within a certain distance of any other In or Out point or the playhead, small triangles appear at that point on the sequence, alerting you that if you drop the clip, it will snap to that position.

Now utilize Snapping by clicking the Toggle Snapping button, which turns it yellow. Grab a new clip from the Viewer and drag it to the sequence where the two clips are. Move the clip around the sequence. As you do so, you will see the incoming clip's edges jump to the ends of the clips already there, as well as to the playhead. As the incoming clip snaps to an end or to the playhead, triangles appear above and below to indicate that the clip has

Figure 4-55 The resulting superimposed video clip at 50% opacity

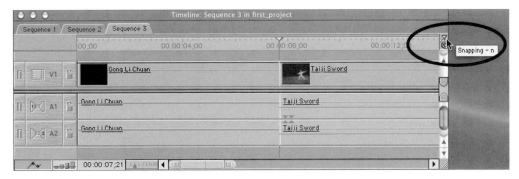

Figure 4-56 The Toggle Snapping button

been snapped to another clip (see Figure 4-57). Pick one of the In or Out points and drop the clip, performing an Overwrite edit. The clip will edit in, snapping tightly to the chosen edit point.

Snapping is a feature that should be used based on your editing situation. It is chiefly useful when your sequence time scale (how much time fits into the Timeline window at once) is rather high—i.e., the sequence shows you 10 minutes rather than 10 seconds. At such times, it is difficult to spot clip edges. In addition, Snapping functions between clips on different tracks. This allows you to make sure that In and Out points of clips join together throughout the sequence without leaving gaps. A nice bonus is that the N key toggle actually works *while* you are holding a clip with the mouse button pressed. If you realize that Snapping is disabled right before you drop the clip, simply hit the N key with your other hand to enable it.

Toggle Linking Button

The button underneath the Toggle Snapping button is called the Toggle Linking button (see Figure 4-58). Linking involves the way a single clip behaves in its relationship with other clips that are connected (linked) to it. When clips are linked, any trimming edits applied to one part of the clip will be applied to the other linked clips. When Linking is enabled, the two chain links on the Toggle Linking button are unbroken and yellow. When Linking is disabled, the symbol becomes a single gray broken chain link. Before learning to efficiently utilize the Toggle Linking button, let's get a sense of what linking does in general.

What is linking? When we capture clips, we do so by capturing video and audio at the same time. Final Cut Express treats the two as a linked clip from the inception, and unless you change that relationship, it will always do so. But the video and audio are really not one integrated clip. The clip really contains one video clip and two audio clips that are linked by Final Cut Express at capture.

Although Final Cut Express does this linking at capture, audio and video clips do not have to stay linked to each other, and they can be in turn linked to other clips. The only restriction to this is that a single video clip can be linked only to either one or two audio clips. Two video clips cannot be linked, and more than two audio clips cannot be linked (although they can easily be grouped by the process of nesting, as we will see later).

Linking is a completely artificial state. You can enable or disable it for clips in a sequence at any time by selecting the linked clips and toggling the Link command in the Modify drop-down menu. Toggling this command this way creates or breaks links between any selected clips based on their current link status; linked clips will become unlinked, and unlinked clips will become linked if they fit the restrictions (you can break multiple clip links at once, but you can only create links based on the one video clip–two audio clips limitation).

Using clip linking, it's easy to link up a video track with other audio sources. This is useful if you are using audio recorded by another device, such as a minidisk recorder, instead

Figure 4-57 These triangles indicate that Snapping is enabled

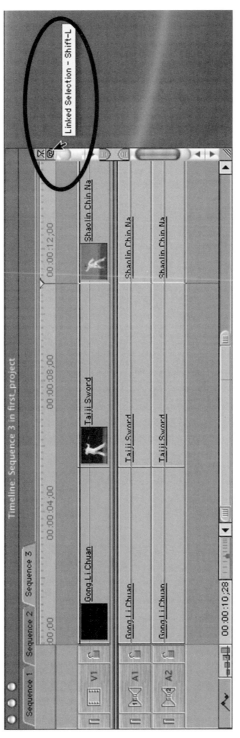

Figure 4-58   The Toggle Linking button

of the camera mikes—a technique called double-system sound. It is useful also if you want to sync up music tracks from an audio CD and make sure they stay locked over time to the video clip.

Linking Operations Demonstrated

Let's quickly perform a bit of sophisticated linking and unlinking. We will take the video portion of one linked clip and link it to the audio portion of another linked clip. We will break all the links between two captured clips, and then we will delete the video clip for one and the audio clips for the other. Finally, we will link together the video clip from the first and the audio clips from the second to form an artificially linked clip that contains the audio and video we want, regardless of what those clips were captured with.

First, clear off the sequence by selecting all clips and deleting them. Next, edit two different captured clips into the sequence. Select both clips using the marquee selection technique or by Shift-clicking them. When they are both selected, go to the Modify drop-down menu, and look for the Link command. Toggle off the links between the selected clips by selecting the Link toggle switch in the Modify drop-down menu (see Figure 4-59). This will break all video and audio links between any currently selected clips.

The Link command in the Modify drop-down menu is actually a Link toggle switch, though only for individual or groups of selected clips. If the Link command is checked in the menu, it means that the currently selected clip(s) in the sequence is linked with other clips. If it is not checked, the currently selected clip or clips are not linked with anything else.

Note that after unlinking occurs, the names of the newly unlinked clips in the sequence are no longer underlined (hit Command-Z and Command-Y, Undo and Redo, respectively,

Figure 4-59 Using the Link toggle switch in the Modify drop-down menu

over and over for comparison). When a clip is linked to another clip, its displayed name in the sequence is underlined to signify its linked status. Although all the clips are still brown, because they are still selected, they are no longer linked to each other (see Figure 4-60).

Click anywhere on the Timeline to deselect all the clips. Then, click any individual video or audio clip. Notice that only the clip you click is selected, not its previously linked clips that were captured with it. Now that all the video and audio clips are completely unlinked, Shift-click to select the two audio tracks of the first of the clips, and then return to the Modify drop-down menu to toggle Linking back on for the selected audio tracks.

Note that the underline returns to the name of the audio tracks when you relink them. If the tracks were originally part of a stereo pair as well, you can also select Stereo Pair from the Modify drop-down menu to reconnect them in that manner (see Figure 4-61). If you reenable the Stereo Tracks toggle for them, little green triangles appear in the audio clips, indicating the special stereo relationship between the two.

Click anywhere on the Timeline to deselect the relinked audio clips, and then click the video clip above them that they were originally captured and linked with to select it. Hit the Delete key to remove that video track from the sequence Timeline (see Figure 4-62).

Marquee-select or Shift-click to select both the audio tracks for the other clip that was also just unlinked, and delete them as well, leaving the video portion of the second clip still sitting in the sequence. Now click the remaining video clip in the sequence, and drag it above the relinked audio tracks. Use Snapping to make sure that the beginning of the video clip you are moving lines up with the beginning of the two linked audio clips. When the video and audio portions are lined up, marquee-select or Shift-click to select the video clip

Figure 4-60   These clips are now unlinked

Figure 4-61 Reconnecting a stereo pair from the Modify drop-down menu

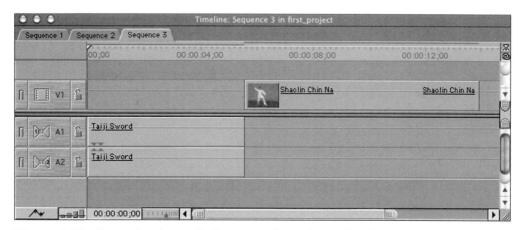

Figure 4-62 Removing the audio from one clip and the video from another

and the two relinked audio clips. When all three are selected, return to the Modify drop-down menu and once again toggle the Link switch (see Figure 4-63).

If you deselect them all and then click any one of them, the others are automatically selected along with the one clicked. Notice that the underline has also returned to the name of the video clip, signifying that it is now linked with audio track(s). This exercise should demonstrate the malleability and artificiality of Linking. Although editors many times take video and audio captured and linked clips for granted, they really are individual pieces that can be broken up and reassembled as needed.

Why, then, offer a Toggle Linking button in the Timeline if Linking can be toggled in the drop-down menu? Because sometimes it will be necessary to quickly unlink a clip or

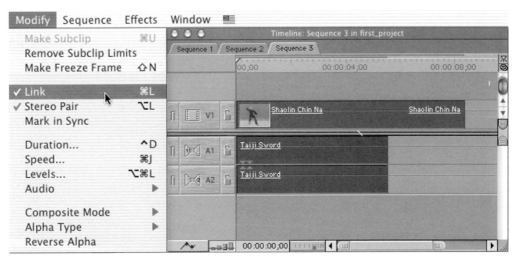

Figure 4-63 Relinking video and audio clips

clips to make a minor adjustment. Rather than physically unlinking many clips and then having to go in and relink them individually in the long process just described, with Final Cut Express you can suspend the links for all clips in a sequence for the moment by hitting this toggle on the Timeline. When you've completed your adjustment, you turn the Linking back on, and everything functions as before. The link between the clips was never lost; it was only disregarded for the moment until you chose to reinstate it.

This ability to quickly unlink and relink clips becomes very useful when you are performing what is referred to as a *split edit* or an *L Cut*. This popular sort of edit involves audio clips beginning before or after their linked video clips in an edit. Often an editor will need the next clip's audio to precede the edit by a short duration. Because we can unlink our clip, extend the In points for the audio clips as much as we want, and then relink them to the video clip, it is very easy to deliver this effect. Audio and video tracks do not have to line up to be linked; in fact, they can be minutes apart from each other on the sequence Timeline.

To perform such a split edit, simply toggle Linking off on the Timeline, then Command-click the two audio tracks' edit points, leaving the video track's edit point unselected. Double-click either audio edit point to load them into the Trim Edit window. Then begin previewing, trimming as the preview plays. Although you didn't load a video edit point into the Trim window, it will still show the visible video occurring in the preview area, thus allowing you to see and hear the split edit you are creating (see Figure 4-64). When you get it the way you like, simply leave the Trim Edit window and toggle Linking back on.

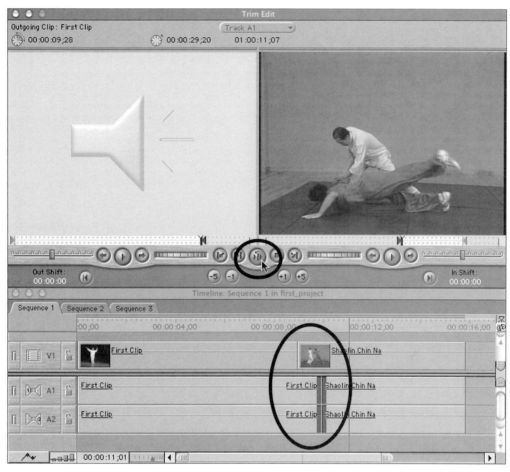

Figure 4-64   Performing a split edit (L Cut)

Sync Issues with Linking and Unlinking Clips

You may be a little alarmed about the ease with which Final Cut Express allows you to link and unlink clips. If you didn't know better, this would be an invitation to audio and video sync disaster. If you unlink a clip, change the position of the video or the audio slightly, and relink, then your sync will be off forever. As long as the two are linked, you cannot move the video or audio without moving the other portion of the clip equally. In truth, the main reason that clips are linked at capture is to avoid such situations, maintaining a rock-solid link between video and audio from capture to mastering to tape.

Fortunately, Final Cut Express throws in another feature as a guarantee against loss of sync, even in the event that your unlinked clips are adjusted and relinked. Whenever audio and video clips are captured together, their media in your Scratch Disk is integrated in special ways. Final Cut Express can sense this, so anytime that two clips were captured together and are placed in a sequence but are forced out of sync, you will see a small red box at the head of each clip stating the number of frames by which the two are out of sync (see Figure 4-65).

Clear off the sequence by performing a marquee-select or Shift-select of all clips and hitting Delete. Edit a captured clip into the sequence (not a relinked clip; the audio and video components of this clip must have been captured together). Visit the Toggle Linking button in the top right-hand corner of the Timeline window under the Toggle Snapping button and disable it.

When you return to the clip and click any of the individual audio or video clips, you will notice that only the individual video or audio clip is selected, just as if you had unlinked them using the Modify drop-down menu Link switch. Click either a video or an audio portion of the clip, and move it over slightly so that its edges overlap the items that it was previously linked to. You will see a small red box appear in each of the items that were previously linked (if an item is selected, its color switches to brown, and the red box also changes, appearing blue).

The number in the red box reveals by how many frames and seconds the items that were originally captured together are out of sync. A positive number of frames indicates that the clip is ahead of its companion pieces; a negative number indicates that the clip follows them.

Final Cut Express offers you a quick tool to get such clips back into sync. Hold down the Control key and click the red "out of sync" box for a moment. A contextual menu will appear offering to Move or to Slip the item back into sync. For the moment, select Move into Sync (see Figure 4-66).

We will discuss "slipping" techniques in the next section, which focuses on the Toolbar. Some care must be taken here for a couple of reasons. The "out of sync" box appears only when such previously linked items in separate tracks actually overlap each other. If the items are isolated from each other over time, Final Cut Express will not assume that they are out

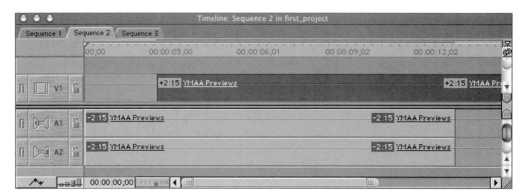

Figure 4-65 "Out of Sync" box indicating the number of frames out of sync

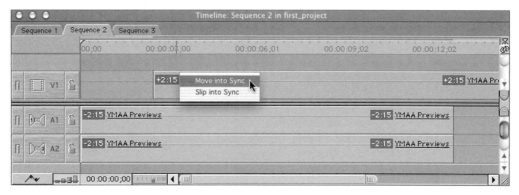

Figure 4-66 Clicking the "out of sync" box to perform a Move into Sync

of sync but that they are simply recurrent uses of the same clip. Further, if you are using the same clip twice in the same stretch of frames in a sequence, Final Cut Express can become understandably confused as to which clip items are supposed to be resynced to which, yielding mixed results.

The Toolbar

The small vertical strip referred to as the Toolbar is full of tools that will make your life more interesting in Final Cut Express. Many of the tools are operational within the Timeline window, although some also have functionality across the application. Some functions cannot be performed unless you switch to the proper Toolbar tool.

Does this mean that you should constantly be clicking back to the Toolbar window to switch tools? Absolutely not. Using the mouse to access that thin, tiny window will do a number on your wrists and isn't a particularly fast way to work, anyway. The answer is the keyboard shortcut. For every tool in the Toolbar, there is a simple keystroke that will change the mouse pointer to the tool you want to access (see Figure 4-67). There's no faster way to work, and you'll find that most experienced nonlinear editors rarely use the mouse for anything other than positioning of on-screen items, preferring to fully utilize the keyboard shortcuts that really speed up the workflow.

If you are just beginning your editing life, memorizing all those shortcuts may seem daunting. There are a couple of options that make that process much easier. Each copy of Final Cut Express comes with a set of keyboard overlay stickers that you can use to learn the shortcuts. Each overlay sticker shows the primary tool that the keystroke will enable. Because the stickers are translucent, you can still see the letters underneath the stickers, allowing you to use the keyboard normally. With all due respect to Apple, using the stickers is a bad idea, because they tend to stick to everything except the keys they are intended to fasten to. Invariably, they end up in a big gummy pile in front of the keyboard.

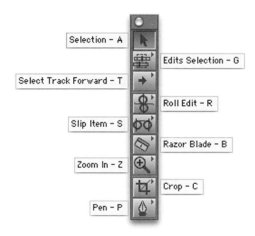

Figure 4-67   The Toolbar and its keyboard shortcuts

What other options are there? There are free keyboard layout charts available that show where the keystrokes are, and if you are willing to spend some money, there are a couple of options. Loren Miller, of Neotron Design, distributes the great, inexpensive Keyguide, which is a laminated sheet with color-coded references to every single shortcut in the application, including the Command/Option/Control/Shift key shortcuts missing from the gummy stickers. For quite a bit more money, another option is the special Final Cut Express/Pro-dedicated keyboards that some companies manufacture. Since they are basically just normal Macintosh keyboards with specially colored and labeled keys, they perform without extra software or hardware. Beginning editors can quickly pick up the functionality of the keyboard in a fraction of the time it would take to learn from accessing the manual. Either way, learning the shortcut keystrokes is very important and will save lots of time over searching for tools in the menus or the Toolbar.

The General Selection Tool (Keyboard Shortcut–A)

The first tool on the Toolbar is the General Selection tool (see Figure 4-68). This is the generic mouse pointer arrow that is enabled when you start Final Cut Express. The Selection tool is simply used for selecting items and moving them around. This tool, as contrasted with the following set of selection tools, is used for selecting individual items. When you want to pick up, move, or load a clip into the Viewer, for instance, this is the tool to engage.

The Selection Toolset and Accessing "Hidden" Toolsets

The Selection toolset button below the General Selection tool on the Toolbar engages a different set of selection tools that are more specific to particular tasks. Although there is only

Figure 4-68 The General Selection tool

one position for each toolset on the Toolbar, Final Cut Express uses a click-and-hold method of choosing the particular tool from any toolset. Click and briefly hold the button. You have a choice of three specialized selection tools here (see Figure 4-69).

Edits Selection Tool (Keyboard Shortcut–G)

Click the first button of the Selection toolset. If you move the mouse pointer over the Timeline window, you will notice that the mouse pointer has switched from the arrow to a small crosshair. This button activates the Edit Selection tool, which performs the same action as double-clicking an edit point between two clips on a sequence. When you click an edit point, it automatically opens up the Trim Edit window containing the edit point you clicked on.

Why use this tool instead of just double-clicking with the General Selection tool as we did earlier? As we saw when discussing the Trim Edit window, we can have more than one

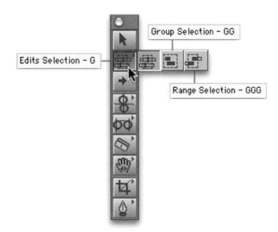

Figure 4-69 The Selection toolset

edit point in the Track drop-down bar within the Trim Edit window if more than one edit point was selected. With the General Selection tool, this meant Command-clicking each additional edit point to add it to the Track drop-down bar to be used in the Trim Edit window.

The Edit Selection tool makes this task easier. Clicking anywhere around the edit points you want to use and marquee-selecting them selects the edit points and then adds them in the Trim Edit window. Instead of Command-clicking around your tracks and then double-clicking to open the Trim Edit window, simply choose this tool and marquee-select around the edit points you want to work with (see Figure 4-70). If you forgot a couple of edit points and want to add them to the current tracks loaded into the Trim Edit window, simply return to the sequence, Command-click and marquee-select the other edit points, and they will be added to the Track drop-down bar in the Trim Edit window.

The Group Selection Tool (Keyboard Shortcut–GG)

The middle tool in the Selection toolset is the Group Selection tool. Once again, the mouse pointer will assume the shape of a crosshair. This tool behaves very much like the General

Figure 4-70   Selecting multiple edit points to trim with the Edit Selection tool

Selection tool. When you click and drag a marquee with this tool, it selects everything it touches, as well as any clips or items linked with whatever it touches. If the marquee you drag with the crosshair touches any part of a clip, that clip and its linked clips become part of the active selection.

Range Selection Tool (Keyboard Shortcut–GGG)

The final tool to the right on this toolset is the Range Selection tool. This unique little tool lets you select a section of one or more clips in a sequence. But unlike the Group or Generic Selection tools, the Range Selection tool does not force you to select an entire clip.

Once again, as with the Edit and Group Selection tools, the mouse pointer displays as a crosshair. To make a selection using this tool, click and drag a marquee over an area inside one or more clips within a track (see Figure 4-71). Unlike the other selection tools, though, the Range Selection tool does not see clip edges and allows you to select a section of a single clip and/or a range of clips. This means that you can select a smaller part of a clip rather than the whole thing. You could, for example, select the last half of one clip and the first half of the next clip.

It does, however see track boundaries, so the range of frames you select with it all need to live on the same track. Because it is a selection tool, it selects linked clips with respect to the way you have the Linked Selection button set; enabling Linked Selection will result in material in the linked audio tracks being selected along with the material you select in the track, while disabling Linked Selection will result in only the one track's material being selected.

The tool is referred to as a range tool because it effectively allows you to discriminate footage over a range of frames rather than based on a clip's In and Out points. This can be very helpful when exporting clips as QuickTime movies or in other situations where you need to isolate a specific section of your sequence, regardless of which clips are included. It is literally a selection of frames in a track, rather than a selection of clips in a sequence.

This tool can be used to load just a section of a clip from the sequence into the Viewer window for manipulation, instead of loading the entire clip. When you select only a portion of a clip, you can selectively apply effects filters to just the section of the clip, rather than applying them to the entire clip. You can also selectively render sections of a clip, as we will do later in Chapter 6, The Audio Tools.

The Track Selection Toolset (Keyboard Shortcut–T)

The next button below the special Selection toolset is another toolset dedicated to selection, but this time the selection criteria is for clips ahead of or behind the sequence playhead within a track. Clicking and holding the button reveals five possible track selection types here (see Figure 4-72).

The arrow pointing to the right will select all items in a track occurring to the right of the frame the playhead is currently parked on. The next button performs the same action,

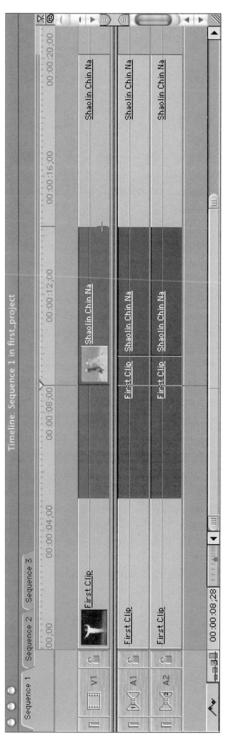

Figure 4-71   Selecting a range of frames with the Range Selection tool

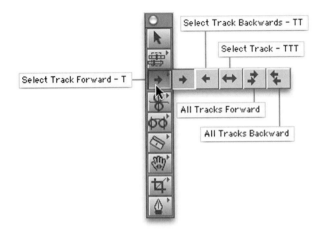

Figure 4-72 The Track Selection toolset

but to the left of the frame the playhead is currently parked on. The middle choice selects all clips in the track. The fourth and fifth choices on this toolset, symbolized by the double arrows on the button, allow you to select all clips on all tracks to the right or to the left of the selection point, respectively.

This tool does not override the Linked Selection button in the sequence, so if all your video clips are linked with audio clips, as they will be after initially being captured, selecting items in the video track using a track selection tool will also select their linked audio clips in the audio tracks.

Ripple and Roll Edit Toolset

The next toolset below the track selection tools contains the Ripple Edit and Roll Edit tools (see Figure 4-73). We have already encountered these functions in the Trim Edit window. The difference is that when these tools are selected from the Toolbar, their trim functionality can be utilized directly on clips in the Timeline window rather than from within the Trim Edit window. By clicking an edit point with either of these two tools, you can trim edit points and dynamically view the results before settling for an edit.

The Roll Edit Tool (Keyboard Shortcut–R)
The Roll Edit tool moves the In and Out frames of the edit points for the two clips chosen in the sequence. Although you do not have access to the large video preview windows and the In and Out timecode tools that are available in the Trim Edit window, when you use the Roll Edit tool, the Canvas window itself switches to a mini Trim window, showing the In and Out point frames as you adjust them. The Timeline is also dynamically updated as

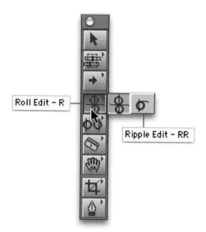

Roll Edit – R

Ripple Edit – RR

Figure 4-73   Ripple and Roll Edit toolset

you drag. Should you wish to use the Trim Edit window for greater precision at any point, double-clicking the edit point with the Roll Edit tool will open it up just as the General Selection tool did.

Edit two abutting clips into the same track on a sequence so that they have an adjoining edit point. Disable Snapping in the Timeline temporarily (hit the N key to toggle it off) so that you can engage the Roll Edit tool from the toolset without imprecise jumping from edit point to edit point. Select the Roll Edit tool from the Toolbar.

Click the mouse pointer on the edit point and drag in either direction. As you drag, keep an eye on the Canvas window, watching the Out and In points change as you move the pointer. Also note that in the Timeline window, as you move the edit point around the clip, there is an indicator line demonstrating where the current Out and In points for the two clips are. Release the mouse pointer, and observe that the clips now meet at different Out and In points, respectively (see Figure 4-74).

As with the Roll Edit in the Trim Edit window, this trimming action shortens the length of only one clip and adds equally to the length of the other. The duration of the two clips combined remains the same. The Roll Edit cannot roll either clip past the media limits of the media file it refers to, thus limiting how far either clip may be roll edited.

The Ripple Edit Tool (Keyboard Shortcut–RR)

The Ripple Edit tool offers the same trimming functions as it does within the Trim Edit window. As with the trimming action there, the Ripple Edit tool only extends or shortens the duration of either the outgoing or the incoming clip, whichever the tool is being applied to. Since the tool is rippling the edit point in only one direction, it affects the duration only of the clip being trimmed; if it affected two clips' durations, it would be a Roll Edit tool! It does, however, affect the overall length of the sequence, because it is adding to or subtracting from the length of one of the clips in the sequence. As the rippled clip is

Figure 4-74　Changing the In and Out points of clips with the Roll Edit tool

trimmed, the rest of the clips in the sequence move over to avoid creating a gap or being overwritten by the duration change of the rippling clip.

In the Trim Edit window, the clip being rippled is determined by which video window the green indicator was lit over. With the Ripple tool in the Timeline window, an edit point will only show either the In or the Out point selected. Clicking near the edit point of either the outgoing or the incoming clip will switch the edit point that is selected to be trimmed. Then moving the mouse pointer over either the left, outgoing clip or the right, incoming clip will switch directions of the Ripple Edit tool's "tongue," indicating which clip of the edit point the trimming action will be applied to.

Select the edit point you want to affect, move the mouse pointer over the clip you want to shorten or lengthen, click and drag, and your clip will be trimmed (see Figure 4-75). As with the Ripple Edit action, the Canvas window will show a continuous update of the new Out or In points the trim action is producing. Not surprisingly, the keyboard shortcuts that applied in the Trim Edit window, the "[" and "]" or Shift-[and Shift-] keys, will work on the Timeline as well, provided the Ripple or Roll tool is activated and an edit point is selected.

Figure 4-75   Changing the In or Out point of a clip using the Ripple Edit tool

The Slip and Slide Toolset

The next toolset below the Roll and Ripple tools is another combination of convenient editing tools, the Slip and Slide tools (see Figure 4-76). These two tools can make quick, one-stop adjustments that would otherwise take several steps and a couple of windows to perform. The Slip and Slide tools allow you to adjust either the length of one clip or the In and Out points of one clip within a group of clips without affecting the overall duration of the group of clips. They allow you to quickly shuffle the length or edit points of a clip so that you see the range of frames you want without changing what can often be a sequence duration predetermined by other factors, such as a client's wishes or the length or rhythm of a musical score.

The Slip Tool (Keyboard Shortcut–S)

If you edit a clip to a sequence and then realize that you wanted to use an earlier part of the master clip than the part you set In and Out points for, instead of reloading the clip in the Viewer and editing in a new version of the clip, you can simply "slip" the

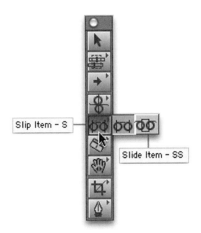

Slip Item - S

Slide Item - SS

Figure 4-76   The Slip and Slide toolset

contents of the clip you already have on the sequence. Thus a clip on the sequence that was edited from the later part of its master clip when it was created in the Viewer window could be "slipped" so that the earlier part of the master clip is now used in the clip. The duration of the clip itself will not be changed, only the material between the In and Out points.

The Slip tool's effectiveness as a fast-and-dirty editing tool is best displayed with a group of four adjoining clips. To line up four clips quickly in a sequence, we will use a technique referred to as storyboard rough cutting.

Storyboard Rough-Cut Technique

Storyboarding is an old film term that describes a comic strip-style panel drawing of different scenes to be shot (see Figure 4-77). Because film and video production is expensive, directors usually "storyboard" the progression of their planned shots in comic-book panels to think out the order and rough look or angle of each shot. These storyboards are then used as a shooting template for everyone in the production. The cinematographer knows how to construct a shot, the art director knows how to arrange the set, and all involved can quickly and conveniently get a sense of what the director wants them to do to produce shots.

Storyboards are more than useful in productions. In addition to keeping everyone on roughly the same page, they help the director actually think out the story line. A short storyboard session prior to a shoot answers most of the on-set questions and eliminates unnecessary surprises.

The usefulness of storyboarding does not end with the shoot. Storyboards also help later to construct the edit, since they also generate a linear progression of the storyline through the series of shots being edited. Once you've captured all the clips from a shoot and they are gathered in a bin in your project, you can simply order them based on their occurrence in the storyboard and create a quick rough cut of the entire project.

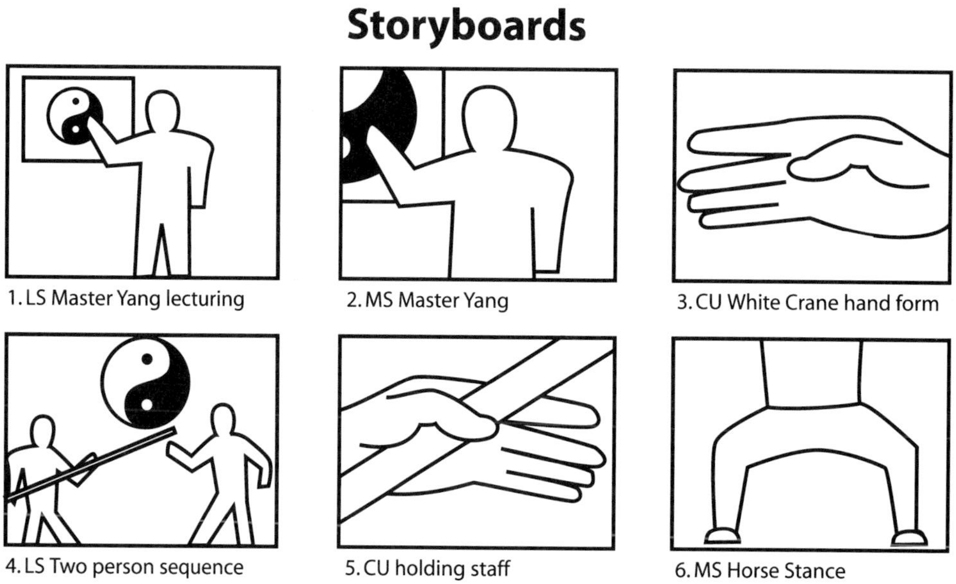

Storyboards

1. LS Master Yang lecturing   2. MS Master Yang   3. CU White Crane hand form

4. LS Two person sequence   5. CU holding staff   6. MS Horse Stance

Figure 4-77   A sample production storyboard

Capture four new video clips, each of which is at least 15 seconds in duration, making sure to include handles of at least 5 full seconds for each clip. Don't forget to use a Capture Bin for these clips so that they get stored in a special bin of their own.

To use the storyboard rough-cut technique, we will use the Large Icons view of the Capture Bin to create a sort of comic strip panel–style storyboard of our clips. We will arrange them in the order in which they should occur, left to right and top to bottom, just like the Sunday newspaper funnies. Then we will take the whole group of clips and deposit them in order on the sequence Timeline in a rough cut. All that will be further required is the trimming actions of the editing toolsets of the Toolbar.

After the capture process is complete, open the Capture Bin and look at the four newly captured clips. With the Capture Bin active, go to the View drop-down menu, select Browser Items, and in the submenu that appears, select As Large Icons (see Figure 4-78). This choice is also available by Control-clicking the bin itself.

Normally, the Browser window is most effective when viewed as a list so that all the detailed information about your materials is available. But when you choose As Large Icons, you are given a thumbnail of each item. This thumbnail, or Poster Frame, by default shows the first frame of a video clip, although you can change which frame it displays by scrubbing the clip and setting the Poster Frame, which is discussed subsequently. Double-click each clip to load into the viewer window. Insert In and Out points such that you have at least five seconds of handles on either side of each clip. Although in normal practice, such

Figure 4-78   Setting the browser to display as large icons

large handles are rarely necessary, we need them in this exercise to demonstrate the functionality of the Slip/Slide Toolset.

Now that your clips are all displayed in large icons in the Browser window, arrange them left to right, top to bottom, as if you were reading them like newspaper comics (see Figure 4-79). With only four clips, you'll only be able to create two rows of two columns,

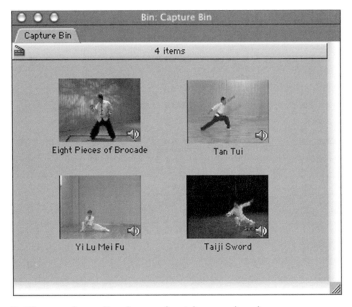

Figure 4-79   Setting up four clips in comic strip-panel order

so if you really want to see this as a functional storyboard rough cut, feel free to add more clips to the Capture Bin. Four clips is just the minimum required to demonstrate the technique. Once all your thumbnail clips are in the proper comic strip-panel order, create a new sequence. Go to the File drop-down menu, select New, and in the submenu that appears, select Sequence.

Click in the Capture Bin window and drag a marquee selection so that all the thumbnail clips are selected. When they are all selected, pick up any one of the clips and drag it to the sequence (see Figure 4-80). When you do this, you will see that all the clips are carried over simultaneously and laid down on the sequence, with no gaps between them. You could also simply pick up the Capture Bin itself from the Project tab in the Browser window and drop it in the sequence for the same effect!

Although we have not done any precise trimming yet, the clips in the sequence are now in a linear order that follows the left-to-right and top-to-bottom order that they maintained in the Capture Bin. All that remains is to go through and individually trim the clips and their edit points to meet our needs.

The Trim Edit window or the Ripple and Roll tools are perfect for editing these clips when you need to add or remove frames of video from the beginning or end of a clip, specifically to shorten or lengthen it. But in some circumstances, the fastest way to make the clip show what we want is simply to slip the contents of the clip so that a different part of the master clip is being used by the clip in the sequence.

Go to the Toolbar and make sure that your Slip tool is enabled. Then go to the sequence where your rough-cut sequence of clips is sitting. Click any clip that is surrounded by two other clips, and click and drag to the left and right. Overlaying the clips on the sequence Timeline, you will see a ghost image of the master clip that the "slipping" clip originated from moving around following the mouse pointer (see Figure 4-81). The ghost master-clip shape is there to let you visually know how far you can slip the clip within the current In and Out points of the subclip on the sequence Timeline.

Move the ghost clip around somewhat and then release the mouse button. You will see that the In and Out points, and therefore the duration, of the clip have not changed in the sequence. However, the portion of the master clip that these In and Out points relate to has changed.

Literally, Final Cut Express is slipping around the clip inside the handles of the master clip it originated from so that you can hone in on the footage you want the subclip to use. This is much faster than reloading the master clip into the Viewer window, setting new In and Out points for the clip, and then replacing the old clip in the sequence.

The Slip tool is primarily useful for what is referred to as B-Roll footage (see Figure 4-82). B-Roll, as a postproduction term, refers to relevant but nonspecific footage you might use to break up long static cuts. For instance, if you are editing a talking-head interview with a school administrator, cutaway shots of kids playing in a school playground and school buses would make excellent B-Roll footage, because they reference the interview but can just be picked up at random rather than scripted out. Interesting and well-shot B-Roll

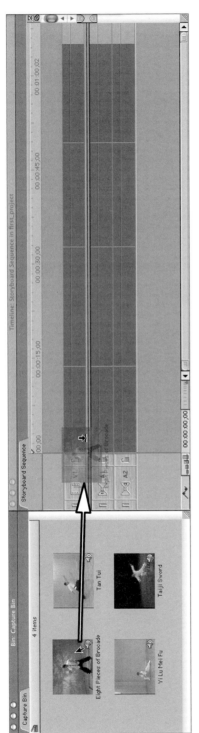

Figure 4-80 Dragging your clips to the sequence

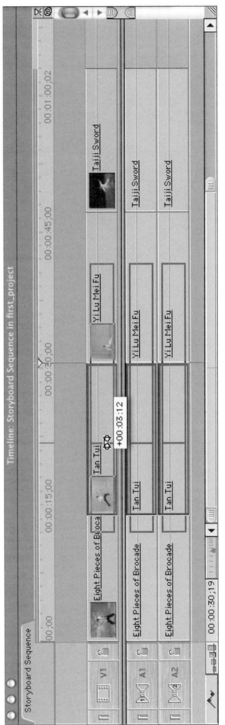

Figure 4-81 "Slipping" to change the part of a master clip used in a subclip

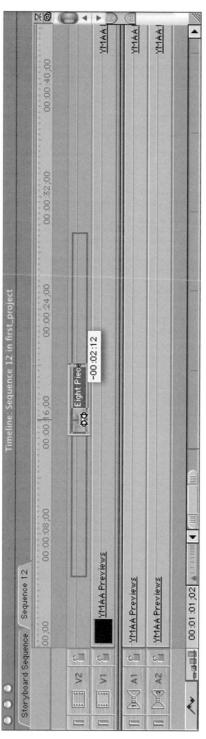

Figure 4-82 Using the Slip tool to adjust B-Roll clips

footage is something you can never have too much of, and it can help smooth out the editing rhythm in a sequence.

With a quick clip adjustment using the Slip tool, all you need initially is your subject footage, long B-Roll clips, and a sense for when to cut away from and back to your main content. The duration that the B-Roll clips should last will largely be determined by your content. If you capture lots of different B-Roll shots in a single master clip, all you need to do is use the same B-Roll clip frequently in your sequence. When you need a specific shot to appear in the B-Roll cutaway, just slip the B-Roll clip around until you get to the specific section of the clip you need. The Slip tool is excellent when your clip must retain its duration but you want to change the video that is displayed between the In point and the Out point.

Slip into Sync

As a final note, it should be remembered that we already encountered the Slip function earlier in the chapter. When we Control-clicked the red "out of sync" box in the Linking example, we found the "Move into Sync/Slip into Sync" box. We chose Move into Sync there to force the clip back into sync with its related clips.

The Slip into Sync choice would have performed an interesting variation on this. Instead of moving the out-of-sync clip to a new position in the sequence to resync it, the Slip into Sync would perform a slip action to the content of the out-of-sync clip such that it is correctly synced, although it does not sit squarely over its companion clips. Although the resynced clip does not change its position on the Timeline, its frames are slipped so that the frames that do overlap the other associated clips are in sync. This can be tricky to work with and can easily make sync matters worse if used improperly, so be careful to select the Control-click option that is appropriate to your situation.

The Slide Tool (Keyboard Shortcut–SS)

The Slide tool is a very convenient tool that also does not change the duration of a group of clips when it is applied to one of their number. But where it differs from the Slip tool is that it moves the sliding clip itself around between the clips surrounding it, lengthening the preceding clip and shortening the subsequent clip so that the edit points of the clip's edges remain intact and no gaps are created between any clips. It's like performing two trim actions on the same track at once!

The In and Out points of the clip you click and drag with the Slide tool stay exactly as they are. In fact, the clip you click and drag is not changed at all, except with regard to where it sits in the sequence Timeline. But in order for the clip to occur earlier or later in the group of clips of which it is a part, the clip preceding and the clip following must have their outgoing and incoming edit points simultaneously trimmed to accommodate the sliding clip.

Select the Slide tool on the Toolbar and click a clip that is surrounded by two adjoining clips. Drag it back and forth, and you will again see a ghost image of the clip you are moving, but this time it will maintain its subclip length and instead show its new, changed position within the surrounding clips (see Figure 4-83).

When you release the mouse button, the clip will jump to the new position you have moved it to, and the edit points for the surrounding clips will adjust so that no gap is introduced. The Out edit point for the clip preceding the sliding clip and the In edit point for the clip following the sliding clip will have shifted, being shortened or lengthened as necessary so that no gap is introduced on either side of the sliding clip.

This sort of tool will also be very useful with B-Roll footage, but this time for maintaining the exact length of the B-Roll clip. If you wanted to make sure that a 3-second and 15-frame B-Roll shot of a school bus would be used in its entirety and that we cut to it as the school administrator says the words "School bus," this would be the perfect tool. Just "slip" the B-Roll clip until the footage of the bus is present and then "slide" the clip right into position at the frame in which the administrator begins the words. Nothing could be simpler or faster.

Monitoring the Slip and Slide Tools in the Canvas Window

When you use the Slip or Slide tool, the Canvas displays the now-familiar small double video window to show you the frames of the clip that you are adjusting (see Figure 4-84). With the Slip tool, the first video window shows the new frame used for the In point of the clip, and the second window shows the new Out point frame, since the Slip tool will change both In and Out frames of the slipped clip. With the Slide tool, the first window shows you the new video frame used for the Out point for the preceding clip, and the second shows you the new frame being used for the following clip's new In point, because the changing frames here will be the preceding and following clips, not the sliding clip itself.

There are limitations to what you can do with this tool, of course. You can't slip or slide past the media limits of the clips you are working with, which is why we made sure that there were adequate handles on each clip in our example. Since the Slip tool will move the In and Out points of the clip you are moving and the Slide tool will change the outgoing and incoming edit points of the surrounding clips, you need to make sure that these clips have enough media to move around in. Final Cut Express will not tell you you've reached the media limits; it will simply not let you move past them. As usual for the trim tools, a small timecode box opens up as you adjust, specifying how many frames you have adjusted for precision work.

The Razorblade Toolset (Keyboard Shortcut–B)

The next toolset on the Toolbar is referred to as the Razorblade tool (see Figure 4-85). This tool is very intuitive and can be picked up very quickly. The Razorblade simply cuts a clip into two separate clips in the sequence at the point where the tool is clicked. This creates two clips from the original: one clip preceding the Razorblade point and one clip following it. The last frame of the first clip occurs right before the first frame of the second clip.

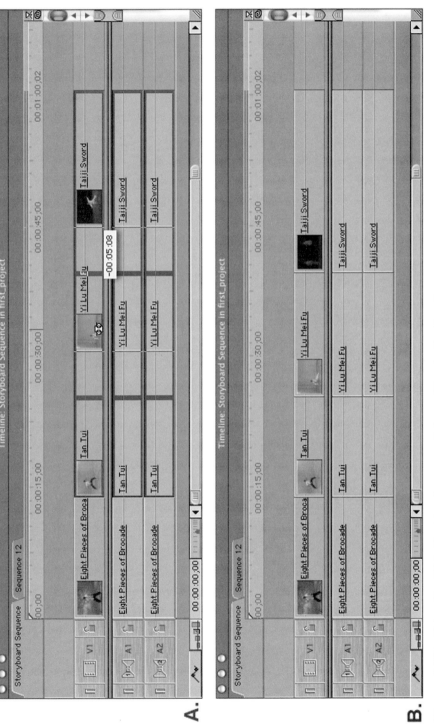

Figure 4-83 Using the Slide Tool to change a clip's position in the timeline

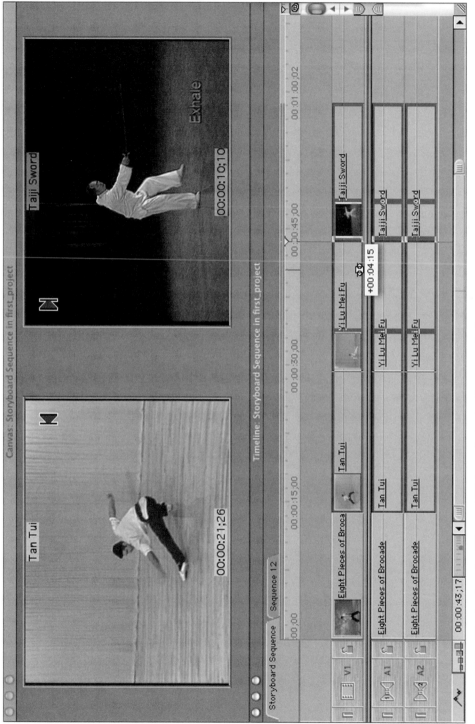

Figure 4-84 Monitoring the Slip and Slide tools in the Canvas window

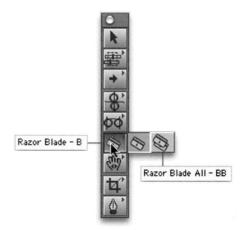

Figure 4-85   The Razorblade toolset

This toolset consists of the tool itself and only one variation on it—the single Razorblade, which performs the cut just described for the single track that is clicked (this includes any linked items if Linking is enabled), and the Razorblade All (keyboard shortcut–BB), which performs the same sort of cut across all clips in all tracks.

Using the Razorblade Tool

To illustrate the Razorblade tool, we will cut a clip. Then, using a shortcut called the Ripple Delete, we will delete the part of the razorbladed clip we don't want and snap the clip following it up to the razorbladed edge, eliminating any gap in the sequence.

Select all clips in the sequence and delete them. Next, perform the storyboard roughcut technique again so that there are contiguous clips in the sequence. In the sequence, move the mouse pointer over any of the clips. Using the J-K-L shuttling technique, find a frame in the clip where you want introduce a cut, making sure that the playhead is parked on the frame where you want to make your cut.

Select the Razorblade tool on the Toolbar, and then return to the sequence. Make sure that Snapping is enabled in the Timeline window, and then move the mouse pointer along the track of the clip you want to cut. As you move the Razorblade mouse pointer along the clip in the track, you will see a small vertical line indicating which frame the tool will cut if it is clicked. Notice that the line appears in both the video and the two audio clips you drag it over. This is because the Linked Selection tool forces the Razorblade to perform the Razorblade action on all linked items. When the Razorblade is near the playhead position in the clip, it snaps to it, enabling you to cut precisely on the frame of the clip. Click that frame, and the Razorblade will cut the clip in two (see Figure 4-86).

Now that the razorbladed clip has been divided into two separate clips, we want to get rid of the second part of the clip that contains footage we don't want. At the same time, we want any clips occurring later in the track to snap to the newly cut clip end to eliminate a gap in the track. If we just selected the second clip and deleted it using the Delete

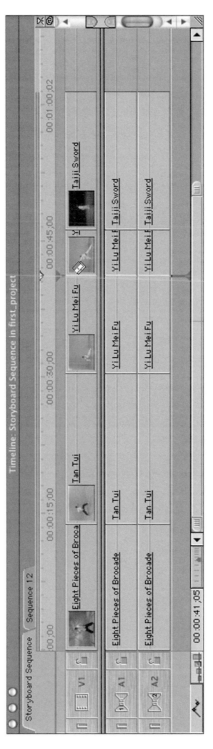

Figure 4-86 Cutting a clip into two with the Razorblade tool

key, there would be a long empty gap between the first razorbladed clip and any subsequent clips in the track. Instead, we will use the Ripple Delete function.

Move the mouse pointer over the second part of the clip in the track that we want to delete. Press the Control key and click this clip. You will be presented with a contextual menu with many options. Choose the option Ripple Delete (see Figure 4-87). When you do so, the second clip will disappear and the subsequent clips in the track will shuffle back to fill in the gap created by the deleted clip. The keyboard shortcut for this is Shift-Delete.

The Zoom Toolset (Keyboard Shortcut–Z)

The final toolset we will be looking at in this chapter is the Zoom toolset. This toolset is a common feature in most image-editing applications. If you click the toolset button in the Toolbar, you will see four options: Zoom In, Zoom Out (keyboard shortcut–ZZ), Hand (keyboard shortcut–H), and Scrub Video (keyboard shortcut–HH), as shown in Figure 4-88. These tools allow you to customize and navigate the windows of Final Cut Express in ways that do not affect the clips and sequences of your project. They help you refine the way the various windows appear and how much of them you can see at a given time. Rather than using the mouse or menus to change the shape of Final Cut Express, learn to take advantage of this toolset.

The Zoom In and Zoom Out Tools

The primary Zoom tool, shaped like a magnifying glass with a plus sign, simply increases the scale of whatever object it is applied to. If you click a sequence with this tool enabled, the scale increases as if you had adjusted the various scale controls of the Timeline window itself. The Zoom Out button next to the Zoom In button provides exactly the opposite effect, shrinking the scale of the window, so that you can quickly adjust the exact scale of any window you are working with. Holding the Option key down while the Zoom In tool is enabled converts it to the Zoom Out tool, making it a quick and precise customization tool. Just hit the Z key to enable the Zoom In tool, and hit the Option key to pull back out if you zoom in too far.

The Zoom In and Zoom Out tools have uses outside the Timeline window as well. The Viewer and Canvas windows can be boosted or shrunk in scale based on a percentage of the actual size of the frame. This number is located in the top center of each window. Generally speaking, this number should be left at the default size, with the window size tab set to "fit to window" for optimized playback. Having the window at 100% can cause playback problems in machines with less video processing horsepower, and 100% is sometimes a bit extravagant when screen real estate is so precious. The default size gives a large enough image for you to look at without getting a headache, it doesn't overtax the processor on playback, and it leaves plenty of room for all the other windows of Final Cut Express. To get your windows back to the default window size, go to the Window drop-down menu and select Arrange>Standard.

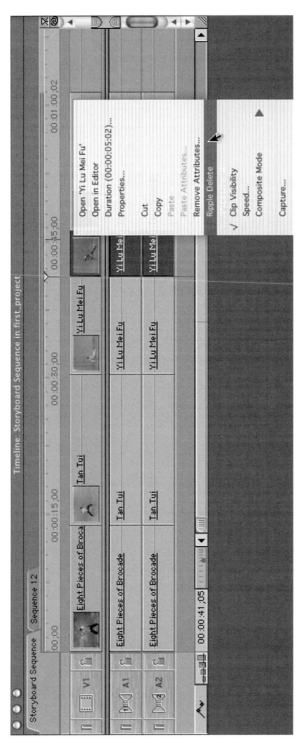

Figure 4-87   Control-clicking to perform a Ripple Delete

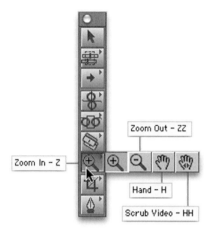

Figure 4-88 The Zoom toolset

The Hand Tool (Keyboard Shortcut–H)

Sometimes it's important to get a closer look at an image you are working with, however, as we will be doing in the following chapter on compositing. So it's possible to zoom in and out much farther than you would normally think necessary. But once you zoom in to 800% in the Canvas or Viewer, how do you navigate around the image to get to the section you wanted to look at? There are scroll bars on the edge of the window, but that will frustrate you as you try to get to a place you can't see using only up-and-down or left-to-right scroll bars.

Predictably enough, Final Cut Express has a tool to simplify this task. The Hand tool simply moves the video frame around so that you can go directly to the part of the window you want without fooling with scroll bars (see Figure 4-89). It does not make any adjustments to clips or sequences; it functions only to move what is visible around the Final Cut Express interface windows.

Load a clip into the Viewer window. Then select the Zoom In tool from the Toolbar. Click inside the Viewer window several times, each time watching the number at the top and center of the window jump in percentage points. Keep clicking till you see the number reach 400%.

By this time you should have noticed that the image is far larger than the window can accommodate. There are scroll bars to the bottom and side, but instead, use the Hand tool from the Zoom toolset of the Toolbar and grab the image, moving it around by clicking and dragging. You may have also noticed that after 100%, the image appears to disintegrate slightly, taking on a blocky appearance that is anything but the beautiful DV image you started out with.

Relax, there's nothing wrong with your television. You are seeing *pixellation*. Each frame of DV is made up of pixels (i.e., picture elements), which are the smallest indivisible sections of a digital image. A single frame of DV NTSC video contains 720 pixels across and 480 pixels high, or 345,600 pixels. When you zoom in to over 100%, you begin to see

Figure 4-89   Moving the video frame around the Viewer window with the Hand tool

these individual pixels as the rectangular colored blocks that they really are, similar to the dots you would see in a newspaper picture if you looked at it under a magnifying glass. Once you zoom back out, you'll see the pixels bleed back together into the lush imagery you were expecting. Just hit the Option key and Zoom Out to return to 50%.

The Scrub Video Tool: Scrubbing a Clip's Thumbnail (Keyboard Shortcut–HH)

The last tool of this toolset is a really handy tool called the Scrub Video tool. Although its use is very specific, it can be a lifesaver if you are doing a lot of clip duplication from one master clip. The Scrub Video tool offers a fast, efficient way to set Poster Frames for your clips in the Browser window as well as a quick way to preview your clip by scrubbing through it in the Browser window. A Poster Frame is the image in the clip you see when your Browser Items are set to display as Large Icons (see drop-down menu View>Browser Items>Large Icons or Control-click the bin). It's also the frame that appears with the clip in the Timeline when thumbnail is enabled in the Timeline tab of the Sequence Settings. The default Poster Frame for any given clip's thumbnail will be the first frame of video in the clip.

This can be very confusing if a lot of your footage looks very similar, especially near the beginning of the clip. If you have five clips that all start with roughly the same shot, the Poster Frames in the thumbnails will all look exactly the same. Changing the image of the Poster Frame to some other more distinct frame from the clip can make it much easier to identify clips at a glance.

There are a couple of different ways to set the Poster Frame for a clip. If a clip is loaded into the Viewer window, you can set it by finding the frame you want to use with the playhead and then going to the Mark drop-down menu and selecting Set Poster Frame (see Figure 4-90), or using Control-P as the keyboard shortcut. But doing this requires that the clip be loaded into the Viewer window. Using the Scrub Video tool, on the other hand, not only allows you to look through the footage of the clip without loading it into the Viewer, it allows you to set the Poster Frame there as well.

Open the bin with your storyboard-style thumbnail clips. If you have reset the bin to display as a list or with smaller thumbnails, set it to show the bin as Large Icons by going

Figure 4-90 Setting the Poster Frame in the Mark drop-down menu

to the View drop-down menu and selecting Browser Items followed by Large Icons or by Control-clicking the bin. Your clips need to be visible as large thumbnails for this example.

Go to the Toolbar and select the Scrub Video tool from the Zoom toolset. Now return to the Browser window and pick a clip that has a fairly wide range of imagery. Click in the center of the thumbnail, and drag to the left and right. As you do so, you should see the thumbnail scrub through the video frames of the clip (see Figure 4-91).

This is a good way to quickly preview a clip before working with it, but it isn't radically faster than loading the clip into the Viewer window, where you could get a much better view of the contents of the clip. The main value of the Scrub tool is not in previewing the footage in the clip but in selecting the Poster Frame. But when you scrub with the tool and release the mouse button, the Poster Frame snaps back to the first frame of the clip. To actually change the Poster Frame, you need to perform a little intricate Control-clicking.

First, click and drag on the thumbnail in the Browser as you just did previously, scrolling through the frames of video in the clip until you find the frame you want to use as the new Poster Frame. When you find the frame, click the Control key while still holding the mouse button on the frame. Finally, release the mouse button while still holding the Control key. Then, release the Control key, and your Poster Frame will have changed to the frame you want to use.

All this may seem like gratuitous effort just to get a little unique thumbnail to look at in the bin window. And with Large Icons view, you lose access to all the great detail information in the columns that you get in List view. Furthermore, you will find that it is far

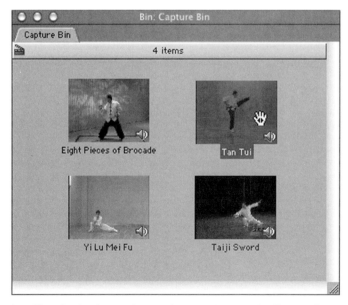

Figure 4-91   Scrolling in the Large Icons view to change the Poster Frame

easier to mentally organize master clips and subclips in the infinitely customizable List view rather than the loose arrangement of the Icons views. Shortly, after investigating the relationships between master clips and subclips and ways of leveraging the List view, we will see that there is indeed a way to get a thumbnail view in our List view, combining the best of both worlds.

Master Clips and Subclips

What are master clips and subclips? A master clip can be thought of as a clip that relates directly to the entire media it references, the media just as you captured it. When you capture video footage, Final Cut Express creates a QuickTime Movie media file and then a clip in your project that references that QuickTime media file. This clip has access to the entire media file that you captured. We call this a master clip. But what if you wanted to divide that master clip into smaller, bite-sized portions? Perhaps the large captured clip contains several different takes, or maybe you just want to use selected bits of the same take repeatedly.

When you load the master clip from the Project tab into the Viewer and give it an In and an Out point to edit with, the master clip in the Browser retains these In and Out points. If you later wanted to use a different section of the clip, you would need to change these and make new In and Out points. This is the way that clips work. They retain edit points until we change them.

But our minds generally do not work this way. It's usually easier to organize a project if you have isolated the various parts of your project in such a fashion that you can look at them en masse. How could you possibly use the storyboard rough-cut edit technique, for example, if all your material were contained in one master clip? Clearly such a method will work only in very small, uncomplicated projects.

A much better way to organize a complicated project with master clips is to create specific subclips and treat them as clips of their own, even though they ultimately reference the same media files as their fellow subclips and the master clip from which they originate. Final Cut Express certainly doesn't care; media files are media files, clips are clips, "parts is parts." The key to successful editing is both project organization and the ability to put the pieces of media together in a pleasing way. You can't have one without the other.

The Final Cut Express Subclip

There are a couple of different ways to create subclips from initial master clips, each of which carries its own implications. The first way is through the Final Cut Express Subclip command. Final Cut Express allows you to do exactly as we are suggesting. When you load a master clip into the Viewer window and set In and Out points, rather than immediately editing with this In and Out pointed-master clip, you can make a subclip based on the In and Out points you added. A new clip appears in the Browser that is limited to just the In and Out points you specified. While the master clip is still loaded in the Viewer, you can continue to create other subclips until you've completely divided and organized the master clip into workable clips.

After switching the bin's view mode back to List in the View drop-down menu's Browser Items, double-click a long clip and load it into the Viewer window. Play through this master clip and set an In and an Out point for what you would consider to be a separate clip within the larger clip. Set your In and Out points wide of the actual frames you want to edit; the Subclip command does not kid around, and considers its subclips as having no access to the rest of the media files they share with the master clip. You will not be able to Trim Edit outside of the In and Out points of the subclip you are creating. There are no handles with Subclip.

After setting the In and Out points in the Viewer window, go to the Modify drop-down menu and select Make Subclip at the top of the list (see Figure 4-92). Instantly, a Subclip icon will appear in the bin with the master clip. A Subclip icon can be distinguished by the shaggy right- and left-hand edges of its icon when viewed in List view mode.

Before moving forward, immediately click the temporary name "Clipname Subclip" and type in a new name for the subclip, identifying which master clip it came from and what it contains. Also remember that there are Comment and Description columns in the Browser window for adding details. There's never a good excuse for forgetting what a subclip is or where it came from.

Double-click the new subclip in the bin to load it into the Viewer. You will see that the length of the clip is exactly the length of the In point to the Out point you set when you created it from the master clip (see Figure 4-93). If you edit it into a sequence, you will further see that the subclip can not be trimmed out beyond the frames you established as the In and Out points.

Final Cut Express regards anything created with the Make Subclip command as if it were a captured master clip rather than a clip carved from a larger master clip. Of course,

Figure 4-92 Making a subclip

Figure 4-93 In and Out points are absolute in a subclip

Final Cut Express offers an override for this limit to the subclip's ability to access the rest of the master clip it was created from. At any time, you can select the subclip, return to the Modify menu, and choose Remove Subclip Limits. This restores the original access to all the media to which the master clip had access. The subclip is still a subclip of the original master clip, but it now references all the media that the master clip does. Of course, when you do this, you lose the range of In to Out that you set up the subclip for in the first place.

So, using this process, you can divide your master clips up however you like. The process can be a little clumsy, though, if you are still in the rough-cut stage, because many times you don't know yet how long a subclip should be. If you create subclips that are too short, there's no way to add a little extra footage to the subclip short of restoring the entire media limits to the clip. That limitation can defeat the purpose of creating the subclip in the first place.

Another Subclip Technique

A second way of creating subclips from Master clips is much simpler and more functional as long as you keep your eye on the ball and watch your naming conventions for your clips. Instead of creating a Final Cut Express Subclip using the command from the Modify drop-down menu, we will simply duplicate the master clip and give the duplicate a new name along with the In and Out points we want to associate with it as a subclip. For the sake of avoiding confusion, "Subclip" capitalized will refer to Subclips created using the Final Cut Express Make Subclip command. The word "subclip" with the lowercase "s" will refer to this alternative method of creating subclips.

Create a new bin in your Project tab, and name it "master-clip>subclips." Double-click this bin so that its window is open and available as you proceed through the next few steps. Select the master clip in your Capture Bin, and load it into the Viewer window. Go to the Mark drop-down menu and select Clear In and Out (see Figure 4-94). This is to clear off any previous In or Out points; you want to start your subclips off as blank slates with no In or Out points.

Figure 4-94 Clearing In and Out points

Once your master clip is loaded in the Viewer and cleared of irrelevant edit points, set an In and an Out point in the master clip just as if you were going to create a Subclip via the Make Subclip command or were going to edit a bit of it into a sequence. Isolate the content you want in the clip, and surround it with In and Out points.

When you have In and Out points selected, grab the clip in the Viewer and drag it to the "master-clip>subclips" bin window (see Figure 4-95). When you drop it there, you will have an exact copy of the master clip but one that contains In and Out points specific to what you want to use in the subclip.

Rename this new duplicate subclip with a name appropriate to the section of the master clip that you want to isolate in it. Technically, the name you give the subclip doesn't matter as much as the fact that it be named uniquely. As you bring more subclips down into the bin this way, each one will carry the name of the master clip until you change it, since you are really only creating a clone of it in the bin, rather than creating a totally new clip with the Make Subclip command.

Return to the Capture Bin and double-click the master clip to make sure it is loaded (rather than accidentally changing the In and Out points of the subclip you just produced). Repeat the steps, setting new In and Out points and then dragging and renaming until you have created as many subclips as it takes to divvy up all the different content in the original master clip. Just remember that each time you make a subclip, you should reload the master clip back into the Viewer.

After you've completed the creation of all the subclips you want in your special subclip bin, double-click one of the subclips and load it into the Viewer. Observe that all the frames of the master clip are still available as handles outside the In and Out points of the subclip, but that each subclip retains the special In and Out points that were set right before you cloned the master clip into the subclip bin (see Figure 4-96). Load other subclips to further demonstrate this fact.

Creating Thumbnails in the List View

You may find yourself asking, "Why can't I have a clip thumbnail in the List view?" All the foregoing processes occurred in the List view mode, where by default there is no clip thumbnail. And although thumbnails are just icing on the cake for the really well organized, there's no reason why we shouldn't help ourselves to as much icing as we can get.

There is a way to enjoy the convenience of the Large Icons view's thumbnails in the List view mode. Although using List view will not allow you to arrange your clips in storyboard fashion as is possible in Large Icons view, many editors find that the List view combination of thumbnails and informational columns, along with the ability to arrange clips by any criteria you can think of, is far more important than assembling storyboard panels. If you need to look at things temporarily from a storyboard perspective, there's no reason you can't switch view modes briefly and then switch back.

Figure 4-95 Creating a subclip by dragging from the Viewer to a bin

Figure 4-96   All the frames of a master clip are still available in a subclip

With your "master-clip>subclips" bin set in the drop-down menu View>Browser Items to List, Control-click the first column header of the List view, which by default is Duration. As you hold the Control key down, a small menu list appears, at the bottom of which is an option for Show Thumbnail.

Select the Show Thumbnail option and release to add a Thumbnail column to the lists (see Figure 4-97). The Duration column simply moves one space to the right to make room. You can now set the Poster Frames for the thumbnails of your new subclips. The Scrub Video tool from the Toolbar will function precisely the same for this thumbnail as it does for the Large Icons view.

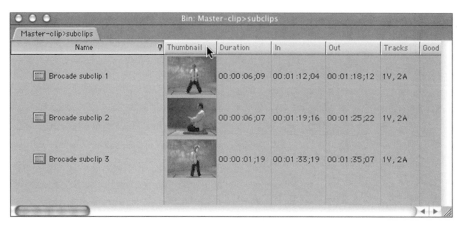

Figure 4-97 Control-click the column header to access Show Thumbnail

The Crop/Distort and Pen Toolsets

The two remaining toolsets in the Toolbar, Crop/Distort and Pen, are best covered in the next chapter, since they relate almost entirely to image manipulation rather than the cutting and trimming functions that define editing.

5 Compositing and Special Effects

What Exactly Is Compositing?

Periodically, we have mentioned the word "compositing" in the course of this book. What does this term mean? *Compositing*, in its most literal sense, means taking a stack of items and making them into one item. Compositing in Final Cut Express involves the process of taking more than one image and integrating or combining those various images into one image. As one Final Cut Express guru put it, "Compositing is everything above Video Layer 1." Compositing is the way that special effects are created. As we discovered when we worked with the sequence, Final Cut Express allows up to 99 separate video tracks (see Figure 5-1). The good news is that in this manner Final Cut Express gives you fantastic flexibility in customizing the way those separate layers work together when they are composited into the final image you see on the video screen.

To be successful at compositing, you have to rework the way you think about making a visual image. Compositing is one of those tasks in which there never is only one right way to accomplish a goal. This is in part because compositing, more than any other element, requires a mental vision of the results. Your uniqueness as a human and an artist cannot help but shine through.

No two compositors generate the same results, just as no two painters use the same brushstroke. Why must you undo your prior knowledge of image making? Because sometimes, adding red to an image is more about taking away green than it is about painting with red. Final Cut Express gives you the ability to obscure or reveal imagery using not only the various features of light—such as opacity (visible to invisible), hue (the shade of the color), and saturation (density of the color)—but also the way that these changes occur over time, also known as *keyframing*.

We'll start with an exploration of layering, track opacity, and the Composite Modes. In the course of setting up and using these effects, we will also learn to use Wireframe, keyframe interpolation, the Text Generator, matte and masking tools, and the alpha channel.

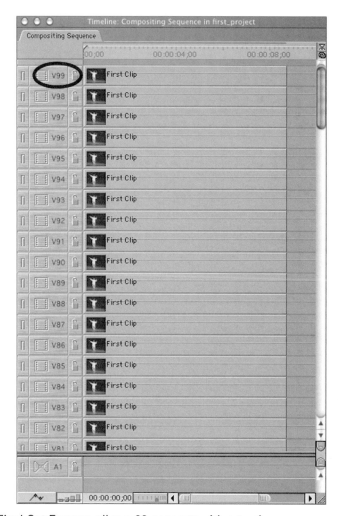

Figure 5-1 Final Cut Express allows 99 separate video tracks

Compositing Layers

From our definition of compositing, we already know that we need more than one layer in a sequence in order to create a composite. Layers in a sequence are stacked, one on top of the other. What you see in the Canvas window is actually what lies in the sequence as seen from the top layer down. Imagine that your sequence of video layers is a messy stack of different types of paper. Some sheets cover others; some are more transparent than others, allowing you to see through them to the next layer underneath. Others may have holes cut in them like a stencil. When you edit video clips into a new layer on the sequence, you are inserting a new sheet onto the stack.

Setting Up a Sequence for Compositing Layers

Create a new sequence in your project. Edit an initial video clip into the sequence in the V1 track. Choose another video clip, drag it to the sequence, position it in the V2 track, and drop it, making sure to perform an Overwrite rather than an Insert edit. You will want the clip on V2 directly above and covering the clip on V1. If no V2 track yet exists, simply place the clip where the track should be, and Final Cut Express will automatically create one.

Make sure that the sequence playhead is positioned somewhere within the clips. A glance at the Canvas window will reveal that the video clip in the V2 layer is covering the clip in the V1 layer. This is because, by default, all video clips have 100% opacity. We have already explored this opacity feature in our discussion of the Clip Overlays button in Chapter 4. When we adjusted the opacity in that chapter, we superimposed a clip onto the Layer 2 track. Then when we lowered the opacity of the top clip, we could begin to see the clip underneath it. We will perform the same operation this time; however, in this process we will also investigate keyframing, or changing the amount of opacity over time.

First, make sure that the Clip Overlays button is enabled in the Timeline window (see Figure 5-2). Remember that the Clip Overlays button, though a part of the Timeline

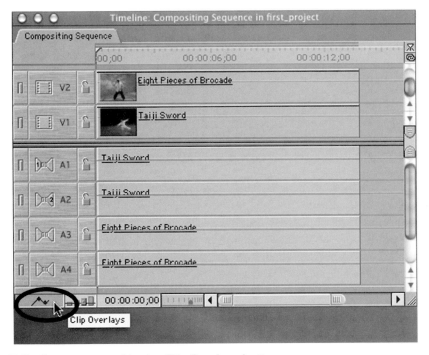

Figure 5-2   Be sure to enable the Clip Overlays button

window, is set differently for each sequence within the Timeline window. Just because it is enabled within one sequence in the Timeline window does not mean that it is enabled in others. If you do not see the rubberband line going through the clips in a sequence, Clip Overlays is not enabled for that sequence.

Choose the General Selection tool (the arrow) on the Toolbar, and adjust the rubberband line of the clip in the V2 layer. As you pull the line down, the red render (or green RT) bar will appear as expected; looking at the Canvas window will reveal that the clip in the V1 layer is beginning to appear through the V2 layer (see Figure 5-3). If you drag the line all the way down to zero, layer 2 will be completely transparent, totally revealing the clip beneath it.

If we render the clip, playback will reveal that the entire clip carries the opacity level at which we set the rubberband line. But how useful could this be in everyday life? Setting a static, unchanging opacity level in a clip might be useful in some situations, but in most, we need to be able to control the level of opacity over time within the clip. To do so, we need to introduce the concept of *keyframing*.

Keyframing in the Sequence Timeline

Keyframes come into use with many visual effects in Final Cut Express as well as in other popular editing and compositing applications. Keyframing means that for a certain feature in a clip, such as opacity, a certain value exists at a certain time. We all have seen scenes in movies where the image slowly fades in from black or fades out to black. This is an example of keyframing. Some quality of the video is changing over time. For instance, we could set a keyframe at the 10th frame of the clip for an opacity value of 25%. But rather than being limited to one value of 25% for the entire clip, by using keyframing, other frames of the same clip could have a different percentage value of opacity. For any frame where we want to establish a specific, definite opacity value, we create a keyframe.

In the digital universe, everything has a value. The example we are working with, opacity, has a value at any given time of 0% to 100%. At 0%, the clip is completely transparent; at 50%, it is half-transparent; and at 100%, the clip is opaque. No keyframes are necessary for a clip to have an initial value; all clips do. But establishing a keyframe and giving a specific frame a value gives us the ability to change that value in a single clip over time.

If we assign the first keyframe in a clip, the value of that keyframe still does not change for the duration of the clip. Even though we have a keyframe, the value of this initial keyframe doesn't change to a new value. The lesson is that one keyframe in a clip expresses only one value. To express a change in values in a clip, you must have two or more keyframes, each one having a different value. We set a keyframe for the value we want the clip to have initially, say, 100% opacity, and then we set additional keyframes farther down the Timeline for the change in values we wish to see over the duration of the clip, say, 50%, then 25%, and then 0%. If we do not want a value to change over time, there is no reason to insert a keyframe at all.

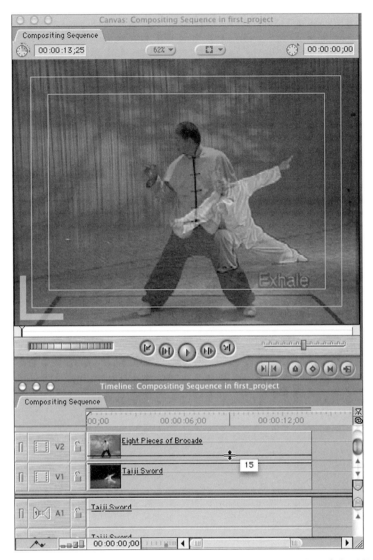

Figure 5-3 Pull the rubberband line down to decrease the opacity of the V2 clip

To insert keyframes into a clip's opacity in a sequence, we need to have two features enabled. First, we need Clip Overlays to be enabled, since this is where our keyframes will be inserted. Next, we need to go to the Toolbar and select the Pen tool. If you click the Pen tool and hold the mouse button briefly, you will see three options: the Pen tool, the Pen Delete tool, and the Pen Smooth tool. We will discuss the Pen Smooth tool subsequently, but for now we are concerned with the Pen and Pen Delete tools. Select the Pen tool (see Figure 5-4).

You may want to go into the drop-down menu Sequence>Settings and change Thumbnail Display from Name Plus Thumbnail to Name (see Figure 5-5). This will remove the thumbnail from the clip in the sequence and will make it easier for you to work with the rubberband line at the beginning of a clip.

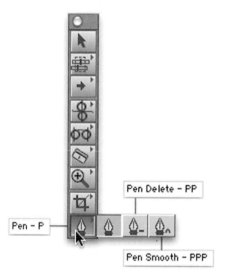

Figure 5-4   Selecting the Pen tool to add keyframes

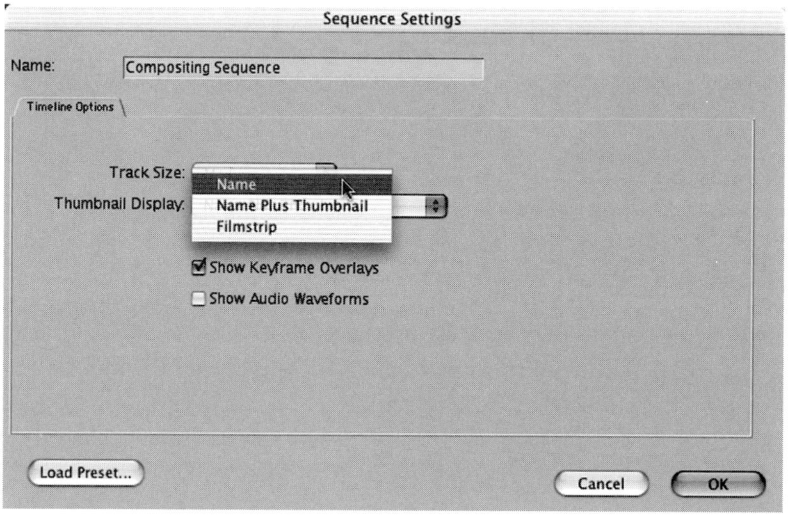

Figure 5-5   Changing Thumbnail Display to Name

Look at the clip in the V2 track that you adjusted the opacity of previously. Move the mouse pointer to the beginning of the clip and place it near the rubberband line. When you move to the beginning of the clip near the Clip Overlay line, the mouse pointer will change from the familiar arrow into the shape of the Pen tool. This indicates that the Pen tool is able to assign a keyframe for the frame you are presently hovering over.

Click that rubberband line, hold the mouse button down, and drag the keyframe up and down (see Figure 5-6). As you do, the value box appears next to the mouse pointer, informing you of the current value of the keyframe you have just created by clicking the rubberband line. Now, without releasing the keyframe, drag it from left to right and back. A timecode value box appears informing you how far you have moved the keyframe from its original clicked position.

As long as you have the keyframe under the thumb of your mouse button, you have total control of the value it represents and the time it occurs within the clip. If you let go of the mouse pointer, but you want to change the keyframe's value or position, simply grab it and drag it again. After you have established a keyframe, the Pen tool displays as a crosshair when suspended over it. Drag the keyframe all the way to the left, so that it occurs on the first frame of the clip. Then before releasing it, drag it all the way up to the top of the clip, so that its value is 100% (see Figure 5-7).

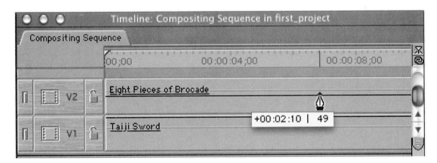

Figure 5-6 Clicking and dragging with the Pen tool to modify a keyframe

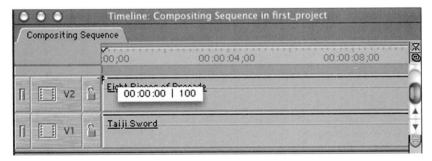

Figure 5-7 Dragging the keyframe to set the opacity of the first frame to 100%

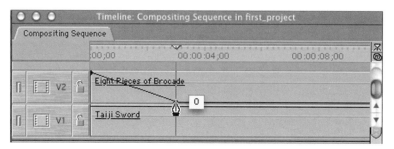

Figure 5-8   Clicking and dragging to set a second keyframe of 0%

Now we have one keyframe set on the first frame of the clip. But as we mentioned earlier, having one keyframe is really no different from having none. To establish a change in value, we need to add a second keyframe that occurs after the initial keyframe. Since our first keyframe is at the beginning of the clip, we will move down the Timeline several seconds to add a second keyframe.

Send the sequence playhead back to the first frame by hitting the Home key on your keyboard. With the Timeline window active, type in "+300," which will move the play-head up 3 seconds from its present position. Move the Pen tool up to the sequence play-head, and watch for the Pen tool to bull's-eye the yellow triangle above the playhead indicator. When you see the Pen tool zero is on the playhead, click to set the second keyframe and drag it down until it hits 0% (see Figure 5-8).

Now you will have two keyframes, each of which contains a different value. The first keyframe is at the beginning of the clip at 100%, and the second is 3 seconds later at 0%. More interesting than this is the fact that between the two keyframes is a long slanting line denoting the change in value of opacity for all the frames in between the two keyframes. Final Cut Express will create all the images that fall between the two keyframes. This is referred to as interpolation.

Keyframe Interpolation

Interpolation is a process by which the computer generates all the values between the two known values, saving you a lot of calculation. We give Final Cut Express the values we want the clip to have at the beginning and ending keyframes, and it figures out the values for each intermediary frame in less time than it would take you to remember where you left your calculator. If you move the playhead through the area of the clip that is between the two keyframes, you will see that the V2 layer clip slowly and evenly goes transparent as the opacity keyframe values go from 100% to 0% over 3 seconds. Each frame between the two keyframes is displayed with a progressively smaller percentage of opacity. And all you need to have for this is the two opacity keyframes that change in value.

Adding Type: The Text Generator

To explore further with compositing, we need a small graphic element to work with. Although any of the effects that we will apply in this lesson could also be applied to video clips, we will be able to see the results a little more clearly using the Text Generator. Adding motion and other effects to text is pretty common practice, so learning to use these techniques is fundamental to taking your productions to the next level.

Final Cut Express ships with the excellent free text generator Boris Calligraphy. Calligraphy is a much more flexible text generator than the native one we will be using in this lesson. But the additional options and abilities also make Boris Title 3D a little more complex to learn. If you want to make use of the Calligraphy text toolset, refer to Appendix D and work through that section.

To generate text using Final Cut Express's built-in Text Generator, we need to bring the generator into the sequence Timeline. Create a new sequence in the Project tab, and double-click it to load it into the Timeline window and Canvas. Edit a video clip into the V1 track of the new sequence so that we will have a video background for our text. Next, click the Effects tab of the Browser window. Make sure you are in View as List mode by Control-clicking inside the Effects tab and choosing "View as List." You should see a list of bins with the names Favorites, Video Transitions, Video Filters, Video Generators, Audio Transitions, and Audio Filters (see Figure 5-9).

This is the drag-and-drop location for all the filters and transitions that are available in Final Cut Express. In the editing and effects work that we will do in Final Cut Express, the drag-and-drop option is often available from the Effects tab of the Browser window. In the Video Generators bin, click the triangle drop-down to look at the contents. You will see a list of the contents: Crawl, Lower 3rd, Outline Text, Scrolling Text, Text, and Typewriter (see Figure 5-10). To use the Text Generator, we want to access it just like a clip, very similarly to the way that we loaded the Bars and Tone clip in Chapter 2.

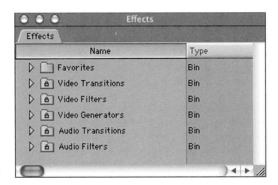

Figure 5-9 The Effects tab

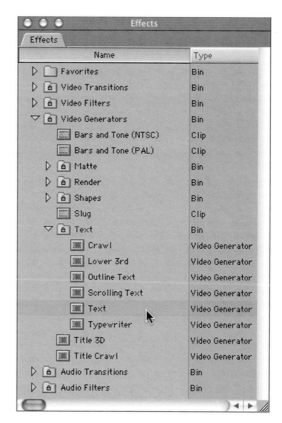

Figure 5-10 The Video Generators bin

This time, rather than load it into the Viewer window directly, as we did with the Bars and Tone clip, grab the Text Generator and drag it into the V2 track of the new sequence directly above the video clip you just edited in. Place the Timeline playhead over the two clips. When you drop the Text Generator clip there, you will see the words "Sample Text" appear in the Canvas window superimposed over the video clip in V1 (see Figure 5-11). "Sample Text" is the default text for the clip until you change it.

To customize the text in the Generator, we need to load it into the Viewer by double-clicking the text clip in the sequence. Take a look in the Viewer window, and you will find a tab we have not seen yet. This is the Controls tab. Click it and take a look at the parameters (see Figure 5-12).

The parameters of the Controls tab will be mostly familiar to anyone who has spent any time using a word processor. At the top is a text entry field, where you can enter the text you want included in the frame. This text entry field acts just like a word processor. Remember that if you hit the Return key, it will include a line break in your text rather than get you out of the entry field. To apply your text changes, either hit the Tab key or

Figure 5-11 Dragging the Text Generator into the V2 track to generate "Sample Text"

click anywhere outside of the text box. To change the size, font, or any other aspect of text you have already typed, you have to select the text first and then make the change.

Let's make some changes to the default text already in the entry field (see Figure 5-13). First select the words "Sample Text" in the entry field. Before typing in new text, click on the Font bar underneath the field. For this exercise, we want a rather blocky piece of text with very thick lines, so choose Arial Black. Take a look over in the Canvas window, where you will see that the Canvas window is being updated globally, meaning that any changes you make in the Controls tab of the Viewer are affecting other windows elsewhere in the application. Keep the Canvas window in view on the Desktop as you work in the Controls tab to monitor how your text looks as you make changes.

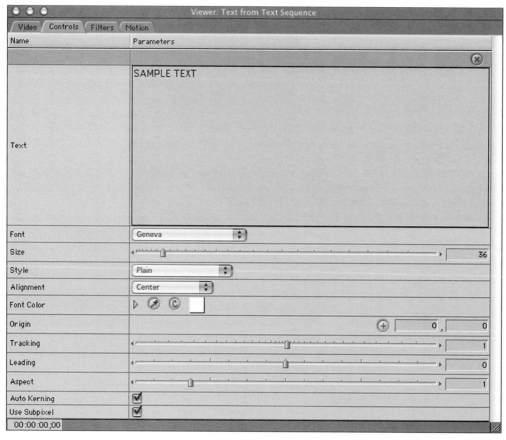

Figure 5-12 The Controls tab

In the Size field, type in 50 numerically. For Style, click the drop-down and look at the options. Since we want to emphasize the blocky nature of the Arial Black font, choose Bold. For Alignment, choose Center. Leave Color set to White.

Origin refers to the position of the text in the frame as seen in the Canvas. This value can be anywhere in the frame and uses two number values corresponding to the X and Y coordinates. We want to use the coordinates 0 and 0 for our text, which will place the "baseline," or the bottom of the line of text, directly in the center of the frame. Tracking refers to how close the letters are to each other horizontally, and Leading refers to the spacing between lines of text. Leading is only a critical issue if you have a line break and thus two or more lines of text in the field. Aspect refers to how squeezed or stretched the letters appear (leave it set to a value of 1 to maintain a normal aspect). Finally, the AutoKerning and Use Subpixel check boxes simply tell Final Cut Express to use its own judgment in positioning and spacing the individual letters of the text, just as any good word processing application does. Leave them checked.

Figure 5-13 Modifying the default text style

After you have ventured through all of those parameters, change the text by typing "Text Clip!" Take a look over in the Canvas window and notice that there is quite a bit of space now. Return to the Controls tab, make sure that the text in the text entry field is selected, and change the Size value to 75. We now have a piece of text for use in the motion effects exercises (see Figure 5-14).

Special Effects: Motion Effects

We have experimented with keyframing of Opacity in the sequence Timeline window, but we have yet to fully explore the functionality of Final Cut Express with regard to the many other physical parameters for a clip and the ability to keyframe them to achieve interesting effects that change over time. We will now move a little further with each of these ideas, learning to fully manipulate a clip within a sequence.

To begin with, we will use the text clip we just created. The main reason we will be using a graphic element like a text clip is that some of the subtleties of the physical properties we are about to adjust are difficult to see in a full-frame, full-motion video clip. This does not mean that the physical properties we will employ here have no effect on video clips; the physical properties we will alter in the text clip are simply easier to distinguish with a small text image. Once you understand how the properties work, you can apply changes wherever you want throughout the system, even to an entire sequence at once.

Figure 5-14 "Text Clip!" ready for use in Motion Effects exercises

The Image + Wireframe Viewing Mode in the Canvas Window

In order to be able to manipulate an image in the Canvas window, we need to first turn on Image + Wireframe viewing mode (see Figure 5-15). Because we will be changing the physical position and appearance of the objects in the Canvas, we need to switch to a viewing mode that allows us to directly adjust them.

In the Canvas, there are two viewing modes. The default viewing mode is Image, which is the mode that you have been using. When a window is in Image mode, you can grab the center of the Viewer window and drag an entire clip into the Canvas or Timeline. You are not adjusting anything in the clip itself; you are just telling Final Cut Express to use the clip in another window.

In Image + Wireframe mode, when you grab the clip, you can move its physical position around *within* the video frame. You are actually changing its position on an X and Y axis, with X values being horizontal and Y being vertical. In practice, you don't have to agonize over the geometry of this. With the Canvas in Image + Wireframe mode, you simply click and drag the object to where you want to place it.

In the Canvas window, click the viewing mode drop-down tab and select Image + Wireframe. In this same drop-down, turn on Overlays as well, since we will need them in this exercise. Next, go down to the sequence and single-click to select the text clip. In the Canvas window, you will see that a blue bounding box with a white X through the center has

Figure 5-15 Setting the viewing mode to Image + Wireframe

become visible (see Figure 5-16). This is the wireframe for the text layer. It is not visible on your NTSC video monitor; it is only a visual aid and viewing mode indicator. Think of the wireframe as a sort of handle that allows you to reposition or in other ways modify your clips in the Canvas window.

Make sure the General Selection tool is active (keyboard shortcut–A), then go to the Canvas, and move the mouse pointer around without clicking. You will see that the mouse pointer has changed into a shape with four arrows pointing in each of the cardinal directions. This is the Move tool and indicates that clicking and dragging will change the position values of the selected clip—i.e., where it sits in the frame. Click the center of the X and drag in any direction. When you drag, the wireframe moves around and follows the pointer (see Figure 5-17). If you pause for a split second, the frame updates to show you the clip's new position. You can drag the wireframe anywhere, even outside the edges of the Canvas's windows! And as long as you see that wireframe or bounding box, you can grab the layer and drag to reposition it again.

You have to be a little careful as you play, though, because of the way that wireframe works. When you switch to Image + Wireframe, it allows wireframes for all objects in the

Figure 5-16   "Text Clip!" and its wireframe

Canvas. Any object that is selected in the sequence will have a visible wireframe. Clicking the object in the Canvas will select the track in the sequence. Such is the global nature of Final Cut Express. You have to be a little careful when you access the Canvas so that when you click, you actually select the clip you intend to select.

In addition to changing the position of the clip in the Canvas window, you can change other aspects of it as well. You have to pay special attention to the shape of the mouse pointer as you move around the wireframe. Move it to one of the four corners of the bounding box. As you move it around the corner of the bounding box, it will alternate between three different shapes: the four-arrow shape we just looked at, a thin crosshair, and a circular arrow.

The thin crosshair is used to change the size of the clip, making it larger or smaller. Place the pointer on any one of the four corners of the blue bounding box. When you see the crosshair, click and drag. As you drag in, the scale shrinks, and as you drag out, the scale increases (see Figure 5-18). You can take this scaling a step further by holding down the Shift key as you drag the scale to shrink either the vertical scale or the horizontal scale separately, yielding interesting stretching and squeezing of the image.

Figure 5-17 Dragging a clip by its wireframe in the Canvas window

The other cursor shape, a circular arrow, is for setting rotational values. Move the pointer to any one of the sides of the blue bounding box. When you see the circular arrow, click and drag in a circular motion, and you will see the clip rotate in the direction that you are dragging (see Figure 5-19). If you hold down the Shift key while dragging the rotational tool, the rotation is constrained to 45-degree angles, meaning that the clip will rotate but will snap to rotations in increments of 45 degrees.

As an interesting combination, holding down the Command key while dragging the scale crosshair will yield corresponding adjustments for both the scale *and* the rotation values, resulting in a sort of spinning appearance. This can yield interesting effects when we get into keyframing of actual motion.

But where are all these values ending up? As you manually adjust these clips, there is a tab on the Viewer window that reflects the exact numerical values of the changes you make. Double-click the text clip in the sequence so that it loads into the Viewer window. Select the Motion tab, then return to the Canvas, and move the clip around as we just did. As you make changes in the Canvas window, you will see the values in the Motion tab of the Viewer window reflect these changes (see Figure 5-20).

Figure 5-18   Scaling a clip with the thin crosshair cursor

You will see a Drop Shadow attribute a little farther down the list. Click the check box to enable it, and then expand the triangle drop-down to look at the possibilities for drop shadows (see Figure 5-21). Set the Offset for 5, which will get the shadow a little closer and tighter to the text it is shadowing. Leave the Angle of the shadow at 135 and the Color at Black. The default setting for Softness at 10 is suitable for this use, as is the Opacity value of 50%. Check out the drop shadow now visible in the Canvas window. There is also a Motion Blur feature below the Drop Shadow attribute, which we will leave disabled for the moment, but which we will return to after completing a motion path.

A chief use of the Motion tab is to be able to quickly and easily reset values for the changes you make to a clip. Note that there is a red X to the right of each attribute on the Motion tab (Basic Motion, Crop, Distort, Opacity, Drop Shadow, and Motion Blur). This is a reset switch that will reset the values of each parameter to the original default value.

Figure 5-19 Rotating a clip with the circular arrow cursor

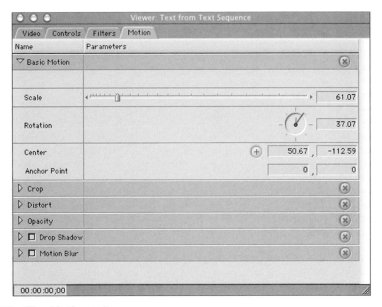

Figure 5-20 The Motion tab

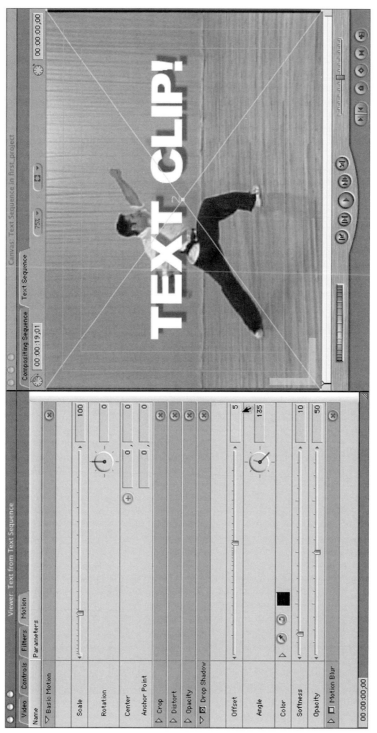

Figure 5-21 Setting and adjusting the Drop Shadow attribute of a clip

Creating a Motion Path

But all of this adjusting has been for a single value on each attribute. Although you could change the scale or position, it stays the same throughout the clip. This is because we have yet to add keyframes. Exactly as with the opacity keyframing we visited earlier in this chapter, we must add multiple known values over time to the attributes we want to change. The only real difference is that unlike the opacity keyframes that were set in the sequence, keyframes for Center (position), Scale (size), and Rotation (degree of turn) must be set in the Canvas.

To create a motion path, we have to set an initial keyframe, meaning we have to tell Final Cut Express where the first position of the text will be. With the Canvas set to Image + Wireframe, Overlays turned on, and the General Selection tool enabled, single-click the text clip in the sequence so that its wireframe becomes active in the Canvas. Next go up to the Canvas window, grab the now visible wireframe, and drag it up into the upper left corner of the video frame. Let go, and the text will stick there (see Figure 5-22).

Remember from our discussion of Photoshop images that with television monitors there is an area of the video frame called "overscan." Although Final Cut Express lets you

Figure 5-22 Placing your text clip in the Canvas

see and work in the entire video frame, a percentage of the video frame will be masked off on the TV sets of your viewer. Although this is less of an issue with actual video from a camera, with text, it becomes critical. If you can't see a word, you can't read it!

Although Final Cut Express can't stop you from making overscan text-placement errors, it does offer you a tool to avoid making such mistakes. Look in the same viewing mode drop-down menu you used to enable Image + Wireframe mode and Overlays, and enable Title Safe (see Figure 5-23). When you do, you will see two white rectangles appear in the video frame. Like the wireframe, these will not be visible when you output to NTSC or PAL video monitors. They are simply guides that allow you a visual sense of when your text is in an area where it shouldn't be.

The smaller of the two rectangles is the Title Safe region. Anything in this region will be completely in the frame and also far enough away from the screen edge to make it readable. The larger of the two rectangles is called the Action Safe, meaning that anything inside that rectangle is going to be visible, though if it is text, it will not necessarily be easy to read. Action Safe can be useful for gauging whether or not an actor is entering the screen on a certain frame. If you used the normal limits of the frame with Title Safe turned off, you might set your edit a few frames too early and make a bad judgment.

Figure 5-23   Setting the Title Safe guides

With Title Safe enabled, take a look at where your text is placed, and make any adjustments so that it appears just inside the edge of the Title Safe zone (see Figure 5-24). If you are previewing your edit out to a true video monitor, observe that this puts your text safely near the edge of the screen.

Setting the Keyframes for Motion

Setting keyframes in Final Cut Express is pretty easy. You set keyframes for position, scale, and rotation by clicking a single button in the Canvas window. Choosing the Add Keyframe button sets an initial keyframe for each and all of these attributes. After setting that initial keyframe, move your playhead farther along your timeline, and set new values (position, rotation, etc.) by making the change directly in the Canvas window using your mouse pointer. Whenever you make a change in the Canvas to an attribute that has an initial keyframe, Final Cut Express will add the new keyframe automatically. If a keyframe already exists on the frame you change the value of, it simply updates that keyframe to what you want.

Figure 5-24 Placing your text clip inside the Title Safe zone

To illustrate this process, in the sequence Timeline, move the playhead to the first frame of the text clip. If the text clip is all the way at the beginning of the sequence, the easiest way to do this is to hit the Home key, which always takes you to the first frame of the sequence. If your clip is elsewhere in the sequence, the fastest way (without using the mouse) is to use the Up and Down Arrow keys, which always move us to the head or tail of a clip.

Make sure that the text clip is loaded into the Viewer window, and switch to the Motion tab so that you can watch it update while you make changes in the Canvas window. Go back to the sequence Timeline and make sure the text clip is selected. Then move to the Canvas window. In the bottom right-hand corner of the window, find the Add Keyframe button, between the Add Marker and Mark Clip buttons (see Figure 5-25). Click Add Keyframe (or hit the keyboard shortcut Control-K), and a keyframe will be automatically added to Center, Scale, and Rotation for the frame you are parked on in the clip, which should be the first frame.

Note that when you click the keyframe button, the X through the center of the wireframe becomes green, indicating that the frame you are parked on now has a keyframe. Because you are not adjusting keyframes on a timeline, as you do for Opacity, it's important to keep an eye on this. Many times you will want to combine two or three different motion effects together, such as changing scale and position simultaneously for a zoom effect. At such times, you will need to know that you are on the same keyframe already used for Center so that you can add a change in the Scale keyframe at precisely the same time.

Another way to easily observe where keyframes exist while you are scrolling through the sequence can be accessed if you have Snapping toggled on (keyboard shortcut–N). If Snapping is enabled, the playhead will snap onto the frame where there are keyframes. Try scrubbing, or dragging the playhead back and forth along the sequence, and you will see it snapping where you have keyframes even though you can't physically see the keyframes themselves. This may make it easier for you to line up any Opacity keyframes set in the sequence with motion keyframes you have already set in the Canvas. Alternately, you can use the keyboard shortcuts Option-K or Shift-K to move forward and backward from keyframe to keyframe.

As we said before, having only one keyframe is no different from having none. In order to achieve motion, we need to have a change in values over time. To set the next keyframe, move the playhead down the timeline 3 seconds. The easiest way to do this is to make sure the Timeline window is active and that no clips are selected (click anywhere in the Timeline to deselect any clips). Then just type in "+300" on the numerical keypad on the right of your keyboard. If no clips are selected in your sequence Timeline, the playhead is automatically moved ahead exactly 3 seconds from its present situation (in timecode, the "3" is for seconds, and the "00" means no frames). If you are at the first frame of the entire sequence, you could also simply type in "300," which would take you specifically to 00:00:03:00.

When your playhead is positioned at the third second of the clip, go to the Canvas again, click the wireframe for the text clip, and drag it down to the bottom right-

Figure 5-25 Adding a keyframe in the Canvas

hand corner of the Title Safe area, roughly opposite to its previous position on the first keyframe (see Figure 5-26). Final Cut Express will automatically set a new Center keyframe for you, and you should now see that the center point of the wireframe has changed to green.

A couple of things will happen after you drop the clip in its new location. First, you will see a bumpy, purple line appear on the screen between the first and the second keyframe you just created. This line is your motion path. It is the direct path the text clip will travel over the 3 seconds between the first keyframe at the beginning of the clip to the second keyframe at the third second, which was created as soon as you moved the clip. There are bumps, or, as Apple calls them, "ticks," on this line that represent the position of the clip as it travels through the motion path in your sequence. Each frame is not represented as an individual tick, but they are there to give you an idea of the speed of the clip moving through the frame. When the ticks are very close together, the clip moves slowly; when they are far apart, the clip moves quickly.

Make the Timeline active and begin stepping back, frame by frame, along the motion path using the Left Arrow key. As you step back through the frames, you will see the text

Figure 5-26   Dragging the text clip into the second keyframe position

clip in the Canvas window inching upward as it returns to the first keyframe position in the upper left corner of the frame. Also note that as you step back frame by frame, the Center value in the Motion tab of the Viewer window changes each time, reflecting the new position of the clip for each frame between the two keyframes. Grab the playhead and drag through the clip in the sequence. Notice as you drag it over the third second where our second keyframe is, a small triangle briefly appears in the clip on the Timeline, indicating the presence of the keyframe where our second keyframe is located.

To add additional motion keyframes for Scale and Rotation, return to the first keyframe, or use the keyboard shortcut for "previous keyframe": Option-K. Make sure that the Motion tab for the Viewer window is up front and the text clip is loaded there. The first keyframe for Scale is the default 100%. We want the text to start out smaller and grow up to 100% over the 3 seconds. We will use the numerical entry here to shrink the text down to 50%. Type "50" into the text field, hit the Return key, and look into the Canvas (see Figure 5-27). The text clip should have shrunk to half its size.

To get the text clip up to 100%, we need to set a new keyframe. When we dragged the text clip to the bottom right corner of the frame at the third second, Final Cut Express automatically added a keyframe for the new Center value. We did not need to hit the Add Keyframe button. But to create new keyframes for Scale or Rotation from the Motion tab, we need to hit the Add Keyframe button on the appropriate frame.

Move the playhead up to the third second where the second keyframe for motion is. Hit the Add Keyframe button in the bottom right corner of the Canvas window. Notice that the X in the wireframe has changed to green. Finally, back in the Viewer window Motion tab, type "100" in the Scale field. If you scrub the playhead back over the clip between the two keyframes, you will now see the Scale interpolate correctly, increasing in size from 50% to 100%.

The only problem here is that now that the text clip begins at 50% scale, it is no longer in the proper position at the beginning of the clip. But you don't have to go through a lot of hand wringing to correct this issue. Remember that whenever you change a value where there is already a keyframe, Final Cut Express simply updates the keyframe there with the new value. To fix this problem, make sure you are on the first frame where the initial keyframe is, then reach into the Canvas and manually move the clip into place a little tighter into the upper left corner of the Canvas.

Next we will add a Rotation to the motion. Once again, use the Option-K shortcut to return to the first keyframe if you are not already on it. Make sure the text clip is selected in the sequence so that you see its wireframe in the Canvas. Go up to the wireframe and float the mouse pointer around the outer corners until you see the circular arrow of the Rotation tool. Once you see it, click and rotate the clip about 40 degrees counterclockwise (see Figure 5-28).

Not sure how far 40 degrees is and which direction is counterclockwise? Easy—make sure the Motion tab in the Viewer window is visible. In the Rotation field, a negative value is always counterclockwise, and looking at the number in the field will tell you exactly how

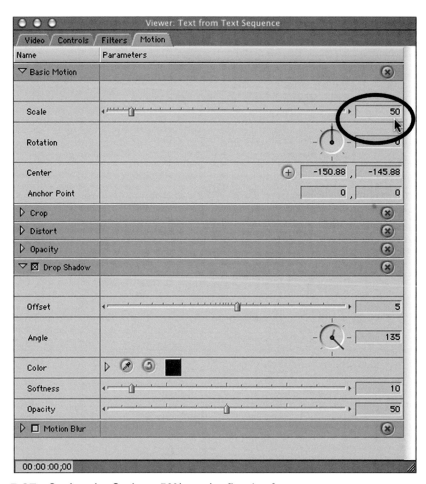

Figure 5-27   Setting the Scale to 50% on the first keyframe

far you have rotated your clip. Of course, if necessary, you can always enter your numbers manually here as with the Scale value.

To get the second Rotational keyframe, move up to the third second and enter "0" in the Rotation field of the Motion tab. Once again, if you scrub back over the clip between the two keyframes, you will see the rotation. To see what this keyframing looks like in motion, render the clip quickly. Select the clip, then hit Command-R, for Render Selection. After the short render, play the clip back. Notice that although the clip is traveling in a straight line, it actually appears to slightly curve because of the combination of the three attributes changing over time.

Figure 5-28   Rotating the text clip on the first keyframe

Nonlinear Interpolation—Adding a Curve

Although the clip appears to curve a little in the motion path, we can add a much more pronounced curve to the motion path. For this, we need to bring out the Pen tool again. Not only does the Pen tool allow us to create keyframes on the sequence Timeline for Opacity, it is also very functional in the Canvas window itself for adding precision to your motion paths.

Make sure the text clip is selected in the sequence, and navigate the playhead to the first keyframe of the clip again. Go to the Toolbar, and click and hold down the Pen toolset. In the first use of the Pen tool, we used it to create keyrfames on the sequence where there were none originally. However, now we are adjusting the keyframes that already exist in the Canvas. For this we need to choose one of the other two tools in the Pen toolset.

The second Pen tool is the Pen Delete tool. Its function is to simply remove errant keyframes from your motion path. This is more valuable than it seems at first. Since with the exception of opacity you cannot actually *see* your keyframes in the sequence Timeline, it's pretty easy to accidentally add a few that you don't want. Errant keyframes you don't know about in between the keyframes that you *do* know about will change the behavior of the clip. To get rid of extra keyframes you don't want, choose the Pen Delete tool, and click the unwanted keyframes in the motion path in the Canvas window (see Figure 5-29). As you would expect, this tool will also delete Opacity keyframes from the sequence Timeline.

To add a curve to the motion path, we need the third Pen tool, called Pen Smooth. Select the Pen Smooth tool, and then move up to the Canvas window. It may help to increase the scale of the Canvas window to 100% so that you can see the motion path a little better. Move the mouse pointer up to the beginning of the motion path where the first keyframe is located. When you see the mouse pointer turn into a Pen tool with a small widget shape, single-click the keyframe (see Figure 5-30).

When you single-click the keyframe, two extra bumps will appear on the motion path line. The first one we are concerned with is the larger one farthest away from the keyframe. Move the mouse pointer over the bump until you see it turn into a crosshair, and then click and drag in any direction (see Figure 5-31). The bump you grabbed will extend out in the direction you tugged, and the motion path will extend out into a broad curve. The bump is what we call a Bezier handle, which describes any tool used to create curves in a line. After you have dragged it into a curve, let go, and frame advance through the motion path with the Left and Right Arrow keys to see how the motion path has changed. If you want to further change the curve, just grab the same bump on the Bezier handle again and tug further.

You may notice that the curve is restricted mostly to the first keyframe we clicked with the Pen Smooth tool. To make a completely round curve, you would also have to perform the same Pen tool action on the keyframe at the end of the motion path. Do so, and tug on the Bezier handle of that keyframe until you have a soft, even curve between both ends of the motion path (see Figure 5-32).

Ease In/Ease Out

There is another type of nonlinear interpolation that you can apply to motion paths to make your motion more natural looking. If you play the motion path back now, you will

Figure 5-29 Clicking with the Pen Delete tool to remove an unwanted keyframe

Figure 5-30 Single-click a keyframe with the Pen Smooth tool to add a Bezier handle

Figure 5-31 Dragging the Bezier handle to create a curved motion path

see that the curve and other motion effects look quite good. But there is one more concept that we see in the real world that is not here: change in speed. In the real world, nothing travels at a constant speed all the time. Things start off moving slowly, speed up, and then slow down as they approach a stop. In the world of keyframing, this is usually called Ease In/Ease Out to describe the fact that your object eases up to speed and then slows down as it gets ready to stop, just like any object in the real world.

It's very easy to get this sort of speed change in your motion path. Simply Control-click the keyframe you want to have that sort of speed variation, and you'll see a contextual menu. One of the options will be Ease In/Ease Out (see Figure 5-33). Set it and it will adjust the speed for you. Do a render and check out how this affects the motion of your text clip. If you find that you don't like the speedup and slowdown, just Control-click the keyframe again and choose Linear instead, which will set it back to normal.

Bezier Handles on the Timeline

Of course, this Ease In/Ease Out capability is available in the sequence, where it is referred to as "Smooth." When we keyframe opacity there, we have the option of making its change

Figure 5-32   Adding a second Bezier handle to create a smoother motion path

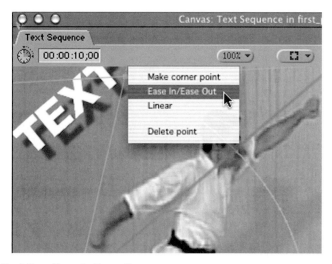

Figure 5-33   Enabling Ease In/Ease Out

nonlinear as well. Let's add a curved change in visibility for the text to match the speed change of the motion path. Return the playback head to the first frame of the clip, and then make sure that the Clip Overlays button is enabled in the Timeline window. Select the Pen tool (keyboard shortcut–P), then go to the first frame of the clip, and click to set your first keyframe.

Remember that if you drag the keyframe, you can reposition it and its value. Drag the keyframe down to give it a value of zero opacity (see Figure 5-34). In the Canvas, the text clip has disappeared from view, but when we set the next keyframe, it will return. Our next move is to find out when the clip should come back to complete opacity. Although we can no longer see the clip, we can see its wireframe bounding box (provided the clip is selected on the sequence!).

Double-click the clip in the sequence to load it into the Viewer window, and then switch to the Motion tab. Scroll through the sequence and watch the wireframe and Scale values in the Motion tab. We want the text to be totally visible when the Scale is about 66%. Depending on how you set everything, the frame may vary, but it will be roughly the 1-second mark. Reposition the playhead at the 1-second mark in the Timeline, make sure the Pen tool is selected, and then click on the Clip Overlays line and drag the Opacity value up to 100% (see Figure 5-35).

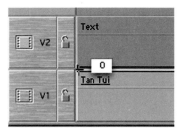

Figure 5-34 Setting the first keyframe to zero opacity

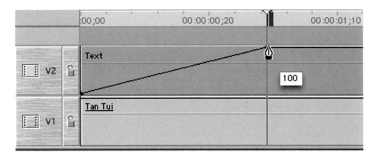

Figure 5-35 Dragging the Opacity value to 100% when the Scale is 66%

We have performed this action before, but now we will add nonlinear interpolation to the keyframes. Hold the Control key down and click the first keyframe. You will see two options: Clear, which will delete the keyframe, and Smooth, which will add a Bezier handle (see Figure 5-36). Choose Smooth. You may want to change Name Plus Thumbnail to Name in the Sequence settings for the sequence (drop-down menu Sequence >Settings), which will make it a little easier to see your opacity keyframe at the head of the clip.

Once you choose Smooth, you will get the Bezier handle for the keyframe. Notice that like the handle for the motion path, the handle here only affects the curve from the keyframe you changed. If you want to make a completely even curve between these two keyframes, you have to make them both smooth. Control-click the second keyframe and select Smooth. Now you have two handles and can make the curve exactly the way you want it (see Figure 5-37). Try rendering both an upper curve, which results in the opacity appearing sooner, and a lower curve, which results in the opacity coming in more slowly at first. You will probably find that in this instance, the latter is the more successful curve, since it allows a more gradual opacity change that synchronizes with the scale change more effectively.

You may also have noticed an unfortunate restriction in the clip overlay method of keyframing. As soon as you create the first Opacity keyframe with the Pen tool, the entire clip needs to be rendered, even if you left the value at 100% (technically the same as no keyframing)! Since we only want about a second of keyframed opacity changes, this results in a lot of unnecessary rendering for the rest of the clip that is basically untouched.

How to deal with this? Pretty easy workaround, actually. Before you set your opacity keyframes, choose the Razorblade tool and razorblade the clip roughly where your last opacity keyframe will be. Since the keyframing will be on a single clip, you won't have to render the bulk of the clip you weren't keyframing.

Before leaving this subject, we should look at a little bit more of Bezier handle behavior in the sequence. This concerns handle interaction between three keyframes rather than two. When you have Smooth selected for a keyframe, unless you override it, Final Cut Express assumes you want the same smooth curve on both sides of the keyframe—i.e., interpolation approaching and departing the keyframe. Thus, if a keyframe is surrounded by

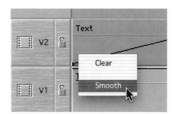

Figure 5-36 Choosing Smooth to add a Bezier handle

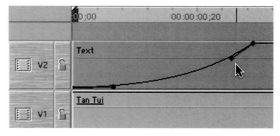

Figure 5-37 Adjusting the opacity curve using Bezier handles

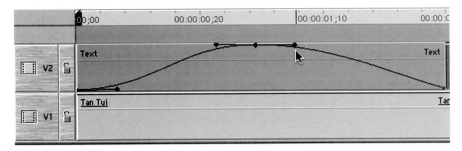

Figure 5-38 Bezier handles appear on both sides of a keyframe

two other keyframes, when you choose Smooth, you get *two* Bezier handles. And they work in unison—tugging on one handle makes an equal and opposite change to the other Bezier handle.

To see this in action, move the playhead up to the second second (00:00:02:00) in the clip (perform a quick Trim to give yourself room if you razorbladed your clip too short in the last action). Choose the Pen tool and create a new keyframe here, this time dragging the value all the way to 100 percent. Although this keyframe is not a Smooth keyframe yet, you can see that the second keyframe before it now has a second Bezier handle on the right side that corresponds to this keyframe (see Figure 5-38).

If you tug on this handle, you will notice that now you cannot change the degree of the angle, only its duration of curve! This is because the two handles are linked and because the value is set at 100%. Click the second keyframe and drag its value down to 75%. Now grab either of its handles and move them around. As you adjust the curve for one, you get an equal and opposite angle from the handle on the other side. This can produce some interesting results, but it isn't always totally useful, either. I usually find that I need to adjust each Bezier handle here totally independently. To do this, you can use either of two shortcuts. If you hold the Command key down, as you click one handle and change the angle, the other handle's angle doesn't change, though its duration does. If you hold down the Command and the Shift keys and adjust the handle, you get completely independent control of each handle (see Figure 5-39).

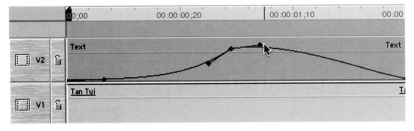

Figure 5-39 Holding down the Command and Shift keys to adjust each handle separately

The Other Motion Tab Tools

There are a few other effects tools on the Motion tab that you will find useful. These are the Crop, Distort, Drop Shadow (which we have seen before while setting up the text clip), and Motion Blur tools. The first two are available from the Toolbar as well as the Motion tab, as we will see next. The second two need to be set up in the Motion tab. In the sequence, Control-click the third keyframe and choose Clear (see Figure 5-40), so that there are only the two opacity keyframes remaining. Double-click the clip to load it into the Viewer, and render it if necessary so that we can proceed with the last few Motion tools.

Crop

The Crop tool is interesting in that it allows you to hide a section of a clip from view without having to insert a matte of any kind. This can be convenient for operations such as displaying only a section of a larger graphic image or video clip inside the frame. Rather than change the scale of an image to make it smaller, which would still include detail you may want to leave out, the Crop attribute simply limits how much of the frame of the clip is visible. The parameters for this are adjustable as a square or rectangle, based on the left, right, top, and bottom edges of the clip.

Switch the Viewer window to the Motion tab and click the widget to drop down the settings parameters for the Crop tool. Click and drag the slider for either the left or right edge and drag it to around 50% (see Figure 5-41). You will see that half of the text clip has been obscured. The other half is not resized, as it would if be you had changed the actual width or scale of the clip with the Distort tool, which we will be looking at in a moment.

The final parameter for the Crop tool is Edge Feather. This allows you to soften the edge you are cropping the clip with so that the image being cut off with the tool fades into the background now visible on the outside of the crop line. This can be displayed by moving the crop line directly over one of the letters in the text clip were are adjusting. Drag the left or right slider such that one of your letters is seemingly cut in half. Set the Edge Feather

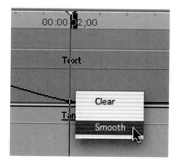

Figure 5-40   Clearing a keyframe

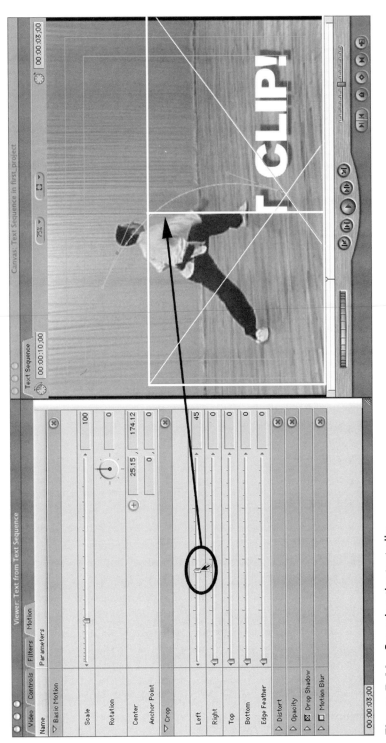

Figure 5-41   Cropping the text clip

at 50% and you will see the cutoff soften such that the letter appears to disappear into the background (see Figure 5-42).

The Crop tool is available on the Toolbar as well. On the Toolbar, choose the second-to-last toolset button, or choose the keyboard shortcut, C (see Figure 5-43). The mouse pointer turns into the common shape of a cropping tool that many different applications use.

After changing to the Crop tool, go to the Canvas window, click on an edge (not a corner—it must be an edge) of the text clip, and drag into the center of the clip (see Figure 5-44). You will find that this has the same effect as moving the slider for that edge in the Motion tab settings for Crop, and indeed, if you look at that tab, you will find it updated to the change you just made using it.

All transparencies, including the Crop tool, are an effect of unseen integrated matting. The soft, feathered edge you are witnessing is the result of Final Cut Express allowing some pixels to be seen and others to become transparent along the edge of the crop. The value you enter into the Edge Feather field simply informs Final Cut Express how far outside of the crop edge to apply the gradual mixture of visible and matted-out pixels. Once you have a grasp of the tool, reset the crop either by hitting its red X in the Motion tab or by dragging the text clip's edges back out manually with the Crop tool.

Distort

The next attribute, Distort, is a powerful tool for altering the very shape and aspect ratio of a clip. Unlike the Crop attribute previously described, the Distort parameters change the actual size and shape of the clip in the frame by altering its physical dimensions rather than by covering them up. The effect is like having an image imprinted on a rubber balloon. If you blow up the balloon, the image on its surface changes its shape. The Distort tool creates very precise distortions based on the amount of stretch applied to the edges of the material.

The first four parameters of the Distort attribute are Upper Left, Upper Right, Lower Right, and Lower Left. These parameters correspond to the corner points of the clip's frame. There is no slider adjustment to these parameters, because the points exist as X and Y coordinates and, therefore, can be assigned to any location in the frame. Interestingly, they can even be set between other points, so that the clip appears to double back on or fold up into itself.

To display this type of clip distortion, enter 0 and 0 as the new X and Y coordinates for the Lower Right parameter. The Lower Right corner of the clip will jump to the center of the video frame, which carries the coordinate value of (0, 0). Not only has the shape of the clip changed, but the text within the clip now appears curved and scrunched as a result of its position in the frame and based on the amount of virtual squeezing of pixels to adjust and fit them all inside the new frame shape (see Figure 5-45).

Notice that although we are still looking at a two-dimensional text image in the frame, the simple change in shape and curvature suggests three-dimensional depth. This is an example of using the alteration of two-dimensional shapes to suggest natural

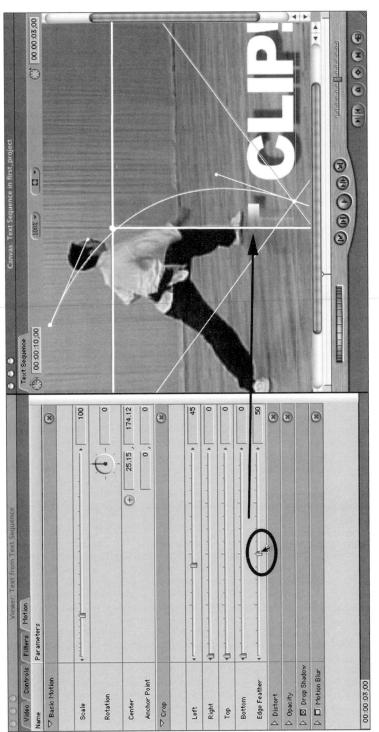

Figure 5-42 Using Edge Feather to soften a cropped edge

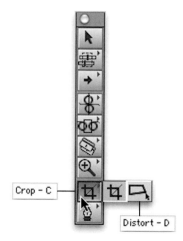

Crop - C

Distort - D

Figure 5-43   The Crop and Distort tools on the Toolbar

Figure 5-44   Using the Crop tool to crop directly in the Canvas

depth perspective. The Distort parameter allows us to mimic the real-world perception of change in size and shape that tells our brain that an object is nearer or farther away. To remove the Distort effect and to return any coordinates of any attribute or parameter back to their original positions, hit the red X parameter-reset button just to the right of the attribute's name.

Just as with the Crop tool, there is a Toolbar version of this Motion tab attribute. Click and hold the Crop tool button on the Toolbar, and you will get the Distort tool option. The keyboard shortcut is D. Choose the Distort tool and move the mouse pointer around the point that you just reassigned to (0, 0) and which is now repositioned right in the

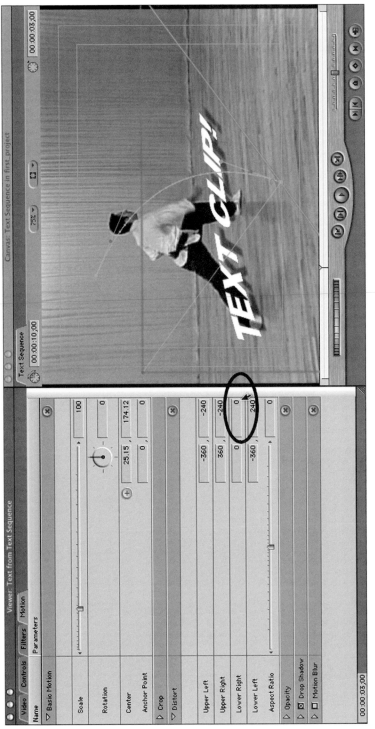

Figure 5-45 Distorting a clip by setting the Lower Right parameter to 0, 0

middle of the text clip's frame. When you see the mouse pointer assume the shape of the Distort tool, click the point and begin to drag it back toward its original location (see Figure 5-46). Drop the point periodically on the way to see it reshape the entire clip as the angle of distortion becomes less extreme.

The last parameter of the Distort attribute is called Aspect Ratio. It is adjusted by a slider, with a default value and unaltered setting of 0. The Aspect Ratio parameter changes the degree to which the clip in the frame is distorted two-dimensionally. Dragging the slider to the left reduces the Aspect Ratio of the clip, making it appear shorter and fatter evenly across the horizontal plane (see Figure 5-47). Dragging the slider to the right increases the Aspect Ratio so that the clip appears taller and skinnier once again, evenly distributed across the vertical dimension.

The reason this parameter is referred to as an Aspect Ratio instead of a "Short/Fat–Tall/Skinny" tool is that it was initially most useful in taking footage shot anamorphically to yield a widescreen, cinematographic look with letterboxing. As described in the Easy Setup section in Chapter 2, many cameras allow you to shoot in a 16×9 mode, which introduces letterboxing at the top and bottom of the frame. The difference in screen shape can yield interesting effects, so many videographers use it when shooting.

Final Cut Express can use and display 16×9 footage correctly; we have already seen in the Easy Setup where and why this is necessary. However, the problem for people using such footage is that once the 16×9 footage leaves the camera, it will appear anamorphically stretched when it hits analog devices such as TVs and VCRs, which have no idea that the original video needs to be squeezed.

Figure 5-46   Using the Distort tool directly in the Canvas

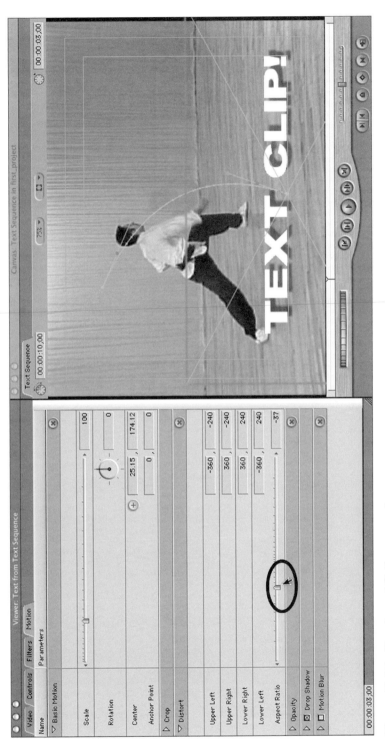

Figure 5-47 The Aspect Ratio parameter

Unless you are using an expensive production monitor, you will very likely have to manually squeeze your footage before sending it out to Firewire and recording to an analog VCR or simply watching it on a TV. In fact, the best way to get 16×9 footage out of your Firewire DV editing arrangement to analog tape is to put your finished 16×9 sequence into a regular old 4×3 sequence (a concept called "nesting," which we will talk about shortly) and then render. When you have occasion to do so, you will find that the Aspect Ratio parameter is changed for you on the fly by Final Cut Express to a value of −33.33, which is the aspect ratio reduction necessary to fit the 1.66 screen shape of 16×9 letterboxed video into a 4-to-3 aspect ratio (see Figure 5-48). Don't let these numbers scare you. Final Cut Express is fully equipped to handle anamorphic video correctly, and if you do your Easy Setup settings and Preferences, it will do most of the conversion process for you. You are only responsible for the render!

Motion Blur

The final attribute in the Motion tab is for Motion Blur. Motion Blur is a unique effect that works only with elements in a composition that move. A clip moving across the Canvas window can display Motion Blur, but a clip that is stationary in the center of the window cannot.

Figure 5-48   Changing 16 × 9 video letterboxed footage into a 4-to-3 aspect ratio

Items such as film and video footage that display natural motion blur in their own original frames will not be affected by Motion Blur settings unless their entire clip moves in the larger video frame of the Canvas. Motion Blur is applied to entire clips rather than any separate part of a clip's frame. Therefore, we will be able to add motion blur to our text image when we move it across the screen, although we could not add it to any object inside the static video clip in the background.

But what is motion blur? Motion blur is a phenomenon that occurs when an object moves faster than the perceptual frame rate of the viewing camera or eye can gather still images. Video and film are simply a series of still images that update so rapidly that the viewer perceives continuous moving objects rather than a series of images. If the frame rate slows down too much, we see the still images individually, and the illusion of continuous motion is broken. Speed up the frame rate, and the illusion becomes stronger and sharper.

At around 24 frames per second, which is the standard frame rate of film, the illusory motion becomes fluid, each frame being nearly indistinguishable from the previous one. Slightly faster, PAL video uses a standard frame rate of 25 frames per second, very close to the film frame rate. NTSC video uses an even faster frame rate, increasing it up to 29.97. Since both PAL and NTSC video are interlaced formats that scan each frame as two separate fields sequentially (see more about this in Appendix A), the true frame rate should be regarded as double this number, as fast as 59.94 individual fields per second.

What does this have to do with motion blur? Motion blur occurs whenever an object passing in front of the camera or eye moves too fast for the viewer to actually record each increment of the movement. If you pass your hand in front of your face quickly, you will see a blur of your hand, because your eyesight is gathering image information at a relatively slow frame rate. In the fraction of a second that your eye gathers an entire frame's worth of visual information, your hand has actually moved several inches or several feet, depending on how fast you move it. For those few fractions of a second, you see your hand in all the places it has traveled since the beginning of your eye's gathering of the single visual frame.

For our eyes, this is nothing new, and aside from some interesting optical illusions based on spinning wagon wheels and such, we are quite used to what our eyes can and cannot perceive sharply. But where motion blur really takes on significance is in the field of image gathering. Photographers and cinematographers must take care that when they record images, the shutter speed, which is the part of the camera that determines how long the image gathering period lasts, is fast enough to overcome excessive motion blur. If the shutter speed is too low, there will be so much movement between the beginning and the end of the exposure that there will be nothing but blur in the frame.

Still photographers have to be more careful than the rest, because the shutter speed for still cameras is a choice to be made by the photographer based on many factors, the most important of which is the desired effect. The photographer can add or take away motion blur by changing the shutter speed. For still photographers, motion blur is an important effect that can be used to deliver a sense of duration and motion in a still image.

As with Drop Shadow, Motion Blur must be checked (on) to be applied to a clip. There are two parameters for Motion Blur: the percentage of blur and the number of samples.

The percentage of blur lets you tell Final Cut Express how intense the motion blur should appear. Final Cut Express creates motion blur by taking a certain number of frames before and after the frame in question and blending them together, just as we said your eye gathers image information about where your hand was over the entire period it gathered a single "frame" of vision.

The result is that you see a mixture of where the object is in the frame now with an image of where the object was just before and after the present frame. Since the blend across the frames is smooth and is reblended with each new frame, you get an effect not unlike what real motion blur does: You are kept from getting a tight focus on each position of the object within each frame.

Although it would seem like a bad idea to obscure focus, motion blur can add realism to moving objects that otherwise appear not to be visually integrated into the frame. We can't help it; when we see motion blur, we assume that an object really moves through space, even if that object is a two-dimensional text image crossing a video screen. Since our job in compositing is to mimic reality on a two-dimensional plane, motion blur is an essential part of any movement we add to our compositions.

The Percentage of Blur parameter increases or decreases blur by adjusting the range of previous frames that the blur blends into the frame when Motion Blur performs the act just described. The scale of percentage ranges from 1,000%, which blends 10 frames of the clip into the blur, to 0%, which blurs none. A value of 100% blends only one frame. The default value of the percentage is 500%, which gives a healthy "standard" blur.

The Sample parameter refers to how detailed the blending process is in calculating the motion blur. More samples will result in a much more fluid blend between the individual frames that are being joined to create the blur. Fewer samples means that the blend may look a little rough, since very few positions between the number of frames being sampled are figured in. The bottom end of fluid samples is 4, which looks pretty rough. A setting of 32 looks fantastic. The trade-off is that the larger the number of samples, the longer it takes Final Cut Express to calculate and render the frame. With 32 samples, this can take several seconds. With 4, the calculation is quick. A setting of 8 or 16 usually gives the best balance between speed and quality.

Check the Motion Blur box to turn the effect on. The default settings of 500% and 4 samples make the clip look pretty choppy, even before we render it and play back. Change the Sample value to 16 (see Figure 5-49). You will achieve a much smoother blur of the text. Render the clip out, and you will see it stretch over the frames as the motion blur is applied to all the frames. You may want to pull back the percentage to 200, since our text moves relatively slowly and thus should have a little less blur.

Effects Filters

You can also apply effects to a clip that are based on the use of filters, also known as plug-ins. In reality, filters are special scripts that are applied to clips to produce special effects.

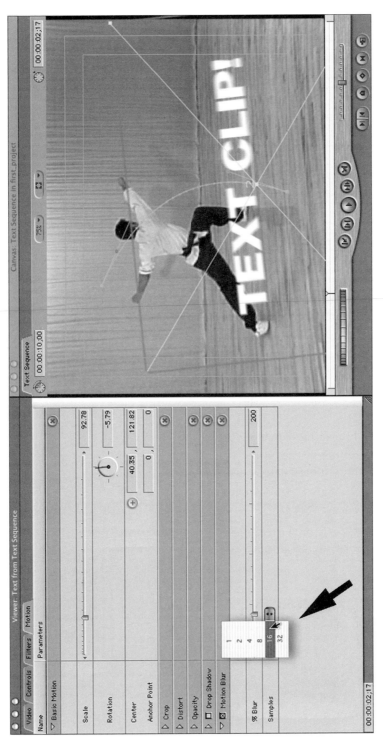

Figure 5-49   Setting Motion Blur in the Motion tab

Rather than adjusting one physical element of a clip at a time like the Motion tab attributes, filters usually change many different aspects of a clip at once. Instead of being designed to change raw physical attributes, such as scale or rotation, filters usually produce a specific type of desired effect dreamed up by a programmer, such as Gaussian Blur or Fisheye. Such filters are often also used to correct problems in your video footage, such as color and brightness or contrast.

The effects filters can be applied in a manner similar to the application of the Transition. You can drag and drop the effect from the Effects tab of the Browser window onto the clip, or you can apply the filter by selecting the clip and accessing the filter from the Effects drop-down menu. In this example, we will use the latter process, although there is no functional difference between the two. Use whichever seems more effective in your personal workflow.

Applying Fun and Useful Effects: The Basic 3D and Viewfinder Filters

Let's apply a couple of effects filters of varying sorts to see how they affect the clip. The Filter parameters must be set in the Filters tab of the Viewer window. As with the Motion tab settings, we will be able to see our work update in the Canvas window. We'll start with the Basic 3D filter.

The Basic 3D Filter

Edit a fresh clip into the sequence and double-click it to load it into the Viewer window. Go to the Effects drop-down window, select the Video Filters submenu, and then select Perspective and Basic 3D (see Figure 5-50). Next, click the Filters tab.

Your clip will not immediately change in the Viewer and Canvas windows. The Basic 3D filter's parameters must be changed in the Filters tab before the clip's appearance is altered. The default settings are for no change at all.

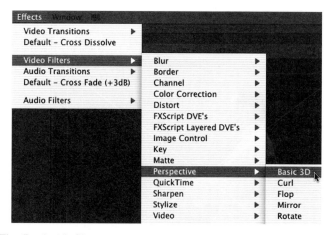

Figure 5-50 The Basic 3D filter

Tear away the Filters tab from the Viewer window. We want to be able to watch our effect change in the Viewer video window as we adjust the parameters of the filter. If you tear the tab away and find no Basic 3D filter present in the tab, either you have misapplied the filter to the wrong clip or you have loaded the wrong clip into the Viewer window.

For a standard captured clip in Final Cut Express, the Filters tab will have two sections: a Video Filters section and an Audio Filters section. The controls for any filters you apply to the clip will appear here. If there are no audio clips linked to the video, there will be no section for audio clips on the filters tab. The reverse is also true for audio-only clips, such as imported audio CD tracks.

Near the filter's name, there is a check box for enabling and disabling it (see Figure 5-51). This can be very handy if you've worked hard to get the correct settings for a filter, but you need to make it disappear for a moment. Rather than deleting the filter by selecting its name and clicking the Delete key, you can simply turn it off at the check box and then reenable it when you are ready for it again. Be warned that disabling the filter with the check box removes any render files associated with it, so you'll have to rerender if you do so.

The 3-D effect is a deep subject, but the Basic 3D filter (being basic, after all) is easy to use. In the parameters for the Basic 3D filter, there are three rotational values: X, Y and Z. In three-dimensional geometry, the X value is horizontal, the Y value is vertical, and the Z value is for depth, or distance from the viewer. If you know the position values for X, Y,

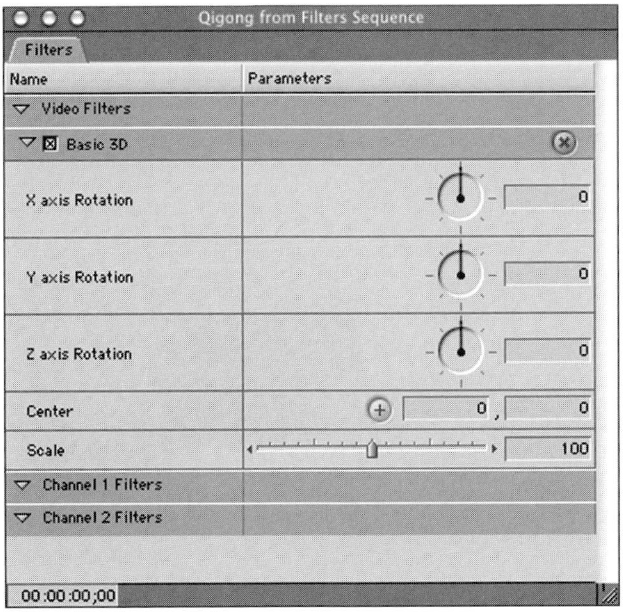

Figure 5-51 The Filters tab

and Z for an object, you can tell its position not only from left to right or up and down, but also how close it appears to be.

Basic 3D allows you to manipulate these three dimensions. The three values of X, Y, and Z in the Filters tab define rotational axis. To use an example, when you change the X value to 45 degrees, the clip is rotated using the X horizontal line for its axis. The result is that the clip appears to tip toward the viewer. If you set the X value to 90 degrees, the clip appears to disappear altogether, because the clip is exactly perpendicular to us. Since the clip has no "thickness," it disappears. Change the value to 91 degrees, and you will see the sliver reappear. Enter 180 degrees, and you are looking at a reverse and upside-down version of your clip, because you are technically looking at the back of the clip; it is completely flipped over!

Type −25 in the X Axis Rotation field to set the initial value. Next, type 25 into the Y Axis Rotation field (see Figure 5-52). The Y value will rotate the object around the vertical axis. The combination of the X and Y rotations yields the appearance that the clip is no longer facing straight ahead but up to the right. The remaining Z value generates rotation values using the Z depth line between the object (clip center) and the viewer for the axis. In practical terms, this means that the clip will rotate just as rotation values do on the Motion tab— that is, rotating either clockwise or counterclockwise, but not horizontally or vertically.

The Center crosshair lets you reposition the starting point for all these axes. In geometry, all axes, X, Y, and Z, must converge at some point, or "coordinate." The Center value you assign here, either by number or by clicking the crosshair, is that coordinate, and it is the value from which the individual axis rotation values are determined.

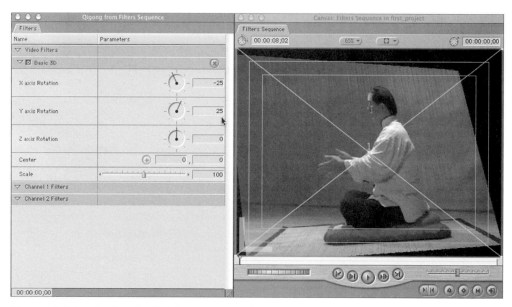

Figure 5-52 Setting Basic 3D parameters in the Filters tab

Finally, there is the Scale value. The Scale value adds depth values that are not based on rotation. Although scale means size rather than distance, when an object is larger, it appears to be closer. Thus, although the clip can't really get closer (beyond the screen toward your face), it can appear to be closer by growing in size. This feature is quite useful when combined with keyframing, such that the clip appears to get larger over time. Unfortunately, as we discover now, no filters in Final Cut Express are keyframeable. That remains the exclusive range of Final Cut Express's older sibling, Final Cut Pro.

The good news is that in most cases, the keyframeable Scale and Rotation values on the Motion tab can be keyframed to go along with the X and Y Basic 3D values on this filter to produce fantastic spatial effects that change over time and jazz up your graphics work. Just set the X and Y values on the Basic 3D filter to taste, then set up your Center, Scale, and Rotation keyframes on the Motion tab to build interesting motion paths.

The Viewfinder Filter

Apple includes a fun graphic filter for simulating the viewfinder of a video camera, appropriately named Viewfinder. You can give your audience a bird's-eye view of the action by applying this filter to your clips. Simply select the clip (or the Viewer window, if that clip is currently loaded in the Viewer window), go to the Effects drop-down menu, and choose Video>Viewfinder. Instantly, you will see two rectangles appear that are the same size and area of the Title Safe and Action Safe overlays we briefly discussed when creating Photoshop titles. Since these rectangles are common in many camera viewfinders, they are included here.

Take a look at the Filters tab under the View Finder parameters (see Figure 5-53). For Mode, you have a choice of the different modes a camera can assume: Play, Stop, Record, Rewind, FWD, Pause, and Custom. Custom allows you to type your own text in the line underneath the Mode parameter, in the Custom Text box. The mode you select controls what appears in the red box on the screen, and in the Viewer and Canvas. You can customize this by choosing the font, size, lamp color, and location of this box with the controls that follow the Custom Text box. The Color parameter refers to the color of the Title Safe and Action Safe boxes that are part of the filter effect rather than the color of the text. The final parameter for this filter is Blink, which lets you set the speed or rate at which the text blinks.

These are only two of over a hundred filters that come with Final Cut Express, and there are hundreds more out there written and sold or given away by the teeming third-party software market. If you do a lot of repetitive work or need very specialized effects or image correction work, you may want to shop around and see what is available; someone may already have created exactly the filter you need!

Composite Modes

The next sort of compositing we need to look at involves the way in which the various luma and chroma values of the images on one layer interact with the values of those on the

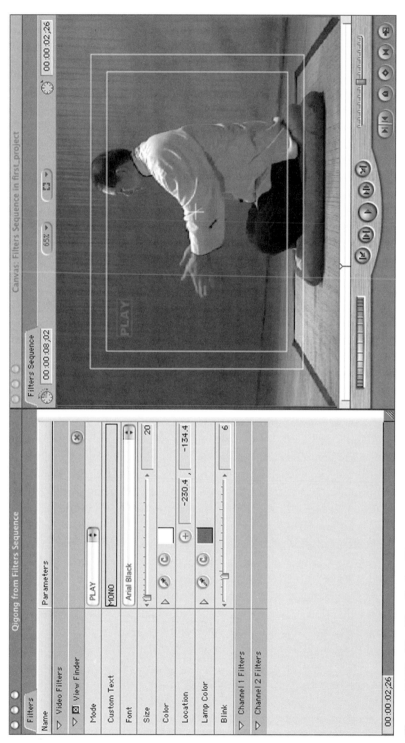

Figure 5-53 The Viewfinder filter

layer underneath. Composite Modes are among the most poorly understood features of Final Cut Express and image editing applications in general. But they should not be avoided, because they provide a tool of incredible flexibility and ease of use when you are generating visual effects.

Part of the confusion about using the Composite Modes is in understanding what they do and what needs to be in place in order for them to show results. The first requirement is obviously that the clip must be in the sequence. Since a Composite Mode is an effect that relies on a clip's relationship with the clip underneath, changing its Composite Mode outside of a sequence will not display its true appearance.

A Composite Mode applied to a clip always interacts with the clip on the layer directly beneath it. This means that when you choose a Composite Mode for a clip, you need to make sure that there is a clip underneath it that will change the clip in the way you want. If no clip exists underneath the clip whose Composite Mode you change, there may be no apparent change in the clip. Using straight black or white backgrounds for a clip's Composite Mode complement could yield unpredictable results or no change at all.

Until you actively change it, a clip's Composite Mode is set by default to Normal. Clear off your sequence from the preceding example and add two stacked clips, one into the V1 track and one into the V2 track. Make sure to select two clips that are different from each other. Single-click the clip in the V2 track to select it.

Go to the Modify drop-down menu and scan to the bottom to find Composite Mode. When you move to this submenu, you will find a list of many different Composite Modes (see Figure 5-54). The Composite Modes are also accessible in a contextual menu by

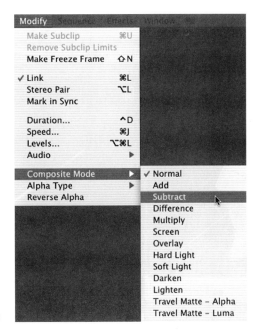

Figure 5-54 The Composite Modes

Control-clicking the clip. Each name describes how the luma and chroma values of the underlying clip will influence the appearance of the clip you apply the Mode to.

The problem for most new users is that the names of the Modes do not accurately describe what the effect on your clip will be. Unlike effects filters such as Gaussian Blur and Fish-Eye, which give some indication of their effect, the Composite Modes only describe the method by which Final Cut Express will take the luma and chroma values of the underlying clip and use them to alter the appearance of the clip you apply the Mode to. This means that the effect resulting from the application of a Composite Mode depends on the contents of both clips and the Composite Mode chosen.

That said, there are some Modes that come into frequent use. Perhaps you want to lighten or reverse the colors in one area of your clip. You may want to enhance the effect of an effects filter by drawing out the luma and chroma values of a clip before applying the filter. Some people are masters at using the Composite Modes as a type of unique paintbrush, one that is able to make complex and beautiful patterns of color and light from the mixture of math and image.

The default setting for a clip's Composite Mode is Normal, which means that the clip is not influenced by the clip below it. If you select any of the Composite Modes other than Travel Matte-Alpha or Travel Matte-Luma, you will begin to see interesting results.

In the Composite Modes submenu of the Modify drop-down menu, select a Composite Mode for the selected clip in the V2 track. Refer to the Canvas window and look at the effect that the Mode creates based on the clip beneath it (see Figure 5-55). Continue choosing Modes from the list for the selected clip, noting how each Mode yields both different and sometimes similar results, depending on the two clips and the Mode.

Some of the Modes show an even mixture of the two images, while others show only the darker sections of the one or the lighter sections of the other. Some reverse areas of similar or different detail, yielding odd color combinations. Some may produce no difference or completely black frames. Each Mode gives different results based on the two clips that you have juxtaposed.

Feel free to change the Composite Mode for a clip as often as you'd like. Of course, any clip that has its Mode changed will require rendering, even for those Macintoshes capable of RT, because the video that is a mixture of the two clips using the Composite Mode does not exist yet. To turn off the Composite Mode for a clip, you must return the Composite Mode to Normal. Composite Modes are not keyframeable and have no controls, although you can certainly change the appearance and performance of any given Mode by changing the appearance of either of the two clips involved. For instance, if you want to reduce the amount of one clip's Composite Mode effect on another, you could reduce its opacity or apply any of a number of effects filters. This variability is what makes the Composite Mode such a flexible tool, even if it is a little tough to get your head around.

Figure 5-55 Subtract Mode

Mattes, Masks, and Stencils

Two of the most valuable Composite Modes were skipped in the preceding section because of their unique function and value to Final Cut Express editors. These are Travel Matte-Alpha and Travel Matte-Luma. These tools offer the ability to frame the images of one video layer inside a shape above another layer. This is great for more advanced picture-in-picture effects, such as the ability to show one video clip through the letters of a word while using another clip as a background, a very common usage. Essentially, the Travel Matte "keys out," or makes transparent, areas that either have a certain luminosity (light vs. dark) or alpha channel, a concept that we will explore shortly.

The effect is rather like using a stencil to paint letters. If you lay the stencil on a background you want to paint the letter onto, you can paint with impunity above the stencil itself, knowing that the paint will reach only the background in the spaces that the stencil allows it to get through. Thus, three layers are involved in the process: the background, the stencil, and the layer of paint that is being used for the letters applied through the stencil.

A stencil is part of a group of tools that all perform roughly this same task. Whether they go by the name "mask" or "matte," these tools are part of a family referred to as *mattes*. Mattes allow you to obscure or reveal areas of an image based on the criteria that defines the matte. In the preceding stencil example, our criterion is very simple. The stencil blocks the path of the paint, restricting it to the shape of the letters the stencil is constructed to paint.

Setting the Travel Matte-Luma

To work with mattes as we have just described them, we need to set up the sequence a little differently. Edit a darker video clip into the V1 track. Perform a Superimpose edit of the text clip we have been using onto the V2 track. Finally, set the target track for V2, and Superimpose edit a lighter video clip onto V3 (see Figure 5-56). This will be used to matte into the text, such that the video from V3 will appear through the text on V2, superimposed on V1. Select a clip from the Browser window that you want to use. Make sure that you use a different clip from the one in the V1 track and that this clip contains footage that is generally lighter in detail.

If both clips are exactly the same or if they both contain footage that is equally bright or dark, it will be difficult to see that matting has taken place, just as if we used a stencil to paint green letters on a green wall. The text clip that we use as a stencil will disappear completely, so don't expect to see the white letters following the next operation.

Select the clip in the V3 track. Go to the Modify drop-down menu, scan down to the Composite Modes, and select Travel Matte-Luma (see Figure 5-57). When you do this, the Canvas window, which was previously showing only the V3 track, will suddenly reveal most of the V1 track, with the exception of the text, inside of which is video matted from your V3 clip.

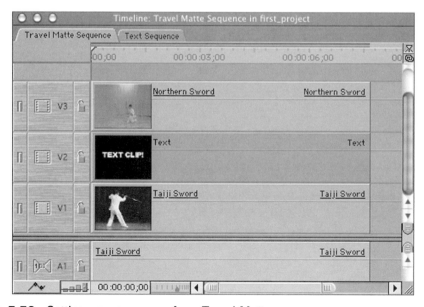

Figure 5-56 Setting up a sequence for a Travel Matte

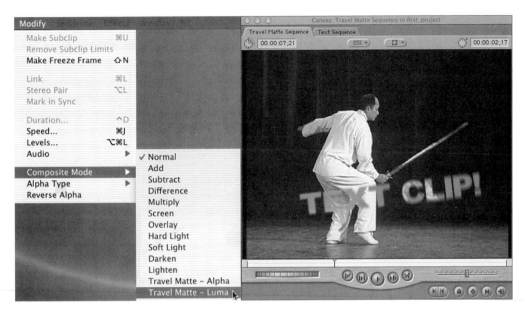

Figure 5-57 Travel Matte-Luma

What is occurring here is that Final Cut Express is using the luma of the text clip values (the white text) to determine what should be used as the stencil. Anything white in the text clip is stenciled and allows the V3 layer clip to show through onto the background clip. Anything that is black (which is all the background of the text clip) blocks the stencil and doesn't let the V3 layer clip show through onto the background clip. It is performing the simple act of matting.

Notice that the drop shadow has disappeared, however. This is because the drop shadow was specified as black, which is not included in the luma key. With the luma Travel Matte, the brighter the values, the more they are matted in. If we went back into the Motion tab of the text clip and set the drop shadow color for gray or white, we would see it begin to appear.

Unlike a normal stencil that either blocks or doesn't block, our Travel Matte performs more like a fine-tunable screen. We can adjust how strong or weak the matte is based on how close to white an element in the clip is. White text such as we created in the Controls tab produces a complete matte, allowing the V3 clip to show through totally. Black, on the other hand, blocks the matte, and all we see is the background V1 clip.

The implication of this is that all the values in between black and white—the grays—have luma values that are not quite here or there. These can be used to yield partial mattes. To see this difference, double-click the text clip in the V2 track of the sequence to load it into the Viewer again and go to the Motion tab. Click the Drop Shadow triangle to reveal the parameters. In the Color parameter, change the color of the drop shadow to somewhere

Figure 5-58   Drop shadow within a Travel Matte-Luma

around middle gray (see Figure 5-58). Return to the Canvas. You will see that the drop shadow is starting to appear on the edge of the matte.

This is because the drop shadow color is not within range of the luma values that the Travel Matte-Luma can translate into a matte. Unfortunately, you also begin to see the limitations of the luma matte itself. The drop shadow, because it is based on the single gray color, is rough edged and uninteresting. Its softness and gradient shading is gone because the matte is simply drawn from its source color, gray. To get a better-looking matte, we will use the Travel Matte-Alpha.

The Travel Matte-Alpha: What Is an Alpha Channel?

The other type of Travel Matte is capable of delivering equally interesting results, but is based on a different method of contributing transparency information to the matte. This is called the alpha channel. The alpha channel is a unique system that includes the transparency information in an image, not simply by using colors within the image (although that is possible as well). Instead, alpha transparency information is included in its own special channel that accompanies an image. There, it performs like a carry-along matte for the image. Any application that can access alpha channels uses the information from the alpha channel to determine what should or should not be transparent.

Some explanation of the RGB system of digital images is necessary here. Digital images generally use a system called RGB to store information about each pixel in the image. R stands for red, G stands for green, and B stands for blue. All the colors that can be displayed by a computer (which includes most of the colors visible to the human eye) can be expressed by some mixture of these three colors. The amount of each of the three colors determines which color is displayed. The scale of possible variations on each primary color in RGB is 256. Therefore, in every pixel, there is a separate channel each for red, green, and blue (see Figure 5-59). Each channel carries a value between 0 and 255 for the amount of that color. The mixture of values for the three channels gives the pixel its color appearance.

Although this doesn't seem like much variation, the combination of 256 possible colors for each of the three primary colors yields over 16 million different colors, from which the term "millions of colors" originates. Each pixel of an RGB image carries bits of data describing what the red, green, and blue values for the pixel are. The reddest possible red in the RGB color scale would carry the value "255, 0, 0," with 0 being the value when none of a particular color is being used in a channel (blue and green in this instance). The luma matte we just created used the RGB values of white (255, 255, 255) and black (0, 0, 0) as well as every shade of gray in between to generate its transparency.

The alpha channel was developed as a system that would not intrude on the original three-color channels but could be used to carry transparency information about the image. A separate channel was devised that is limited to variations of strictly luma information. The alpha channel uses 256 levels of gray to communicate whether or not a pixel should be transparent, regardless of its RGB color data. Because this alpha information can be expressed as grays as well as completely black or white, a pixel can also be partially transparent, depending on how close the alpha level is to black or white.

This may sound very similar to the luma matte that we created earlier, and in fact the same process is used. But the difference is that we needed two images to complete the luma

Figure 5-59 RGB color

matte: the text clip for the matte and the actual image we were matting (not counting the background the matte was being stenciled onto). But an image that contains an alpha channel carries the matte inside of it as a channel. Thus, an image with an alpha channel is like two images in one: our color information that we see as image detail, and an unseen channel of grayscale information that determines only what parts of the image are transparent (see Figure 5-60).

Many applications, Final Cut Express included, can read and utilize alpha channels, and many use alpha channel transparency information for processing transparencies, just as we are doing, without informing you that the process is taking place. A good example of this is the text clip we have been using all along. Although we didn't have to tell Final Cut Express we wanted the rest of the frame to be transparent, it understood this and applied alpha transparency to the text clip in those areas where there is no text.

Unfortunately, the Apple DV codec that makes Firewire DV possible does not support alpha channels. Although we are working with them in Final Cut Express, the media files on our Scratch Disk actually do not contain alpha channels. Final Cut Express is adding them to the clips only for use in the application. If you need to export a video file for use elsewhere in another application and you want to send an alpha channel with that file, you need to export it using a codec that does support alpha channels (e.g., the Animation codec), as shown in Figure 5-61.

Although an alpha channel does use grayscale luma information to carry transparency data about the image, it is not the same sort of matte as a luma matte. We will use our text clip again as an example of the way that alpha channels can show information that does not display when a luma matte is being used.

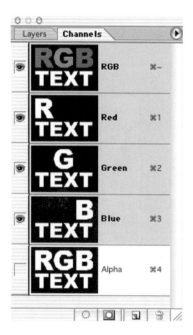

Figure 5-60   The alpha channel

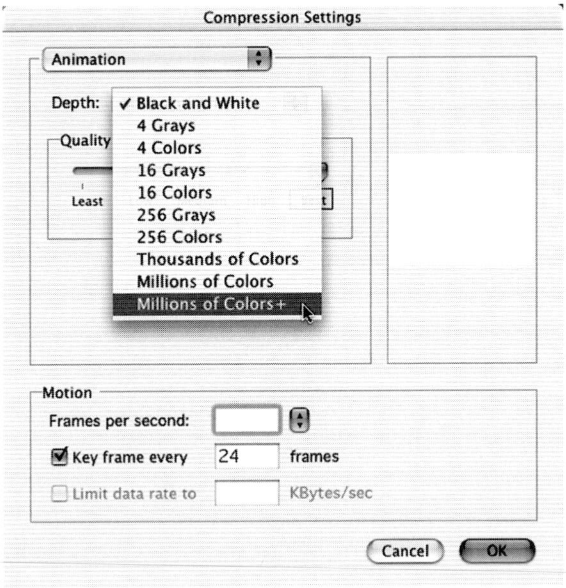

Figure 5-61 Exporting as Millions of Colors +

Final Cut Express can easily detect and access alpha channels. They exist typically wherever transparency is needed. One exists in our text clip. It is what is giving us the ability to overlay the text clip on top of video and see around its edges. Wherever you do not see text in the text layer, you are seeing (or, rather, not seeing!) alpha channel transparency. And because this alpha channel information is dedicated to how transparent a pixel is rather than how dark or light it is, we can achieve much higher-quality results using it for things like drop shadows in our Travel Matte.

At the moment, the V3 clip is still set for the Travel Matte-Luma. Control-click it and choose Travel Matte-Alpha from the Composite Mode submenu (see Figure 5-62). The change is immediate and satisfying. The soft gradient of the drop shadow returns, but this time it is a gradient transparency rather than simply darker or lighter.

Speed and Duration

Another effect that you can apply to video and audio clips is Speed. It is easy to change the speed of a clip directly. Because of the flexibility of the Speed control dialog box, it's also easy to coordinate the new speed with a specific duration so that you can slow the clip down to match another element in your sequence.

To change the speed of a clip, we want to load it into a sequence first. Although you can change the speed of a clip by simply selecting it in the Browser or loading it into the Viewer, this will actually apply the speed change to the original clip, which is more than

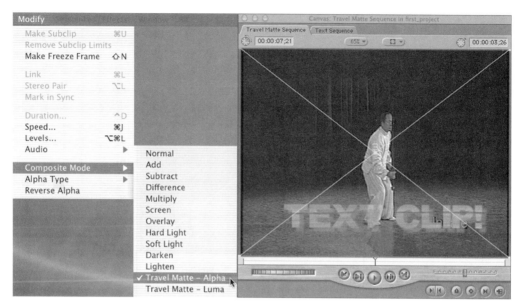

Figure 5-62 Switching the Composite Mode to Travel Matte-Alpha

likely your master clip. Clips that have had their speed adjusted must be rendered to play back correctly, and rendering can only occur in a sequence.

Edit a clip into a fresh, empty sequence. Adjust the Time Scale of the sequence so that the entire clip is visible on the sequence Timeline. With the clip selected, go to the Modify drop-down menu and select Speed. When you do so, you will receive a dialog box that allows you to customize the resulting clip generated by the Speed command. Type 50% into the Speed field, and watch the Duration field double in length (see Figure 5-63).

The first field is for the percentage of speed. The default, 100%, is normal speed. Lowering the percentage will decrease the speed; raising it will increase the speed. Below this is a Duration field. Notice that if you hit the Tab key after entering a new value into the Speed field, the Duration field updates, revealing the new duration of the clip. Reducing the speed to 50% will result in doubling the duration, while doubling the speed to 200% will result in halving the duration.

By the same token, changing the Duration field will give a new speed percentage value. This is probably the most valuable tool for wily B-Roll video editors who want to make the most of every frame they have, and who aren't afraid of adjusting the speed of a clip to make it fit just right into its edit slot. Although Fit to Fill, one of the Canvas editing overlay boxes, also performs this function automatically, you can't check the speed change before committing to the edit. With the Speed command, you enter the duration you

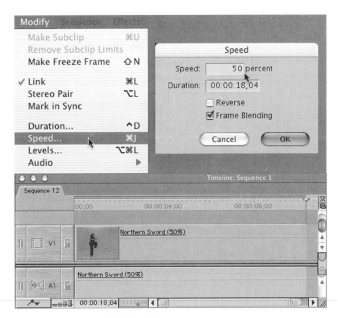

Figure 5-63 Changing the speed of a clip

have for the clip, and you can immediately see the speed change that your clip will be subject to when processed before you commit to it. The Reverse check box simply applies a negative value to the percentage. This means that in addition to any speed changes made, Final Cut Express will reverse the order of the frames in the clip, making it run backward.

Frame Blending should always be enabled. When you speed up or slow down a clip, you are removing or creating frames of video to make the video appear faster or slower. This can cause strobing or stuttering if the new set of frames do not appear to be as continuous or sequential as the original set were. Frame Blending creates new intermediary frames that are a blend of the frames removed or added by the speed change. The result is smoother and cleaner speed changes.

Set the percentage to 50%, enable Frame Blending, leave Reverse disabled, and hit OK. The clip in the sequence will have doubled in length and will require rendering. If you render, you will observe the very smooth slow motion.

Bear in mind that any change in speed will require a render, since no video media file yet exists for the speed-changed clip. Interestingly, if you change the speed and then change it back to 100%, or normal, the speed change will not require rendering, since the second speed change simply refers the clip back to the original clip media. When you change the speed, the clip in the sequence will be marked with the percentage of the speed as a handy reminder that the clip is modified.

Nesting and Effects, the Final Cut Express Way

Up to this point, we have only discussed how effects work with single individual clips. This is fine, but of course situations will arise where you need to apply the same effects filters equally to all the individual clips in a sequence. Or perhaps after completing an edit of a sequence, you want to apply Motion tab-type effects to a sequence in its entirety rather than its individual constituent clips. This would be impossible to do with the sequence's clips on a one-to-one basis.

The answer lies in *nesting*. Nesting simply refers to placing a sequence inside another sequence so that the first sequence is treated as a single clip. You can manually move one sequence into another by simply dragging and dropping it just as you edit in a clip. You can load a sequence from the Browser window into the Viewer window just as if it were a clip and then edit it into another sequence. And you can apply effects to a sequence as if it were a clip. About the only thing you can't do with nesting is to nest a sequence inside of itself.

You can create very interesting picture-in-picture effects by nesting that would be practically impossible without nesting. If for instance you wanted to have a series of scaled down video clips move across the screen in a line, you could use nesting to apply the same motion path to all the clips rather than create a motion path for each clip.

Start out by creating a new sequence and name it "inside." Edit a video clip into V1 and another clip into V2 of "inside." Trim the longer of the two so that they are of equal duration. Double-click one of the two clips to load it into the Viewer. While the clip is loaded in the Viewer, click the Motion tab and set the Scale value to 25%. Now double-click the other and perform the same Scale setting.

In the "inside" sequence, select the clip in the V2 track. Once it is selected, make sure the Canvas window is in Image + Wireframe mode, and look for the wireframe of the clip you just selected in "inside." Finally, Shift-click the wireframed clip and drag to the right or left. Shift-clicking and dragging clips in the Canvas window "constrains" the direction of movement to either a horizontal or vertical direction. This allows you to line up one of the clips either directly above or directly next to the other. When you have one clip lined up next to the other, drop the clip (see Figure 5-64).

Now Control-click in the Project tab to create a new sequence. Name this one "nest," and double-click to open it into the Timeline window. Edit a video clip in the V1 track of "nest." This will be the background video clip of our picture-in-picture effect. From the Project tab, grab the "inside" sequence and drag it onto the V2 track of the "nest" sequence. Look in the Canvas window, and you will see that the two scaled-down video clips from the "inside" sequence are superimposed over the background clip in V1 of "nest."

It gets even better. Because the "inside" sequence is acting like a clip in the "nest" sequence, we can also perform keyframing and Motion tab adjustments to it just as we did earlier in the chapter to the text clip! Hold down the Option key and double-click the "inside" nested sequence on V2, and it will load into the Viewer window. Click the Motion tab to access its attributes. Check the Drop Shadow on and leave the default settings for

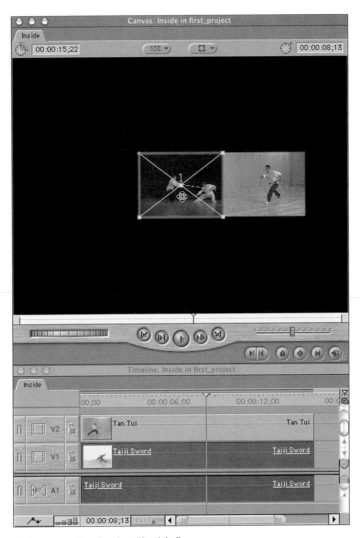

Figure 5-64 Lining up clips in the "inside" sequence

these fields: Offset, 10; Angle, 135; Color, Black; Softness, 10; and Opacity, 50. Also click the check box and enable the Motion Blur, and leave its default settings.

Now move to the Canvas window to keyframe a motion path. Make sure the "inside" nested sequence is selected and that the sequence playhead is on the first frame of the "inside" nested sequence. In the Canvas, pick up the wireframe of the "inside" nested sequence, position it in the lower left third of the frame, and set a keyframe. Next, in the "nest" sequence, move the playhead to the last frame of "inside." In the Canvas window, Shift-click and drag the "inside" wireframe, and drag it to the right to create a motion path (see Figure 5-65).

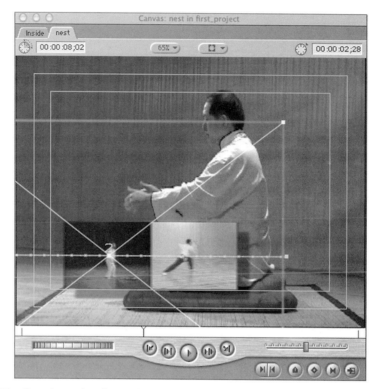

Figure 5-65   Creating a keyframed motion path on a nested sequence

Now, if you hit the Left Arrow key and move the playhead back into the "nest" sequence, you will see the "inside" sequence moving across the frame just as a clip would if keyframed. The big difference here is that both the clips in the original "inside" sequence are moving in exact unison based on the motion path created by the single nested sequence. This is a faster way to work, since you only had to create one set of keyframes to get any number of clips in motion. Once you start putting together more complex keyframed effects, you will find that many composited effects cannot be performed without nesting as we have just done, particularly ones that rely on rotation values.

6 The Audio Tools

Adjusting Audio in Final Cut Express

OK, so not everything is going to be perfect after your recording session. Sometimes people will speak too loudly or softly, or, worse, they will do both during the same recordings. There will be some noise, no matter what you do. And frankly, you're going to want to change things that aren't technically bad audio, just because, well, because you want them to sound differently. Of course, you should always strive to record the highest-quality audio you can while shooting. To find out more about how to improve your recording techniques, check out Appendix D.

Final Cut Express does have some tools for addressing audio issues. Similar to the opacity effects, audio levels can be adjusted and keyframed in the sequence. Unlike with the opacity effects, however, you can actually keyframe audio in the Audio tab of the Viewer window, though generally it's a little easier and more intuitive to do so in the sequence. Final Cut Express also has audio filters that can be used to clean up a number of common issues. Finally, there are some pretty cool tools that make it easy to get quick, classy voice-overs into your productions.

Fixing Audio Levels

First, we'll take a look at the basic audio tools in Final Cut Express. In your project, open up a new sequence in the Timeline window and edit a clip into it. Select the clip and go to Modify>Stereo Pair (see Figure 6-1). When Final Cut Express captures your video and audio, it links them together in a single clip so that it is easy to maintain video and audio sync. But it also can create a special relationship between any two individual audio tracks that are above one another in the sequence or are linked to each other as a capture clip. This special relationship is the *stereo pair*.

To understand the difference between a stereo pair of audio clips and a couple of mono clips that are simply linked together, you have to understand the difference between mono and stereo sound. Mono sound is unidirectional. In simple terms, this means that the sound you hear is flat and appears to be generated from all directions at once. It does not have an identifiable source location. If you are listening to a mono AM radio broadcast and you

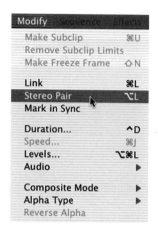

Figure 6-1 Making a stereo pair

close your eyes, for instance, you can easily tell where in the room the radio is. The radio's sounds all seem to originate from the same single speaker source.

Stereo, on the other hand, uses two speakers to simulate depth, and thus position, in the sound field. Sounds emitted by stereo speakers, if mixed properly, do not appear to originate directly from the speakers, but rather somewhere between them. Stereo sound mixing can spread a single sound between two speakers, putting less of the sound in the first speaker and more of the sound in the second speaker, which makes the sound source appear to be closer to one side than the other. It is this variance of levels of a single sound to two different speakers, or "stereo mixing," that gives stereo its depth, realism, and presence.

When you make two audio clips stereo in Final Cut Express, as we have just done, you add this mixing option. But even if you don't intend to do any heavy mixing, making tracks stereo can benefit you with a special sort of convenience when setting and adjusting audio levels. Since it is assumed that you want to increase stereo channel levels equally, when you make two audio tracks stereo, any level adjustment you make to one is automatically applied to the other. A stereo pair will appear on a single Audio tab in the Viewer window. Any audio filters are automatically applied to both audio clips. In the sequence Timeline, two little green triangles appear at the head of the audio clips to indicate that these two audio clips are linked in a special way. Even if you "unlink" your clips using the Toggle Linking button in the Timeline window, the two clips will still be locked together in this special relationship.

After selecting the new "stereo-ized" clip, double-click to load it into the Viewer window. Look at the tabs and find a tab labeled Audio. Click it and you will see a window that contains two wavy, jagged lines (see Figure 6-2). These are called the *waveforms*. The waveform is essentially a graphic representation of the levels of the audio in the clip. Where you see spikes in the line, the audio level is higher; where the jaggies are shorter, the levels are lower.

These levels correspond to the levels you may have already seen in the special Audio Level Meters window and in the clip in the Timeline when waveforms are turned on. The

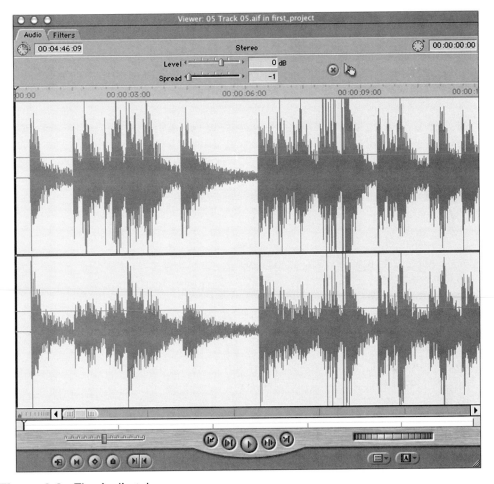

Figure 6-2 The Audio tab

Audio Level Meters is a small, thin window that normally resides next to the Toolbar when the windows are laid out in the default arrangement. It looks very similar to an audio meter on a stereo sound system, and in fact it does the same thing. It simply shows you how high the levels are at any given moment while the audio is playing. If you hit the spacebar to begin playback, you will hear sound and see the level meter registering the rise and fall of the audio levels.

Of course, we are not limited to the levels that we have when we capture. We can lower the levels of audio that is too loud. We can also raise the audio levels to a certain extent, though there is a limit to this, because at some point the audio will begin to *clip*, or generate digital noise that sounds totally unacceptable. If you look at the top of the tab, you will see a slider marked Level. This red slider corresponds to the red horizontal level line down in the waveform area of the tab. To change levels, you can either move the slider left or right, or you can use the mouse pointer to move the level line in the waveform tracks up and down. Use the mouse pointer to grab the red line in the waveform track and drag it up. As you do, you will see a small box appear with a number and "dB" (see Figure 6-3). The abbreviation dB stands for decibel, a unit of measurement for force that is often used to describe sound and audio levels. When you see "8 dB," let go. You'll see the slider follow it.

This audio level rubberband line can also be found in the sequence. In the Timeline window, enable the Clip Overlays button. The clip's audio tracks will display a similar level line. If you grab that line with the mouse pointer, you will see that it is also at the 8 dB level. If you drag it back down to 0 dB, you will see the lines in the Audio tab in the Viewer window follow it. And we can also view the actual waveform of the audio clips in the sequence Timeline. To enable the waveform view in the Timeline, click the Timeline to

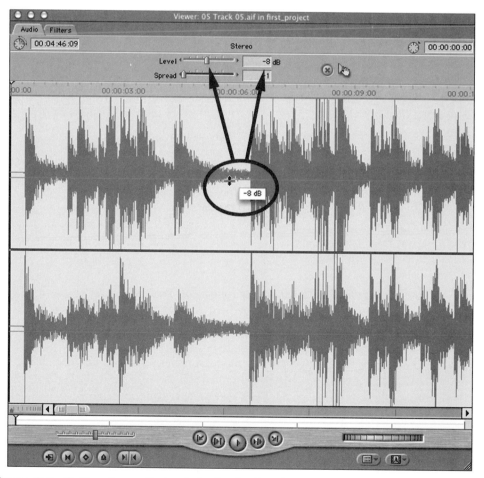

Figure 6-3   Setting the audio levels in the Audio tab

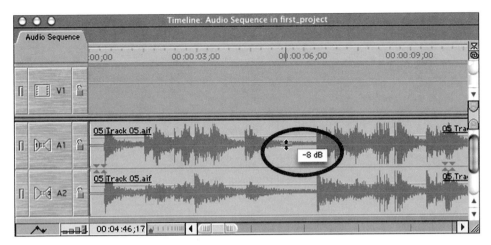

Figure 6-4 Viewing the audio waveform on the Timeline

make it active, and select Command-Option-W. The waveform will appear in the audio tracks. The same keyboard combination toggles waveforms off (see Figure 6-4).

Keyframing Audio Levels

Of course, we are not limited to just raising or lowering the levels of an entire audio clip. We have already learned how to keyframe Opacity levels in the sequence. We'll use the Pen tool again to change the audio levels. With both Overlays and Waveforms turned on, select the Pen tool (keyboard shortcut–P), and then proceed to the audio clips in the sequence. Position the mouse pointer over the rubberband line in the audio tracks, click, and create the first point. As with Opacity, you need two points to create a change in values, so click elsewhere, either before or after this first point, and drag up or down. As you do, you will also see the little "dB" box appear, informing you how much you are raising or lowering audio levels (see Figure 6-5).

Also notice that this keyframe you are adjusting can be dragged and repositioned on the Timeline (left or right). When you change the position of the keyframe in the sequence, the line between the two points extends, and just as with Opacity keyframing, the transition between the two audio level values takes longer. So, for instance, if you wanted to slowly increase an audio track from quiet to loud over 4 seconds, you would set the first keyframe at a relatively low "minus dB" value at the first frame where the audio starts. Then set the last keyframe at the fourth second at a higher, more suitable audio level.

There are a couple of frequently encountered uses for this sort of audio keyframing. Because you can easily and quickly drop audio levels, it's easy to tailor the beginning or end of an audio track to the beginning or end of a visual scene. This creates an *audio transition*. If you want your audio to softly and gently fade out as the picture fades to black, keyframing your audio *fades*, as they are called, directly on the sequence is the simplest way

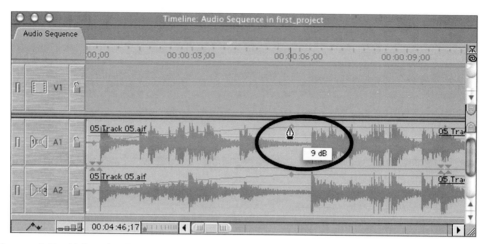

Figure 6-5   Using the Pen tool to keyframe audio levels on the Timeline

to get the timing just right. Although there are audio transitions that are very similar to the Cross Dissolve transition we worked with in Chapter 4, many times it's faster just to hit the P key for the Pen tool, reach up into the sequence, and set two keyframes.

Of course, the other use for such keyframing is to tailor your mixes in various ways, such as removing unwanted, objectionable noises. Keyframing allows you to gently transition from the captured audio for a clip, to substitute audio replacement clips and then go back to the original audio clip without your audience ever being the wiser. Since the first audio is being reduced at the same rate and level that the replacement clip is being increased (a technique referred to as *cross-fade*), the listener never notices the switch-out. Editors often use *room tone* replacement audio clips to clean up their noisy audio tracks. For tips on recording audio and information regarding room tone and its uses, see Appendix D.

It is also useful for quickly equalizing levels between music tracks that you may have introduced to your project from CDs, voice-overs, or other sources. Because you will generally want to fade music in and out based on "visual cues" (a 25-cent term meaning "what is going on on-screen"), it helps to be able to grab the Pen tool and set your audio fades on the fly, and then bring them surging back at the appropriate moment without having to set faders or other annoying interface items.

Using the Audio Filters

Audio filters are very similar to video filters in that you apply them to an entire clip. These filters are used to correct audio problems or add effects such as echo. When you apply the filter to the clip, its controls appear in the Filters tab in the clip's Viewer window. There are a lot of filters to choose from, each with its own particular function. We'll look at a few of the more important ones and figure out what they do and how to set them for your individual clip's needs.

The Three Band EQ

An *equalizer* is an important tool in cleaning up audio. To understand what it does, you have to know a little bit about audio itself. Audio and sound are composed of two important features that make them "sound" the way they do. The first, amplitude, describes volume levels as we have been adjusting them. Amplitude describes how powerful, or loud, a sound is. In the waveforms we've been looking at, the higher the spike in the wave, the louder the sound. This is the amplitude of the sound or audio wave.

The second feature is the frequency. Frequency is the number of waves that happen over a period of time. Don't confuse this with the sample rate, which has to do with how frequently your camera samples the audio waves. Frequency here means how many different waves happen per second in the sound you are hearing. Higher frequencies result in higher-pitch sounds like whines, lower frequencies result in lower-pitch sounds like rumbles. The combination of frequency and amplitude determines how loud and what pitch the sound is.

Knowing this gives us a little leverage for fixing sounds. The EQ, or equalizer, is a tool that allows you to adjust the audio levels of a clip, but instead of adjusting all frequencies at the same rate, it allows you to change the loudness of individual frequencies in the sound. For instance, you may have audio in which the high-pitched sounds are where all the noise is, but you want the middle pitch, or midrange, and the lows to remain the same. With an EQ, you would simply lower the audio levels for the high-pitch noises, while leaving the midrange and low-pitch sounds untouched.

The number of bands an EQ has determines its precision in addressing ranges of frequency. A 12-band EQ, for instance, will split the whole range of human hearing (20 Hz to 20 KHz) into 12 sections, allowing you to effectively have four different bands of EQ for all three ranges—high, middle, and low. That's a lot of precision. There are even 24-band EQs that can isolate very small bands of frequency without touching others. Of course, with that level of precision comes a big price tag.

The very lowest number of bands you are going to encounter in an EQ is the Three Band EQ, simply because this is the fewest number of bands that can be effective when you are separating frequencies. To apply the Three Band EQ, edit a fresh clip into your sequence, and then double-click to load it into the Viewer window. Go to the Effects dropdown menu and select Audio Filters>3 Band EQ (see Figure 6-6).

You will immediately see one of the biggest problems with using this filter in Final Cut Express. You will see a red render line appear in your sequence above the clip. This means that in order to hear the effect of the filter, you will have to render each time you change the settings of the clip. That can make it pretty difficult to get it right.

Fortunately, there are ways to make this process a little less painful. Rather than constantly rendering the entire clip every time we make a change in the settings, we will select

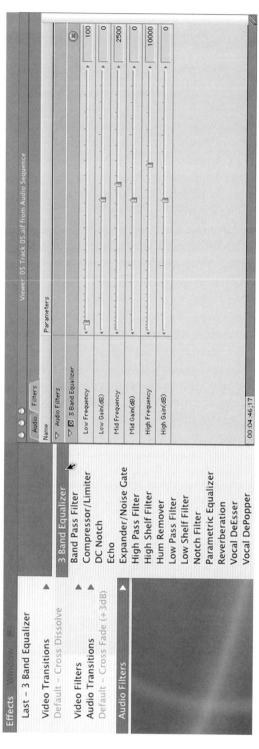

Figure 6-6 The Three Band EQ filter

only a small part of the clip containing both the noise we want to get rid of and the sound we want to keep (for instance, the sound of a pause between words of dialog containing lots of hiss, plus a little of the dialog so we can hear what happens to the voice when we equalize out the hiss). This way, we only render a couple of seconds every time, which is nearly instantaneous with a G4 processor.

In the sequence, locate a short section of a clip that contains a passage as described in the last paragraph. Then in the Toolbar, choose the Selection toolset (second from the top) and choose the third button on the toolset, the Range Selection tool. Go to the clip in the sequence, click inside the body of the clip, and drag. You will see that you are selecting only a portion of the clip (see Figure 6-7). Make sure that you've selected the area of the clip that you want to use for a test (you only need a few seconds).

After you've selected the area, go to the Mark drop-down menu and choose Mark Selection, or use the keyboard shortcut, Shift-A. This will put an In and an Out point for the range of selected frames in the clip. To render the selection, choose Command-R. If the range of frames between the In to Out points becomes deselected, hit Option-A for Select In to Out. To play from the In point to the Out point only, choose Shift-\, or Play In to Out.

Basically, the workflow is like this. You make a change in the audio filter settings and then immediately hit Command-R to render. Then hit Shift-\ to play the selection you just rendered. Listen to what happened, make another change, render again, and then play again. You keep this up till you get it right. The render is unbelievably fast when you limit it to a few seconds, and you find after a few rounds of this that it's pretty automatic.

Take a look at the Filters tab and the controls of the Three Band EQ. They are divided into the high-, mid-, and low-frequency ranges. For each range there is a frequency setting to specify and a "dB" level adjuster. To set the EQ, you want to choose the frequencies that

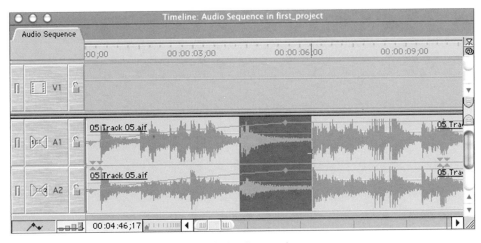

Figure 6-7 Selecting with the Range Selection tool

need help; then reduce the levels of those frequencies. Remember that you won't hear any difference until you actually lower the "dB" level for the frequency.

What sort of settings should you start with? Here are a few very common frequencies of annoying sounds that you will have to address at some point.

- 8,000 Hz—Electronic hiss, the kind of hiss that doesn't exist in the room, but is generated by the electronics of your microphone and the camera.
- 15,734 Hz—Television refresh whine. If you record too close to a television monitor, you will very likely pick up this high-pitched whine, too high to easily hear, but there and very annoying.
- 60 Hz—A very low hum originating from problems in electrical wiring and grounding in the location you are plugging your equipment into. It's also difficult to hear when recording, but painful when you are trying to get rid of it in your tracks.
- 20–200 Hz—Low rumbles, often structural vibrations and noise that you can't "hear" but that is recorded to tape and interferes with other frequencies.
- 1,000 Hz—A very common frequency for room hiss, and annoying sounds like heating and air conditioning vents. Unfortunately, this frequency is also right in the middle of the human vocal range, so be careful!

Apply these settings and experiment. It will take a while, but you will find that in Final Cut Express, this is the most useful tool for eliminating hiss at one stroke.

The Parametric EQ

The Parametric EQ works from a similar methodology. It isolates a frequency range and then lowers the level by the amount you tell it to in the controls. The difference here is that you only have one band in the Parametric EQ filter, rather than the three in the Three Band. To make up for the deficit, the Parametric EQ allows you to select the frequency band you are adjusting, plus it lets you make that band of frequency larger or smaller. In other words, you can only affect one group of frequencies, but you can make that group of frequencies cover a range as large or small as you want, to focus on eliminating the noise you hear.

Click the check box in the Three Band EQ filter controls to turn it off, then go to the Effects drop-down menu and choose Audio Filters>Parametric EQ. When you see this filter appear in the Filters tab (see Figure 6-8), you may also be surprised to find that it doesn't need to be rendered. Final Cut Express can process the Parametric EQ on the fly and incorporate the changes you make in the settings without requiring a render. This makes finding good settings very much faster than with the Three Band EQ.

Unfortunately, the Parametric EQ pays for this through only accessing one band of frequencies. If, for instance, you needed to cut down the high frequencies and the low frequencies simultaneously without affecting the midranges (which is in fact the most common audio cleanup situation), you would have to apply two separate applications of the

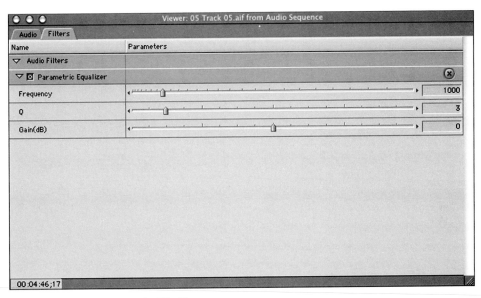

Figure 6-8 The Parametric EQ filter

Parametric EQ. You would then find that it can only can handle one Parametric EQ filter without requiring an audio render, because this stretches Final Cut Express's real-time audio mixdown capabilities to the extreme.

Take a look in the controls and you will see two sliders that you would expect. The second slider control, however, is new. Q is the control that determines how wide the range of frequencies you control is. When it is set to 1, it is as nearly as wide as the entire frequency range! When it is set to 20, it is covering a very narrow frequency range. The smart way to work is to set it at around 3 (which is very wide), set the "Gain(dB)" control to − 20, and start moving the Frequency control around as the clip plays until you hear the noise disappear. Once you find that range of frequencies, start adding to the Q value and bumping the Frequency control until you get Q up to about 10 and you are still hearing relatively little noise. Evaluate how the rest of your clip sounds with this EQ setting and then make more changes if necessary.

The Reverberation Filter

The Reverberation filter is a very important filter, especially for those who keep a sharp eye on their audio and who are concerned that their audio be appropriate to the video on the screen. Reverberation is the secret weapon for editors who need their subject on the screen to mesh into their background more effectively. It's a great tool for giving sound more presence, making it sound more like a place and less flat and monotone. That said, reverberation, or reverb for short, is a very delicate tool, and it's easy to overdo it. Too much reverb, and your tracks become muddy and unintelligible.

What is reverb, anyway? Reverb can be thought of as a very fast echo. The technical definition of reverberation is sound waves that have reflected off of surfaces so many times that we can't tell the original direction they came from, otherwise referred to as "sourceless sound waves." When you yell out in a large cathedral, the sound waves travel in all directions, reflect in even more directions, and interfere with each other, and eventually all anyone can hear is a blurry mess. If you've ever sat in the back of an auditorium during a speech, you'll be familiar with the concept. The closer you get to the speaker, the clearer the sound gets. That's because the closer you get to the sound source, the more direct the path of the sound waves, and the lower the amount of interference that occurs between the sound waves trying to make it to you.

So you'd think reverb is a bad thing. But you'd be wrong. Controlled reverb is one of the things that give us an immediate understanding of the size of a space. Imagine that you were standing in the middle of an auditorium, but the sound was as quiet as a telephone booth. Even when there is no real source of sound, like someone talking, you still subconsciously hear the room environment, picking up clues about how large the space you are in is.

This isn't just true for real life. Sound designers in Hollywood are paid the big bucks for their ability to manipulate things like room tone and reverb to give your ears something subconscious to work from as you watch the screen. Step back from the viewing experience for a second, and you'll realize the impact reverb has. A great exercise to demonstrate this is to attempt to listen to a fantastic movie, such as *Apocalypse Now*, without watching it. Even without seeing the images, you get an incredible feel for the visual space the camera is moving around in, even when we are listening inside the main character's head!

How do you use reverb? First you have to apply the filter. Eliminate the last two filters from the Filters tab of the clip, then go to Effects>Audio Filters, and choose Reverberation (see Figure 6-9). This filter, like the Three Band EQ, requires rendering to hear the effect, so use the same method described there to quickly evaluate the effect.

The controls in the filter are Effect Mix, Effect Level, Brightness, and then Type, which is a drop-down tab containing an enormous number of presets representing the type of space you want to simulate. Brightness is a control for how fast, tight, and short the "echo," or returning part of the reverb sound, is. It's usually best left at zero unless you really need to mimic large and unusually reflective walls, such as metal and bathroom tile.

The Effect Mix and Effects Level controls are necessary for the reasons we stated when talking about the auditorium example. Although the speaker is in the auditorium, the listener might be farther away or closer, meaning that the amount of reverb will be greater or lesser depending on how far away they are. Effect Mix and Effect Level let you adjust how much reverb you hear from the preset you use in the Type control.

For instance, if we choose Tunnel, which is the most extreme of the Type values, but then we pull the Effect Mix down to 25, it will still sound as if we are in a tunnel, but it will sound as if we are very close to the sound source, rather than far away, where the sound

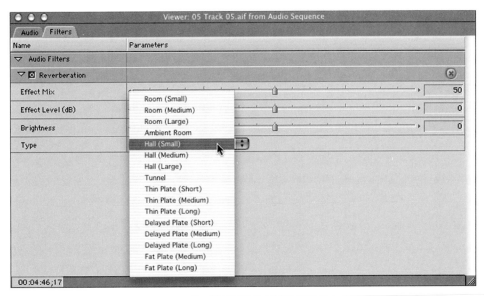

Figure 6-9 The Reverberation audio filter

would be muddier. A good setting to add a little life to a talking head might be to set Type for Room (Medium), Effect Mix at 25, Effect Level at 0, and Brightness at 0, although the correct setting will depend on the room the viewer sees behind the subject! The key to using the Reverberation filter successfully is to watch your video and experiment with the mix until you get it right. At some point, you will find the perfect amount for the size of the space in the camera's view and the distance from the object making the noise.

The Voice Over Tool

A great audio tool provided in Final Cut Express is the Voice Over tool. This tool makes it a snap to add classy, high-quality voice-over tracks to your video productions without having to juggle complicated audio equipment or even recording devices! Although you still have to be careful about how and where you do this recording, you won't have to find an audio professional to lay down tracks for use in your editing. The Voice Over tool is very easy to master and incredibly easy to integrate into your workflow.

Even those who don't need voice-overs for dramatic effect will find it useful. If two or more people are working on the same project, it's a great way to leave messages and commentary about the way to deal with certain footage. Nothing could be more convenient than having a separate audio track that is especially reserved for notation. Need to tell someone else how to handle an edit? Bring up the Voice Over tool, select the target track, and talk away. It's as easy as that.

Setup and Things to Consider

Setup is pretty easy. The Voice Over tool can access nearly any audio input device that works with your Macintosh as long as it is compatible with Sound Manager, the QuickTime engine in the Macintosh operating system that makes sound possible. Most USB Mike input devices qualify, such as Griffin Technologies iMic, as does the old microphone input on older G3s and G4s. PowerBooks all have a built-in microphone mounted on the lid of the laptop; iMacs have a built-in mike as well. You can even hook up your DV camcorder through Firewire and use it. There are, of course, the expensive add-on PCI card solutions, which may or may not work, depending on compatibility with Sound Manager, but in general there are plenty of ways to get audio into the Voice Over tool.

To access the Voice Over tool, go to the File drop-down menu. Choose the Voice Over tool. When you do so, the Voice Over tool will appear in a new window (see Figure 6-10). The first thing you need to check is whether your audio input device is available. Look in the lower half of the window for a drop-down tab labeled Source. Depending on your Macintosh and what you have connected to it, you may see a number of options.

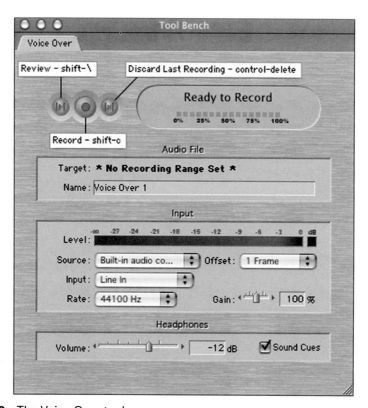

Figure 6-10 The Voice Over tool

The likely choices will be Built-in Audio Controller, DV Audio, and USB Audio. The Built-in Audio Controller refers to the built-in 16-bit sound card that all Macintoshes have on their motherboard. Depending on the Mac you own, this Built-in Audio Controller may have a microphone input. If so, you can certainly use it for creating voice-overs, though you will need to connect a microphone to the input. PowerBooks, as we said earlier, have such a microphone built into the lid of the laptop, and the iMac models also sport a built-in mike. The Input drop-down below this will list the possible inputs that are available using the Source. If the Source drop-down is set for Built-in Audio Controller, then the available Input choices will be variously Internal Microphone (for built-in mikes as in the PowerBook) and Line In (if such an input is available, such as a built-in mike input).

DV Audio refers to a DV device potentially connected to your Firewire port. This will show up regardless of whether there is actually a Firewire device connected or not. However, if there is no such device connected, when you select it in the Source drop-down menu, you will receive a message stating that it is missing. Don't engage this option unless your DV camera or deck is connected and turned on, not in VTR mode as is normal but in record mode. In addition, remember that you need to set Final Cut Express to Real-Time and not Firewire in the View>Video drop-down menu (see Figure 6-11). Because the Firewire cannot pass video or audio in both directions at once, you have to disable Final Cut Express's Firewire output so that the voice-over audio can be captured by the Voice Over tool.

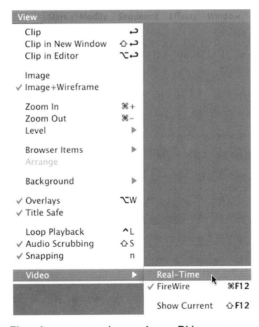

Figure 6-11   Disable Firewire output when using a DV camera as a mike

Capturing voice-over audio through your camera or deck is both better and worse than capturing through the Built-in Audio Controller. It is better than the Built-in Audio Controller because its sample rate can be set at 48 K, higher than the 44.1 K limit of the built-in sound card. In addition, the native 48 K that is brought in from the camera will exactly match the sample rate of your sequence, unlike the 44.1 K clips brought in from the built-in sound card. On the other hand, it is worse because on-camera mikes are some of the worst sounding mikes on the planet. They tend to pick up more noise than true mikes, and because they are attached to a bulky camera, cannot be easily positioned for the best possible sound recordings. In general, this will work in a pinch, but if you really care about the quality, you won't use either of these first two Sources.

Rather, look into the large number of USB audio interfaces that have saturated the market in the last two years. USB audio capture devices are uniformly inexpensive, have reasonably reliable standardized drivers built for Mac OSX, and generally have quite good recording capability. Most feature at least 48 K audio sampling and the ability to get a lot farther away from your loud, noisy, buzzing computer than the Built-in and Firewire Inputs would. If you are going to do this regularly, it's worth looking into.

At the bottom of the Voice Over box, you will see a section labeled Headphones. It is strongly advised that you monitor your voice-over delivery through headphones. As you will see when you begin to record your voice-over, Final Cut Express lets you hear the audio tracks already present on the sequence that your voice-over will accompany when you are finished. In addition, it gives a countdown, a series of beeps that let you know when to start talking and when you should stop. If you let these sounds come through the Macintosh built-in speaker, they will bleed over into your recorded voice-over track. You can adjust the level of audio feeding into your headphones here; it will not affect the recording at all. You can also disable the beeping cues, although this is a pretty bad idea, since you'll be losing the ability to easily tell when you should start your delivery.

Setting the Offset

One important item you should initially set up when you start using a new audio input is the offset. This is going to be different for the various audio inputs available to you, so you need to check whenever you start using a new input. The offset is the delay caused by the various electronic and digital pathways that the audio must take before it is finally recorded by Final Cut Express. USB, DV Audio, and the internal sound card all have different delays, so you need to run a quick test with whichever method you are using.

On an empty sequence, navigate to the 10th second by typing in the number "1000" and hitting Enter. Then hit the I key to create an In point. Type the number "2000" and hit Enter to navigate to the 20th second. There, hit the O key to enter an Out point. Now, hold the recording microphone up to the headphone speaker and hit the Record button in the top left corner of the window. You will be letting the Voice Over tool record its own cue beeps.

Continue holding the microphone to the headphone speaker until the voice-over recording has completed. After a moment, the newly recorded track will appear on the sequence Timeline. Use the Command-Option-W keyboard shortcut to enable waveform previews on the sequence (unless you already had them enabled). Use the Up and Down Arrow keys to navigate to the end of the voice-over clip. Use the Command-+ keyboard shortcut to zoom in on the sequence until you are seeing increments that are individual frames.

Make sure that your playhead is on the frame "00:00:20:00" and then count the number of frames after the frame number that the last beep's waveform ends with. The number-of-frames difference here is the correct number to use in the Offset drop-down tab in the Voice Over tab (see Figure 6-12). After you set this, do another quick test run to

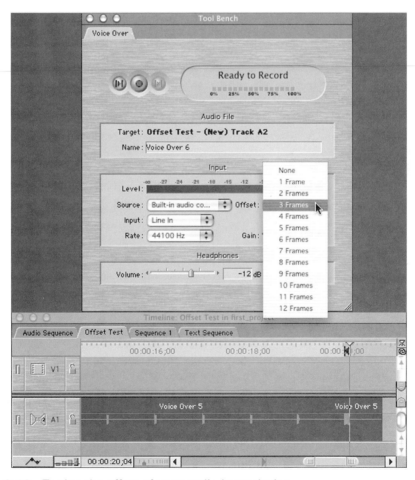

Figure 6-12 Testing the offset of your audio input device

make sure that this was the correct offset. After you get it set, you can be sure that your delivery will be right in sync with the video you are doing a voice-over for. Apple states that USB audio input devices tend to have an offset of one frame, while DV cameras and other Firewire input devices may have offsets of up to three frames. Make sure to check the offset if you are using one of these options.

The Rest of the Voice Over Window

The buttons at the top (see Figure 6-12) are important for the operation of the Voice Over tool. The one farthest to the left is like a run-through. When you hit it, Voice Over tool will run through the exact range of frames included in the In to Out points. If you have not set an In to Out point range, it will use the current position of the playhead as the In point and the last frame of the sequence as the Out point. Clearly, it's a good idea to limit your range of frames to just what you want to cover.

We have already used the red Record button to test the offset of our mike and input device. Next to it, on the right, is the Discard button. This button is only available just after you have completed a *take*, or voice-over recording. If you want to immediately toss the last attempt, you can hit this button. A warning will come up telling you that this is an irreversible act. And it is. The take will be wiped from the disk, so make sure you don't want to keep it. To the right of this is the progress meter. In this box, you will receive messages telling you how much longer you have, as well as a percentage meter informing you how much time is left during the voice-over take.

Underneath this is the Audio File section. This box informs you of the currently set target track where the voice-over clip will be sent. The Name text field underneath the Target label is for assigning a name that will be applied to the voice-over clip to be created in the sequence. If you don't enter a name, the Voice Over tool will use the last name that was assigned plus a number.

Finally, in the Input section, in addition to the Source and Input tabs, there is a level meter so that you can detect any clipping in the recording you are making. If you see clipping, first make sure you are not speaking too close to the mike! Many mikes are very sensitive, and you need to add a little distance in order to get a good recording. If the levels are still too high, you might drop the Gain control somewhat and see if the results are more successful. Finally, look at the Rate tab and make sure you have selected the highest sample rate available, since some devices can use several different ones. If you have options, 48 K is the preferred sample rate, since this will match the rate we are using in the sequence.

Using the Voice Over Tool

To put the Voice Over tool to work is very simple. First, you need to set the range of frames you want to record the voice-over on. Find the frame where you want to start your delivery in the sequence, and hit the I key to insert an In point. Navigate up to the frame where you want the voice-over to end, and set an Out point (see Figure 6-13). Unless the

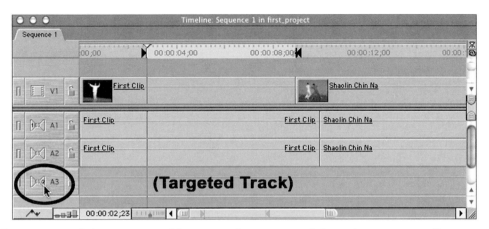

Figure 6-13 Select a range of frames and target a track for voice-over recording

delivery must be in one unbroken piece, consider breaking the range up and doing several individual voice-overs.

Once you have set the In and Out points, take a moment to figure out where the voice-over clip should be sent. It is not critical to specify this. Final Cut Express will never record a voice-over into a track where there is already a clip present. If a clip is in the way, Final Cut Express will create a new track for the voice-over and bump the tracks already containing clips down into new tracks. No audio sync will be threatened. But it's a good idea to organize and plan ahead. In general, for organizational purposes, you should dedicate a couple of tracks out of the way of your normal audio tracks that are linked to your video tracks.

The rule is that Final Cut Express will always use the second yellow target track. This is not Audio Track 2 necessarily; this refers to the yellow target track indicator. If, for instance, you have set Audio Track 5 as the second yellow target track, the Voice Over tool will select Audio Track 5 as the target track for the voice-over clip. If there is currently a clip in the target track, the Voice Over tool will select the next track down. If there is also a clip in that track, the Voice Over tool will leave the target set for the track but will bump these tracks down a step out of the way.

To begin the voice-over recording, put on your headphones and hit the red Record button. You will immediately hear a countdown start beeping. It will stop a few seconds before the frame you wanted to start your delivery on. In the background, Final Cut Express starts recording a few seconds before you indicated you wanted it to in case you begin a little early, so that you don't accidentally cut off the beginning of your first word. It also continues for two seconds after the last beep to make sure you aren't cut off.

The Canvas window will play through the frames of video that your voice-over is to accompany. In the progress meter, you will see the countdown to the end of the voice-over. If the voice-over range is more than 15 seconds long, at 15 seconds before the end of the voice-over you will be given a warning beep. Then, in the last 5 seconds of the voice-over range, you will hear five warning beeps, followed by a "finished" beep. If these beeps get in the way of a decent voice-over delivery, feel free to disable the "sound cues" check box in the headphone. Just be careful to monitor the progress meter so you know where you are in the recording session.

After the recording is finished, the clip will appear in the track. You can give the track a quick listen, immediately discard it, or temporarily mute it using the keyboard shortcut Control-B so that you can have another go at the voice-over without hearing the previous take. Immediately discarding the take can be a bad idea; usually, you will not get an entirely perfect take in one go. If you complete several takes, you may be able to piece the best parts of each take into the perfect voice-over; you'd be surprised to hear that this is frequently the way that professional voice-over tracks are cobbled together!

After you get the voice-over completed, you can eliminate the takes you don't want to use, and trim the ones you do want to use. You can move the good takes up into more accessible audio tracks. As a final note, you might want to be careful to back up these voice-over tracks. Unlike your video and audio tracks from your camera, these voice-over tracks have no timecode. If anything happens to your hard drives, you will have lost the voice-over tracks forever. Use the export techniques described in the next chapter to export the voice-over audio, and then burn them to CD-ROM or other backup media for safekeeping.

7 Getting Your Project Out of Final Cut Express

There are two basic ways of sending your material back out to the DV deck to record onto DV tape. We call such copies *master copies* because they come directly off of the editing station in the first-generation dub and are therefore of the highest quality. Actually, the term originated with analog recording systems and is less relevant for Firewire DV editors these days, because the master copy you record out through Firewire to DV tape can then be duplicated to other DV tapes with no generational loss. Thus, any digital copy or dub you make of the first generation can still be considered "first generation." But we still cling to the term, because it means that this is a finished copy that you want to archive and preserve, regardless of its lack of susceptibility to generation loss. It is your master copy.

Once you've finished editing your video production, you're ready to output the results to tape via the Firewire connection. Printing to video is incredibly easy. If you've been sending the video and audio out to Firewire all along for preview as you edit (by attaching an NTSC or PAL monitor to your camera/deck/device for Firewire viewing), you've already completed half the Print to Video tasks! Recording the material to tape is simply a matter of deciding how much you want to automate that process.

The first and simplest way to record your finished production out to Firewire and DV tape is to put the tape in the deck, park the playhead at the beginning of the sequence, hit record on the deck, and then hit the Spacebar to play in Final Cut Express. There is no real difference between this method of Firewire output, which you've been using all along to preview the edit on an NTSC or PAL video monitor, and the following method, Print to Video, aside from varying degrees of automation. This simpler method may prove best for editors using DV converter boxes or those who are using cameras and decks not yet supported or controlled by Final Cut Express.

If you intend to use the "playback from the Timeline" method, it is highly recommended that you use Mixdown Audio from the menu (see Figure 7-1), rendering the audio in your sequence. This will ensure that the tracks play back with no fluctuations in the data rate, regardless of how many tracks of audio you have included in the Timeline. If you have been using the Low setting for Audio Playback Quality in the Preferences, you will want to set this to High and perform the subsequent render if you get a red render line in the sequence. The Print to Video method always uses High settings anyway, but crash recording by simply playing your video directly from the sequence and hitting the record button on your DV deck relies on your present settings!

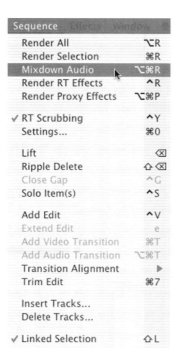

Figure 7-1 Be sure to use Mixdown Audio before crash recording to DV

Output to Firewire: Print to Video

The second method is for customizing your master copy that gets recorded to DV tape and is called Print to Video. This simple yet powerful tool allows you to define what goes to tape. You can define leader material such as color bars and tone, slate information, special countdowns, and the amount of black that occurs before your sequence begins playback and after it ends. You can specify whether the entire sequence or just a portion of it is played back. You can have Final Cut Express play the sequence back as a defined number of loops, inserting black space between each loop. You can also add trailer black onto the end of the recorded sequence so that your recorded product doesn't end on blank video, resulting in a timecode break. And you can keep tabs on exactly how long the final recorded piece will be, based on the amount of extra time you've added to include the features just described.

To start the process, make sure that your deck or camera is connected to the Macintosh's Firewire port and powered on. Select a sequence in the Project tab or the Timeline window that doesn't require rendering or has already been rendered. You can also set In and Out points in your sequence to use Print to Video for only a section of the sequence. Now go to the File drop-down menu and select Print to Video.

Customizing Print to Video

When you select Print to Video, a dialog box will appear named Print to Video (see Figure 7-2). This is the window that lets you customize the output. The top section of the box, labeled Leader, contains any elements that you may want to include prior to playback of the video in your master tape. You enable or disable each element using check boxes.

Color Bars and Audio Test Tone

The first Leader element is for Color Bars and Tone, essentially the same as the Bars and Tone clip we used at the beginning of this book to explore the various windows of the application. Here, Final Cut Express will automatically output color bars and audio test tone to tape right before your project. Color bars are the reference colors that are always included in any tape used in the broadcast industry or in any situation in which calibrating video monitors or decks is necessary. Once your video leaves the DV tape, it is no longer digital and exact. The color settings on almost all televisions and video monitors are different. Many times, these settings are so far apart that the color relationships in the video footage can be completely wrong. This means that although a color on your videotape is

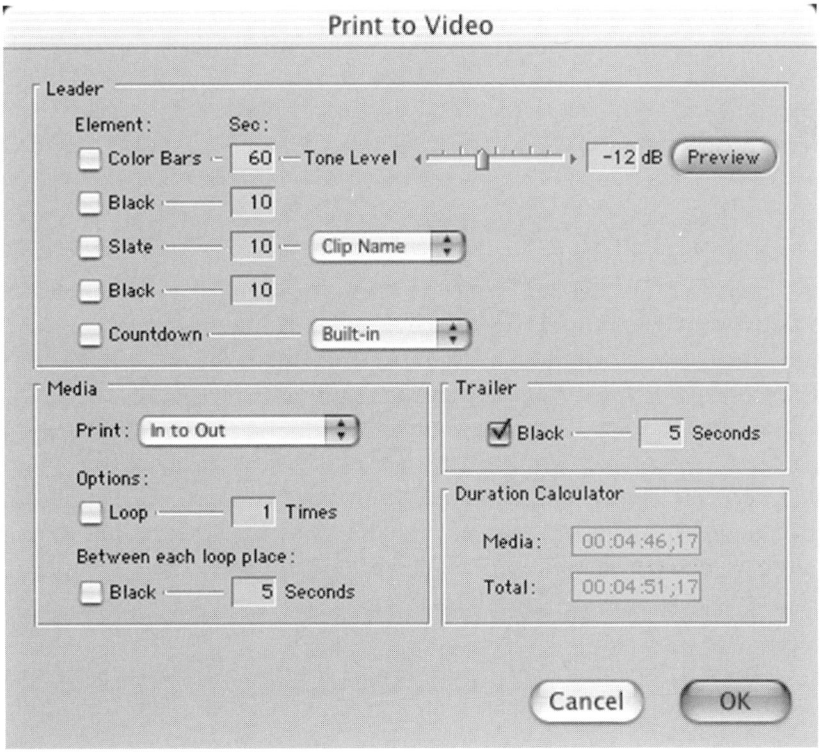

Figure 7-2 The Print to Video dialog box

blue, it may be closer to green or red than it should be on the video monitor that it is passed to.

Most video monitors are not *calibrated*, or set to display colors exactly as yours does. Thus, the color displayed as blue, for instance, on your monitor may appear as a different hue or saturation on someone else's. This is where calibration comes in. Color bars contain each of the colors necessary for establishing the correct color balance of a video monitor. Since the color bars are digital and are preconfigured to be correct, when piped through a video monitor they reveal how far off the monitor's color settings are. Using color bars, it's easy to see that a color is not being displayed correctly and that an adjustment must be made in the monitor's color and brightness controls.

Color bars are not only useful for calibrating your own video monitors, they are also necessary in the broadcast industry for making sure that your video fits within the broadcast specification for video. Such specifications are referred to as *broadcast legal*. When you send a tape to a television station, the video engineer passes the tape through two video devices—the *waveform monitor*, which measures the luma values, and the *vectorscope*, which measures chroma values—that check to make sure that the luma and chroma values of the video signal are not too extreme for broadcasting.

If luma and/or chroma values exceed this broadcast-legal specification, the engineer can then arbitrarily clip the chroma or luma to make it fit the specification, resulting in loss of fidelity to the original. A better alternative for the engineer is to adapt the luma or chroma more gently so that it fits within the specification. But the engineer cannot do this adaptation without a reference to what is "legal" on your tape. Using color bars and audio tone at the beginning of a tape, you can make changes based on the waveform monitor and vectorscope assessments, resulting in legal video that more closely resembles what you wanted it to look like.

Without reference color bars on your tape, you are always at the mercy of having your video displayed incorrectly wherever it is played back. Including them is always a good idea, even if you think you may never need them. Most stations require a minimum of 60 seconds of color bars prior to slate information on the tape. Remember that tape is always cheaper than embarrassingly bad-looking video, even if your family is the only group that will ever see it. The beauty of Firewire DV editing with Final Cut Express is that perfect quality is easy and cheap; the sad thing is that some folks are either too lazy or disinterested to take full advantage of that fact!

Final Cut Express also includes a reference audio tone with the color bars. In essence, the reference audio tone performs the same function as the color bars. The reference tone is a standard 1 KHz tone you've probably heard a thousand times when a television station finishes its programming for the night. This standard tone lets the engineer check to make sure that what your tape thinks is 1 KHz agrees with what the station's equipment thinks is 1 KHz. If the level of your reference audio tone is set at −12 dB, the engineer will know how to adjust your audio tracks when mixing them with other audio sources. It will be possible to boost or lower the signal with great precision so that your audio is reproduced faithfully.

Even if you never intend to have your material pass through a television station, the −12 dB reference tone allows you to set the volume on the monitor you are using at the optimum level before playback. Just play the tone back through the system it will be played on. When you hear the tone on the tape playback, set the volume on the video monitor or television accordingly, and you can be sure that the audio levels you worked with in your project will be in the same intended neighborhood when played back.

This system of matching audio levels between the recording side and the playback side using a reference tone is referred to as *gain staging*. It has far more important benefits than those listed earlier, especially with respect to avoiding distortion and clipping when the audio is rerecorded through analog or digital systems later on down the road. Just remember that anything you record without reference color bars and audio tone leaves you operating in the dark about the state of your video and audio. You will have no way of gauging how the product looks or sounds when reproduced on another video monitor or when rerecorded later.

Below Color Bars and Tone is an option is for black. This option is offered between each leader option for the purposes of making your leader smoother, more predictable, and easy to use later on. You can customize the amount of black in seconds here. Enable the Black check box and insert 10 seconds of black.

Slate

The third option is for a slate. Slates are simply text or graphic images that appear before your video piece plays back. They can give information about the format of the video and audio, the title of the piece, who produced it, what it is for, the reference bars and tone, and anything else you want to include. Often, production facilities have specific policies about what they require in the slates before a submitted piece of video. Make sure you know what should and should not be there, as well as how long the slate should appear.

There are three options for the slate. You can use Clip Name, the default setting, which includes just the name from your project being recorded. If you are recording a sequence, the name of the sequence will appear in the slate. If you are outputting only a single clip, its name will appear. Clip Name is the default setting because the other two choices, Text and File, require you to enter information or select a file, whereas Clip Name will just use the name of the object you are printing to video.

If you click the Slate drop-down bar and select Text, a small text box appears to the side of the bar (see Figure 7-3). You can type all the relevant information here, and it will appear as the slate during the Print to Video operation. This is the fastest way of getting information into the slate prior to recording, since it requires no external file preparation but is capable of including far more information than the simple clip name. Be careful when using this, though. It's easy to forget to change this text, and you will find yourself using slate information from a previous recording session if you do not change it, since the text remains the same until you disable or alter it.

Finally, the Slate drop-down bar gives you an option for File. If you choose this, a small folder icon appears next to the bar. Clicking the icon allows users to navigate to the file

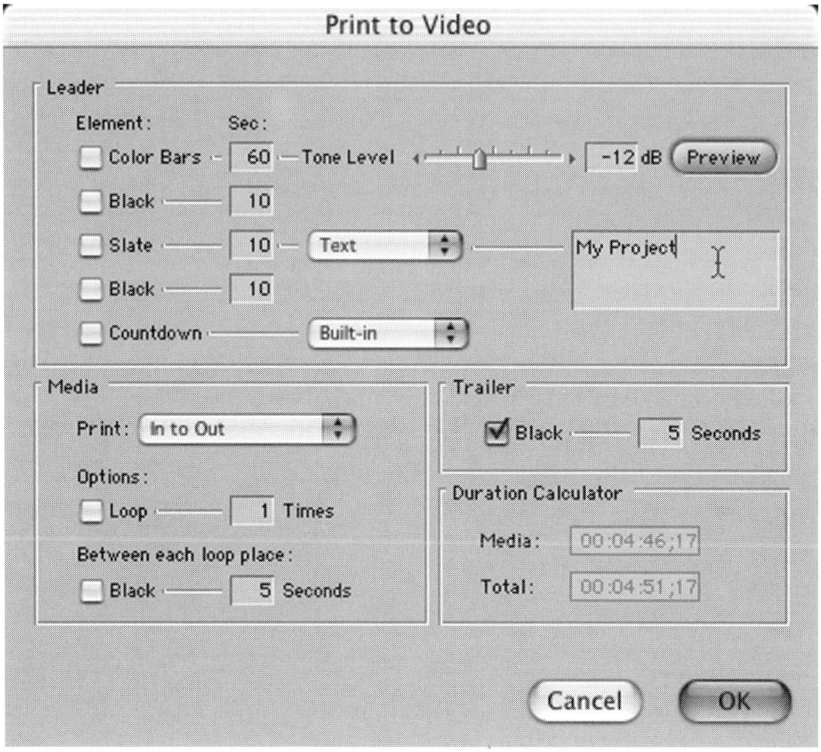

Figure 7-3   Using the Text option for the slate

they have created for a slate. This option is very useful if you wish to use a standardized company logo image or you have a specific design you want to use that cannot be achieved using the limited text box of the previous bar option.

The File option allows for the use of standard PICT files, Photoshop images, or any of a number of QuickTime still image file types. Remember that the nonsquare pixel rules are still in effect here as discussed earlier in the book and that you need to prepare image files such that they are displayed correctly without appearing squeezed or stretched.

If you choose to include a slate in the playback, there will be a slight render delay before playback for recording is possible. Since the slate will be played back as video out to Firewire, it must be rendered, just like any still image in your project. The length of the render delay depends on the duration of the slate as well as the type you use. The Clip Name and Text options result in very fast renders because they are using a standard black-and-white text format that processes and compresses very quickly. If you use the File option, the render may take longer because Final Cut Express converts and then processes and compresses the video. In either case, the render of still images in Final Cut Express is rather fast and is well worth the wait if you want the benefit of sharp-looking handmade graphics that say more about your product than just what its name is.

Enable a slate, set it for 10 seconds, and then choose Text from the bar. In the text box, type in "This is the Print to Video text slate." Below this is another optional Black field. Enable the Black check box and insert 10 seconds of black.

Countdown

The final option of the Leader options is for Countdown. This option also contains a drop-down bar for selecting the source of the countdown. There are two options: Built-in, which is a standard countdown file that comes prepackaged with Final Cut Express, and File, which gives you the ability to create your own custom countdown movies. The built-in countdown is precisely clocked for 10 seconds, in which each second is displayed with a clock wipe showing the passage of the second. When the countdown reaches second 2, there is a "pop" (a "2-pop," as it is called) that makes it easier for audio to be synced with the video should there ever be the need. Countdowns are imperative for precise editing situations and broadcast facilities that must cue up tapes with a great degree of accuracy.

You could also select your own customized countdown QuickTime Movie file by changing the drop-down bar to File and then navigating to the new countdown file. You can use Final Cut Express itself to create your custom countdown file; just create and export a suitable movie file and save it in a safe place for use when you need it. But remember that using a custom-made countdown file does not guarantee that it is accurate to a 10-second countdown. You have to arrange that yourself when you create the file. The Print to Video settings box will not constrain your file to fit a 10-second countdown. It will simply play the file you select. Enable the countdown and select Built-in from the bar.

Media

In the bottom left corner of the Print to Video window, there is a box labeled Media. This box lets you customize what gets sent to tape through the Firewire tube. Although the practice of sending media through Firewire is no different from simply playing from the Timeline, the Print to Video window allows us to automate the process and create seamless master tapes based on our individual needs. This can include looping the media, choosing to record only a specific portion of the sequence, or including pauses between the loop repetitions.

The first option is a drop-down bar named Print. The two choices on the bar are In to Out and Entire Media (see Figure 7-4). In to Out allows you to create a range in your sequence or clip defined by In and Out points on the sequence Timeline or Viewer window. Then choosing In to Out in the Print bar will restrict playback to those edit points. This can be very useful if you are only backing up sections of your sequence to tape and are not yet mastering the entire sequence.

Choosing Entire Media, on the other hand, plays the whole clip or sequence from the first frame to the last frame of the last clip. Although this is a good, quick way of printing your finished sequence, it can be messy as well. If you have forgotten about orphaned clips late in the sequence that are separated by gaps from the parts that you do want to record to tape, Entire Media will cause Final Cut Express to play all the way until it has played

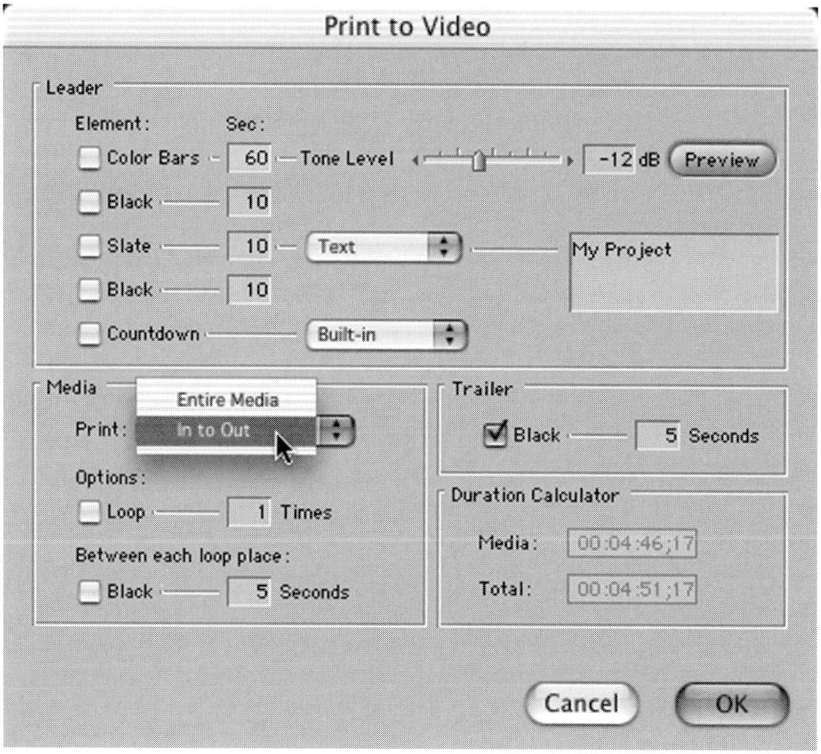

Figure 7-4 Print In to Out or Entire Media

these orphaned clips as well. The use of these two options is rather like the Voice Over tool in the previous chapter; if you set an In point to Out point range in your sequence and choose In to Out, Final Cut Express will apply Print to Video to only that range. If you choose Entire Media, Print to Video ignores any In and Out points and records the contents of the entire sequence from the first frame to the last.

Of course, none of this is really ever out of your control. You can always stop the Print to Video by stopping the recording at the deck and/or hitting Escape on the keyboard. Print to Video does not involve Device Control; you are the one who tells the deck to actually begin recording. The only difference between Print to Video and simply playing from the Timeline and hitting the record button on your deck is that Print to Video allows you to add all this useful leader and trailer content. Print to Video will not start or stop the recording on your deck.

Below the Print bar are two options. The first check box is for Loop, which is accompanied by a numerical field for establishing the number of looped repetitions. Beneath this is a check box for a black pause between repetitions and a field for determining the length of the pause. For the Media settings, select Entire Media from the bar, and then disable the Loop and Black between Loop check boxes.

Trailer

To the right of the Media box is the single option for Trailer. You may include black following the end of your recorded product, and you may define the length of this black trailer.

Do not be fooled by the seeming unimportance of this one box. It is very important that you insert a black trailer at the end of your recording. Always tack on at least 30 seconds of recorded black trailer at the end of your program. At the end of the Print to Video, the Firewire output will switch from the Print to Video back to displaying whatever frame the playhead was parked on when Print to Video began. Thus at the end of your emotionally touching video, the recording could instantly switch to a video frame currently sitting in the Viewer window that shows your crazy uncle doing something embarrassing.

This is no big deal, and you could certainly just park the playhead over a black area of the sequence before printing to tape, but it is much better to get into the habit of manually including black frames at the end of your productions. A more important reason for including this black trailer is that if you do not add some sort of recorded material after your piece, the timecode on your tape may end up suffering from a timecode break. Remember that when we captured video, we had to be very careful about capturing around timecode breaks. They could be just as bad or worse for you on your master tape. But if you always record 30 seconds of black at the end of your Print to Video, you will always have some video at the end of your piece to tag the next recording onto, therefore avoiding any possibility of timecode breaks. For the Trailer settings, enable Black and enter 30 seconds into the numerical field.

Duration Calculator

Finally, the box underneath Trailer is the Duration Calculator. The two timecode fields refer to Media (the length of the actual sequence or clip) and Total, which is the sum amount, down to the frame, of all the leader, media, and trailer footage, including any looping of the media. This is just a short idiot check to make sure that you have enough recording space on the tape for the duration that you have prepared to print to tape. It will also keep you from accidentally looping or including far too many seconds of leader if you make a mistake entering those parameters.

Your Duration Calculator should show the length of your sequence in the Media field and that same amount plus 2 minutes and 20 seconds in the Total field, that being the sum of the leader and trailer features you have tacked on to the piece.

Print to Tape

Once these settings are correct, hit the OK button to begin rendering the slate and the countdown. Since the built-in countdown is not a still image, it takes a bit longer to render. While the render process is completing, cue up a DV tape in the deck, or if you are using an A/D converter box or other pass-through device, prepare whatever deck you are using to record.

When the render process is completed, you will be greeted by a message box reading, "Start the video recorder now and click OK to begin playback" (see Figure 7-5). This is your cue to manually begin recording on the deck or camera. Let the tape record for at least 8 seconds of pre-roll, and then click OK. The video will start feeding down the Firewire tube, showing you the leader, your product and finally the trailer black footage. Near the end of the trailer black, press "stop" on your deck, and you will have completed your first mastering-to-tape process. Remember that you can stop the process at any time if you realize that you have made a mistake. Pressing the Escape key always aborts Capture or Print to Video functions immediately.

Exporting

You don't have to restrict yourself to printing to tape. Although DV is a fantastic way to make video for full-frame, full-screen viewing, you can also use the Export function to produce QuickTime Movie files for use in Web, CD-ROM, DVD, and many other functions. To explore all the possible variations of exporting is far beyond the scope of this book, but stepping through several of the more important options should get you through the initial stage and give you the tools for further experimentation.

There are two primary purposes for exporting media from Final Cut Express: (1) to create media files optimized for such specific purposes as the Web, CD-ROM, or DVD development and (2) to create media files that are unchanged from the source for external manipulation in another digital application, such as iDVD, Adobe After Effects, Pinnacle Commotion, or Discreet Combustion. Each of these two purposes requires a different strategy, and, predictably, Final Cut Express has developed a convenient workflow for dealing with each option.

Export for Distribution: Optimizing the QuickTime Movie

The first option we will discuss is exporting to optimize a media file for use in specialized distribution. The most common use for this is to create multimedia files for use in Web, CD-ROM, or DVD distribution. In this instance, we are actually creating a new media file that contains the content of the media we are exporting from Final Cut Express but using different parameters to allow it to function elsewhere.

There is much you can change about a file while exporting it. Depending on the codec (Apple DV, MPEG-4, Animation, MPEG-2, etc.), the frame size, aspect ratio, and frame rate, you can change the media to suit your needs specifically. Which option you choose when exporting will determine how you can manipulate the media as you export it as a file. But to export the file as we want it, we need to first specify the file format, which will determine how the media will be exported into the new file.

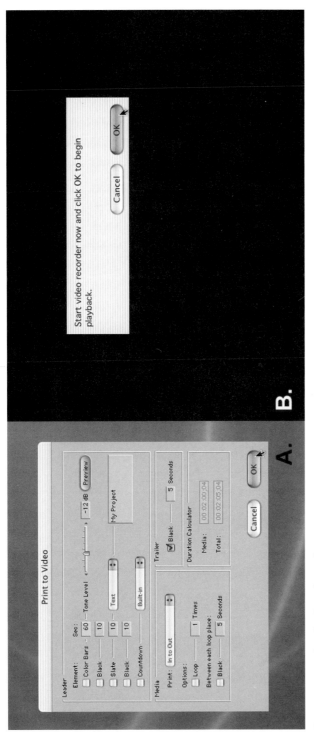

Figure 7-5 Beginning the print-to-tape process

Choosing the File Format

Select a clip that you want to export. Make sure the Viewer is active and the clip is loaded into it. For this exercise, we are exporting a single clip, although you could also set In and Out points in the sequence and export as an In to Out range. Next go to the File drop-down menu and select Export. When the submenu pops up, you will see the two Export options: Final Cut Movie and QuickTime.

For this first exercise, select QuickTime. An Export dialog box will pop up asking you to specify the settings for the QuickTime Movie (see Figure 7-6). Remember that QuickTime is an engine, not a specific file type. Just as a skyscraper and an outhouse are both buildings, there is a world of difference between the two. There are many variations between the different types of QuickTime export possibilities.

Underneath the Save As field and the Where (file location) box, locate the Format option drop-down bar. The options on the list have their specific purposes, and independently purchased codecs can add even more flexibility, such as the Sorenson set and DVD Studio Pro's codec, which gives the ability to export MPEG-2s suitable for advanced DVD authoring. The formats we want to work with in the first exercise are QuickTime Movie and MPEG-4. If you are looking to export video for use in iDVD, we will be using another option later in the chapter that is more suitable for that job. For Web or CD-ROM video, we will take advantage of the special features of QuickTime.

Underneath the Format bar is a Use bar with Export presets for the format you've chosen, but it is rarely a good idea to settle for presets where you have the option of customizing the file manually to match your specific purpose.

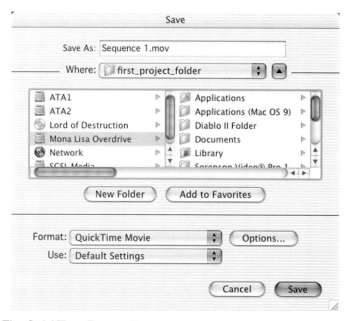

Figure 7-6 The QuickTime Export dialog box

Choosing and Setting the Compression

The main issue at stake for creating media files for Web and multimedia functions is to keep the data rate low. The data rate is the amount of data that your Macintosh must process per second to show every frame of video correctly. For the DV codec we are using in Final Cut Express, the data rate is a steady 3.6 MB per second. Unfortunately for users viewing QuickTime Movies from the Web and CD-ROMs, the data rates shouldn't exceed a maximum of 128 KB per second, and for most low-bandwidth Web surfers, the data rate should be even lower. This is far below the current data rate of the DV media in our project, so we need to optimize the file as we export it, simultaneously dropping the data rate and creating a separate file for use elsewhere.

From the discussions in Appendix A about codecs, we know that there are several issues involved in lowering the data rate of a media file. The initial issue is the codec we choose to utilize for the video. We know that the codec determines not only how much data is included about each frame of video but other factors, such as the size of the frame and its aspect ratio.

For instance, the DV codec we use for Firewire DV requires that the frame size be exactly 720×480 pixels for NTSC and 720×576 pixels for PAL. It also requires that the frame rate be a standard 29.97 and 25 frames per second, respectively. This means that the data rate cannot dip below 3.6 MB per second and still account for all those pixels.

Other codecs are more flexible in this regard. Most software codecs will support different frame sizes and frame rates, and the data rates will adjust lower accordingly. There are a host of other factors for each codec as to how it trades off image quality and size for data rate, so there is always a particular codec that is best suited for the job of getting the data rate lower. In addition, it must be remembered that the same codec must live on the machine that exports the file and the machine expected to play the video file back. So selecting the proper codec must involve a little soul-searching as to what the file needs to do and where it needs to go.

For this exercise, we will use two common multimedia codecs: Sorenson 3 and MPEG-4. These codecs are cross-platform, meaning that they are equally functional on both PC and Macintosh systems. Sorenson is fairly flexible at offering different frame sizes and frame rates, and delivers very small data rates, enabling widespread use in Web and multimedia applications, though it is not quite as good as MPEG4 at getting great images for such low data rates. MPEG-4 is a new cross-platform standard that is becoming popular but is not yet in widespread use. Its quality is staggering, though, in view of how successful it is at delivering beautiful quality at very low data rates. We will use both to export a file suitable for multimedia distribution.

Select QuickTime Movie from the Format list, and then look for the Options button in the dialog box. After hitting the Option button, you will be presented with a dialog box that lets you optimize each facet of the soon-to-be-exported Movie file. At the top is the Video section. The default compressor, or codec, is Video. Beware—Video is the name of a codec in the list, not just a general title! You need to change this. Since we want to use Sorenson 3, click the Settings button. You will be presented with the Compression Settings

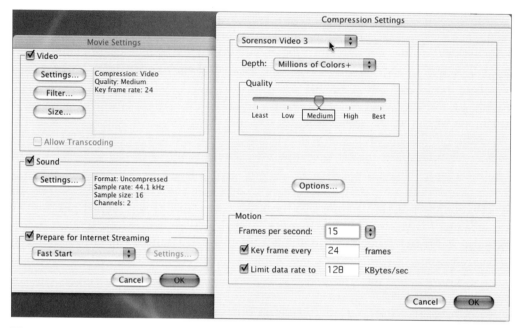

Figure 7-7   The Compression Settings dialog box

dialog box (see Figure 7-7). Click the compressor drop-down bar and select Sorenson Video 3 from the list. When you do, the options for the codec will appear below the bar.

First, since we want to shrink the data rate enormously, enter 15 in the Frames Per Second (frame rate) field or select 15 from the frame-rate selection bar. Although this means the codec will throw away many frames from the video file, 15 frames per second is still enough to give a pretty good illusion of the moving image, and it will shrink the size of the exported file radically, eliminating over half the visual data at one go.

The other two settings involve the way that the codec will operate on the video frames and determine which data is relevant and which can be thrown away. The two methods are referred to as *spatial* and *temporal compression*. Some codecs use one method, some use the other, and still others use both as a means of eliminating excess data from video frames.

Quality, or Spatial Compression

The Quality slider represents the amount of spatial compression you are applying to the file. Spatial compression looks at each frame of video and throws out a certain amount of detail in order to achieve a specific amount of data reduction in the frame. The Quality slider does no comparisons between groups of frames for important or recurrent detail; it just evenly lowers the detail quality for each frame a certain amount based on how low you set the slider. Set the Quality slider at Medium, which will cut the data rate radically without losing too much detail.

Keyframe Every, or Temporal Compression

The next setting is called Keyframe Every and represents the temporal compression technique. This keyframing is not to be confused with the keyframing we worked with in the sequence and Canvas window, although they do approach their separate tasks from the same universal idea of the amount of change between two frames. Temporal compression sets a keyframe at an interval established by the value you insert in the box. Each keyframe frame is compressed only using your setting for Quality, or spatial compression.

However, all the frames occurring between the two keyframes, called *interframes*, are compared with the initial keyframe. Any differences between the interframes and the keyframe are retained, whereas any similar pixels are discarded, thus further lowering the amount of data in the frame. If your video contains areas of the frame that do not change at all over time, such as static backgrounds around talking heads, much of that data can be thrown out without affecting the image quality of the interframe at all. The result is that the data rate shrinks dramatically as the amount of data in each interframe is lowered, while the image quality isn't affected very much.

Of course, this compression type is effective only if you do not have a lot of changing imagery in the video footage for the keyframes to keep track of. If you establish keyframes every 90 frames, this means that major changes in footage over roughly 3 seconds will not be tracked. If your keyframes are too far apart, a lot of important movement could be discarded as the interframes get farther away from the keyframe. As the distance between keyframes increases, the image quality drops.

The option of entering a lower number in the Keyframe Every setting, thus decreasing the distance between the keyframes and making them closer together, results in higher-quality interframes. Unfortunately, it also defeats the purpose of the keyframing temporal compression, since the more keyframes you have, the fewer the frames that are processed as interframes and compressed.

The key, of course, is to shoot and select your video with an eye toward the compression issues you'll encounter later. If you are going to compress video for the Web, make sure to get rock-steady tripod shots, and don't allow excessive camera or subject movement. Other codecs, such as Cinepak, offer different mathematical procedures for the compression, but the parameters for codecs are largely limited to spatial and temporal compression.

Leave the Keyframe Every setting at the default value of 24 frames. The final setting in the Compression Settings box is Limit Data Rate To. This lets you set a ceiling for the data rates, just in case your compression settings are not sufficient to bring the overall data rate down. Set the data rate ceiling at 128 KB per second, a data rate ceiling for slower CD-ROM drives and faster DSL/cable modem connections. Click OK and return to the Options box.

Other Factors: Frame size, Audio, and More

Now that we have set the compression, the next setting is Filter, which would allow us to apply effects filters directly to the clip as it is exported. In most cases, you will not want to apply such filters; it's far better to apply such image manipulation in Final Cut Express as you edit, and then export it directly. The next button, Size, will be necessary to visit, though. Because the video file is likely to be viewed on a computer screen, it is not necessary to stick religiously to the large 720×480 frame size our video currently uses. Cutting the size of the video frames will cut the data rate enormously, since fewer actual pixels will be included in each frame of video.

Click the Size button, and you will enter a dialog box labeled Export Size Settings (see Figure 7-8). The two check box options are for Use Current Size and Use Custom Size. Click the dot next to Use Custom Size, and the Width and Height fields will appear. You can resize according to whim, which may result in a stretching of the video frame. To choose a new frame size, simply divide the starting dimension in halves or quarters, or however small you wish to shrink the frame.

Don't forget that the pixel shape, square or nonsquare, is determined by the codec in use. The DV codec your footage is originating from used nonsquare pixels, resulting in a 720×480 or 720×576 frame size. But the codecs you are likely to use with Web and CD-ROM exports will be in square pixels. Therefore, the half frame size for this export from DV to Sorenson would be from 720×480 to 320×240, that being half the frame size for the square pixel video file the Sorenson compressor generates. For the Size setting, select 320×240 pixels, and then hit OK to return to the Options box.

The next section to set is for audio. We do want to include audio with the file, but we definitely need to change the settings from the default uncompressed version. Although audio data rates are smaller than video data rates, they can still be far higher than necessary for such uses as Web and CD-ROM, where every byte counts. Click the Settings button in the Sound section of the Options dialog box to enter the Sound Settings, or audio compressor, dialog box (see Figure 7-9).

In the Compressor bar, select the IMA 4:1. This is only one of a number of excellent audio compressors on the market as well as the ones freely supplied with the QuickTime compression system. Each audio compressor has a specific targeted function, such as optimizing the data rate for human voices, midrange music, and many other specific issues. Most audio compressors are expressly for use with the Web and multimedia. Because audio

Figure 7-8 The Export Size
Settings dialog box

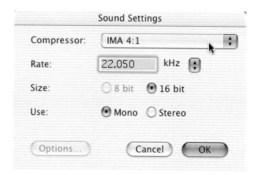

Figure 7-9 The Sound Settings dialog box

data rates are generally so low, compared with DV video, we never compress audio there. But for streaming video and other Web and multimedia work, compressing audio is just as integral a process as compressing video.

Setting the sample rate lower, to 22.050 KHz, will also contribute to a lower data rate. Although 22.05 KHz would be considered unacceptable for inclusion in the DV video we are editing, it is more than enough for low-bandwidth options. With the IMA 4:1 codec, the bit rate is fixed at 16, while you can choose between a stereo or mono file. Select Mono and hit OK to return to the Options box.

The last option in the box is for Fast Start. Fast Start refers to file coding that can be inserted in the exported QuickTime file to facilitate Internet streaming functionality. If your QuickTime Movies are to be sent to a server for streaming download, contact the administrator of the server and find out how the Fast Start settings need to be optimized for use. If you have no plans for streaming the video file, you can safely disable the feature.

Hit OK to return to the QuickTime Movie box, check your settings, and then click OK again to return to the Export dialog box. Now all that remains is to navigate the Save location to a suitable place. This will depend on your exported file. If the QuickTime file were of a high data rate and comparable in size and compression to the DV files you edit with in Final Cut Express, you'd want to save the file to a dedicated media drive just as if it were a captured clip. If, on the other hand, the file had a very low data rate for use on the Web, like the export we are working with here, saving it to the Desktop and playing from there would do no harm to your system. Since our exported QuickTime Movie will be heavily compressed with a very low data rate, we will save it to the Desktop.

Navigate the Save location to the Desktop by clicking the Where tab and choosing Desktop. Name the file, using the .mov suffix in case any of your PC pals want to access it, and then click Save. Final Cut Express will begin rendering out your QuickTime file. Depending on the amount of processing and the codec you use, the render can be very short or very long. Once the render process is complete, you can double-click the exported file on the Desktop to view it in the QuickTime Movie Player application already installed in your Macintosh with the operating system.

MPEG-4, MPEG-2, and You

Before we move on, it might be a good idea to address a couple of formats that are likely to be the new standard in compression of video for distribution on the Web as well as for viewing on a television screen. These are a set of compression formats referred to as MPEG. There are various types of MPEG formats, each relating to a particular type of media and distribution format. MPEG generally offers such flexibility and quality at such low data rates that it is a shoo-in to be the most popular format for some time to come.

But the most amazing feature of MPEG is that it is a standard rather than a single proprietary child of one corporate parent. In other words, no company owns MPEG; MPEG specifications (or what an MPEG must be able to do) are developed by a consortium of industry professionals, who then develop their own versions of MPEG products. This assures the consumer that Company A's MPEG-compressed files will play back on Company B's player device. No one company can hold the standard hostage, since no one company "owns" MPEG.

Some of the MPEG formats are already in widespread use, though working in the background. The MP3 audio format is part of the MPEG system. Its name is somewhat misleading; it is not MPEG-3 but rather MPEG-1 Layer 3, hence the short term MP3. Although it was developed as a complement to an MPEG video format, its audio compression quality was so excellent that it has come to be almost universal in the function of music compression and distribution.

Of course, the other widespread use of MPEG is MPEG-2, the video file format used in DVDs. This special format offers exceptional quality at incredibly low data rates. If you purchased your Macintosh with a Superdrive DVD-R burner, you would be able to create DVDs playable in a desktop unit using either the iDVD application that comes free with the Superdrive burner and contains its own compressor, or with the much more flexible (and expensive) DVD Studio Pro application. DVD Studio Pro actually installs a special codec option in the QuickTime Export format options to allow you to choose suitable compression settings for the MPEG-2s you will need to author in that application. iDVD, on the other hand, comes with its own automatic MPEG-2 encoder, so that you don't have to work with compression settings. To use it, you should export your video as a Final Cut Movie, to be covered in the next main section.

There is another MPEG format that you probably see every day without realizing it. Most cable and satellite television is transmitted using MPEG-compressed video. Its quality is just as high as, if not higher than in some cases, the previous analog video transmission systems that cable relied on in the past. But, being a digital system, it has the ability to carry even more options, such as extra channels and interactivity that were impossible a few short years ago. MPEG, as a system, is very much changing the way video and audio are distributed.

Before moving on, though, we should visit an MPEG format that promises to be the most successful format in history in terms of quality, compatibility, and flexibility: MPEG-4. Although it is possible that MPEG-4 will always remain a format for online Web distribution where data rates must stay very low, its fantastic quality and universal acceptance by every platform and system make it extremely attractive to deliverers of digital content.

It must be stated, though, that MPEG-4 is still in its infancy and is just beginning to stake its claim in the world of video distribution. Currently, in order to view MPEG-4 content using the Macintosh OS you need QuickTime 6 or later. Obviously, this will not be a problem on your Final Cut Express editing station, since QuickTime 6 or later is required for Final Cut Express to run. But you have to remember that not everyone out there is running the most current operating software on any platform. If you are going to encode content using a compression format, you want to take into account who will be accessing the content. If some of your viewers are using older systems and do not have access to MPEG-4-capable computers, you may need to offer the same content using older, more compatible, if less impressive-looking, compression formats.

Exporting with MPEG-4

That said, let's step through the process of exporting MPEG-4 QuickTime Movies. First, line up a clip for export using the same steps used earlier for the Sorenson-compressed export. When you get to the step of choosing the format in the QuickTime Export dialog box, click the Format list and choose MPEG-4. Then hit the Options button to configure the export.

The Options box offers a series of tabs that allow you to get specific about what sort of trade-offs you are making to lower the data rate. On the General tab, set the Video Track to Improved and the Size to 320×240 (see Figure 7-10).

MPEG-4 uses a series of "profiles" to give more flexibility with regard to quality, data rate, and streaming options when compressing, but not all MPEG-4 decoders can read all the profiles. In addition, if you select the largest frame sizes and higher frame rates, the

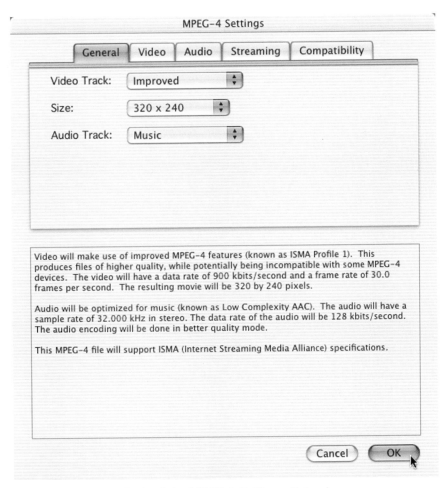

Figure 7-10 The General tab of the MPEG-4 Settings dialog box

computer that receives the file will also have to be able to decode them, and that might be a lot to ask from an older PC. With the free MPEG-4 compressor that comes with Quick-Time 6, the only audio options are Music and None. Obviously, we want audio here, so select Music. In the next couple of tabs we will optimize the settings for the best possible quality.

Click the Video tab (see Figure 7-11). The default data rate for the Basic video setting is 64 kilobits. Beware—this is kb, or kilobits, not KB, or kilobytes! There are 8 bits to the byte, so divide 64 kilobits by 8 to get only 8 KB. The average DSL or cable modem connection can get between 70 and 128 KB per second, so this gives us a lot more bandwidth and will allow us to get much better quality than the default setting. We'll set the bit rate for the worst case scenario of DSL/cable. Assuming the end user is getting a connection speed of 70 KB per second, this would give us a bit rate of around 560 kb per second. On

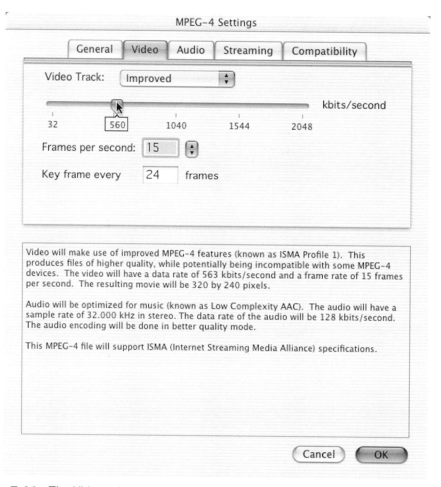

Figure 7-11   The Video tab

the Video tab, drag the slider up to a value of around 560. The frame rate should be set at 15 frames per second, and we will set the temporal, or Keyframe Every, to 24 frames as well for a starter.

Unfortunately, if you had set the initial video track profile for Basic rather than Improved (with Basic providing the widest compatibility for streaming), you would have discovered from reading the information about your settings in the box below the settings controls that bit rates in excess of 64 kb per second do not fit into the Basic profile that guarantees the widest compatibility among MPEG-4 players. In addition, the frame size of 320×240 would also have been invalid. Although the widest compatibility is nice, it doesn't give you much bandwidth to make good-looking video.

On the Audio tab (see Figure 7-12), leave the audio bit rate set for 128 kb and change the Channels setting to Mono. The only use for stereo would be if you had actually made

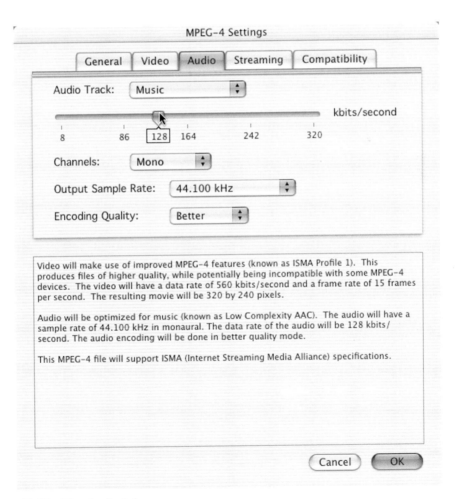

Figure 7-12   The Audio tab

interesting use of stereo in your project (such as sounds that are only present in one channel or the other, or music from a CD). If not, the stereo file is basically just two mono channels, which means you are using twice the data rate that you really need! When you change the setting to Mono, the lowest sample rate you will be able to achieve is 44.1 KHz. Lower sample rates will mean lower data rates, so select 44.1 KHz. Interestingly, if you choose Stereo for Channels, you can select 32 KHz, which is still an acceptable sample rate quality. Finally, set the Encoding Quality for Better, which is a decent trade-off between quality and bit rate.

You should leave the Streaming tab (see Figure 7-13) alone until you can get to your network administrator, who will inform you of any settings necessary to prepare your content for streaming. It must be said that streaming technology is a rapidly evolving area. At this point, many content providers still prefer the older reliable method of Progressive

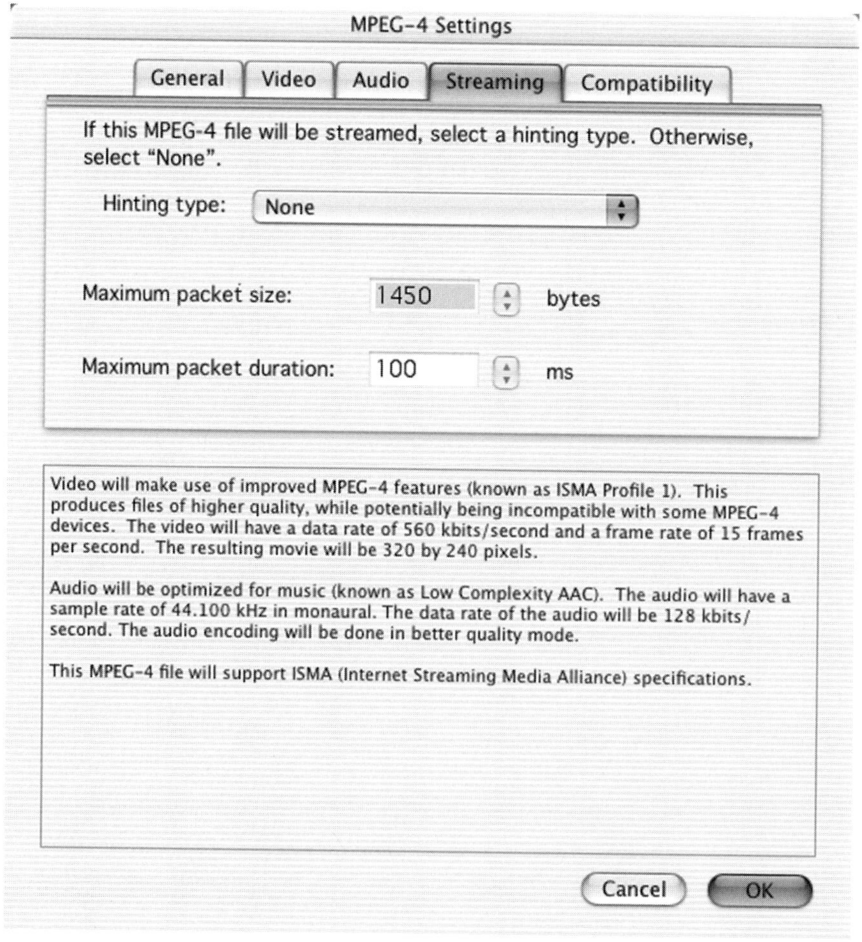

Figure 7-13 The Streaming tab

Download for the highest quality and reliable playback, as opposed to Realtime Streaming. Seek more information about your server and what you need to do if you want to implement this option.

Finally, on the Compatibility tab (see Figure 7-14), leave the compatibility profile drop-down set to ISMA. If we had chosen Basic earlier for compatibility and still chosen our high data rates, we would have needed to set this to None to avoid an invalid combination of settings. Because we set our data rate and frame size too high for compliance with the standards for ISMA streaming protocols, the MPEG-4 compressor compability would have to be set to None.

Hit the OK button to return to the QuickTime Export box, and then hit OK to begin the Export. Once it is complete, go to the Desktop and double-click the .mp4 file to start up QuickTime Player and watch your movie. Although the frame rate might

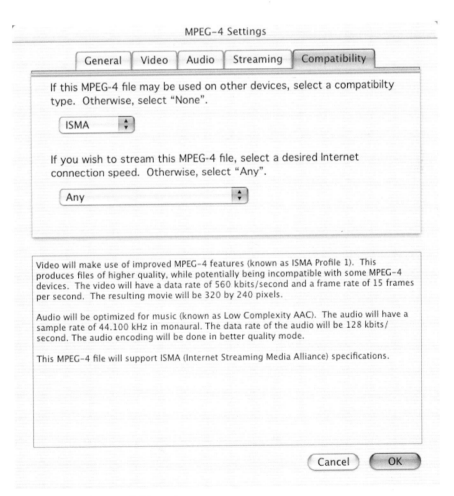

Figure 7-14 The Compatibility tab

be a little jumpy because you have reduced it to 15 frames per second, you should be pleasantly surprised by the quality, even in comparison with the Sorenson compressor we used earlier.

Export for Lossless Transfer—The Final Cut Movie: Self-contained vs. Reference Option

Although the previously described Export is much more common, there is another export method that is specially designed for postproduction purposes. Postproduction is a wide-ranging term that generally refers to anything done to a film or video after it has been shot. The issue for postproduction is definitely not reducing the data rate or the quality of the editing materials. Quite the opposite—there is a necessity to retain the highest level of quality and fidelity to the film or video while editing and manipulating it.

It is often necessary to pass sections of a clip or sequence out to be manipulated by another application. There are numerous applications, such as Adobe After Effects and Pinnacle System's Commotion Pro, that use specialized toolsets to further develop the same matting and keyframing techniques we worked with earlier in Chapter 5. Although Final Cut Express has a great set of compositing tools, professional postproduction often requires styling that only specialized applications can deliver.

Other applications, such as Discreet Cleaner, are more streamlined and flexible at batch processing compressed QuickTime Movies for Web and multimedia use. Although you could use the previous section's method for exporting compressed QuickTime Movies, many content producers opt for the different feature sets other applications offer for this activity.

As mentioned in the section on MPEG technology, many Final Cut Express editors will want to use the simple iDVD application to burn DVDs of their projects. Since iDVD uses an automatic encoder to produce the MPEG-2 files it needs to burn a DVD, you actually can't export your video into the proper MPEG-2 format manually. So you need to bring your clips and sequences out of Final Cut Express at the highest quality, without passing them through a compressor and lowering the data rate and image quality.

These are only a few of the many possible applications that can accept video files for further processing and manipulation. The material exported to these application needs to maintain the highest fidelity possible. Since the new application will be processing and manipulating the video files, it needs to receive video that is as close to the original as possible. And why shouldn't we be able to fulfill that requirement? We are working with digital media after all. Digital media does not have to lose generations of quality when copied. It should be no problem at all to maintain the highest fidelity to the original when we are exporting a copy for either preview or manipulation.

There is a complication in the premise that digital media cannot lose a generation when being copied, and it has to do with the fact that we are working with codecs, which selectively discard image information. Anytime Final Cut Express renders media, it applies the codec currently in use in your sequence presets. That means that when you render a section of a sequence, it is compressed using a codec, which in our case would be the Apple DV codec. Compression discards image data, and discarding image data lowers image integrity.

Before the reader begins to feel cheated or alarmed, consider that the second generation of compression with the Apple DV codec yields results of extremely high quality. Any rendering of effects that you complete on the sequence Timeline is likely to blend seamlessly with material that has never been rendered and recompressed, and it takes something of an expert to track the image degradation.

You also don't have to worry about second to third renders of the same material in a Final Cut Express sequence, because each successive render of a section within a sequence just rerenders the section, replacing the previous set of render files. Each render is considered a "first-generation" render. Rendering inside a Final Cut Express sequence, except in extreme cases of images that are very susceptible to compression artifacting, produces visually seamless results.

The problem we are addressing here results from the fact that the export we are proposing in this section is of material that needs to remain free of additional compression. If it is of the utmost importance that we work with the intact original image, we must make sure that the image is not recompressed upon export. The media will be exported, manipulated, and rendered in another application and then reimported into Final Cut Express for inclusion in the project.

If we use the previously described QuickTime export process, our clip will end up having passed through two sets of compression. The first will be compression applied as the QuickTime file is saved using a codec. Then it will likely be compressed a second time as it is rendered in the other application to which we exported the movie. Any time Final Cut Express creates media that does not already exist, it must render that media, and rendering with a codec requires compression.

There are two ways to overcome this problem. The first is fairly obvious: If you don't want to involve compression in the export, use a lossless codec that doesn't discard data! In Appendix A, we describe three codecs: Animation, Cinepak, and the Apple DV codec. For a couple of reasons that are explained there in painful detail, the Animation lossless codec is not acceptable for our uses; in particular, it involves a waste of time and drive space.

The media we want to export without compression already exists in our Scratch Disk folder. It is already digital, and it is already compressed. Why recompress digital media, when it is already sitting there on the media drive? Creating more copies of the same media on our media drives is a waste of space, particularly if the redundant copies are generated by a codec like the Animation codec that explodes the data rate tenfold.

Beyond this, we have already seen that rendering takes time. When you render, Final Cut Express has to analyze and process each frame. No matter how fast your Macintosh's processor is, that takes time. Decompressing the DV codec source material, then applying the lossless Animation codec, and saving it to disk is a process that will have you looking at the progress bar far longer than you would if you could simply access the relevant parts of the media file already sitting in your Scratch Disk folder.

What if you could simply produce the equivalent of a Final Cut Express clip that can function outside of Final Cut Express? A clip in a Final Cut Express project is simply a reference to the original media file back in your Scratch Disk folder. When you work with it in the Viewer or Canvas, you are simply telling Final Cut Express how you want to work with the media file being referenced by the clip, rather than working with the media itself. This is what makes nonlinear editing possible and what sets digital video editing apart from old linear analog tape editing.

What Is a Reference Movie and Why Use It?

Final Cut Express includes an export feature that is sometimes referred to as a *reference movie*. A Final Cut Express Movie is very similar to a QuickTime Movie; indeed, most applications will see it and treat it as such. But the Final Cut Express Movie offers an option that a standard QuickTime Movie export cannot: the choice between a self-contained and a referenced exported file.

In the QuickTime Movie export earlier in the chapter, we were creating what are called stand-alone or self-contained movies, since those movie files contain all the video frames in the file themselves. Remember that the reason we were trying to reduce the data rate was to make the file size smaller by reducing the amount of data in each frame. But a reference movie is very different. It does not contain any frames of the video in the file, but instead references the frames of video from the Final Cut Express project from which it was exported. It references media from the Scratch Disk just as a clip in a Final Cut Express project does.

A Final Cut Express Movie file that is not self-contained is treated like a normal Quick-Time Movie by any application that can access such files. But instead of being a self-contained file that has been processed by a codec, this movie acts just like a Final Cut Express clip and refers to the media files in the Scratch Disk folders. And because the exported movie may be from a range of clips in a sequence, it even accesses any render files that might have been created if you rendered an effect in the sequence.

Since a self-contained movie file is not being created, no rendering is required, and the reference file export is nearly instantaneous. No more waiting on progress bars. And because the file is merely a reference to the media in the Scratch Disk folder, the reference movie file actually takes up very little drive space—in most circumstances, less than a single megabyte. Thus this reference movie export function allows you to work with material that has not been recompressed with a codec, does not delay you with excessive render times, and takes up nearly zero drive space. This is clearly the best method to use if you want to take your media to another application, particularly iDVD and Discreet Cleaner. It will be seen that we can even include Chapter Markers in our Final Cut Movie for use in iDVD!

Special Limitations

That said, there are a few tweaks and special rules that apply. It's important to follow the correct process in generating the reference movie to make sure that you are benefiting from all that the feature has to offer. To create the Final Cut Express reference movie, first create a range of frames that you want to export in a sequence Timeline, using In and Out points. Make sure that the range of frames does not require rendering. If it does, render it before attempting to export. If you export material as a reference movie that requires rendering, Final Cut Express will render the material prior to creating the reference movie and then embed the render files in the reference movie itself, resulting in a render process that takes time but does not actually apply to the sequence material you are exporting. In addition, the size of the reference movie itself grows, because the render files are included rather than really being referenced. Always render your sequence before exporting a referenced Final Cut Movie.

Also, you must be very careful not to "orphan" your reference movie by accidentally eliminating or moving media files referenced by the movie. This means that you need to keep the reference movie on the same workstation that the media files for the project are on. Unlike a sequence in a Final Cut Express project, the reference movie is never updated after it is exported, so if you change anything about its media, it will lose its links and become worthless. This applies particularly to render files in your Final Cut Express project. If you make a change to a sequence that has been rendered, the new render files will not work with any previously created reference movie. This is not a step that can be undone, so proceed with caution when working with a project that you know has been used to create Final Cut reference movies.

The Export Final Cut Movie Dialog Box

Select a sequence and the range of frames using In to Out points. Then go to the File drop-down menu, select Export, and in the submenu, choose the top option, Final Cut Movie. When you do so, you will be presented with the Final Cut Movie Export dialog box (see Figure 7-15). You must configure this box correctly to achieve the goal of a true reference movie, since Final Cut Express will allow you great flexibility in generating an exported movie file.

At the top of the dialog box, you will find the familiar Save location tools. Because the reference movie is not a true media file, it is less imperative that you save it to your media drive. Give yourself an export folder on the Desktop and store your reference movie there. After you navigate to the appropriate Save location, name the file, making sure to specify in the file name that it is a reference movie—i.e., "xxx.ref.mov."

The setting Include bears a little discussion. A limitation of the reference movie is that only video files can be indexed; audio files are not indexed by a reference movie. If you leave the Include bar set at the default Audio and Video, the resulting reference movie will actually embed the audio tracks, just as it embeds render files that are not rendered prior to export. Selecting Video Only eliminates this problem, because only the video files will be included in the reference movie.

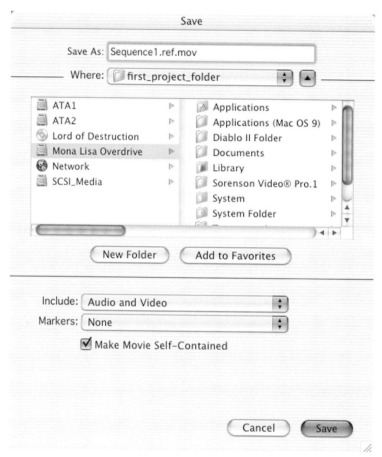

Figure 7-15   Final Cut Movie Export dialog box

If you need to include audio in the reference movie (for instance, if you are using this as an export for use in iDVD), do not hesitate to set Include to Audio and Video. Remember that audio data rates are very low, and the inclusion of the audio data in the index file will not radically increase the file size. Just remember that you may want to store such reference movies that include audio on your media drive, since they contain audio files that have to be accessed at the requisite high speeds of a true media file. For our exercise, set the Include bar at Video Only.

Underneath the Include bar is another drop-down tab, named Markers, which by default is set for None. In most cases this is suitable. But we should look at it for the options it offers to those looking to work with iDVD and other DVD authoring tools. Because Apple knew that many Final Cut Express editors would be using the Final Cut Movie option to move sequences between Final Cut Express and iDVD, they included the ability to insert

Chapter Markers in the sequence and then carry them out with the sequence in a Final Cut Movie straight to iDVD.

Where do the Chapter Markers come from? If you remember the discussion on capturing clips in Chapter 2, in the Capture window we had the option of inserting Markers that would stay with the captured clip once it was brought into the project. Although this Marker could not be seen on the video output to the DV camera or deck, we could use any notes we included in the Marker for reference purposes. Another use for Markers is to carry Chapter Markers from the sequence to iDVD. In the sequence, you simply hit the M key twice (the first time creates the Marker, and the second one opens up the Edit Marker dialog box so you can change its contents). One of the options in the Edit Marker dialog box (see Figure 7-16) is the Chapter Marker. When you insert a Chapter Markers (which appears in the Edit Marker text field as "⟨Chapter⟩"), it will be included in the Final Cut Movie export. Once the Movie is imported into iDVD, the Chapter Markers will be read and interpreted.

After this, there is a check box option that warrants special attention. This is the Make Movie Self-Contained box. If this box is enabled (the default setting), Final Cut Express will create a stand-alone movie file for the export. But this is inimical to our pursuit here, because we want to create a reference movie that simply indexes the original file. Creating a stand-alone file would be duplicating media that already exists. Deselect Make Movie Self-Contained to create the reference movie (see Figure 7-17). Click OK to save the file.

Unless you have chosen to include audio or you are making a self-contained stand-alone Final Cut Movie, the process should be nearly instantaneous. Hide Final Cut Express (by Option-clicking the Desktop or hitting Command-H), and locate the exported Final Cut Express Reference Movie. If you select the reference movie and hit Command-I, you will see that it is indeed quite small, compared with the same thing exported as a stand-alone QuickTime Movie of equal quality.

The icon used for Final Cut Movies is a variation on the Final Cut Express icon. If you double-click the Final Cut Express Movie icon, you will see that it opens the file up as a

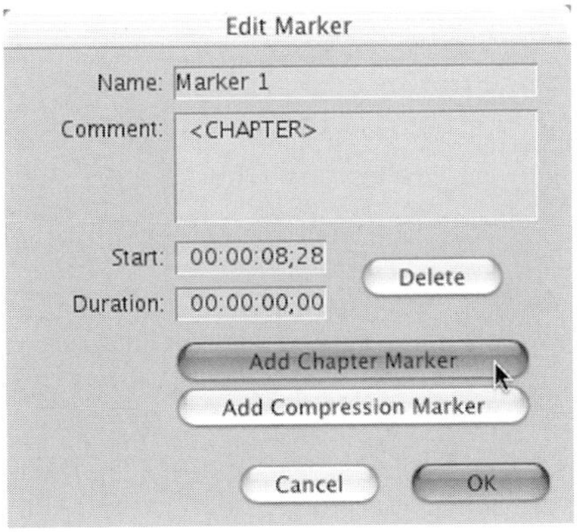

Figure 7-16 The Edit Marker dialog box

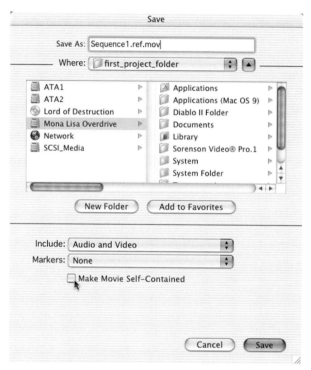

Figure 7-17 Deselecting the Make Movie Self-Contained check box

clip inside of Final Cut Express instead of opening the QuickTime Movie Player application that the QuickTime Movie file we exported earlier opened. This is because the file contains code establishing that it was created by Final Cut Express. This information is used by the Macintosh OS to decide which application to open when the file is double-clicked. Have no fear—applications that can use QuickTime Movie files, such as QuickTime Player, iDVD, and Adobe After Effects, will recognize the reference movie and utilize it just like a QuickTime Movie.

Appendix A
What Is Digital Video, Anyway?

How Video Works

To understand digital video, we have to know how digital video differs from analog video. Analog video is still the most common format used in television and consumer videotape recorders. Like film, video works by the rapid display of many still images, one after the other. This creates the illusion of real motion because the still images replace each other on the screen more quickly than your eye can register. In film, the rate of these images is 24 frames, or individual images, per second. NTSC (National Television Standards Commission) video, has a frame rate of 29.97 frames per second and is used in the United States, much of South America, and Japan. PAL (phase alternating line) video, has a frame rate of 25 frames per second and is used in most of Europe, China, and countries that were under European colonial control late into the 20th century. Standards in other countries vary between the two, based on the system of electricity in use (the US and Japan use 60 Hz, while Europe uses 50 Hz).

This concept of illusory motion is where the similarity between film and video ends. Film creates the illusion of motion by shining light through celluloid material to create a projected image on a flat reflective surface. Each frame is created on-screen as a result of light passing through the emulsion, or the material coating the celluloid film. Each frame is projected through the lens of a projector completely at once, top to bottom, side to side (see Figure A-1).

Video, on the other hand, is an indirect system of display. A video signal is an electrical wave that travels through a cable—say, from your VCR to a television. This electrical wave carries the visual information for each frame to your television. On receiving the wave, the television interprets this information and uses an electron gun to shoot a beam of electrons at the inside of the television screen. The electron beam charges up phosphors on the inside of the television screen, producing the glowing images you see on the front. It does this at the frame rate established by the video standard in use, 29.97 or 25 times per second for NTSC and PAL, respectively. The origin of the term *analog* comes from the fact that video's electrical waveform is an analogy, or corresponding likeness, of the original image.

The process of directing the electron beam to the television screen is called *scanning*. Instead of illuminating the entire screen at once as film does, the electron gun must draw thin horizontal lines, one after another, all the way down the screen. When the beam has

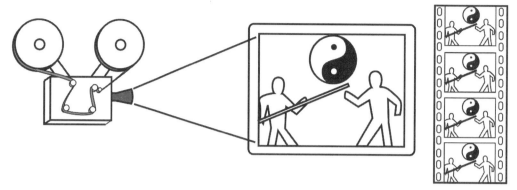

Figure A-1   A film projector displaying frames of film

crossed the video screen horizontally once, we say it has scanned one line. After it scans a single line, it moves to where the next line is to be drawn a little farther down the screen.

A single frame on an NTSC video screen is composed of 525 of these separately scanned horizontal lines, which we call the *vertical resolution*. When the scanning of 525 lines on the screen is complete, we say one frame of NTSC video has been scanned. Then the process begins again, repeating this action at the rate of 29.97 times per second for NTSC and 25 times per second for PAL, which is composed of 625 lines.

To make matters a little more confusing, a video frame is scanned in two sweeps, or two separate scans of the video frame. The two sweeps are referred to as fields. The electron gun in the television monitor does not go directly from the first scanned line to where the second one should be. Instead, it skips a line before it performs the horizontal scanning process again. While scanning a single frame, the electron gun scans all the odd-numbered lines first, and then on reaching the bottom of the screen, it returns to the top to scan all the remaining evenly numbered lines (see Figure A-2). It does this very quickly so that the scanning process is not detectable by the human eye.

This process is referred to as field interlacing, because the two separately scanned fields when viewed together form one interlaced frame. Although the precedence of one field being drawn before the other, or *field dominance*, can vary between digital video systems, for the moment it is enough to know that electricity is driving the video signal, that the electrical waveform for each field of the frame determines what you see on the screen, and that this scanning action occurs at the rate of the video standard in use in your area. For NTSC, there are 29.97 frames per second, each frame being composed of two separate fields, yielding a field rate of 59.94 fields per second. For PAL, there are 25 frames per second, each frame being composed of two separate fields, yielding a field rate of 50 fields per second.

Knowledgeable readers will recognize that this field rate corresponds to the system of electricity in use in the country in question. In electrical measurement, one hertz equals one cycle or wave per second. Countries like the United States and Japan, which have a

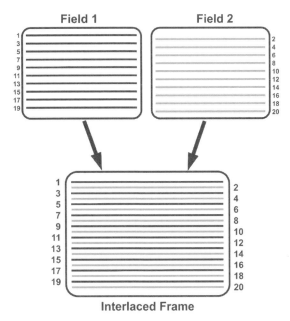

Figure A-2   Interlaced scanning lines on a television monitor

standard electrical current of 60 Hz, have a field rate of 59.94 times per second, while European countries, which use an electrical current of 50 Hz, use PAL, which has a field rate of 50 times per second.

Generation Loss and Digital Video

"Great," you say, "it works, and that's all I care about." What is the need for digital video if we have a perfectly good analog system? The answer lies in what is referred to as *generation loss*. Because the analog video signal is an electrical wave, it is a physical thing. It is composed of physical electrons that move up and down in waves that then travel through a cable, thus transmitting the necessary information to the video monitor so it can display images. The quality and integrity of the image you get is totally dependent on the quality and integrity of the electrical wave that is the video signal.

The problem is that every time the signal passes through a medium—for example, when it passes through a cable from your consumer VCR to your video monitor—the electrical wave changes a little, or a lot! The electrical wave that makes it to your television is never quite the same as the electrical wave that was magnetically stored on the videocassette and played back. The slight distortion in the wave from its transmission through the cable results in a change for the worse in the picture quality generated by the wave.

We call the decay of the electrical wave when it passes from medium to medium generation loss. Every time you make a copy of a videotape or even simply pass it through a cable, you lose a generation. After a few generations of passing between even the highest-quality analog equipment, the electrical wave will deteriorate until the quality of the video image and the audio is poor indeed.

Here digital video comes to the rescue. At some point during the recording process, the analog video electrical wave is converted into a sequence of binary numbers that can be stored as digital data, essentially no different from a word processing file. Unlike analog video, which is an electrical wave and is therefore subject to waveform deterioration, the digital file has only a numerical value, which never alters until we ourselves choose to change the numbers. The quality of the digital video data will remain intact regardless of how many times it is copied.

Think of it this way: The number one has the value of one. Copying the number one always results in an exact copy, because it is a value and not a physical thing. An electrical wave (or a zebra or a goldfish), on the other hand, can never be exactly copied, modern cloning processes notwithstanding. Some subtle difference will always be introduced in the copy of analog video, and those subtle differences turn up as signal noise, the evil result of generation loss. The digital copy, however, being numerical and immaterial, is theoretically never subject to such loss.

Another bonus of the digital video system is that the technology is remarkably plug-and-play, provided your digital video system is configured correctly. Broadcast-quality video editing prior to the advent of the new Firewire-based DV editing technology involved expensive and difficult-to-configure analog components that required users to have a relatively high degree of technical experience to run properly. You will find that Apple Final Cut Express software, the Apple Macintosh desktop computer, and a DV deck or camera constitute an inexpensive, elegant, and simple solution that produces quality results that a few years ago were possible only with an astronomically expensive solution.

Before we lose our heads in revolutionary hyperbole, it is important to note that we will not be completely free of analog devices for quite a while. All-digital DVD and HDTV technology is rapidly ascending, but most consumer televisions and VCRs are still analog video devices (as are your eyes!), and that situation is unlikely to change anytime soon. So chances are that your new Final Cut Express editing station will contain a mix of analog and digital video devices, since most of the people you will want to distribute your edited products to will be using analog devices as well.

Your television (or a dedicated NTSC or PAL video monitor, if you have one) and your VCR or DVD player are two of the analog devices that are still necessary; we will use them to monitor what we have edited and to distribute the final product to a world that does not yet widely own DV decks. VHS, though old as the hills, is still the predominant format for easy, cheap distribution of video content. We can also easily produce DVDs, but you will find that DVD players are also connected to your television through good old analog video cables.

The Macintosh desktop computer and the DV device (e.g., a DV deck or camera) will constitute the digital devices in your editing system. Between the Macintosh and the DV device, you will be able to capture and edit video without incurring generation loss. When

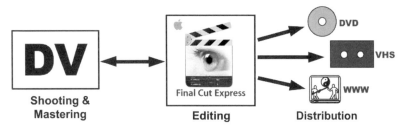

Figure A-3   Shooting, mastering, and distributing with Final Cut Express

you have finished editing, you will be able to output your edited material to a DV tape, which will keep a perfect digital copy always available for further work and for archiving. Provided you have the necessary hardware and software accessories, you will also be able to store your DV production on DVD discs both as data backup and as a disc playable in many common set-top DVD players. Finally, you will be able to pass video out from the DV device to analog videotape so that you can share your handiwork with the rest of the world (see Figure A-3).

Your DV device is the hardware center of your editing system. It is more than simply a record/playback unit for DV tapes. It can pass digital footage directly to the Macintosh through its Firewire connection. In addition, the deck or camera acts as a conversion device from digital video to analog video. That means that while editing digitally in Final Cut Express, you can watch the results on your NTSC or PAL video monitor instead of squinting at a postage stamp-sized box in the computer monitor. The DV camera you own is now worth twice the price you paid for it!

Where Does Digital Video Originate?

How does DV work? How does the video become digital in the first place? How exactly does light become the series of numbers that are safe from generation loss and deterioration? Let's take a look at a video camera. When light passes through the lens of the camera, it is evaluated for its luma and chroma, or bright/dark values and color values, respectively. The luma and chroma information is collected on light-sensitive chips called *charged coupled devices* (CCDs). The luma and chroma information is gathered from the chips at the same rate and in the same manner as we saw with the electron beam in the back of the television set. It is essentially the same operation in reverse, the television generating light from electrical information, and the CCD generating electrical information from light (see Figure A-4).

This much of the process is really no different whether a digital or an analog video camera is being used. Both generate luma and chroma information from CCDs. The difference is in what happens after that information has been generated. In the analog camera, generally speaking, nothing more is done with the signal. The electrical wave created by

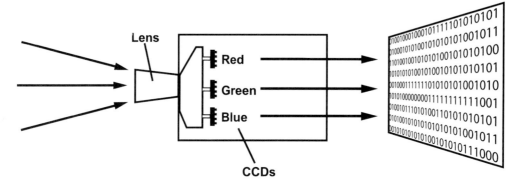

Figure A-4   The lens and light-gathering CCDs of a DV camera

the CCD passes directly to the destination videotape, where it is stored magnetically for later playback.

The digital camera, on the other hand, digitizes the electrical signal. It quantizes, or assigns numerical values, to the various qualities of the light, translating the luma and chroma values into data that can be stored on DV tape (see Figure A-5). As a result, although both analog video and digital video end up being recorded to tape, the digitally recorded video is never recorded as a raw electrical waveform. It passes from CCD to the recording tape as pure data.

Sampling and Compression

It sounds very easy. The camera magically changes light into numbers. In reality, the process is quite mechanical and predetermined. First, the luma and chroma values are subjected to a process called sampling. It turns out that, perceptually speaking, bright/dark values are

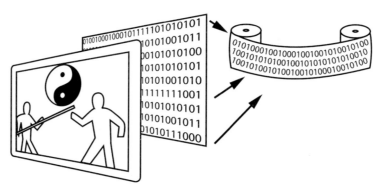

Figure A-5   Digital data recorded onto DV tape

far more important to the human eye than color information. You need a lot more luma information to make out detail in an image than chroma. Consequently, the chroma values are recorded in camera less frequently than the luma values.

As the camera scans a video line and gathers luma and chroma values, it does so at a ratio of luma values to chroma values. Since the luma values are far more important to the image than the chroma values, all the possible luma values are recorded, or sampled. But because the chroma values are less important, they are sampled less frequently. The actual ratio between the luma and chroma sampling depends on the camera and the system of processing the digital video data that follows this sampling.

There are three common ratios in use in digital video. Since ratios generally work best in whole numbers (and for other, more complicated, reasons we will not go into here), the ratios list the luma value first, designated as Y, and assign it a value of 4. This yields the following three ratios: 4:4:4, 4:2:2, and 4:1:1. In these ratios, the 4 designates that the luma value is always sampling all the possible values for bright/dark. The other two numbers in each ratio refer to two of the three primary colors for video: red and blue.

Thus, in a 4:4:4 sampling ratio, all luma and chroma are sampled: four Y, four red, and four blue. In a 4:2:2 ratio, however, the red and blue values are only sampled every other time in comparison with the full four samples of the Y, resulting in four Y, two red, and two blue. And finally, in the 4:1:1 ratio, the red and blue values are sampled only every fourth time (see Figure A-6). The third primary color, green, never needs to be sampled, because its value can be determined easily by calculating, by process of elimination, using the two sampled colors red and blue and the luma value, Y. We call this system of determining the value of a third color from the factoring of two colors and luma the

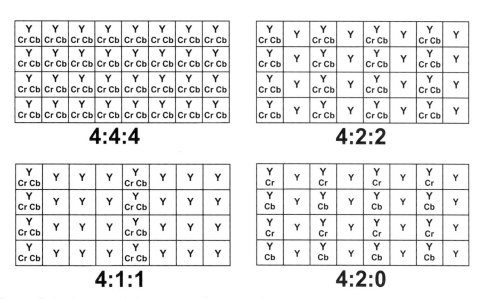

Figure A-6   4:4:4, 4:2:2, 4:1:1, and 4:2:0 color sampling ratios

color differential, the most common method used in making component video (a video standard to be discussed later in Appendix B).

Few systems other than computer monitors are robust enough to sample at the full 4:4:4 ratio, and there is very little need to do so in nearly all circumstances. A 4:2:2 sample ratio is perceptually indistinguishable from a 4:4:4 ratio for most purposes. The 4:2:2 ratios characterize the bulk of the high-end equipment in use in the broadcast industry, where very high quality is demanded. Our DV prosumer systems ("prosumer," an informal term concocted from the words "professional" and "consumer," is used to describe the many devices on the market that are of substantially higher quality than consumer gear, but that are not considered to be of the absolute highest quality) use the 4:1:1 sampling ratio. Although not nearly as detailed an image system as the far more expensive 4:2:2-based cameras and decks, 4:1:1 provides a fairly high-resolution sampling at a fraction of the price. In comparison with the video quality of prosumer, and even professional, video gear from years past, DV's 4:1:1 sampling ratio is vastly more detailed and ensures much higher fidelity to the image being recorded.

The digitizing process is not complete with the sampling process, however. The next key element to the process of digitizing video is the application of the codec, a basic fact of digital life that has important implications in every aspect of digital video. The codec is the key to efficient digital video acquisition and editing. As we shall see, the codec is the link that makes all digital video possible in the camera, the desktop editor, and in every other use you can create for it.

The previously described sampling process generates an astounding amount of information. In order to create a single scanned line of a digital video frame, we must sample 720 individual values, or pixels, for luma. And then, depending on the sampling ratio involved, we must also sample a large number of values for red and blue. Beyond this, we must gather 480 or more such lines per frame and then repeat this 29.97 times per second for NTSC and 25 times per second for PAL. Even with the great speed of today's advanced cameras and computers, this is far more information than can be juggled by prosumer electronics and computers.

The amount of data generated by the sampling and compression process is its *data rate,* which is expressed in terms of megabytes per second. The excessively large data rate coming directly from the sampling process can exceed 24 MB per second. To put that number into perspective, the sustained data rate of the stock hard drives in a Macintosh G4 generally clocks in at around 10 to 14 MB per second and peaks at around 16 MB per second. The hard drive solutions of the standard inexpensive desktop computers we intend to use for DV editing cannot match the data rate of the video coming right out of the sampling process.

There are two ways to deal with this situation. One solution is to speed up the data rate of our computer with faster hard drive systems. In higher-end editing systems in which the absolute optimum quality is necessary, hard drive storage solutions are employed that can match or exceed the requirements of enormous data rates. The downside, of course, is that these superfast drive solutions are also radically more expensive and probably far out of the price range that most of us can afford.

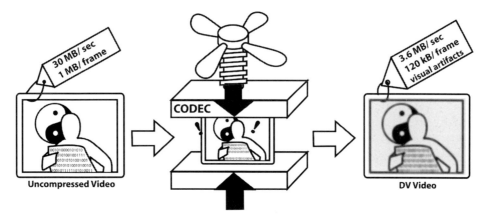

Figure A-7   A codec compresses video data

For our low-cost system, however, there is a better way of dealing with the issue—reduce the video data rate to something more manageable. In the Firewire-based Final Cut Express DV editing system, this latter method is employed through a process called *compression*. The initial staggeringly large video data rate is brought down to a respectable 3.6 MB per second, which is well within range of the inexpensive stock drives of your Macintosh.

This data rate reduction is made possible by the *codec*, a term that combines the words "compression" and "decompression." A codec's main function is to reduce the amount of data in a video frame while at the same time maintaining the integrity of the image (see Figure A-7). When a video frame is initially compressed, the codec throws away excess digital information, retaining only what it deems will be necessary to decompress, or reproduce the image again later. The result is a much smaller amount of data for each frame, a correspondingly lower data rate, and, hopefully, an image that more or less resembles the original uncompressed source footage.

Types of Compression

There are many different codecs, and they accomplish the previously described task in as many different ways. In Chapter 7, we investigated the primary methods by which various codecs do their compression magic. Here we want to look into the two main criteria to judge a codec: (1) how effective the codec is at reducing the video file's data rate and (2) how well it maintains the image's integrity while doing so. To illustrate the relationship between these factors, we can take as examples three popular codecs available through your Macintosh operating software and Apple QuickTime: Animation, Cinepak, and the DV codec.

The Animation codec is a completely lossless codec. When video is compressed and decompressed using it, there is zero loss of image detail (see Figure A-8). In terms of image

Figure A-8   The Animation codec

integrity, it is as if no codec had been used. Indeed, the size of the compressed file tends to be only slightly smaller, and the corresponding data rate is still very high. Thus, we say that Animation is an impractical codec, even while admiring the image integrity. Great image quality with large data rates will not serve our general DV editing purposes.

The Cinepak codec, on the other hand, discards huge amounts of image data, reducing the data rate enormously in the process. In fact, the data rates are so low that it is valuable as a codec for Web distribution of video content. But as a consequence of the heavy compression, the image quality suffers terribly, resulting in visible artifacting and loss of detail (see Figure A-9). Thus, we say that Cinepak is also impractical, although we might accept the low image quality in exchange for the very low data rates that will make CD-ROM and Web applications easier to implement.

The DV codec is our happy medium for editing. It discards a vast amount of image data on compression, generating a very satisfactory data rate that is well within the limits of what our inexpensive Macintosh's hard drives can handle. And decompression (i.e., playback of the compressed material) reveals that we are left with very acceptable image quality (see Figure A-10). The DV codec is in many ways the perfect codec for the DV editor, because it generates very good image results with a very low data rate, and it doesn't break the bank doing it. Although the DV codec is not perfect (and the trained eye can find evidence of the codec's artifacting quite easily), it is in the ballpark with the codecs used by editing systems costing many times more than the amount you will spend on your Final Cut Express editor.

Figure A-9   The Cinepak codec

After comparing lossless, high data rate codecs such as Animation with lossy, low data rate codecs such as Cinepak and DV, we can further group codecs into three categories: software-only, hardware-only, and software/hardware hybrids. This simple division explains much about the way codecs function within computer systems. The proper performance of your Final Cut Express editing system and the ability to maintain the highest possible quality in your video productions depends on how well you grasp what happens and when.

The first type of codec, software-only, is a compression/decompression process that is accomplished entirely by software calculation. The Animation and Cinepak codecs described previously are good examples of software-only codecs. Video is analyzed by the software codec, and data is discarded, redistributed, and reformulated according to the calculation method used by the codec. The calculation method is generally very flexible for software codecs, allowing the user to determine how lossy the codec will be, how low the data rate will be pushed, and even how many colors are used to reconstitute the image.

The major trade-off is in processing speed. Software codecs are, without exception, the slowest at compressing and decompressing video. The computer's operating system must process each pixel of each frame, and decisions must be made as to whether the data must be kept, changed, or discarded. Such processing is slow and relies entirely on the desktop

Figure A-10   The DV codec

computer's built-in hardware. When you compress less and have a consequentially higher data rate, the built-in hardware may not be able to process the video fast enough to achieve the high frame rate, a phenomenon known as *choking* or *underrun*. At higher compression levels, the image quality is sacrificed beyond what we would regard as acceptable for broadcast video.

Most software-only codecs are used exclusively for Web and CD-ROM applications, because the files they produce must be accessible by computers that do not have specialized software or hardware. Any file compressed by a codec must be decompressed by the same codec to be played back, so the same codec must live on both the computer that compresses the video and the computer the video is distributed to. Whether PC or Macintosh, most computers have such software-only codecs preinstalled in their system files and are able to decompress these files. This makes software-only codecs very attractive to the Web and CD-ROM distribution markets.

Hardware-only codecs are not so common. A hardware codec is a specialized piece of electronic circuitry that takes an analog video signal and converts it to or from digital video. There is little or no variability involved. The video is digitized with a set of parameters that are usually optimized for a specific level of quality whereby little or no editing or manipulation of the video will take place before playback. Since little variation is built into the system, the hardware is simply converting electrical values into digital ones and back in a rigid fashion.

One example of a hardware-only codec system is the digital video conferencing system, such as those produced for corporate and industry use. With such devices, the only objective is getting digital video data from point A to point B intact, usually at fixed, relatively high data rates. Although the image quality of these solutions is quite acceptable, they are constructed expressly for data transfer and cannot be made to work with an editing station.

Another example is the so-called all-in-one-box video editing solution, in which the editor gives up the wider options of codec quality control for the ability to simply plug analog video into the connectors of a box and edit away. Such systems usually offer limited transitions and effects but are not built to function as completely expandable postproduction solutions. The lack of flexibility makes them useful in simple editing situations but impractical for projects that are very complicated or where many people are involved in the edit process.

Hardware solutions function in a manner referred to as *real-time digitizing*, meaning that unlike the software codec, there is no appreciable delay in the conversion of the analog video signal to digital data. The circuitry of the hardware codec is designed to compress or decompress the video electronically rather than mathematically, almost instantly producing a digital video image. Since the hardware is constructed specifically with this purpose in mind, the quality depends on the hardware system, but you can expect to pay heavily for acceptable quality.

The third sort of codec is a hybrid of software and hardware. This type of codec uses both the high quality and speedy results of hardware codecs with the variability and control of software interfaces. These are usually more expensive solutions, such as Avid Technology's Avid Xpress and Media 100's Media 100i, and they tend to be proprietary solutions, requiring one to use the company's own editing interface to utilize the hardware card. Apple Final Cut Pro, Final Cut Express's older sibling, also can make use of a number of excellent hardware expansion cards, such as the AJA Kona, Aurora Igniter series, Blackmagic Decklink, Digital Voodoo, and Pinnacle Systems Cinewave.

Generally speaking, regardless of who manufactures the analog capture card and its corresponding software, the function of the hardware/software combination is ultimately the same. A hardware digitizing card is used to convert analog video from a source such as a video deck into digital data using a flexible compression scheme; it is usually capable of generating very low compression and high data rates. The software interface that works with the hardware card gives the user subtle control over how much compression takes place, giving the option of better image quality or smaller data rate and file size, depending on the editor's needs.

Much less lossy compression and higher image quality schemes can be instituted, because the hardware codec is taking care of the processor-intensive actions that would otherwise have bogged down the system. In most cases, the hardware capture card is also making use of the higher-quality sample ratio of $4:2:2$ we mentioned earlier. This sort of system has been considered the standard in broadcast digital video editing for a number of years; such systems have offered the best quality and highest reliability available. Even today, where the absolute highest image integrity is necessary, and where the budget is not the first concern, software/hardware hybrids offer the only real solutions.

The problem, of course, is that such a hybrid of hardware and software is often very expensive. In addition, many of these solutions are strictly proprietary. If you use the hardware capture card from an Avid or Media 100 system, you can decompress only using that same software/hardware codec. Since these expensive software/hardware combinations will generally burst the seams of most modest budgets, the likelihood of distributing files created with the expensive systems' codec is slim to none. The few smaller-scale editors who can afford such an editing solution operate as stand-alone editors, digitizing material from tape and then outputting to tape when the editing is complete.

Some analog capture cards, like the modestly priced Final Cut Pro-compatible capture cards mentioned earlier, can use a more universal M-JPEG compression or even uncompressed formats that can be accessed without a particular hardware codec, but being able to decode and decompress the hardware codec is only part of the expense. Even the more universal M-JPEG compression format carries a very high data rate if the quality is set to an acceptable level. And high data rates require the fast-drive storage solutions that, in turn, equal sticker shock as the price of your turnkey DV editing station grows.

And expensive these storage solutions can be. Although prices have dropped drastically during the past few years, the price tag of these software/hardware solutions remains out of range for most users. After you tack on the price of the superfast storage solutions necessary to take advantage of the low compression and high data rates, you end up with a system that most of us simply can't afford to own. Even at the most cost-efficient end of the spectrum, $1,000–$5,000 for an appropriate capture card, $300–$600 for a fast SCSI card, and another $2,000 or more for the drives themselves really add to the overall cost of the investment.

There is another game in town these days, however. The DV codec used by Firewire-based DV editing applications is a unique hybrid. It exists as both a software and a hardware codec, but independently. Material can be compressed and decompressed using either a software-only version of the codec, such as the Apple DV codec that Final Cut Express uses, or a hardware version of the codec. Material that has been compressed using the hardware codec can be played back with the software version and vice versa.

The hardware version of the codec is closer at hand than you think. You may already own it. It lives in your DV deck or camera. As you are shooting and recording video onto DV tape, the video is being sampled using the 4:1:1 ratio and is then immediately compressed by the hardware DV codec in the DV deck or camera. When we need to edit, instead of having to purchase an expensive digitizing card to access a special hardware codec, we simply plug the Firewire port of the camera into the Macintosh, accessing the camera's built-in hardware codec for our editing purposes.

The Firewire cable going between the DV deck or camera and the Macintosh is simply a data tube that transmits digital information from one device to the next (see Figure A-11). The potential data rate for this tube is more than high enough to transmit the DV codec–compressed video from deck or camera to Macintosh and back. It is this Firewire

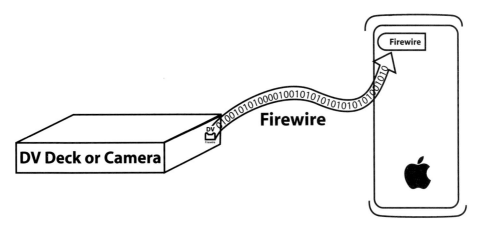

Figure A-11   A DV camera's Firewire cable is a data tube

connection between the Macintosh and the DV deck or camera that allows digital video to be translated to analog for viewing on a video monitor. It also allows the digital video previously recorded on DV tape to be passed through to the Macintosh, where it will be accessed by the Macintosh's QuickTime software version of the codec, making it possible for you to play back and edit the material.

What About Digital Audio?

We've described how video is compressed and sent down the Firewire tube to be accessed by a DV codec on the other side, but obviously there is another piece of the puzzle. Video without audio would make for very uninteresting viewing. Digital audio is also included in the Firewire data stream. In order to understand how it is available to the Macintosh, we need to understand how sound becomes *digital audio*.

Sound becomes *analog audio* when sound waves in the air encounter a transducer, such as a microphone, thereby producing an electrical waveform that is an analog of the original sound wave (see Figure A-12). This process is similar to that of analog video. Analog

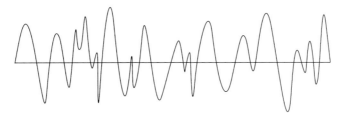

Figure A-12   An analog audio wave

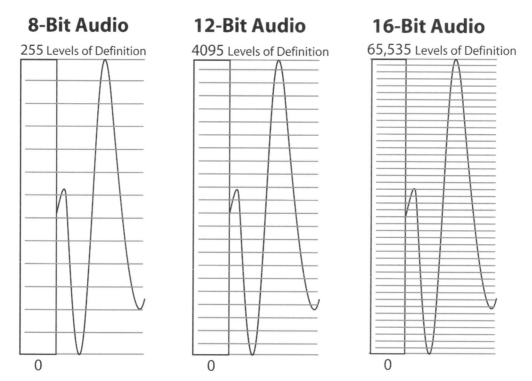

Figure A-13   Bit depths of digital audio

audio at this stage is usually directly recorded to analog tape. When the tape plays back, the electrical waves recorded on the tape are converted back to sound.

As with analog video, the audio waveform experiences deterioration through generation loss. Digitizing audio eliminates this problem, just as digitizing video does. Digitizing audio involves a procedure called sampling. In audio sampling, the digitizer analyzes the audio wave and assigns numerical values to describe each variation of level and frequency in the audio waveform.

There is a further breakdown of digital audio. Each sample is composed of a number of bits. There are four common bit depths of digital audio: 8, 12, 16, and 24. The number of bits per sample and the way they are utilized in the sample yields some interesting flexibility in manipulating, recording, and playback. Bit depth also plays a role in the digital audio quality itself, since the fewer the number of bits per sample, the less information that is retained about the audio when it is digitized (see Figure A-13).

Of course, as we saw with sampling video, sampling audio is a variable task. You can sample both video and audio more or less intensively. Unlike video, however, audio data rates are far lower, so audio really never needs to be compressed for acceptable playback performance. Digital audio for use in editing DV footage is never compressed, and its quality is determined by the frequency of the sample rate and the bit depth.

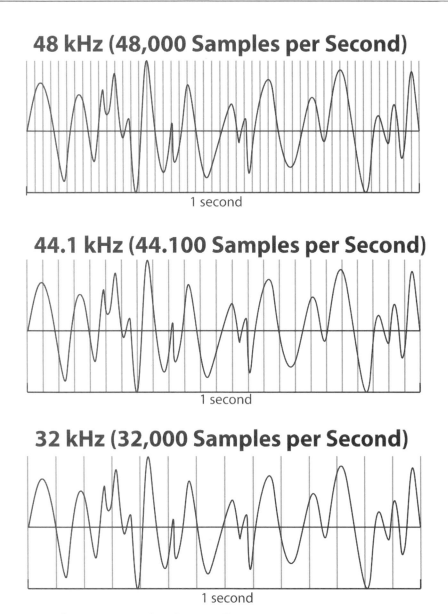

48 kHz (48,000 Samples per Second)

1 second

44.1 kHz (44.100 Samples per Second)

1 second

32 kHz (32,000 Samples per Second)

1 second

Figure A-14   Sampling rates for digital audio

Sampling and Digital Audio

This sample rate is described in kilohertz, or thousands of cycles per second (one hertz equals one sample or cycle per second). A higher sample rate results in more finely detailed information about the original audio wave and thus a higher-quality digitizing process (see Figure A-14). It follows that the higher the number of samples per second, the larger is the amount of available information about the recorded audio, and thus the better the quality

Table A-1 Sampling Rates and Their Applications

48 KHz	32 KHz	44.1 KHz	22.05 KHz
DV, DVD	DV	Audio CD	CD-ROM, Web
16-bit	12-bit	16-bit	8- or 16-bit
2 channels	2 or 4 channels	2 channels	1 or 2 channels

and the higher the necessary data rate. There is an increase in the data rate and quality of digitized audio when the sample rate is increased. As always, the more information a digitizer has about the material, the better the job it is going to do when digitizing it.

There are standard sample rates that are commonly used in the world of media production today, as shown in Table A-1. Audio compact discs, for example, use a standard sample rate of 44.1 KHz, or 44,100 samples per second. This is adequate definition for high-quality two-channel stereo recording. Another common sample rate is 22.05 KHz, which is a lower-quality sample rate used in multimedia CD-ROMs and for the Web because its file sizes and data rate are small enough for delivery over low-bandwidth Internet connections. The quality is quite horrible—better than the quality of telephone audio, but not much better.

The two sample rates that concern us here are the native sample rates for DV decks and cameras: 48 KHz and 32 KHz. The 48 KHz sample rate is very high quality. It exceeds the quality of audio CDs and provides very accurate reproduction. It is a fully professional sample rate, and not long ago it was available only through expensive digital audio tape (DAT) recorders. It is a testament to the power of the prosumer market that such quality acquisition is available at such low prices today. Currently, 48 KHz is one of the two native sample rates available in nearly all DV cameras and decks, and it is your best bet for recording audio.

Why then, you ask, would we use a lower sample rate of 32 KHz, when 48 KHz is so much better and available on the same camera or deck? Some cameras and decks allow you a really interesting option when recording your audio. With some cameras, if you shoot video and record the audio at 32 KHz, you can simultaneously record four tracks of 32 KHz audio, or even go in later and overdub the two extra tracks to accompany the two tracks you already have on tape.

The reason this is possible has to do with the different bit depths that are allowed with the use of the two sample rates; 48 KHz and 32 KHz are referred to as 16-bit and 12-bit, respectively, in DV cameras. Bit depth, as mentioned earlier, describes how many of these bits are recorded at each sample and, therefore, how much information is gathered at each sample.

The 48 KHz rate gives us 16 bits of audio per sample, which is enough to provide two tracks of very high quality stereo audio. But most DV cameras can also be set so that the audio is recorded at 32 KHz, capturing 12 bits of audio per sample. The twist is that this distribution of 12 bits can be organized on the tape to allow four separate tracks of 32 KHz 12-bit audio instead of the two allowed at 48 KHz 16-bit.

Multitrack audio recording on digital videotape using the 12-bit/32 KHz audio setting is a highly underutilized feature, one that many people aren't even aware exists in their camera. But it can be useful in event videography, such as weddings and ceremonies, where more than two microphones must be used and where separation must be maintained between sound sources. And despite what you might assume, 32 KHz is of reasonable quality and may be acceptable for such applications. Only you can judge if the quality is high enough for you through testing.

Sync Adjust Movies and Sample Rates

Digital audio is audio that has been sampled and then digitized. The quality of the digital audio file and the fidelity to the original source from which it was created depend on the number of times per second that the source audio was sampled, or its *audio sample rate*. In DV cameras and decks, the two sample rates used are 32 KHz and 48 KHz, referred to in most cameras as 12-bit and 16-bit, respectively. Unfortunately, some prosumer cameras and decks are not actually sampling at the exact rate of either 32 KHz or 48 KHz. Some DV cameras and decks actually sample the audio at slightly different rates than the target 48 K or 32 K. Thus, an audio sample may actually be at 48,007 Hz instead of exactly 48,000 Hz. This is not a setting on the deck or camera; it is the inaccuracy of the deck or camera's sampling clock. We do pay a small price for the low price of prosumer gear.

In ordinary playback in the camera or deck, this isn't an issue. The problem is that Final Cut Express at the outset is unaware of the actual, not-quite-standard sample rate of the audio you are capturing. The application only sees the standard audio sample rates of 48 K and 32 K. Of course, the difference between 48,007 and 48,000 samples per second is very minor and nearly imperceptible.

The problem is that the video and audio were recorded together. But if after being captured into Final Cut Express, the video is playing back at the correct rate, but the audio is playing back slightly too fast or slow (because Final Cut Express thinks there are more or fewer samples to play than there actually are), the result over a long period of time is that the two can go progressively out of sync with each other. This is noticeable only over extremely long stretches of footage, since it takes many seconds for those 7 out of 48,007 samples per second to generate a serious audio/video sync issue.

The Sync Adjust Movies feature causes Final Cut Express to calculate the exact number of samples for the captured audio clip rather than assume that it is precisely 32 KHz or 48 KHz. This probably sounds like a great thing to have enabled; more precise calculation of audio sampling means less chance of audio/video sync errors. Certain cameras, such as the Canon XL1, actually require Sync Adjust Movies to be turned on (see Figure A-15) if a clip is to be longer than 5 minutes, because of the disparity between the assumed and the true sample rate.

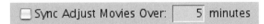

Figure A-15   Sync Adjust Movies adjustment in the Preferences

If Sync Adjust Movies is such a great feature, why would Apple give you the option of turning it off? There are a couple of instances where this feature could cause you problems, even though you're doing all the right things. One issue lies in a serious chink in the Sync Adjust Movies armor. If footage is being captured and a timecode break or area of the tape that contains no video or audio is encountered, a wildly incorrect number of audio samples are registered inside the audio file's data. If the timecode counter number on your camera or deck resets to zero while the tape is playing, you probably have timecode breaks on your tapes!

With Sync Adjust Movies enabled, Final Cut Express is counting the number of audio samples encountered. But because it can't count frames of blank footage, it comes up with crazy numbers for the sample rate and can result in clicking, crunching audio artifacts, as well as completely out-of-sync audio/video. Although this may not be overtly apparent at first, use of the Sync Adjust Movies feature in this instance can yield a complete lack of sync between video and audio. This is a very easy mistake to make, particularly for those new to shooting video who do not prepare their tapes with continuous timecode.

To avoid such a situation entirely, always "prestripe" your DV tapes prior to shooting with them. The process of prestriping is surprisingly simple. Put a blank DV tape in your camera, put the lens cap on, and hit record. This will put unbroken timecode all the way through your tape. When you shoot later with this tape, the camera will "regenerate" the timecode on the tape, meaning that it will start recording using the timecode numbers that are already on the tape. If you accidentally start in a different place on the tape than you stopped recording previously (for instance, if you were fast-forwarding or rewinding and weren't careful about where you returned to), there will always be continuous timecode wherever you initiate recording!

Another problem that can crop up is the "mysterious beeping syndrome," which has to do with how Final Cut Express deals with the Sync Adjust Movies' newly calculated sample rate. When audio clips have a sample rate that does not exactly match the sample rate of the sequence they are playing in, Final Cut Express must resample the clip on the fly to match the sequence settings. This means that in addition to displaying the video frame and any other audio clips you may have present, the processor must slow down or speed up the audio clip that has a nonstandard sample rate. If it's a little hard to get your head around this concept, just understand that you may be forcing the Mac to work harder than it should. When your hear a beeping noise on top of your audio playback, Final Cut Express is telling you it requires an audio render to make everything stay in sync.

The worst part of that scenario is that, in most cases, the amount of sync loss from common small nonstandard audio sample rates is so small you'd only notice it in a clip that is extremely long! This is why you can set a minimum number of minutes of capture before the Sync Adjust Movies audio resample feature kicks in to recalculate. To make things even a little more complicated, the quality of Final Cut Express's audio resampling feature has been improved from the quality level that its older sibling, Final Cut Pro, used in previous versions. The improvement in quality means that when Final Cut Express resamples a non-standard sample rate, it requires even more processor power to do so. Thus, you are even more likely to get the beeping audio render alarm if you use Sync Adjust Movies on every clip. Although you could simply set the Audio Playback Quality setting in the Preferences to Low to avoid the beeping, that doesn't fix the problem. Later on, you will still have to render to correct a problem you could have avoided in the first place by choosing the appropriate setting here.

Which setting is correct? That depends on the camera or deck you originally recorded the tape on, your working habits, and the reliability of your tape's timecode, among other factors. Generally, if you are using the Canon XL1 camera, leaving this feature on and set for 5 minutes is recommended, since that camera's sample rate clock is known to be rather nonstandard. If there is any aberration in the sample rates, it will be caught and recalculated automatically. Other decks and cameras do not appear to require Sync Adjust Movies, even on massive clips of over an hour in length, and the feature can be safely disabled. Although theoretically the feature should not cause problems with other cameras, the chance of accidentally capturing over timecode breaks and other such anomalies makes it unwise to risk having it on all the time when there is no real reason to have it enabled.

If there is the slightest likelihood of a timecode break or video dropout on tapes, capture using Sync Adjust Movies could result in a serious sync issue and the feature should be disabled. Those using an analog digital converter box or a pass-through device of some kind and who are therefore not using Device Control in the Capture window would be best advised to leave the feature disabled, since it is fairly easy to accidentally capture blank video footage. In addition, remember that if your clips are shorter than 5 minutes or so, the sample rate irregularities will be completely unnoticeable, making the feature a moot point. Sometimes the best idea is just to keep your clips short and sweet.

What Are Timecode and Device Control?

We mentioned Firewire earlier in reference to transmission of video and audio data between the DV deck or camera and your Macintosh desktop computer. But what exactly is Firewire? Firewire is Apple Computer's proprietary name for an industry-agreed-on engineering specification called IEEE 1394 (see Figure A-16). The IEEE 1394 standard was developed so that the many companies developing high-bandwidth digital interfaces would be more likely to construct machines and software that could talk to each other. Sony's proprietary name I.Link refers to the same IEEE 1394 specifications. This is why you can use so many different decks and cameras with Final Cut Express. Although not all DV devices are officially tested and supported by Apple for use with Final Cut Express, they are all based on the same technology. The engineering specification allows for a certain amount of digital information to pass from one device (say, your deck) to another device (say, your Macintosh) at a specific rate and using certain wiring and data transfer protocols.

A newer version of the IEEE 1394 specification is currently being implemented in new Macintoshes and Firewire drives. The IEEE 1394b specification, called "Firewire 800" in Apple-speak, boasts a much higher potential data rate than the IEEE 1394 specification

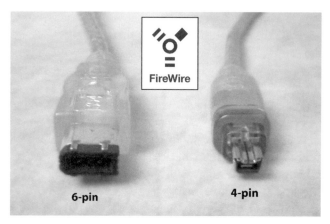

Figure A-16   Firewire (IEEE 1394)

while conferring the benefits we are talking about here. It is also backward compatible with IEEE 1394, so if you have a new Macintosh, you don't have to worry that your machine is unable to work with DV cameras and decks. For more information about IEEE 1394b and Firewire 800, refer to Appendix C.

What this means is that through just one cable you can pass both digital video and audio between the deck or camera and your Macintosh. But it also allows for other data to be transferred. *Timecode* and *Device Control* data is passed between computers and decks, and cameras as well. Final Cut Express is capable of manually controlling any of the devices that Apple Computer specifies are supported, as well as a good many more that they simply haven't gotten around to testing. How it does this is really not a new process for those experienced with video production, but it is very important information for new users who have never encountered the concept of timecode.

Timecode: Analog and DV

We said earlier that there are 29.97 frames per second in NTSC video and 25 frames per second in PAL. But how can we track each and every frame when they pass that quickly? When we get into the editing process, we will see that sometimes the difference between making a cut plus or minus one frame can make a serious difference in the success of the edit. Clearly, it is important to be able to access and manipulate video at the level of frames rather than seconds. But anyone who has ever tried to edit with a VCR using a time scale based on seconds will tell you that it is an impossible task. How can you expect to do exact editing when there's no way to get a deck to record or play with any degree of accuracy by pushing buttons on the fly?

The answer lies in *timecode*. Timecode uses what is referred to as video frame addressing. When the video footage recorded on a tape is accompanied by timecode, we say that each frame of the video has a specific and unchanging address. When you insert a tape with timecode into a deck that can read timecode, the deck will display the frame number of the tape that is currently queued up on the playhead of the deck. Each frame of video on the tape has a frame number that is unique to it.

For simplicity, it is a standard that this numerical frame address follows the universal convention of the digital clock—that is, in the form of hours:minutes:seconds:frames; for example, 01:23:45;15. Although the real-world clock does not contain frames as a unit, video does—at a fixed rate to the other elements of hours, minutes, and seconds. Thus the NTSC timecode clock runs up 29 frames and the PAL timecode clock counts up 24 frames before each turns over a second, in the same way that a real-world clock runs up 59 seconds before racking up a minute.

The benefits of this system should be obvious. If we wish to make an edit at such and such a frame, we simply start recording and playing based on that frame's exact timecode address. Fine and dandy, but we are still obstructed by the fact that our fingers can't move with that degree of accuracy. Luckily, the frame address system of timecode confers another bonus on our tired fingers. Because the frames we want have immutable assigned numbers as addresses, it is easy for computers and decks to automate the process of play, record, and capture. As long as there is timecode, your computer and decks can do this precise work for you, getting exactly the results you want without your lifting a finger.

There is an important distinction that applies only to NTSC. This is the difference between *drop frame* and *non–drop frame*. What are drop frame and non–drop frame time-codes? The difference has to do with the slightly odd frame rate of 29.97 frames per second of NTSC video. Remember that this is the rate of frames being seen per second. But there is no such thing as a fraction of a frame; all video frames are whole, intact entities. And the function of timecode is to count their progression over time using a clock of hours:minutes:seconds;frames.

Unfortunately, we need a whole-number system to do this. We cannot use the fractions that exist in the actual NTSC frame rate, which would result in a time scale using incre-ments of .999 frames instead of 1! This is not a problem for PAL users, since the PAL frame rate is exactly 25 frames per second, but for NTSC users the issue is critical. If we take the most obvious path and just round off the frame rate from 29.97 to 30 frames per second, at the end of an hour you end up with a disparity of 108 frames between the real-world clock and the timecode clock, which at a frame rate of 29.97 frames per second equals more than 3 seconds!

Here's the math:

60 minutes × 60 seconds × 30 frames = 108,000 frames (if we use the rounded-up, incorrect 30 fps)
60 minutes × 60 seconds × 29.97 frames = 107,892 frames (if we use the correct 29.97 fps)
108,000 frames − 107,892 frames = 108 extra frames

Imagine the consternation at the television broadcast station. The timecode standard of counting 30 whole frames per second slowly and progressively throws off the relation-ship between when the show should end and when in fact it does end. As the timecode values get further away from the real-world clock values, hours get longer, and if the union watchdogs weren't awake, workers at the station would be putting in an extra 30 seconds of free labor in an 8-hour day! But, more important, broadcast schedules would go completely out of whack after only a few hours.

Think of it this way. There have been many calendars in the history of the world, but they haven't always been as accurate as our 365 1/4-day calendar. We know that a solar year is the amount of time it takes for the Earth to go around the sun once. Unfortunately, that one revolution doesn't fit exactly right with the number of days it takes to complete that revolution. It takes that extra quarter day to complete the revolution.

How does the calendar compensate for one quarter of a day? Does the sun stop rising once a year at 6:00 AM and start over? Do we have one day of the year marked with only a quarter-of-a-day marker? No, instead we use a leap year. Every four years, we add a day to the calendar to make up for four years of missing one-quarter days. That way, over many years, the calendar doesn't go completely out of order and we don't watch the Superbowl in the middle of the summer.

So how do we get an exact whole number for each frame of NTSC video without the numbering system going out of whack? The Society of Motion Picture and Television Engineers (SMPTE) developed an ingenious system that allows all NTSC video frames to fall on a whole number for a frame address without losing sync between the real-world clock and the timecode clock. Instead of adding a leap year, we are periodically subtracting a "leap frame" from the timecode.

The system is called *drop frame timecode*. In drop frame timecode, the numbering system is based on the frame rate of 30 whole frames per second. Then, over the course of 1 hour, exactly 108 frame numbers are left out. Although the real, true, honest-to-Joe frame rate of the video is 29.97 frames per second, the drop frame timecode numbering system actually labels the frames with the progression of numbers at the whole-number rate of 30 frames per second. Then to keep the frame address numbers from exceeding the actual clock time of the hour, it periodically skips numbers.

Which numbers are left out of the count? It isn't random at all. Frame numbers 0 and 1 are skipped in the first second of each minute, unless the minute number is divisible by 10. Thus after 10 minutes, 18 frame numbers have been skipped, leaving a progression of numbers like 00:01:59;28, 00:01:59;29, 00:02:00;02, 00:02:00;03. . . . It is important to remember that no actual video frames are ever left out; there is only a skip in the number chosen for a frame's address. Just as street numbers for houses are rarely in perfect sequence but the houses are all present, timecode address numbers are skipped, though each frame has a numerical address.

Non–drop frame timecode does not take the 108 frames per hour discrepancy into account and always uses 30 frames per second as its numbering system, never skipping any frame address numbers. Remember that the actual video frame rate of both drop frame and non-drop frame timecode video is 29.97 frames per second. Of course, as mentioned previously, this issue relates only to NTSC, since PAL does not suffer a frame rate based on fractional values.

Drop frame and non-drop frame timecode are easily distinguished in the timecode number. Drop frame timecode always uses a semicolon instead of a colon to separate seconds and frames—for example, 01:02:03;15. All NTSC DV timecode is drop frame and exhibits this. Sony's proprietary format DVCAM can record either drop frame or non-drop frame in the rare circumstances where it is required. PAL DV, not having a drop/non-drop frame issue, always uses non-drop frame signatures.

Unlike its older sibling Final Cut Pro, Final Cut Express has a more relaxed relationship with the timecode you use in a project. After capture, each clip's timecode starts with zeros for ease of reference. Even so, the true timecodes for all captured clips in a project are present in your project and can be used to completely recapture your project automatically in case of disaster.

Device Control

DV timecode utilizes the revolutionary new protocol that made lossless digital data transfer available on the consumer level. This protocol, the IEEE 1394 Firewire specification, includes video, audio, and timecode streaming data along with Device Control. Thus, when you connect the Firewire cable from your camera or deck to the Macintosh, you not only enable the Macintosh to access the video and audio on the tape, you also gain access to the timecode information of that video, and you get remote control of the deck through the Device Control data. That's a lot of control when you get into the process of production.

Why is that? Because, in addition to other benefits, it adds the element of safety to your production. Timecode and Device Control give you the power of automation when you are working. Once you have arrived at the perfect edit of your video, you will want to record it to tape. But what would happen if your drive failed or any of a number of horrible accidents happened, wiping all your hard work away? Without the timecode numbers from all those edits, you'd have nothing left but the fond memory of your project. This is one of the chief benefits of using a professional editing application such as Final Cut Express, rather than Apple's iMovie or similar amateur editors. Such inexpensive (or free!) editors often do not access timecode data and offer no recapture capability. But since you are working with a computer and an application that does, you can use the timecode numbers embedded in all those edits to retrieve the appropriate material from the original tapes and place it in order in your project exactly as you originally had it. This is available only when you are using the full resources of Firewire: video, audio, timecode, and Device Control. And, of course, keeping ironclad backups of your Final Cut Express projects.

Appendix B
DV Formats and Devices

DV Decks and Cameras

"Do I need a deck, or is using the camera OK?" This is probably the most frequently asked question about Firewire and Final Cut Express, by new users and experienced editors alike. One of the grandest accomplishments of the DV revolution is that for such a small amount of money, you can get a turnkey, or complete video editing, solution that also includes a high-quality three-chip camera. This is about a third of the price of a system with similar functionality a few years ago, minus the camera! So it's a pretty good deal all around. Still, there is faint grumbling among initiated editors that using a camera as a deck is not such a great idea. Strictly speaking, they are right. In the long run, using a DV camera for a deck can be a bad idea. Let's take a look at the arguments for and against using a camera as a deck.

The arguments for using a camera as a deck are pretty obvious. The cost savings of using a camera both for footage acquisition (a 25-cent term meaning shooting) and as an editing deck are enormous. A decent-quality DV deck runs into the thousands of dollars, so if we can accomplish the exact same deck functions with a camera we already possess, we drive the total price of our system down into the bargain basement. Most would find this a hard argument to beat, especially those for whom video editing is simply an interesting activity and who don't want to break the bank doing it.

There are, of course, other good reasons for using a small DV camera as a deck that have little to do with saving money. There's nothing quite like the luxury of capturing and editing freshly shot tapes in the field. The convenient size of a DV camera and the fact that most can run on batteries instead of having to be plugged into a wall socket make editing possible in ways that were unthinkable a few years ago. The staggering number of consumer- and prosumer-level cameras that have been approved for use with Final Cut Express makes this an attractive potential use. It's hard to believe that you can fit a fully functioning nonlinear editor and deck on the dinner tray of a coach-class airline seat (assuming you have the PowerBook laptop with you and not the minitower!).

The rough-and-tumble videographers often tell a different story, and for those who intend to use their equipment very intensively, paying attention to their logic and experience would be wise. Any videographer who has experience with intensive use of equipment will tell you that portable camera packages, and especially prosumer and consumer packages, are not designed for the heavy logging and capturing work that is often a major part of editing. Camera tape transports, the little motors and parts that the tape moves around on, are designed for long life, assuming that the majority of that life is spent rolling at a consistent playing speed or performing high-speed rewind and fast-forward.

The "stop, start, rewind, frame-advance, play, stop, fast-forward, pause" actions that typify the log and capture editing process really stress out the transport mechanism of the camera. Think of it like this: Your car can be put into reverse and then back into a forward gear in order for you to operate it on public roads in normal use. Normal use means shifting it to reverse perhaps a few times a day, or at most a small percentage of your actual mileage on the car. You can drive for 100,000 miles in normal use without running into transmission problems.

However, the transmission is not meant to be repeatedly shifted between reverse and the forward gears every 20 seconds, and if you do this, you can be sure that you will soon wear out the transmission's hardware, as well as become very dizzy. The car's transmission allows reverse as a convenience in many situations, but it is not a long-term driving solution. The high costs to repair or replace transmissions can exceed the worth of the car, making such driving patterns unwise.

Such is true of the DV camera as well. And the analogy holds true even for costs, in view of the fact that a really nice DV camera can sell for as much as a used car. Wearing out the tape transport mechanism of a camera is a sad waste of a high-quality imaging device. Most DV decks, on the other hand, are constructed precisely to withstand the constant back-and-forth shuttling that would eventually destroy the transport of even the sturdiest DV camera.

Such issues may be less relevant since the release of Final Cut Express. One of the new features included was a tool called DV Start/Stop Detection. This feature allows users to capture whole sections or even an entire tape, then automatically divvy up the single captured clip into separate clips based on when the recording was paused or restarted during shooting. This feature, also referred to as Scene Detection, could potentially allow the user to avoid the heavy stress of normal logging and capturing, since capturing an entire tape at one go involves simply playing the tape back at normal speeds, something we know that cameras are generally constructed to do well.

Still, you should plan ahead and think about what a year or two of work will do to your equipment. Another important thing to check for when shopping for a deck is the transport itself. Some lower-end DV decks use a tape transport mechanism that is not much more solid than the generic camera tape transport. Be careful to check the deck and make sure that you get what you pay for. It is also important to make sure that the various DV formats are compatible with each other and that they get along well with Final Cut Express.

DV Formats: The Many Faces of DV

Just what do we mean by format? Although we saw that DV uses a standard codec and that Firewire uses a standard communications protocol, there are still proprietary recording formats for DV that will affect your choice of DV device and its relationship with Final Cut Express. Although the DV codec used and the data rate generated by these devices is the same, some use a different tape recording speed and what is called *track pitch* when recording to tape. The formats to be discussed are DV, DVCAM, and DVCPRO (see Figure B-1).

The track pitch is based on the angle at which the record head is positioned on the tape crossing it. Track pitch is the distance between recorded tracks, measured in microns. The greater the angle and track pitch, the greater the amount of data that can be stored per frame of video as the tape crosses the head (see Figure B-2). Of course, the consequence is that the tape speed must be higher if the track pitch is greater. Thus, some material

Figure B-1   MiniDV, DVCAM, and DVCPRO tape

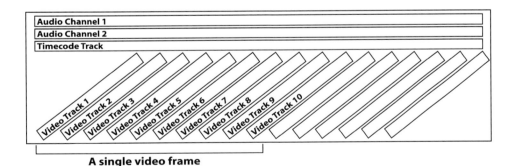

Figure B-2   Track pitch on DV videotape

recorded with a higher track pitch might not play back correctly on decks that do not offer multiple playback speeds. In addition, track pitches that require higher tape speeds also lower the amount of recording time that can be recorded on the same tape.

MiniDV

The first and by far the most common DV format is referred to simply as DV or MiniDV. Many cameras use this standard tape speed and format, making it the only format that isn't the proprietary child of a single corporate parent. The MiniDV cassette size is the most common cassette size for DV cameras, although some DV cameras also take advantage of the greater runtime lengths of larger DV cassettes.

MiniDV runtimes generally top out at one hour. Although many decks and cameras also feature a *long playing* (LP) recording speed that extends the recording length of a tape up to 90 minutes, it is *highly* recommended that you avoid using this feature. LP record speeds are not only nonstandard among decks and cameras; they increase the risk of tape dropout and other recording errors that could jeopardize your footage.

DVCAM

The next of the formats is DVCAM. DVCAM is Sony's proprietary DV format. Cameras that do not display the term "DVCAM" generally cannot play DVCAM-recorded material correctly, although some do, including most of Sony's own non-DVCAM products. And some non-Sony products not only play Sony DVCAM-recorded tapes, they can record at a track pitch and tape speed comparable to that of DVCAM.

What is the difference between MiniDV and DVCAM, and why are some non-Sony devices compatible with it? The main difference between MiniDV and DVCAM is that both the speed and the track pitch of DVCAM are markedly higher (see Figure B-3). As

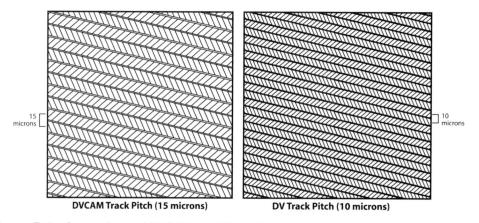

DVCAM Track Pitch (15 microns)   DV Track Pitch (10 microns)

Figure B-3 Comparison of DVCAM and DV track pitch

we said earlier, higher track pitch results in shorter recording times per tape. But more videotape crossing the playhead per second also results in more information being recorded to tape, and more information recorded is always desirable.

DVCAM decks, without exception, use the same cassette size and tape stock as MiniDV; however, a larger cassette size is available to DVCAM deck users with decks that can use them. Many DVCAM decks and some cameras have a larger tape-loading bay and can accept a special DV cassette size that offers dramatically longer runtimes, up to 184 minutes per tape. There is no difference in the tape stock itself inside the cassette casing, or in the quality of the footage recorded (except, of course, the difference in the imaging sections of the camera!). The difference between non-DVCAM MiniDV and DVCAM is the speed and track pitch with which the tapes are played and recorded. In addition to DVCAM, other deck and camera manufacturers are increasingly offering products that use a higher track pitch and tape speed than MiniDV as well. Although some can play back the higher track pitch of DVCAM but can record only at the lower track pitch of MiniDV, higher track pitch will continue to work its way into prosumer camera and deck units.

Since the track pitch of DVCAM is greater, there is a corresponding required increase in the tape speed. Recording tape speed/track pitch in a DV deck is usually a transparent function, with the exception of a few Sony decks and cameras that allow the user to select either DV or DVCAM. A deck or camera records at the speed at which it is built to record. This means that a generic DV tape, when used in a DVCAM deck, lasts only 66% of the advertised runtime length. In other words, a DV tape labeled "60 minutes" will record for only 40 minutes in a DVCAM deck, because the higher speed of the DVCAM deck will run through the length of the tape faster than a DV deck would.

Sony's own DVCAM tape stock is basically standard DV or MiniDV tape, with the exception that the tape speed for DVCAM is correctly labeled on the packaging (in fairness, it must be stated that Sony does have its own proprietary tape stock formulas; the implication in the preceding is simply that other tape stocks, including Sony's own non-DVCAM tape stocks, will function correctly in a DVCAM deck or camera, minus the tape speed variation). Sony MiniDV-sized DVCAM tapes are sold in 40-minute lengths instead of 60-minute lengths, because the amount of tape in the cassette is the same but the recording speed is faster. Although the tape stock itself is no different in technical specification, the intended playback and record speed is. This means that normal DV tapes can be used with a DVCAM deck; simply do the math to figure out how much time your DV tape will lose based on the faster record speed.

One note of caution for new shooters and editors is to follow an old videographer's rule for avoiding tape head problems. Find a brand of tape stock you like or trust and stick with it. Minimize using just whatever tapes you can get your hands on, and try to stick with one tape manufacturer. Although all tape specifications are adhered to by manufacturers, they sometimes use proprietary materials in fabricating their tapes. These can include oils and other materials that over time build up on your tape heads as you play or record. That is normal and common, and you should own a tape head cleaner to periodically run over the heads.

But the problem is that sometimes the proprietary gunk from one tape stock chemically reacts with the proprietary gunk from another tape stock as they mix on your tape heads. This can cause huge problems, from dropout on your tape to faulty heads. It's a rare occurrence, but if you are getting frequent dropout and you've been mixing tape brands in your camera, you might want to clean those heads off and stick with one brand. This is not something that tape manufacturers will ever admit to; it is something that videographers have learned to deal with, and so should you.

You may wonder why Sony would create a different track pitch and tape speed in its product line and introduce a potentially incompatible format, when there is a popular existing standard that much of the industry agrees on (including Sony, which has quite a few non-DVCAM products). DVCAM is not simply a different format; it includes an improvement on the existing DV format. The quality of the DVCAM format is no different from that of DV, because this is determined entirely by the optics, imaging chips, and hardware codec of the camera, not the record speed.

The added benefit of DVCAM is its robustness and resilience in comparison with DV. DVCAM uses a redundancy technique in recording the DV data. If data is lost, damaged, or corrupted on what are, after all, rather fragile tapes, the redundancy of the data may resolve the problem. You pay a price for this redundancy in the increased track pitch/tape speed/format incompatibility, but if you require absolutely no surprises in your shooting/recording, that price may be a small one to pay for the peace of mind that DVCAM's data redundancy provides. As mentioned before in the section on timecode and Device Control in Appendix A, DVCAM also supports the recording of non-drop frame timecode, if such is necessary.

DVCPRO

The final format of DV is called DVCPRO. Panasonic's DVCPRO is generally more expensive and is consequently more rare as a format in consumer and prosumer markets. It uses a completely different cassette casing and a still greater track pitch than DVCAM or MiniDV. DVCPRO originated prior to the advent of DV Firewire editing, antedating the Firewire port on the Mac itself. Originally, it was developed as a high-quality, convenient, and robust format to be used happily along with analog-based systems. With the development of Firewire DV, DVCPRO has shown itself to be valuable on that front as well, bringing lossless editing to a market of users who invested in DVCPRO before such editing possibilities existed. The greater track pitch and robustness of the format is a result of its being designed for rough-and-tumble field acquisition. DVCPRO tape even includes a spare audio track for the inclusion of extra non-DV analog timecode.

A bonus conferred by the greater track pitch of the DVCPRO format is that it can play back any of the three DV formats. Since DVCPRO is almost a universal format, DVCPRO decks can play back both DV- and DVCAM-recorded material, although they can only record in DVCPRO. DVCPRO has a comparatively long history in professional applications, as reflected in the higher prices DVCPRO decks and cameras fetch. And the

DVCPRO format, in another variation of DV beyond the scope of this book, is being used as a tape format for recording HDTV, although such HDTV DVCPRO cameras will be far out of reach for most of us for a very long time.

Is DVCPRO a necessary option for you? The real issue is probably whether you will need to be able to access DVCPRO tapes from other sources. Since the video and audio quality is no different for the three formats, the extra expense is likely not to be worth the investment unless you need to be able to use all three DV formats. If this is not the case, and money is an issue, the lower prices of the prosumer DV and DVCAM formats may make for a better investment.

Features to Consider when Purchasing a DV Device

Knowing the specifications of DV formats is not enough to make a solid decision on the particular DV deck or camera for you. The features, functionality and price all need to be considered so that you don't waste money on features you will never use. At the same time you want to make sure that the device you buy fulfills your needs, even ones you may not be able to predict at this moment the main issues you need to consider are: the format, the analog compatibility and whether a converter box is a better solution.

Cassette Size and DV Format

There are three distinct formats of DV that you may encounter in your adventures. This implies that there are incompatibility issues you must take into account, both as you purchase your equipment and afterward, as you send your finished tapes into the world to be played by other decks and cameras. The issues to keep in mind are cassette size, which means that you need to make sure you will be able to play back any cassette size you want to edit with, and tape speed/track pitch, which means that you know that your deck or camera can play back and record in whichever format that you may need to access.

In general, DVCAM is an excellent choice if you can afford it, because it can access the two most widespread formats: DV and DVCAM. DVCPRO, although an excellent format as well, represents a much smaller proportion of the market and may not justify the extra expense, especially for those who know that 99.9% of their source footage will be generated by their own non-DVCPRO deck or camera. Do not assume that a DV deck can or cannot play back the DVCAM-recorded tape, however, because many manufacturers are building the ability to play DVCAM track pitch tapes into their own decks. Do the homework, test the decks yourself, and figure out the best deal based on your needs.

Analog Video Format Compatibility

In addition to the format issues already discussed, there are other features that you should consider in your search for the perfect deck for your money. One of the first things you should look for is the analog video inputs and outputs. Even though you may be shooting with a DV camera and mastering to a DV tape in the deck, you will at some point want to share your products with the rest of the world.

The analog video signal leaving the deck should be as high quality as possible, and not all video signals are created equal. If you are combining this DV deck with other video equipment, you should take pains to make sure that the analog format of the output of the DV deck matches that of the equipment you want to record with. There are three main types of analog video connections currently available on DV decks. You will find that the type of analog video outputs present on the deck and the quality of the signal both increase in proportion to the price of the deck.

Composite

The most common analog video format is *composite*. Composite video requires only one RCA or BNC cable for the video signal (see Figure B-4), and the quality is correspondingly low, though acceptable enough for most consumer-level uses. A composite signal is one that contains all the luma and chroma values in one electrical waveform, thus requiring only one cable. The corresponding compression of the waveform means that the generation loss will be more extreme, resulting in nearly half the resolution of the frame being lost in the transfer. This is why VHS tapes look so poor in the second generation. Although it is a widespread analog format and is used for most of the video we are familiar with, VHS is pretty horrible for serious dubbing purposes.

Y/C, or S-Video

It is unlikely that you will even be able to find a DV deck that only offers composite out; almost all DV decks also offer what is referred to as *Y/C, or S-Video* in common parlance. Y/C is a step up from composite video and offers much higher quality by using two

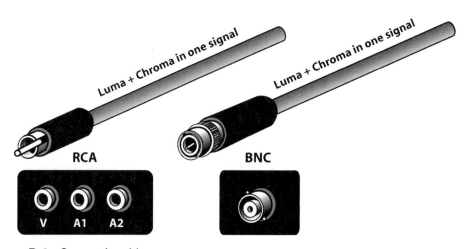

Figure B-4 Composite video

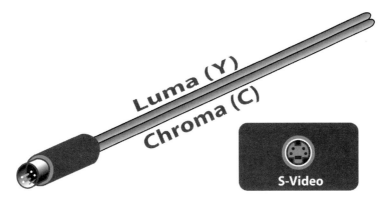

Figure B-5   Y/C, or S-Video

separate wires (though usually both are included in a single cable) to transfer a video signal from one deck to another (see Figure B-5). The Y in Y/C refers to the luma values, and the C to the chroma. Although the chroma values are still composited into a single electrical wave, they are at least kept discrete from the luma values, thus delivering much higher resolution in a dub. The resolution loss over a generation is much less extreme, resulting in only a quarter of the detail being dissolved.

Although the quality is much higher than that of composite video, Y/C is still considered a prosumer format and is affordable enough to be available to most editors. This is a great analog format for making dubs, and anyone editing video using prosumer-priced equipment should look into purchasing an inexpensive SVHS deck for dubbing their DV products down to a distributable tape. Although the generation loss is still greater than in the component format, the next format to be described, it looks fantastic in comparison with composite video and is priced modestly enough to make it available to most DV editors.

Component

The final format to be considered here is that of *component video.* Component video is the highest-fidelity format of analog video. It is something of a universal analog format for applications requiring the cleanest, highest-integrity analog video recording. And it is expensive as analog recording formats go. Even used analog component decks cost at least several thousand dollars, which is between 10 and 20 times more expensive than an S-Video deck that is limited to Y/C and composite connections.

Component decks generate this high level of quality by using three separate cables to transfer the video image. The cables correspond to the three separate electrical waves of the video signal: one for Y, and then one each for red and blue chroma (see Figure B-6). The Y signal is intact, as it was in the Y/C connection, but the color definition of the chroma is not composited into one cable, instead using one cable for red and one for blue. Alternately, some systems may use the three cables for red, green and blue, or even for both types

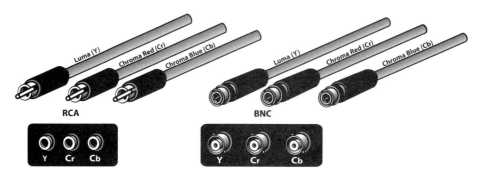

Figure B-6   Component video

of component color, as some Sony decks can. The integrity gained by keeping the chroma signals discrete and intact translates into the richest analog video images available. The quality is fantastic, but the cost is prohibitively expensive for most.

This sticker shock goes not only for the analog component video deck, but also for any DV decks that include component inputs and/or outputs. Most affordable DV decks are limited to Y/C and composite in/outs, which are of prosumer quality. To attain all the benefits of component-quality video dubbing, both the source and destination deck must have component video connectors. Therefore, in addition to needing an expensive analog deck, you might have to pay much more to acquire a DV deck that inputs and outputs this analog format.

Once again, as with the initial choices to be made about whether a DV deck is necessary as a supplement to your camera and which DV format you should be building your system with, your choice of a destination analog format should inform your purchases. If you restrict your editing to family fun days, you may never miss the resolution you are dropping by using only composite connections and a standard VHS deck for your dubbing purposes. Even so, the price gap between composite VHS and Y/C S-Video decks has narrowed dramatically, and even the most miserly would do well to consider the quality increase available for very little expense.

For professionals who intend to make a living (or at least happily pad their present living) with their editing, the investment in component equipment is one that should be considered. If you expect to receive and deliver the highest-quality formats, then you have to have the equipment to do it with, and component equipment is the highest standard of analog video there is. Even though you will have to configure things a little differently and invest more capital in your system, the end may justify the means. When that gold mine client walks in and says, "Can you work from these Betacam tapes?" you want to be able to pop them right in, rather than dubbing them down later when the client leaves and hoping she won't see the noise introduced by the generation loss. Just make sure that you also invest the time and forethought in arranging all the pieces of your system so that they serve you best.

But, on the other hand, don't be convinced by reading this section that you won't be taken seriously if you don't have component decks or if you aren't shooting in DVCPRO. I know videographers who make an excellent income using one MiniDV camera and a three-year-old Macintosh. And it isn't always a question of making money, either. If your tools make something creative for yourself and the rest of the world to enjoy, then that's professional in my book, too. To put it rather bluntly, "professional" is an attitude you take to the projects you engage in, not the equipment you use.

Film production has been around for 100 years now, and television and video for more than 50. Not having access to the awesome image quality of the video tools of the past few years never stopped any of the great film and video makers of the 20th century from producing great work, and not having an $8,000 Betacam deck shouldn't stop you, either. Firewire DV editing, using inexpensive cameras and decks, is high-quality gear. Just don't forget that it's what you *do* with the DV that makes a project professional, not what the format inherently is.

Analog/Digital Conversion Boxes

While discussing decks, we should address another category of devices, that of *analog/digital DV converter boxes*. Although not a deck, the DV converter is a device that accepts analog video and/or audio on one side and generates a DV data stream on the other (see Figure B-7). Because it's a converter box, it can also work in the other direction, accepting a DV data stream and converting this to an output analog signal. These devices run the price range from a few hundred dollars to several thousand, but they all do one thing: convert analog video and audio to or from DV for access through Firewire.

The DV converter can be a really useful piece of equipment, in particular for those who have lots of legacy format tapes to work with. If you have a huge stack of Hi8, 3/4-inch, VHS, or other analog media, a DV converter can provide a very convenient means to access them all in Final Cut Express. For those who simply need to bring in little bits of media and who are not engaged in deeply complicated editing, this may also be a very cheap and simple answer to your needs. For professionals who need to interface expensive component video equipment and high-quality audio gear with their system, this may be a great option for integrating DV and Firewire-based editing into your system without a major equipment upgrade.

The functionality of any given DV converter is very evident in its price, and you get a lot more features in a converter costing several thousand dollars than one costing a

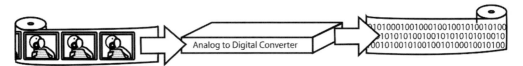

Figure B-7   Analog/digital DV converter

Figure B-8 Canopus ADVC-100

Figure B-9 ProMax DA-Max+

few hundred. Although, as stated earlier, all DV converters do the same thing, not all are created equal. At the bottom end of the chain, barebones DV converters such as the Canopus ADVC-100 (see Figure B-8) offer a simple in/out solution. For very little money, you get Y/C and composite in/out and two unbalanced RCA audio in/outs for stereo sound. On the Firewire side, you get a selector for changing the sample rate from 48 KHz to 32 KHz and a Firewire port. The whole thing is the size of a small clock radio, and it runs on an AC plug-in adapter. It's a very simple solution that will get you through the night.

On the other end of the scale, there are the richly featured converters such as the Laird Blue Flame and the Promax DA-Max+ (see Figure B-9), costing thousands of dollars but offering necessary interfaces that professionals often need. Most are rack mountable and carry balanced XLR audio inputs. Many feature not only component video input/outputs and extra Firewire ports, but also audio level meters and in/outs for other professional digital formats such as *serial digital interface* (SDI). For editors who perform offline editing, the lower DV resolution in comparison with such high-end formats may not be an issue, but the ability to get any sort of media into your system could be.

Of course, we have to remember that with the use of the DV converter, we give up the use of DV timecode. DV timecode is written onto DV tape as video is recorded there. When you stream analog video into a converter box, there is no DV timecode accompanying it, so we lose the ability to recapture, should we run into trouble. While we could still recapture the same material through the converter box, we would have to start from scratch and reedit the entire thing.

Using DV timecode originally captured from a DV tape, on the other hand, we would be able to put all the pieces back together automatically using the Capture Project option in the Capture window. This may not be an issue for people whose media needs are uncomplicated and who could easily manually recapture and reedit any media that is lost accidentally. But accidents can be a real heartbreak for the editor engaged in more complicated assignments; in this instance, working with timecode is imperative.

Appendix C
The Hardware for Editing with Final Cut Express

What You Need for Final Cut Express: The Basic Firewire Setup

What is necessary for a complete turnkey Final Cut Express nonlinear editing station? That is a loaded question, and the answer depends primarily on what you want to do with it. But if what you want is a base-level editing station that captures, edits, and outputs loss-less video through Firewire, then here is the bottom-line configuration that is required for Final Cut Express to perform correctly.

- An Apple Macintosh Computer with a 300 MHz or faster G3 or G4 processor and built-in Firewire ports (additional processor speed required for RT effects)
- Mac OSX version 10.2 or later
- Apple QuickTime version 6 or later
- 256 MB or more of RAM (512 MB or more is highly recommended)
- Two or more physical hard disk drives, one for the operating system and the other for media
- A Firewire DV device, such as a DV deck, camera, or DV converter
- Apple Final Cut Express software

The reader will notice that the words "or later" and "or faster" recur constantly in the list. This is because, like many applications, Final Cut Express can function under different versions of the operating system or of QuickTime. Apple is constantly tweaking and perfecting the operating system as well as the QuickTime video engine and even Final Cut Express itself. The Apple Macintosh is a very adaptable machine that you can customize to suit your needs. When the time comes to upgrade or change your system configuration, you will find that it is much easier and less expensive to do so than to purchase a whole new configuration. Macs last forever. The preceding list simply gives the minimum requirements. Generally, you want to be running the most recent version of the operating system and QuickTime software for Final Cut Express to function optimally.

Welcome to the Macintosh

The Final Cut Express nonlinear editing station is composed of four principal parts:

- The Macintosh Minitower, PowerBook, eMac, iMac, or iBook computer hardware
- The Macintosh operating software (Mac OSX)
- Apple Final Cut Express software
- The external DV device (deck, camera, or converter)

These parts must all work together correctly for editing to take place. Although advances in software and hardware development have made much of this configuration transparent, there are still tweaks that you must make for best results. Final Cut Express likes its tummy scratched in certain ways to deliver best performance.

Unlike its older sibling, Final Cut Pro, Final Cut Express works exclusively with DV footage. Although these two applications share nearly identical workflows and toolsets, the big difference between them is that Final Cut Pro, when properly configured, can edit almost any format of video in current use. New hardware and software products are being developed and released on a daily basis, and by the time you read this, new ones that the author could not possibly predict are likely to have hit the market. Such is the nature of the world of technology. This obviously makes Final Cut Pro a more robust and functional editing application.

Still, Firewire DV editing with Final Cut Express is here to stay. The format of DV and Firewire is one that will remain constant and popular for quite some time, so we can focus on its major features to determine the best way to arrange and configure the hardware and software. The bonus of a Firewire DV-only editing configuration is that it is far simpler and faster to set up.

Let's take the system apart and look at what is involved in the Macintosh's hardware. The first item, the Macintosh computer, is obviously necessary. A G3 or G4 processor with 300-plus MHz and built-in Firewire ports are required for Final Cut Express. In addition, we will see that Final Cut Express features certain real-time effects that do not have to be rendered to be previewed on-screen. For such effects to be available, the minimum requirement is a 500-plus MHz single processor, 450-plus MHz dual processors, or 667-plus MHz PowerBook. Apple's current Macintosh models, including the Minitower, Titanium Power-Book, eMac, and iMac, sport Altivec-enhanced G4 processors, which Final Cut Express's program code has been optimized to take advantage of.

Earlier Macintosh models with G3 and G4 upgrades are not supported by Apple for Final Cut Express. Although enterprising hackers will no doubt come up with a way to get them to work, this is not the path for the inexperienced. As with most hacks, some knowledge of the implications of the hack is a necessity, and for those with little experience in these matters, the result is usually frustration. A hack that seems to offer new life to an old machine or increased features on an unsupported Macintosh is also likely to deliver spotty performance. Just remember that using a hack makes poor machine performance your problem, not Apple's.

The wise recommendation is to invest in a system that is already completely functional and supported. This book assumes you are following such a path. Apple software development has an excellent record of supporting machines that are three or even four years old, which is astronomical in this day of rampant obsolescence (the minimum machine that can run Final Cut Express, for instance, is the old G3 Blue and White Minitower, which was introduced in January 1999!). Hardware and software qualifications are there for a reason: to guarantee that your system will work as advertised.

The Four Primary Areas of the Apple Macintosh

The neatly arranged insides of your Apple Macintosh computer are composed of four major areas:

- The processor/motherboard
- The Macintosh operating software (Mac OSX)
- The storage (RAM and hard drives)
- The input/output buses (AGP, PCI, Firewire, etc.)

Although this description is vastly oversimplified, it is the most general blueprint of the computer. The interaction of these parts results in a working computer capable of running Final Cut Express. Although most of the items to be discussed are built into the motherboard and the computer cannot be purchased without them, it really helps to understand how the whole package works together so that you can make more intelligent decisions about your system when the time comes to add new components or troubleshoot existing ones.

If all of this tech talk seems a little overbearing, relax and just absorb as much as you can. You do not have to be a computer technician to edit with Final Cut Express, nor should you trade your precious editing time and skills for a fixation on hardware and software issues. But it will make your life easier if problems do crop up to know exactly what everything does, where it goes, and so forth. The difference between getting back to work in about a half hour vs. paying $200 to Apple technical support should encourage most folks to get a little more familiar with the insides of their Macintosh. If you can't get through this discussion, just make sure that your system has the necessary hardware and software listed earlier.

The Processor and the Motherboard of the Macintosh Minitower

The processor located on the Macintosh's *motherboard* (all of that circuit board electronics inside the Macintosh) can be defined as the brain of the computer. It receives instructions from the Macintosh operating software and acquires data resources from input/output buses. As one would expect, the processor must be very fast and efficient to perform all of this at once. Indeed, your Macintosh needs to have a G3 or G4 300 MHz or faster Power PC processor in order to be certified to run Final Cut Express.

The discussion in this section will assume that the user is working with a Macintosh Desktop Minitower model. Although Final Cut Express can easily work with properly configured iMac minidesktop, Titanium PowerBook, eMac, and iBook laptop units, the vast majority of editors are likely to be using the Minitower. If you intend to work with a model other than the Minitower, the system requirements are still in effect, and there may be other issues to address, such as hard drive options and RAM. Make sure that you take such issues into account before purchasing a machine. In particular, be aware that the laptops in the Macintosh line are much trickier when it comes to adding RAM and hard drives, and while the PowerBook has the same essential components as the Minitower, it may not be as easy to upgrade them.

The Macintosh Minitower is the flagship of Apple's Macintosh line and always sports the latest in Apple's processor development. The Minitower is also the most easily and thoroughly upgradeable in all respects. Adding new drives, more RAM, and new hardware cards is almost too easy, and there is far more interior space to do so than with any other Macintosh. Any new improvements to the Power PC processor will be included immediately in the Minitower, while for various reasons they may not show up in iMacs, PowerBooks, or iBooks for generations.

Of course, the Minitower is more than a name, it is a descriptive term. This is not a portable computer. It is built to be a stationary workstation that is permanently part of an integrated solution accommodating the hundreds of accessory devices developed for use with it. It weighs in at a good 30 pounds and has a side latch for uncommon ease of access to its interior (see Figure C-1).

The Macintosh Minitower is currently configured with several different motherboards (see Figure C-2) sporting varying speeds of dual- and single-processor units. All the different configurations of G3- and G4-equipped motherboards are suitable for use with Final Cut Express, and your choice of configuration should mirror what you intend to use it for.

Dual-processor models will offer vast speed increases if you intend to do effects work that requires a great deal of rendering, as will faster processor speeds. Dual processors can really make a difference in rendering speeds, but they can also make a real difference in the wallet, especially when rendering isn't a burning issue. Of course, Final Cut Express will function just fine in a single-processor unit (which of course includes PowerBooks and iMacs as well), if a little more slowly on the processor-intensive functions such as rendering effects or exporting files. And since Apple is always developing its software titles to take advantage of current hardware, dual processors will eventually unlock more and more features in upcoming software releases.

In addition, Jaguar, Apple's term for Mac OS 10.2, runs with much more spunk on a machine that has dual processors, processor speeds in excess of 800 MHz, 512 MB of RAM, and AGP video card slots (to be described in the next section). Although Apple doesn't *require* these features, you will find that performance drastically improves with machines configured as such.

Figure C-1   Macintosh Minitower side view: door open

Figure C-2   Macintosh Minitower motherboard from above

Inside the G4 Minitower, you will find room for four extra hard drives in addition to the start-up hard drive that the Macintosh ships with. Adding new drives is a snap with the Minitower and takes less than a few minutes. Before the advent of the "Mirrored Drive Door" model in the summer of 2002, the Macintosh included two ATA drive buses that could contain a total of two devices each. The upper ATA bus contained the DVD/CD burner/player (depending on what you purchased it with) and an optional Iomega Zip drive. The lower ATA bus contained at least one stock ATA hard drive—the start-up drive that ships with your Mac—and could easily take another. The other empty drive bays can be utilized with the installation of inexpensive PCI expansion cards that allow for the inclusion of more hard drives and other devices.

The newer Mirrored Drive Door model contains three ATA buses, one of which is dedicated to the CD/DVD drive. The front panel includes room for a second optical (CD or DVD disk) drive, making copying from CD/DVD to CD/DVD a snap. This second optical drive requires an ATA address on one of the other two ATA buses. The lower ATA buses can take two drives each, one address of which is likely already taken up by the stock start-up drive. The bonus, though, is that since it already contains a second lower ATA bus, you can install several extra internal drives before you need to add PCI ATA expansion cards.

If you order a Power Macintosh with the SCSI option instead of the ATA drives, the system will come with a SCSI card installed in one of the PCI expansion slots, to be described later in this appendix. This is a slightly more expensive option and although it is completely acceptable, SCSI must be set up a little differently. Contrary to popular misconceptions held by some editors from yesteryear, SCSI is *not* required for video editing, particularly for low-data-rate DV editing. Although high-data-rate systems with capture cards usually require a special SCSI configuration, Firewire DV editing works just fine with inexpensive stock ATA drives, which we will investigate shortly.

There are either three or four RAM slots, depending on the G4 Macintosh model, allowing easy installation of additional RAM chips. Your system will come with a certain amount of RAM preinstalled, but you can easily upgrade the RAM to either 1.5 or 2 GB (1,024 MB equals 1 GB), depending on the particular model of Macintosh you own. How much RAM you should have installed and why will be addressed shortly in the discussion of storage.

Also located on the motherboard are the various input/output buses. They are the pathways from the processor to the rest of the computer's parts through which data is brought in or sent out. The largest of these are the *PCI expansion slots* and the *AGP slot*. Your Macintosh will arrive with one stock video card in an AGP slot, which is dedicated to your computer monitor. The PCI expansion slots are for adding additional components such as extra video cards for multiple monitor support, SCSI cards for inclusion of SCSI devices, professional audio cards, and beyond this just about anything else you can imagine.

In addition to these PCI and AGP buses, and located on the outside and to the rear of the Minitower, are the remaining input/output buses. Standard buses on the Macintosh are the Firewire ports, *universal serial bus* (USB) ports, an Ethernet connection, a modem connection, a speaker jack, and, depending on the Macintosh model you own, a microphone input jack.

Data Storage: RAM and Hard Drives

There are two different categories of storage on your Macintosh: *volatile* and *nonvolatile*. Volatile refers to data storage that is lost when your Macintosh is powered down. When you shut down your Macintosh, whatever was stored in volatile storage is lost, but whatever was stored in nonvolatile storage is saved until you reboot the computer. RAM, or *random access memory*, is volatile storage. Physical hard drives of whatever flavor are nonvolatile storage. Each has its place and function.

RAM: Random Access Memory

RAM is the superfast storage where your system software, applications, and opened files load up and operate. It is the fastest storage device in your system and is where the computer does most of its work. RAM chips (see Figure C-3) are integrated circuit chips that hold electrical charges while the machine is powered up. RAM is incredibly fast, which is why the active parts of the OSX System load up into and run from RAM at start-up. RAM is also the storage space where applications live and perform their functions while you are running them. When you quit an application, it gives up the space it was using in RAM, making that space available for other uses.

Typically, Macs ship stocked with 256 or 512 MB of RAM installed, but you can easily install up to 1.5 or 2 GB, depending on the Macintosh model you own. RAM chips are sold in sticks of 128, 256, and 512 MB. Since you have only three or four RAM slots, it behooves you to purchase larger sticks so that in future years you may add more as you need it. If your Mac has four RAM slots and you have four 128 MB sticks rather than one 512 MB chip, you will have to throw away 128 MB in order to add more RAM.

In purchasing additional RAM, keep in mind a couple of considerations. First, make sure that you are purchasing RAM from a company that sells Macintosh-dedicated and guaranteed hardware. Apple uses a higher technical standard for RAM chips in its motherboard than manufacturers of PCs. As such, at start-up the Mac OS tests all the RAM chips installed. Cheap RAM chips that do not meet Apple's specification are ignored. This

Figure C-3   RAM chips and slots

is very much a good thing, since RAM chips are so critical to consistent, trouble-free performance. The Mac OS is just making sure that the installed RAM can keep up with it without making mistakes and crashing your system!

Also, make sure that you purchase your RAM from a vendor that guarantees hassle-free, instant replacement of faulty RAM chips and a lifetime warranty. The last few years have seen a steady decline both in the price of RAM chips and in their quality and reliability, and it's not uncommon at all to get at least one faulty chip during your lifetime. This very likely isn't the vendor's fault, or Apple's, but some nameless contractor company three steps up the marketing food chain. Just make sure that if you determine the chip to be faulty, you know the company will immediately send you a replacement. Not every company does this, and sticking with the ones that do will often be worth the extra few dollars you spend for the initial purchase.

Obviously, more RAM is better than less; you can't have too much RAM. The average system running Mac OSX uses anywhere from 70 to 100 MB of RAM just for itself. If you had only 256 MB installed on your system, there would not be enough left to run Final Cut Express, which requires a minimum of 192 MB of RAM just for itself and really should have access to 256 MB of RAM or more. Although Final Cut Express might actually start up and begin running (because of virtual memory kicking in, a concept to be described shortly), you would very quickly run into severe performance issues.

Mac OSX, in keeping with the UNIX system it is built on, no longer requires the user to set RAM allocations for each application manually. The Mac OS itself dynamically allocates RAM resources, meaning that it is constantly giving and taking RAM to and from active applications as necessary. When an application needs more RAM, the OS just doles it out, no more no less. All applications always have as much RAM as they need at any given moment. No more crashing the system because there is not enough RAM to go around!

Unfortunately, this can also cause a problem. If you do not have as much real physical RAM as the applications you are running demand, the OS must somehow come up with the RAM resources. The OS performs what is called a *pageout*, a function also referred to as virtual memory. What virtual memory does is simulate the existence of more RAM in your system by using a hard drive as if it were RAM. Using virtual memory from 10 GB of hard drive space provides a nearly unlimited amount of pseudo RAM. Instead of writing information into the real RAM chip, it does a pageout, or writes out the information to a location on a locked-off section of a hard drive. Under Mac OSX, virtual memory, being controlled by the Mac OS, cannot be disabled, as was possible under the old-world Mac OS 9.2.2 and earlier.

You might think that this is a bad thing. "If it is problematic, why take away the ability to turn off virtual memory, as you could in the earlier Mac OS?" you might ask. The reason Apple instituted dynamic memory into the Mac OS was to provide a great benefit to the user called *protected memory*. This simply means that the Mac OS itself is controlling each megabyte of RAM, rather than leaving such management to the applications actually using the RAM.

If one application doesn't play nicely or runs into trouble and decides to crash, it can only crash itself. Protected memory makes it impossible for one crashing application to affect others. Gone are the days when one crashing application locked up your entire machine. You can safely force quit (Command-Option-Escape) any running application without crashing the whole system or any other application. Although you would lose any unsaved work in the application you are force quitting, you won't lose everything else you were doing and most likely won't even have to reboot your machine. Mac OSX dynamic memory management makes this possible. This alone is enough to make most old-school Mac enthusiasts upgrade to Mac OSX!

Why is virtual memory a bad idea then? RAM is, of necessity, very fast storage. The processor on the motherboard can access it at nearly instantaneous speeds. But your processor can work only as quickly as it is provided data, so the Macintosh is as slow as the slowest link in the chain. If the processor is receiving data from bona fide RAM chips, your Mac will work at its fastest. If, on the other hand, you are using virtual memory, your processor will at times be forced to receive information only at the dramatically lower speed of the hard drive. For instance, the theoretical data rate of a DDR 2100 RAM chip (the type of RAM chip used in the Power Macintosh Dual 867 MHz Minitower) is an astounding 2.1 GB per second. In contrast, the stock hard drive on your Macintosh might keep a sustained data rate of 6 to 16 MB per second at best. The operations that Final Cut Express and the Mac OS need to perform at lightning speed occur rather more like molasses, and you immediately begin to see bad behavior.

The importance of using real RAM in processor-intensive applications like nonlinear editors cannot be overemphasized. Use of virtual memory is to be avoided in video editing. Unfortunately, since you can't turn off virtual memory in Mac OSX, you need to make certain that pageouts do not kick in and that virtual memory is never engaged. You will also find that other applications work much faster when you have plenty of extra RAM to go around. Take advantage of the rock-bottom prices on RAM and settle the situation correctly.

Hard Drives

In the category of nonvolatile storage, we have the large and sometimes confusing range of hard disk-based drive solutions. As nonvolatile storage, disk-based storage is capable of retaining data saved to it after your Macintosh is shut down. Unlike RAM, which is functional only when turned on and receiving power from the computer's motherboard, the disk drive is its own physical magnetic medium. When you write information to it, that information is stored as magnetic data and will remain intact even when the unit is shut down.

The manner in which the computer actually accesses that data on the drive is what spawns the bewildering diversity of disk-based storage solutions. There are solutions that are appropriate for only one specific purpose, and there are good all-around solutions that function well under many circumstances. Since prices of hard drives can run the gamut from very inexpensive to ruinously expensive, it is important to understand what standards are necessary for Firewire DV editing with Final Cut Express so that you get the best deal available.

The two most important criteria with which to judge a disk drive are its storage size and its sustained data rate. Your own particular needs with regard to the first issue, the storage capacity, can be determined by considering the data rates we looked at in Appendix A. We know that the data rate of the Apple DV codec we will be using is 3.6 MB per second, which gives us a storage need of roughly 5 minutes per gigabyte, (1,024 MB of drive storage per gigabyte and 3.6 MB per second × 60 seconds × 5 minutes = 1,080 MB). Drive fragmentation, a concept we will explore later, requires that we cut this number down to about 4.5 minutes to the gigabyte. Thus a 20 GB drive will hold just under 90 minutes of DV codec video. The need for large drives should be abundantly obvious.

The second criterion to be evaluated is that of sustained data rates. As we will see, there are a number of different ways for a drive to transfer data back and forth between itself and the motherboard of the computer. These differing methods produce limitations on how fast a drive can deliver or accept data. No matter how fast the drive itself is, it can function only as quickly as the interface with the motherboard of the computer. The sustained data rate of a drive depends not only on the drive's internal capabilities, but on the type of bus it uses to communicate with the processor/motherboard. This concept, referred to as bandwidth, is rather like saying that only so much water can pass through a hose at a time. The larger the hose, the more water can pass through per second. No matter how much water is on either side of the hose, only so much can travel through it per second. Similarly, the larger the bandwidth of the drive interface, the higher the speed with which data can be passed through from one side to the other.

First, we'll look at the types of drive solutions by location, (removable, internal, and external) and then by standard. The major standards appropriate for Final Cut Express Firewire DV editing are ATA and SCSI, as well as the popular variation of the Firewire drive.

Types of Drive by Location: Removable Disk

The first category of hard drives is that of removable disks. The lower-end scale of removable disk drives involves smaller and slower disk types such as the Iomega Zip disk. These disk types are valuable primarily for their ability to move small amounts of data quickly between machines. With a limit of less than a gigabyte of storage and a very slow data transfer rate of around 1.5 MB per second, the Iomega Zip disk and its colleagues are clearly not acceptable for use in the capture, playback, and storage of DV footage. Their use is generally limited to saving and backing up projects, documents, and other smaller relevant files.

Types of Drive by Location: The Internal Drive

The next category of hard drive solutions is that of internal drives (see Figure C-4). The stock hard drive that came as the start-up drive for your Macintosh is just such an internal drive. Internal drives may be either ATA or SCSI, the two major standards we will describe, and their only real limitation is the amount of space inside your Macintosh. Internal drives, sometimes also referred to as "bare," are the least expensive drive solution, because they require only a connection cable, a few screws, and a power supply cable. They do require a little work on the user's part, though, since they must be manually installed. This installation is quite simple, however, particularly with the Macintosh body design.

The two major drawbacks to filling your Macintosh with internal hard drives are portability and heat. Because you are seating the hard drive in the Macintosh's belly, you can't easily move it to another Macintosh should you need to do so. Installation and removal are easy, but not that easy. An internal drive is to be considered a fairly permanent item in the Macintosh.

The second drawback is heat. The inside of the Macintosh gets very hot, much hotter than you think. The more items you have installed in it, the hotter it runs, taxing the cooling fan system built inside the Macintosh. Overheating systems can exhibit strange behavior or simply melt down completely. Although the built-in cooling system should keep your internals at an optimum temperature, be aware that filling the Macintosh up to the brim with drives and then running it in a 100° Fahrenheit room may eventually cause problems.

Types of Drive by Location: The External Drive

An external drive is simply an internal drive that has been prepackaged in a resilient casing, with an input/output interface based on whichever standard it uses. The user simply pulls

Figure C-4   3.5-inch internal drive

it out of the box and connects it to the Macintosh with no muss or fuss. Of course, the user pays for this ease in price. Expect to see the price for the same amount of storage to double for an external drive solution put together for you by a retailer. If you know what you are doing (and the process is quite simple), you can purchase your own drives and external cases and put them together yourself for much less than most retailers charge. Just make sure that you investigate the latest in drive and case developments before investing in the materials, since, along with the rest of technology, they change on what seems like a daily basis. Remember that the old saying "You get what you pay for" fully applies and that a deal too good to be true usually is.

Why choose an external drive rather than an internal? There are some benefits to using an external drive that may be less than obvious. As stated before, there is a limit to the number of internals one can fit in the Macintosh. For externals, there is only the limit of your storage standard, since some standards, such as ATA, which can have at most two drives on one ATA bus, are more limited than others, such as SCSI and Firewire, which can have many more. If the standard you are using is nearly unlimited, so too will be the number of possible drives. Although the ATA drive standard does not exist as an external option, both SCSI and Firewire external drives are in heavy use. A Macintosh can technically connect to up to 63 Firewire drives at the same time. The larder knows no limit.

External drives are obviously spared the heat issue that can affect congregating a large number of internals inside the Macintosh. Although an external drive also needs cooling resources, generally the casings are designed so that a fan is not necessary, or one is included in the case.

External hard drives also may be considerably more convenient in terms of mobility. Although no hard drive is designed to withstand the heavy shocks of being banged around constantly, it can be moved much more easily than doing so with an internal. Moving an external hard drive to another system is as simple as unmounting the drive from the desktop (i.e., dragging the drive icon to the Trash) and disconnecting and then reconnecting a cable. Moving an internal drive will require some surgery, regardless of how simple that surgery can be.

Types of Drive by Standard: ATA, IDE, or EIDE

There are four primary standards of connectivity with your Macintosh, each of which can be used for communication with drives. These are the input/output buses that will be described in the next main section. But since each of these buses determines the standard for the drive we connect through it, it is necessary to look briefly at them. The four, in order of popular usage, are ATA, SCSI, Firewire, and USB.

Each of these standards simply does one thing: It transfers data between two devices— for instance, your drive and your computer. The maximum data rate of the hard drive at the end of this connectivity is limited by the highest possible data rate that the standard supports. No drive or set of drives ever reaches the theoretical limits of its specifications, but some come very close. Our job is to look at what we need for Firewire DV editing with Final Cut Express and see how far we can make our money stretch.

The first and most popular standard is ATA (see Figure C-5), also known as IDE or EIDE. This is the most inexpensive drive solution on the market, offering enormous amounts of drive space for the lowest prices. As standards go, ATA is the best deal around, and, with some reservations, it is a very suitable drive standard for Firewire DV editing.

The ATA drive interface does, of course, have some limitations that are a reflection of the bargain prices per gigabyte of storage. The first and most serious limitation is that the cables that connect ATA devices must be shorter than 14 inches. This means that there are no external ATA drive solutions. If all ATA drives must be internal, then there is a practical limit to the number of ATA drives one can have in one's system. ATA drives are further limited by the fact that the standard internal ATA bus built into the motherboard of pre-2002 Macs (the one the start-up drive is located on) can hold only two devices. In addition, as of this writing, the standard ATA buses on Macintoshes limit any ATA drives to 137 GB sizes, making the largest ATA drive accessible the 120 GB models. As we will see in the section on buses, this may imply further expense inasmuch as PCI expansion cards may be required to increase the number and size of ATA drives inside the Macintosh.

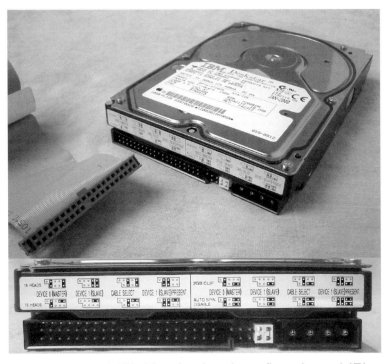

Figure C-5   3.5-inch internal ATA drive showing pin configuration and ATA connector

Although the specifications for ATA data rates change with the technology faster than my printer can keep up with, generally speaking, the sustained data rate for an ATA individual drive (given the many possible variations among drives, Macintosh units, and fragmentation) tops out at around 16 MB per second. Since the data rates required for Firewire DV editing are around 3.6 MB per second, the ATA standard is well within the range of suitability for use with Final Cut Express. The low cost and acceptable data rates make the internal ATA drive a logical choice for most Firewire DV editors.

Types of Drive by Standard: SCSI

The next popular standard of connectivity for storage is SCSI, which stands for Small Computer Systems Interface (see Figure C-6). SCSI is a very old standard that has gone through many variations and contains several different levels of data rate and access. A few generations back in the history of the Macintosh, the SCSI interface was the standard for connection with drives of all kinds, and a SCSI connector came built into the Macintosh's motherboard.

These days, the cost-effectiveness of the ATA standard has eliminated most of the lower-end usage of the SCSI standard. But SCSI has remained in higher-end applications, where its flexibility stands superior to ATA in every way. The SCSI chain can be a very wise invest-

Figure C-6 3.5-inch SCSI drive showing pin configuration and SCSI connector: external SCSI RAID

ment consideration when one will potentially be using much higher data rates, especially in upgrading their Final Cut Express editors to Final Cut Pro and the professional video capture cards that Apple also supports.

The acceptable SCSI cable lengths, while still limited to a certain length, are far longer than those of ATA. This means that external drive solutions are possible. In addition, the main SCSI standard in use allows up to 15 possible devices on a single SCSI bus, as compared with two devices for the ATA bus. And most SCSI cards allow for internal as well as external drives to be used simultaneously. Add this to the incredible potential data rates that SCSI card and drive manufacturers currently offer and you have a very impressive standard for connectivity. Depending on the SCSI card type, drives, and formatting software system, data rates of 160 MB per second are possible.

The catch, of course, is the price. Even bare internal SCSI drives can cost up to and sometimes more than three times as much as a comparably sized ATA drive. And since the Macintosh does not carry a built-in SCSI bus on its motherboard as it does an ATA bus, an add-on PCI SCSI card must be figured into the price of the system, further driving up the cost of the storage solution. The cost of a lower-end 120 GB solution using the SCSI interface could easily amount to $800, whereas a bare 120 GB ATA drive could be had for around $150. Of course, the savings would appear later, because the SCSI interface easily accepts more and faster-configured drives, internally and externally, whereas the ATA bus is completely filled with only two (unless you have an ATA PCI expansion card installed, a subject to be addressed shortly).

SCSI prices tend to fluctuate less and remain at a premium, partially because of their popularity in higher-end solutions and partially because of their special flexibility in terms of expansion and configuration. The prices of ATA drives continue to plunge as each new development in drive technology nudges up the data rates and storage capacity of the individual ATA drive. Whether SCSI or ATA is a better solution depends on your long-range plans, but ATA is generally the drive of choice for Firewire DV editors, while SCSI is the system of choice for higher-end production stations using uncompressed video and HD, for which flexibility and the ability to handle extreme data rates are basic requirements. In short, SCSI is a wonderful, if expensive, standard that will not cause you problems, but it is not technically necessary for editing with Firewire DV material. Its suitability generally lies within the realm of high-performance video editing, rather than the Firewire DV that Final Cut Express is limited to.

Types of Drive by Standard: Firewire

Special mention must be made of an external solution that exists in the Macintosh market today, that of Firewire drives (see Figure C-7). Although we have discussed Firewire as a system of transferring digital video and audio, the Firewire connectivity is simply a data transfer system that is fundamentally similar in function to ATA and SCSI. Although radically different in design, the standard is simply a technical specification for transferring data between one end of a cable and the other.

Figure C-7 3.5-inch Firewire drive

IEEE 1394 Firewire has a specified data rate ceiling of 400 megabits (mb) per second. Since there are 8 bits per byte, this delivers a maximum possible data rate of 50 MB per second. The recently implemented IEEE 1394b specification, referred to as "Firewire 800," has a theoretical limit of 800 mb per second, giving a potential data rate of up to 100 MB per second!

Of course in practice, this is higher than the actual possible rates achievable with the present hardware available to use with the Firewire interface, although the Oxford 911 chipset in widespread use approaches it. A Firewire drive that uses the Oxford 911 chipset in its Firewire-to-ATA bridge and at least a 7,200 RPM ATA drive makes much more efficient use of the Firewire bus. When purchasing a Firewire drive, ask to make sure it has the Oxford 911 chipset by name; Firewire drives that do not sport this chipset may be plagued by slower data rates, and frankly the cost difference is minimal. Once again, saving a few bucks will only result in headaches. As the Firewire 800 specification is further implemented in the industry, other Firewire bridges will be developed, as, for instance, the third generation of Oxford bridges, the Oxford 922, accesses the IEEE 1394b potential. Make sure you research the current capabilities before you purchase!

High data rates are not the only bonus conferred by the Firewire interface standard. Firewire shares and expands the connectivity gains inherent in the SCSI standard and allows for long cable lengths, enabling it as an external solution (see Figure C-8). Devices can be daisy-chained, allowing up to 63 possible devices on the Firewire bus. As a bonus, Firewire connectivity confers the ability to hot-plug Firewire devices. Hot-plugging means the user can disconnect a device while the computer is still running, something potentially disastrous for either ATA or SCSI devices.

In reality, there is no such thing as a "Firewire drive." Firewire drives are basically external drive boxes containing an ATA drive and a bridge that converts the Firewire data stream to and from the ATA data stream (the Oxford 911 and 922 chipset "Firewire-to-ATA bridge" described earlier is such a bridge). Thus, the cost of the Firewire drive is determined by the low price of the ATA drive, the increasingly low price of the ATA-to-Firewire

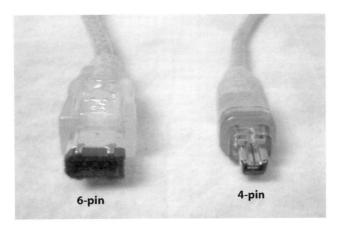

Figure C-8   Firewire cables: 4-pin and 6-pin connectors

conversion bridge, and the box that holds it all together. There are several do-it-yourself kits on the market that allow you to purchase and install your own drive for use in a Firewire case. Just remember that the drive you install in the case is the weakest link in the chain, and that you shouldn't depend on a drive that you wouldn't want as an internal unit. A slow drive in a fast Firewire chain equals a slow Firewire drive. Make sure the drive inside the Firewire case is at least 7,200 RPM.

Given the benefits of using the Firewire interface for storage, you may not want to use anything else for DV editing purposes. The convenience, portability, and rich feature set of Firewire drives make them very attractive, and their reliance on very inexpensive drives makes them a cost-effective solution.

Types of Drive by Standard: USB

The final standard for connectivity in data transfer is that of the *universal serial bus* (USB), as shown in Figure C-9. The USB standard delivers a very low data rate that does not exceed 1.5 MB per second. While this data rate is acceptable for less intensive uses such as floppy disks and the Iomega Zip drive, it is far below what is needed for editing with the DV codec and Final Cut Express. The USB standard is not recommended for editing purposes, although it has its uses elsewhere in the Macintosh system, as we will see in the discussion of input and output buses.

The next generation of USB, USB 2.0, sports a radically faster data rate, one that is theoretically as fast as or faster than Firewire! It may come to pass that in the future, the USB 2.0 standard becomes a staple for DV editors. Unfortunately in the meantime, the USB drivers in the Macintosh operating system do not allow the USB ports to operate at such high data rates, and there is no real indication that they will do so in the near future. In addition, USB interconnectivity is a rare feature in the DV cameras that are half of the Firewire DV editing revolution, and thus USB 2.0 does not appear to be a good idea for

Figure C-9   USB connector powered and unpowered

committed editors looking to make a solid investment. Firewire drives will generally be a smarter choice wherever a choice is to be made between the two, if for no other reason than built-in support and widespread compatibility.

The Input and Output Buses

The input and output buses of the Macintosh constitute the way in which it receives and delivers data to and from the outside world and other parts of the Macintosh. There are several such buses, and each one is dedicated to a specific task. The primary input/output buses are AGP, PCI, ATA, SCSI, Firewire, and USB. In addition to these, there are other specialized input and output ports (e.g., the Ethernet, the Internet modem, and the external speaker).

The AGP Bus

The *accelerated graphics port* (AGP) is a dedicated expansion slot on the motherboard of the Macintosh (see Figure C-10). It is a very high speed interface that is designed to communicate with the primary video graphics card controlling the computer monitor you use with your Macintosh. The Macintosh comes standard with one such video card in the AGP slot. The AGP card is also the engine that drives the high-intensity graphics requisite for the proper functioning of Final Cut Express and other applications.

Figure C-10   AGP slot on the Macintosh Minitower motherboard

The AGP port is a relatively new feature of the Macintosh, and it is possible that users with the earliest G4s will not have an AGP port or card. This is no cause for alarm; the AGP is not required for Final Cut Express to function correctly, although it will deliver improved performance and flexibility. Mac OS 10.2 is optimized to offer massive performance increases based on the presence of the AGP slot and video card. It should be noted that many video cards are not AGP cards and that such cards will not fit in the AGP slot. Attempts to make them fit will damage the card, the motherboard, or both. Make sure you are buying the appropriate card for your needs when shopping for a new video card for a second monitor.

The PCI Bus

The second bus is the *peripheral component interconnect* (PCI) bus. These are the expansion slots lined up next to the AGP slot on the motherboard (see Figure C-11). Different models of the Macintosh include different numbers of PCI slots, from an all-time high of six slots in the old Power Mac 9500/9600 to four slots in the present-day model. PCI slots are one of the most useful items on the Macintosh motherboard because they allow the user to easily install a completely customizable set of input and output devices, such as SCSI and ATA expansion cards, extra video cards for multiple monitor support, and a host of other

Figure C-11   PCI slots on the Macintosh Minitower motherboard

third-party items such as professional audio cards and video capture cards, the list of which grows by the hour.

One of the most appealing things about the AGP and PCI buses is that, in contrast to their counterparts on the PC side, they are completely plug-and-play compatible. This means that although you may have to install a software driver of some kind, you do not have to worry about hardware conflicts and addresses as you would with a PC. The Macintosh hardware and software is able to locate and work with AGP and PCI expansion cards with no fuss, provided the proper software drivers are installed. PC users who discover this are usually amazed at the ease of installation they encounter in the Macintosh, compared with the nightmare of IRQ settings and hardware conflicts of other operating softwares.

If the Macintosh was purchased from Apple with a SCSI drive system installed, one of the PCI slots will be occupied by the SCSI card. Since the Macintosh no longer comes with a SCSI interface, a PCI slot and SCSI card are necessary to use SCSI devices. Once again, installing and utilizing a SCSI card is painlessly simple. Most SCSI cards can service SCSI drives inside the Macintosh as well as external SCSI devices simultaneously, making for a uniquely flexible solution. And the SCSI standard is not limited to drives. Items such as scanners, archival data tape backup units, and CD or DVD burners are all available with SCSI connectivity.

ATA expansion cards are also available that allow users to add more than the previously stated limit of two ATA drives of some Macintoshes. If you are not the owner of a

Mirrored Drive Door Minitower, which contains an extra ATA bus, an inexpensive ATA controller PCI expansion card adds two more ATA buses to the Macintosh. This would allow you to install up to four more ATA drives internally, conveniently filling up the remaining four drive slots inside the Mac. ATA expansion cards are very inexpensive compared with SCSI cards and may prove the best expansion alternative for low-end users looking for more internal drive capacity. In addition, ATA 133 PCI controller cards will enable you to use ATA drives with capacities larger than 136 GB, which is the limit for ATA drives running off the stock ATA bus.

Beyond the SCSI and ATA expansion possibilities lies a range of third-party cards, each of which performs a specific task. Extra video cards for multiple monitor support are inexpensive and painless, most of them not even requiring the installation of software drivers. Both the AGP and PCI slots are situated so that the connector side of the card installed in the slot will peek out of the rear of the machine, making connections to computer monitors and external hard drives a snap.

The ATA Bus

The ATA bus is a dedicated bus that sits directly on the motherboard of the Macintosh. Unlike a SCSI bus, which is a card that requires a PCI slot, the ATA bus is already connected directly to the processor and is hardwired to the motherboard. It allows the connection of a total of four ATA devices, which can be hard drives or anything else that uses an ATA interface. On Macintoshes that were not purchased from Apple with the SCSI option, one of the two devices will already be in place, that being the stock start-up ATA drive. Macintoshes purchased with the SCSI option are likely to have no ATA drives preinstalled on this bus.

As stated before, there are two ATA buses included with every Macintosh motherboard. One (the ATAPI bus) is dedicated to the CD/DVD burner/player and an optional Iomega Zip drive located in the front panel of the Macintosh. Although it is technically possible to remove these and replace them with hard drives, this is not generally recommended. It would be rather counterproductive to run a Macintosh in the 21st century without a CD or DVD drive, since this is how the bulk of software is installed. As for the Iomega Zip drive bay, it is narrow in the extreme, and getting a drive to fit comfortably in that space is difficult even for a professional. For more internal drives, consider an expansion card, or look into the external options.

With the introduction of the Mirrored Drive Door Minitower G4s in the summer of 2002, a second CD/DVD drive bay was included, allowing the user to install a second optical drive. This makes it easy to burn copies of one CD or DVD onto another CD or DVD. To do this, one simply installs the optical drive and connects it to one of the extra ATA addresses available. As stated earlier in this appendix, the newer Mirrored Drive Door Minitowers come with three ATA buses rather than two. One is dedicated to the CD/DVD burner that comes stock, leaving two free ATA buses, which can hold two devices each. If the start-up drive occupies one of those addresses, the Minitower could take three more devices, which could be hard drives or a second optical drive.

Each ATA bus requires that the two devices on each bus have distinct addresses. One address is called the Master and the other the Slave. There are two different ways that the addresses are assigned to the devices. In pre-2002 Macs, there is no difference in the inter-action between the Master and Slave addresses, and it makes no difference which device is which. This is simply a way for the Macintosh to differentiate between the two devices on the bus. If there is only one drive on the ATA bus, it can be either Master or Slave, but if there are two, they cannot both be Master or Slave. The determination of this address is set with small plastic jumpers, based on the drive manufacturer's conventions. These are usually printed on the side of the hard drive itself for convenience.

As of the release of the 2002 Mirrored Drive Door Macs, Apple uses a mode called *cable select*. All ATA hard drives have their jumpers set for cable select, rather than Master or Slave. Then the position of the drive on the ATA cable determines its address. One must be careful, though, because cable select requires a specific type of ATA cable as well as the special jumper settings. Make sure you use the ATA cables provided by Apple and your computer to avoid damaging your equipment.

The Firewire Bus

The third type of bus included in the Macintosh is the Firewire bus, a high-speed input/output port that is the basis for our whole system of Firewire DV editing. It con-nects the Macintosh with DV cameras, decks, DV converters, Firewire drives, CD burners, and potentially any other device that also has a Firewire connection. The Firewire bus has two separate ports, located on the back of the Macintosh, to communicate with any exter-nal devices you connect to it. A wide range of devices can be connected at once, regardless of their function. You can have a DV deck, a Firewire hard drive, a scanner, and a remov-able drive all connected at once without fear of failure for any of them. Hubs are also avail-able that allow the user to connect devices to a central breakout box rather than stringing them together in a chain.

Firewire devices can be connected in a daisy chain of up to 63 devices, any of which can be connected or disconnected without powering down the computer or device (making them hot-swappable). They do not require special addresses or IDs and can usually be used by the system without the installation of software drivers. Even so, to prevent corruption, care must be taken that the Macintosh is aware that the drive is going to be disconnected. Simply dismounting the drive by dragging it to the Trash on the Desktop will make it safe for disconnecting.

Because there are two types of Firewire connectors, care must be taken in selecting the proper cable for use. There is a 6-pin connector, known as a bus-powered connector, and a 4-pin connector. This makes three possible cables: a 6-pin–6-pin cable, a 4-pin–6-pin cable, and a 4-pin–4-pin cable. The connectors on the Macintosh are of the 6-pin variety. Most deck and camera jacks are of the 4-pin variety, so unless your Macintosh comes packaged with the proper 4-pin–6-pin cable, you may need to obtain one. Many CD burners and other devices such as Firewire hard drives utilize the 6-pin connector, so check to make sure you have the correct one before attaching equipment.

The bus-powered 6-pin connector enables you to pass electrical power to Firewire devices that can accept it, meaning that in some cases you may not need to plug a device to a wall AC circuit. This feature is relatively rare and is almost exclusively the domain of pocket-sized portable Firewire drives. Make certain that any device you own can function with bus power before you rely on it.

As of 2003, Macintoshes come with the Firewire 800 bus, rather than just the previous Firewire 400 bus. There is no need for concern; the IEEE 1394b specification includes the 400 specification, so your legacy Firewire 400 devices, including cameras, decks and drives, will work just fine. Be aware that Firewire 800 does use a new special connector cable; while it is backward compatible with Firewire 400, you will need to find an appropriate cable/adapter.

The USB Bus

The USB is a slower data rate connection used for input and output of devices that do not require massive streams of data. Your keyboard, mouse, some printers, and graphics tablets are very undemanding devices, and the USB has more than enough bandwidth to handle them. The present standard for the USB maintains a data rate of roughly 1.5 MB per second.

There are a large number of devices on the market that can utilize the USB connection. Floppy disk drives, lower-end SCSI adapters, and even CD burners and audio and video capture devices have been designed for the USB interface. Like the Firewire bus, USB can carry power to a device. Hubs are also available in both powered and unpowered varieties. Some devices, such as printers, that do not actually use the power from the USB connection still require a powered connection, so be careful to select a powered hub should you be in the market for one. Like Firewire, USB connections are hot-swappable, giving the standard some excellent flexibility compared with the older serial standard that it replaced on the Macintosh. In general, however, if you can get a Firewire device for roughly the same price as a similar USB device, you are better off with the Firewire device every time.

With Macintosh OSX, universal USB drivers are preinstalled with the OS. In many cases, installation of special drivers is unnecessary, and USB devices will work immediately when plugged in. If you do install a third-party USB device, check to see if the manufacturer has developed custom drivers for OSX. Although your USB device will likely work fine without them, custom drivers might enable extra functionality intended by the third-party manufacturer.

Various Other Inputs and Outputs

The remaining connections on the rear of the macintosh are mostly concerned with network connectivity and multimedia access.

Ethernet and Internal Modem

The Ethernet and modem connections that come stock on the Macintosh (see Figure C-12) allow it to communicate with the outside world of other computers and/or the Internet. The software that operates your Ethernet and modem is built into the Mac OS, so networking with a Macintosh is a shockingly simple. To network multiple Macintoshes, simply connect them together either directly or through an Ethernet hub/router/switch, using a Cat-5 Ethernet cable. The built-in modem is also a snap to use, and the initial start-

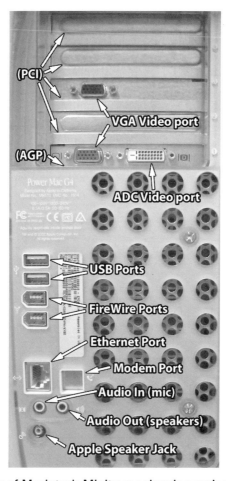

Figure C-12   Rear view of Macintosh Minitower showing various inputs and outputs

up of your Macintosh will walk you through the process of either accessing your present Internet account or starting a new one. And luckily for us, 99% of all viruses propagated throughout the Internet only affect the Windows platform, so connection to the greater world can be accomplished with a lot more confidence.

Apple Pro Speaker Out and Headphone Out

Unlike with most PCs, a high-quality 16-bit sound card is built into the motherboard of every Macintosh, allowing you to run excellent stereo-quality audio out to speakers from your system. As with the Ethernet and modem connections, the sound is controlled entirely by the Mac OS software and requires no extra configuration for audio output. The Apple Pro Speaker connector, despite its appearance, is not a stereo mini one-eighth-inch connector. The port labeled with the speaker should only be used with Apple Pro speaker sets. If you wish to connect a standard multimedia speaker set to the Macintosh, simply plug its one-eighth-inch stereo mini jack into the headphone jack and get back to work!

Checking the Pieces: The Apple System Profiler

Although there are an infinite number of other items that you may have installed with your system, the list at the beginning of this appendix states the bare minimum for bulletproof performance. Although you may have purchased your system preconfigured as an out-of-the-box editing solution, you should still take a moment to check through the process of installation, as detailed hereafter, to make sure that your system is optimized and prepared for editing.

To check on almost everything relating to your Macintosh's hardware and software, access the Apple System Profiler (see Figure C-13). In Macintosh OSX, the Apple System Profiler is hidden away in the Utilities folder of the Applications folder. The Apple System Profiler is a little application that gives the hardware and software status of your entire system at the moment. It is an excellent tool for quickly checking whether a device is present and doing what it should be doing.

The first tab of the Apple System Profiler shows the System Profile. It describes the version of the currently loaded system software, the start-up drive and its bus and address, the amount of installed RAM and its distribution amongst the RAM slots, etc. It describes the major areas of your system all on one tab.

The second tab, Devices and Volumes, is a detailed map of all hardware components currently connected to your system (see Figure C-14). Each bus is represented, along with a hierarchical chart of what is connected to each bus and the settings, if any, of the device or volume at the location.

The next two tabs give a detailed listing of all the Frameworks and Extensions in your Macintosh OSX System. Frameworks and Extensions are special collections of files that drive the operating system's components, many of which are installed with third-party soft-

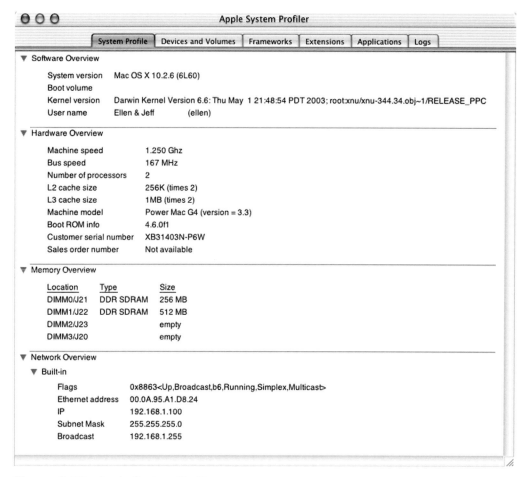

Figure C-13   Apple System Profiler

ware and hardware. The Applications tab displays every application program on your system. This can include many smaller applications that are included in the installed package of larger application sets. In general, you should stay out of your Mac OSX System folder and allow it to keep its own house clean. The usefulness of the Apple System Profiler is that if you do run into trouble at some point down the line, you will be able to evaluate what software is installed to root out the issue.

In addition to being informative to the user, the Apple System Profiler is an invaluable tool for technical support or long-distance troubleshooting. You can save a copy of your

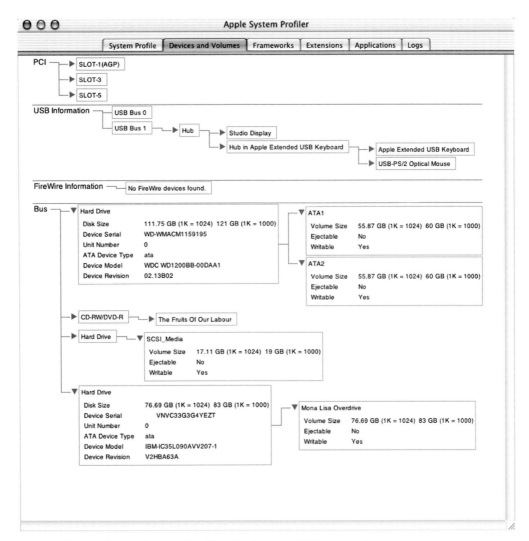

Figure C-14   Apple System Profiler, Devices and Volumes tab

Apple System Profiler as a report to print out or e-mail to a troubleshooter, eliminating the need for the troubleshooter to be present to look at your system. Simply glancing through the Apple System Profiler and looking for known issues can solve many problems, both hardware and software.

Appendix D
Assorted Tips and Tricks

Regular Operating System Maintenance

Your Macintosh is a computer, and computers, like cats, tend to bite you when you refuse to pay attention to them. No matter how much buzz you hear about systems that never have to be shut down and that never fail, you just know that your experience will not be like that. You are correct—it won't be, unless you regularly follow some maintenance procedures to make sure the computer is keeping its nose clean.

But what maintenance is proper and when should you do it? Apple's own resources are relatively vague about the periodic maintenance techniques that will keep the whole system happy. Partially, this is because the Mac OS does many of the tasks. Mac OSX is built on a UNIX system that is programmed to clean up after itself periodically. That UNIX core gives it the ability to repair and maintain itself to a limited degree. It also hides many of the files that are doing a lot of the work, so that you can't "see" them in the GUI (the graphical user interface, the "desktop" and windows you use) even if you could figure out what to do with them in the first place (the short answer is absolutely nothing). To make matters more confusing, OSX uses file permissions, essentially allowing only certain users access to certain files.

Is there anything you can to do to keep your system happy? Yes, you still have to do a regular maintenance routine to keep things in order. The good news is that this is very simple and that much of it can be automated, except in extreme situations. What follows is a good system to follow on a weekly basis to make your editor bulletproof, or at least easy to restore in case disaster strikes.

Repair Permissions

UNIX ushers in a whole new idea for old-school Mac users: permissions. With UNIX, all files and folders have access permissions determining whether a user can read and/or modify a file or folder. This is very secure and is one of the reasons that multiuser logins in OSX work. Unfortunately, this can be confusing for the user who is trying to clean up their system or improve performance. A "user" isn't always your weird friend who accesses the same machine you do. In fact, the operating system itself is a user. A whole host of users and groups is acting in the background to make sure that any part of the system that needs access to any file or folder can get it when necessary.

Unfortunately for us, these permissions are largely transparent. When permissions are set incorrectly or are corrupt, the machine doesn't die, it just gets weird. It may begin to operate very slowly. You may hear your hard drive start spinning at top speed when the machine is doing nothing. You may suddenly be locked out of hard drive directories or be unable to start certain applications, and then tomorrow have access to them again. Most importantly, your machine will slow down dramatically.

To avoid this, you should periodically repair permissions. Go to the Utilities folder in the Applications folder on your System drive. Locate and start up the Disk Utility application. On the left, select your Mac OSX system partition (where the System and the User folder are located), click the First Aid tab, and choose Repair Disk Permissions (see Figure D-1). You can repair permissions only on the partition you are booted from, and only if it is a true Mac OSX boot partition. After initiating a repair-permissions action, get some coffee, walk the dog—this process takes a long time (10 to 15 minutes, give or take). Repeat it until you are only getting the initial repair report that ends in "New permissions are

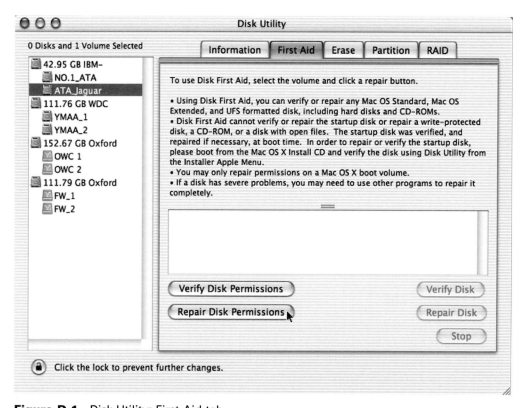

Figure D-1 Disk Utility: First Aid tab

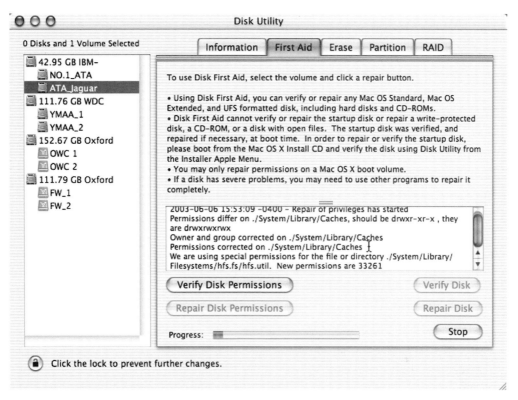

Figure D-2   Permissions running

33261," followed by the date (see Figure D-2); this will always appear, even if there is nothing wrong with the permissions on the partition.

Obviously, you can't repair permissions on an OS 9—only or nonsystem partition, since permissions affected by this tool only exist on a Mac OSX partition. Although files on removable and other drives in your machine can have permissions, the repair-permissions action works *only* on Apple-installed or—configured files; it doesn't touch files or folders it didn't create, so you don't have to worry about it messing up permissions of your personal stuff.

As a side note, it is a good idea to eliminate the option of permissions on extra media volumes you are using for storage rather than system/applications (don't do this to *any* volume or partition that has a Mac OSX system installed—only to media and scratch disk volumes). You can easily accomplish this by selecting a volume or partition and hitting Command-I, for Get Info. Open the Ownership and Permissions tab, and look to the bottom for the "Ignore Ownership on this volume" check box. Check it, and now all files created there will always be read-and-write accessible to anyone. This is particularly important for Firewire hard drives that you may be using on several different systems with different users accessing the same media.

Repair permissions at least once a week if you use your machine a lot (more than 5 hours per day). You will likely see a tremendous speed boost the first time you do this, and that speed will stay consistent if you regularly repair them. It's also a good idea to repair them anytime you install any applications, since apparently that's frequently a time when permissions get misassigned. Either way, you cannot do damage repairing permissions, so once a week is a good idea.

Single User Mode

The way the Mac OSX file system works, you can't run any sort of disk utility on a disk partition while booted up to that partition. If you open up Disk Utility, which we just used, your drives and partitions are listed on the left side of the window. If you select your Mac OSX boot partition from the list and then click the First Aid tab, you'll see that the Verify Disk and Repair Disk buttons are grayed. Although you can use Verify Disk and Repair Disk for any partitions or volumes that are not the current boot partition, you can't repair a partition you are running from. That makes fixing disk problems difficult, if not impossible, when you only have one boot partition with both OSX and OS 9 installed there. Booting from a CD to repair disks is so painfully slow with OSX that there must be a better way.

Of course there is. Apple allows you to enter a mode called Single User Mode. Restart your machine and as soon as you hear the "bong," hold down the Command-S keys. Continue holding them down until you see some rather obnoxious-looking old ASCII text go streaming down the screen, and then release the keys. This text means the Macintosh is booted up outside the Mac OSX GUI and can directly perform file system repairs. Once you get to a cursor prompt (a solid white box that doesn't blink), type in the following without quotes: "fsck –y" (note the blank space before the " –y"). All this means in code is "File System Check; yes, repair any problems you find." It will immediately start running through your boot partition, looking for and correcting any problems. This can take a while; the Mac OSX file system has tens of thousands of files.

When it is finished checking the disk, it will give you a one-line report. If it found problems, it will state, "Disk X has been modified." If no problems were found, it will state, "Disk X appears to be OK." If you get the ". . . modified" statement, run "fsck –y" again repeatedly until you get the ". . . OK" statement. I have seen this process take up to four times to repeat in a system with serious problems.

When you get the ". . . OK" message, type (without quotes) "Reboot –n" (see Figure D-3). This will restart your machine (the "–n" tells the system not to perform a certain memory operation) and return you to the User GUI you know and love. Perform this once a week or whenever you smell trouble. It can't hurt you and it might help catch a problem before the problem catches you.

```
standard timeslicing quantum is 10000 us
vm_page_bootstrap: 189430 free pages
mig_table_max_displ = 64
COLOR video console at 0xa4008000 (1280x1024x8)
IOKit Component Version 6.6:
Thu May  1 21:45:00 PDT 2003; root(rcbuilder):RELEASE_PPC/iokit/RELEASE
_cppInit done
IODeviceTreeSupport done
Recording startup extensions.
Copyright (c) 1932, 1936, 1989, 1991, 1993
           The Regents of the University of California. All rights reserved.

using 1966 buffer headers and 1966 cluster IO buffer headers
USBF: 27.975 [0x244c000] USB Generic Hub @ 1 (0x9)
USBF: 27.975 [0x244c000] USB Generic Hub @ 1 (0x8)
Local FireWire GUID = 0xa27ff:0xfeda5de8
USBF: 28.852 [0x250ba00] USB Generic Hub @ 2 (0x100000)
devfs enabled
IOKitBSDInit
From path: "/pci@f2000000/pci-bridge@d/mac-io@7/ata-4@1f000/@0:10,\mach_kernel', Waiting on <dict
ID="0"><key>IOPathMatch</key><string ID="1">IODeviceTree:/pci@f2000000/pci-bridge@d/mac_io@7/ata-
4@1f000/@0:10</string></dict>
USBF:  29.122 [0x250bc00] USB Generic Hub @ 2 (0x1100000)
Got boot device - IOService:/Core99PE/pci@f2000000/AppleMacRiscPCI/pci-bridge@0/IOPCI2PCIBridge/
mac-io@7/KeyLargo/ata-4@1f000/KeyLargoATA/ATADeviceNub@0/IOATABlockStorageDriver/IOATABlockStorageDevice/
IOBlockStorageDriver/IBM-DTLA-307045 Media/IOApplePartitioinScheme/NO.2_ATA@10
BSD root: disk1s10, major 14, minor 21
devfs on /dev
USBF: 33.470 AppleUSBKeyboard[0x2423800]::start USB Generic Keyboard@3 (0x1100000)
Jun 6 11:08:49 mach_init[2]: Started with uid=0
Fri Jun 6 11:08:49 EDT 2003
Singleuser boot -- fsck not done
Root device is mounted read_only
If you want to make modifications to files,
run '/sbin/fsck -y' first and then '/sbin/mount -uw /'
sh-2.05a# fsck -y
**/dev/rdisk1s10
** Root file system
** Checking HFS Plus volume.
** Checking Extgents Overflow file.
** Checking Catalog file.
** Checking multi-linked files.
** Checking Catalog hierarchy.
** Checking volume bitmap.
** Checking volume information.
** The volume ATA_Jaguar appears to be OK.
sh-2.05a# reboot -n
```

Figure D-3   Single User Mode: "fsck –y," then "reboot –n"

When Single User Mode Doesn't Fix It

On rare occasions, your system may be so completely messed up that "fsck –y" won't clear the problem even after repeated doses. In that case, get out your Mac OSX installer CD and boot up from it in the time-honored method of restarting and holding down the C key. When you have booted to the Apple CD, look under the Apple menu, and access the Run Disk Utility option. When Disk Utility opens, access the First Aid tab and run Repair Disk and Repair Disk Permissions for all volumes and partitions until they come clean (see Figure D-4). Then reboot and see if the problems have cleared up.

There have been rare instances where even running Repair Disk while booted from the Apple CD did not clear up serious problems. On such occasions, it may be necessary to invest in some form of third-party disk maintenance software. Alsoft's DiskWarrior is a great example (see Figure D-5); it can rebuild a damaged disk directory that even Apple's tools can't correct. I have seen it pull both Mac OSX boot partitions and Firewire drive partitions back from the dead when no other software tools could rescue them.

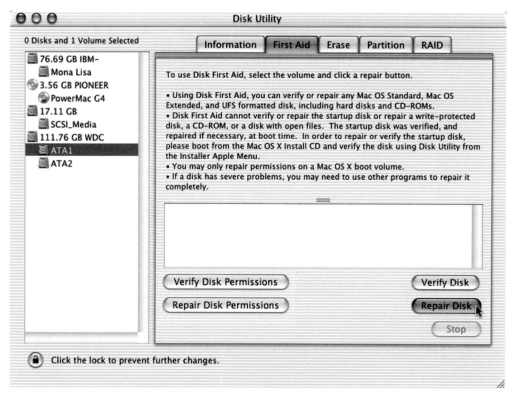

Figure D-4 Running Disk Utility from the installer CD

Cleaning House

UNIX is unique in that it performs its own system maintenance on a regular basis without prompting. Although it isn't going to fix any disk-related trouble for you, it does do things like dump temporary cache files and logs that can get bloated when the system doesn't throw them out as it should. But there's a catch, of course. UNIX only performs these activities in the wee hours of the morning (when it assumes all the IT people are home and no one needs the processor or the files it will be doctoring). There are daily, weekly, and monthly tasks that UNIX schedules for these early-morning hours.

Now, many folks, especially those from pre-OSX days, shut their systems down when they are finished working. Mac OS 9 liked a regular reboot anyway, and not everyone is willing to leave a machine on 24 hours a day. I'm not going to discuss those merits here; that's your choice as a machine owner. But you have to know that the UNIX autocleaning isn't going to happen if your machine is off or asleep.

There is a way to beat this. Although you could figure out the command-line code to perform these actions, it's easier to find one of the nice shareware apps out there that give you a GUI to accomplish the same thing. Go to the Apple Web site and investigate the Mac OSX page for links to freeware and shareware applications that will perform these

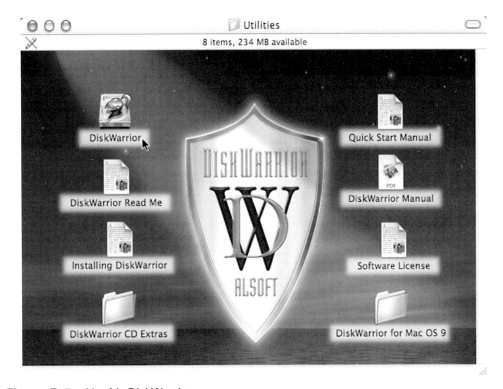

Figure D-5   Alsoft's DiskWarrior

actions for you. In particular, check out MacJanitor from Brian Hill Software, which gives a nice, simple push-button interface to perform each of these UNIX cleanup tasks whenever you feel like it (see Figure D-6). Basically, you can have MacJanitor initiate the UNIX cleanup scripts for you at the push of a button, rather than having to type in code or leave your machine on all the time. And MacJanitor, as of this writing, is free!

Another great tool to check out for regular maintenance is Cache Out X, from NoName Scriptware (see Figure D-7). It performs a bit of maintenance that MacJanitor leaves out. Mac OSX, in normal operation, creates many different "temp" files. These files are intended to be in existence only for the short time they are in use; thus, they are "temp," or temporary. However, sometimes the applications that create them forget to delete them after they are no longer useful. This can lead to unexplainable missing disk space and even constant crashing. Because temp and cache files are often invisible, there is no easy way to find them and delete them.

Applications like Cache Out X (and there are a few others, though not all of them are completely free), simply delete all cache files they find. Generally this requires a restart of the Macintosh, because they also clear out cache and temp files for the operating system itself. This doesn't hurt your system; it may help it in fact, because it can catch and delete corrupt temp files before they become a problem to your system.

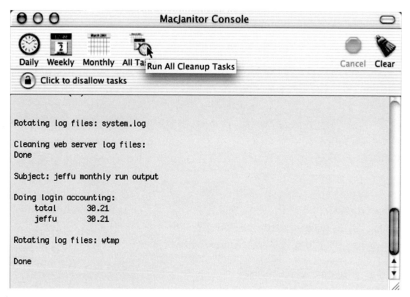

Figure D-6   Brian Hill's MacJanitor

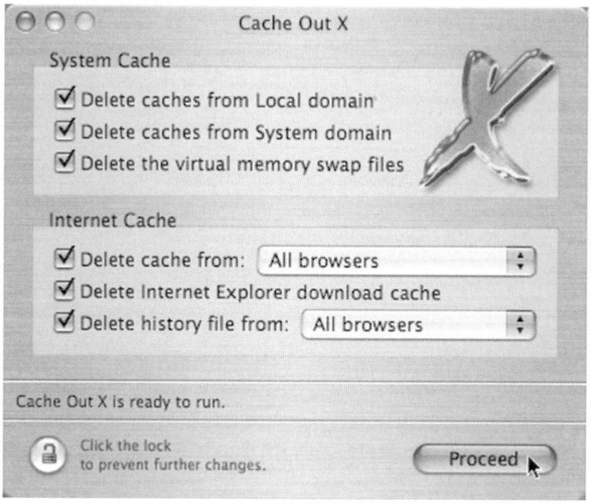

Figure D-7   NoName Scriptware's Cache Out X

Backing Up Your System

Gone are the days of the easily copied System folder. In the previous Mac OS 9, you could back up your system with a single drag-and-drop of a folder. You could create a bootable backup CD by dragging one group of folders into Toast. Mac OSX, on the other hand, has many little invisible files and structures that don't copy over when you drag a volume's contents. This means you can back up normal data with no problems, but you can't just duplicate your drive by dragging and dropping it.

There is, thankfully, at least one way to safely back up a partition these days, and it's one of the coolest shareware applications out there today: Carbon Copy Cloner (see Figure D-8). This application, created by Mike Bombich, clones one partition onto another partition. The clone carries all those invisible files and makes a perfect duplicate of the original partition that is even bootable (although most of your System Preferences get reset; they will need to be visited again when you boot to that cloned partition). It's very handy; you will use it more than once if you try it. If you download this software, pay the man. We have saved many gray hairs with this simple GUI application.

Here's the method you can use for a regular, bulletproof backup. First, run all the previously described maintenance routines, such as repairing permissions and entering Single User Mode. You don't want to clone a start-up partition that has problems! Then, get a small, cheap, dedicated Firewire hard drive and hook it up to your system. Use it with Carbon Copy Cloner for a regular, portable high-speed backup. In the Carbon Copy Cloner Preferences, you can even set the application to schedule this cloning to occur when you are sleeping and to perform sync actions that don't overwrite data you want to keep continuous on your backup drive.

Do this process once a week. If your system ever goes south at a bad time, you can just boot to the backup Firewire drive and get your work done until you can take the time to run Repair Disk and Single User Mode and let them do their jobs. This has allowed me to

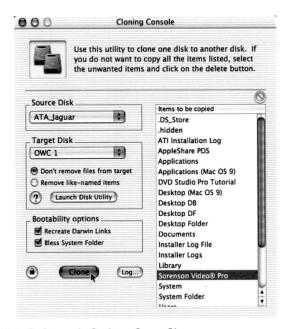

Figure D-8   Bombich Software's Carbon Copy Cloner

hit deadlines with work when one of my machines decided to behave badly at a clutch moment.

If you have several systems, as I do, you can partition this backup Firewire drive such that there is a different backup partition for each computer. When you want to back up a particular computer, plug the Firewire drive in to mount the partitions, start up Carbon Copy Cloner, and set it to clone to the partition that you dedicate to that computer. Since you are cloning to one of several partitions on the drive, you won't affect the other backup partitions. This is a good regimen; it will keep downtime to a minimum even if you do run into problems.

Conclusion

This is not the absolute last word in Mac maintenance, but it's enough to keep your system in good working order and at its best performance level. Do these things consistently and regularly, and even if you do rarely run into problems, at least they won't keep you from working. Schedule your maintenance so that it happens while you are sleeping or otherwise occupied, so that you don't waste half your workday doing something the machine can do by itself just as well. You want to keep the thing working without sacrificing editing time, so be realistic, schedule your maintenance, and then actually do it.

Backing Up to CD-Rs

All new Macintoshes ship with either a CD or DVD burner. You can use a single CD-R optical disk to back up in excess of 600 copies of your project. The bonus is that CDs are far cheaper and more reliable than floppy, Zip, and other removable disks as long as you don't scratch the shiny side. You can use either the Apple Disk Copy application in your Utilities folder or a third-party application such as Roxio's Toast to burn the folder holding the project file. Although Toast costs a little extra, you will find that it is very useful for other functionality, such as burning video CD and DVD disks, as well as audio CDs and data disks.

Regardless of which you choose, simply change the name of the project folder on your Desktop to the date and time each time you burn a copy of it. After doing this a couple of times per edit session, you will end up with an imperishable copy of your project as it was at every stage of your edit. If you need to return to your project at any stage of its development, you can simply pop the CD in, grab the appropriate folder, and launch it. This method, combined with the Autosave Vault feature addressed in the Preferences, is the best way to work for those who don't want to have to redo entire projects after an accident.

Using Apple Disk Copy

To burn a copy of this project folder using Disk Copy, start the Disk Copy application (found in the Utilities folder in the Applications folder of your Macintosh hard drive), and then choose "New>Image from Folder or Volume" from the File drop-down menu (see Figure D-9). In the dialog box, choose Desktop from the Where drop-down tab, and then find and double-click the project folder you want to back up.

This will lead to a new dialog box wherein you are asked to save the disk image you will be burning. Choose Desktop as the location again, select "compressed" from the Image Format choice bar, and click Save. Once the image has been saved, return to the File menu

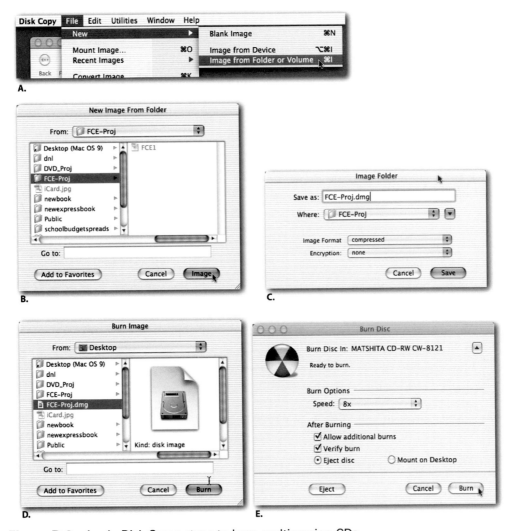

Figure D-9   Apple Disk Copy: steps to burn multisession CDs

and choose Burn Image. In the dialog box, select the image you just created. When you select it and choose OK, you will be given the option of making this a "multisession" CD by selecting Allow Additional Burns. A multisession CD allows you to burn additional images to the CD-R after the first one. If you do not make it a multisession CD, you will have to burn a fresh CD every time you back up your project. If you choose multisession, you can probably fit nearly 600 backups on one 700 MB CD-R!

Using Roxio Toast

If you already own Roxio Toast, you may want to use it instead. The setup for burning is much more streamlined and easy. In addition to the backups you can perform as we describe here, Roxio Toast adds a great deal of flexibility that will come in handy as you start to send your productions out into the world. Toast can burn special VCDs (video compact discs that can play back in most consumer DVD players), audio CDs, and data CDs of all types. It's even a snap to duplicate your homemade DVDs that you produce in iDVD and DVD Studio Pro without having to remaster them from the original projects!

To back up your project folder in Toast, start up the application. Make sure that the Data button is selected in the top of the window, as opposed to the Audio, Copy, and Other buttons (see Figure D-10). When it is running, you will see the Toast window. Grab the project folder off of the Desktop and drop it into this window.

A CD will appear in the window. Its name will be whatever the name of the folder was. If you want to change this name—say, to the date and time of the burn—just single-click this name and change it. As a last step, click the triangle to see the contents of the CD. Select the file named .DS_Store and click the Remove button at the bottom of the window. This file will cause verification errors after the burn is complete.

Once you have this set, insert a blank CD-R. Click the Record button. After a moment, you will enter a final dialog box in which you select the speed and tell Toast how to burn the CD. Generally, burning at a speed other than the fastest possible leads to fewer coasters; waste a few extra seconds, and you may end up with fewer coasters. Select Make Session rather than Make Disk to make this a multisession CD, as described in the previous section.

When you choose Make Session, the burn will begin. After it is complete, make sure you verify the disk. You want to know if there is any chance of corrupted data on the disk. A backup CD isn't worth much if the data can't be used! After the verification, hit Eject, and your backup is complete!

Vectors and Bitmaps: A Primer

To understand the problem of integrating Photoshop's unique shading, texturing, and contouring layer effects into Final Cut Express, we need to understand a little about the difference between vector-based and bitmap-based graphics. Vector-based is from Mars,

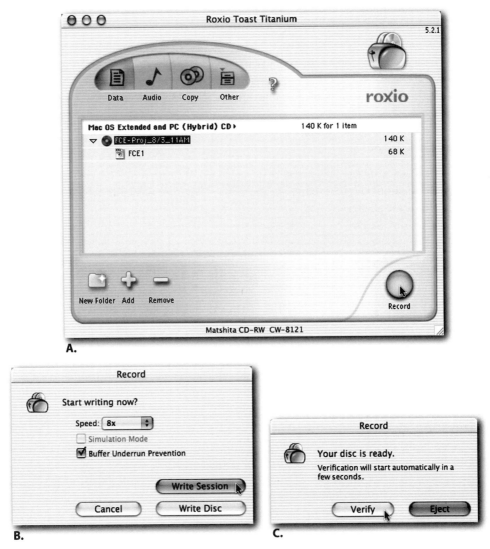

Figure D-10   Roxio's Toast: steps to burn multisession CDs

bitmap-based is from Venus, and you are sitting here on Earth. With the exception of a few rare interesting examples, applications cannot deal directly with both types of graphics, because they measure and plot space in a distinctly different way. The vector-based method describes the world in a series of geometric shapes, since all complex shapes, like the human body, can be broken down into many smaller, less complex shapes. The bitmap method, on the other hand, is an atomic model, based on the earlier described pixels, in which image matter is composed of an exact number of indivisible individually colored dots.

These two methods of generating an image are at loggerheads. There is no such thing as a single reducible geometric shape. As your high school geometry teacher might have drilled into you, "A point is not a shape." Shapes are possible between points. With a vector-based graphic, you have a point A and a point B. To describe a simple shape such as a line, all you have to know is that it is the shortest distance between A and B. To make things more complex, just add another point, or vector, C, and now you've got a triangle. The more vectors you add, the more complex the shapes get, until at some point you aren't looking at geometry, you're looking at images.

If you look around at naturally occurring shapes, it's difficult to escape the notion that vector geometry is a natural science, as well as a thoroughly artificial one. Infinitely thin lines and small points aren't physically possible, but nature does generate uncannily geometric patterns. Philosophical pondering aside, it is important to note that vector geometry is an exceptional way of creating computer graphics, one that allows a lot of flexibility and efficiency in adapting shapes in such applications as Adobe Photoshop and Illustrator.

Geometric shapes do not exist in the bitmap universe. Neither does empty space, which in a vector space would be an area with no points. This is the primary difference between the bitmap and the vector. With a bitmap image, each space of the image is occupied by a pixel. The color of that pixel determines what you see in that section of the image. The larger the number of pixels squeezed into an image, the higher the detail (resolution) of the image, since there will be more opportunities for pixels to change color over a distance.

But that is the key; no matter what color the pixels are, they are there, completely filling the image. Vector images, on the other hand, are shapes created from points in an empty space. You see a geometric shape because it has an inside and an outside. A bitmap has no outside, unless you go outside the image file entirely. Vector-based images tend to get ridiculously complicated once you get to the level of detail we think looks acceptable for broadcast video. The simplicity of describing images with geometric shapes isn't really worth much when you have to express a geometric shape with 6,000,000,000,000,000,000,000,000 different vectors. That could take years just to express one frame of video.

But in the bitmapped view, there is no such thing as empty space. A complicated shape takes exactly as much information to record as a simple one. The vector-based model has to record all the different points in the shapes it is describing, making simple shapes easier to record and complicated ones difficult. A bitmapped image uses exactly the same amount of information to record both.

The problem with vector-based images for video should be obvious, and in fact, it is only used in multimedia-delivered content such as Macromedia Flash files, where the limit of image complexity is more easily controlled. The problem with bitmap as a system is that if you don't have enough pixels squeezed into the image—in other words, the resolution—you get less and less detail. It takes a lot of resolution, or pixels per inch, to generate a respectable bitmap image.

Thus, video usually uses bitmapped frames, since it is easier to describe the wildly fluctuating colors and luminance levels using individual pixels rather than vectors, which are better at describing fairly continuous values.

Using the Boris Title 3D Text Generator

Although it is not an Apple Final Cut Express text generator per se, the Boris Title 3D Text Generator comes free, bundled with your Final Cut Express license. Its functionality and quality far exceed that of the standard text generator that ships with Final Cut Express. It offers many more controls and text customization options than are available with the standard title generators found in Final Cut Express.

Because it is a bundled product, you do have to specify that you want it installed when you install the Final Cut Express application itself. If you did not do this, get out your installer CD and choose install. You will be offered extra install options for Boris Calligraphy (which is the umbrella name for the Title 3D and Title Crawl generators) as well as the CGM FX Script DVEs (another nice bundle that we will not cover here but that offers interesting functionality and control in the video filters). You do not have to reinstall Final Cut Express to install the Boris plug-ins; simply check the Boris Calligraphy box and install. Make sure to hit the Boris FX Web site for updates and freebies to augment the bundle that comes with Final Cut Express.

To generate a text clip using the Boris Title 3D Text Generator, go to the Effects tab of the Browser window. Double-click and open the bin named Video Generators. Locate the generator clip named Title 3D and drag it to the Viewer window (see Figure D-11). You can also load this generator into the Viewer window by clicking the Effects drop-down button at the bottom right corner of the Viewer and selecting Title 3D.

When you do this, the Viewer window loads the Title 3D generator as a clip. Although it's easy to think of the text generator as an effect, titlers, slugs (black footage), and color bars, which are available in the Effects tab, all belong to a family of effects called *generators*. They provide standard shapes, colors, and patterns for use in your production that are always available and customizable. Such generators always act as clips and as such must be loaded into the Viewer and edited into a sequence just like a clip, rather than being applied to clips, as other effects from the Effects tab are.

Arranging the Title 3D Clip Using the Control Tab

The way that the Boris Title 3D generator operates in conjunction with the Viewer window can be a little confusing at first. The first time you access it from the Effects tab or the Effects drop-down tab in the Viewer window, its text customization box will automatically open. After the text customization box has loaded the first time, you will have to access it through the Controls tab in the Viewer window to make changes. The first time that you load it, you should be looking at a window with a text entry area and some formatting tools in the bottom of the window.

If you are not seeing this, you may need to manually open the text customization box. With the Boris Title 3D generator loaded into the Viewer window, click the Controls tab. At the top of the tab you will see a box labeled "Title 3D: Click for Options."

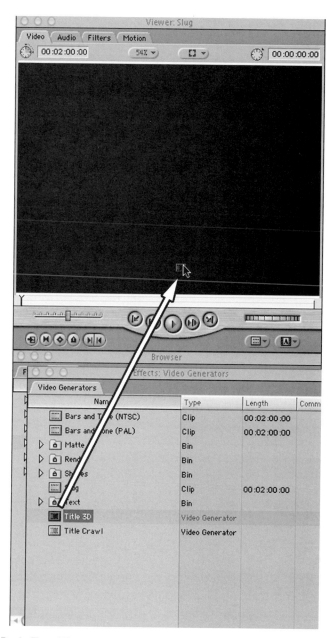

Figure D-11   Boris Text 3D generator: moving it from the Effects tab to the Viewer

Clicking this box will lead you to the text customization box, where you'll enter text (see Figure D-12). It is this interface that you use to define exactly how the text will look, right down to the drop shadows.

First we need to add a bit of text to the text entry field to see what we are doing. The Title 3D is a very flexible tool with a huge feature set. Although we will not cover every feature, make sure that you read through the accompanying Calligraphy manual for a great quick introduction to all the possibilities. At the top of the box is a field in which to enter your text. Type in the words "Boris Text." Hitting the Return key after your text entry would be a mistake here, since it would just result in a hard return line break in the text field. The text entry field acts just like any word processor; any typing will register in the text field.

Also, just as with any word processor, after typing text in, you must select the text to change any of its style formatting. If you apply a text formatting or style change and do not see that change reflected in your text, make sure you selected the text first. Why is this so? One of the nice things about the Boris text generator is that you can apply different formatting to individual items of text in the field, something that is difficult, if not impossible, to do with other text generators. For instance, you could give only some of the letters a drop shadow or give each letter a different color.

On the far left-hand side of the interface box, you will see five tabs that correspond to each of the areas of text customization available to you (see Figure D-13). They are, from top to bottom, Text Formatting, Wrapping, Fill, Edge, and Drop Shadow. You don't have to visit each one of these tabs if you don't want to change the settings you have already, but you are encouraged to spend some time investigating the possible variations. In particular, the Edge and Drop Shadow tabs allow you to store up to five presets you regularly access. In addition to this, once you get text looking just right, you can save the settings as presets in the Style Palette. For more details on fully exercising the Style Palette, as well as infor-

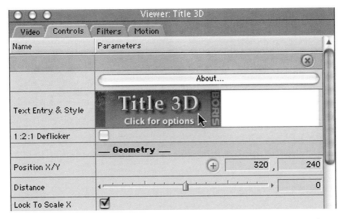

Figure D-12   Double-clicking the Title 3D box in the Viewer to open the text customization window

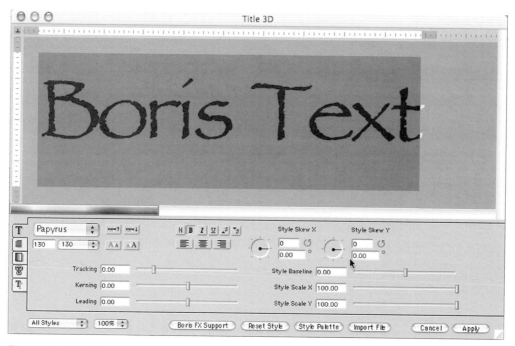

Figure D-13   The first tab in the text customization box

mation on where you can get tons of free styles, consult the Boris FX Web site and look for Freebies.

Make sure the text in the text entry field is selected, then click on the Font tab (symbolized by the letter T), and choose an interesting font. If you want to browse the fonts and see how your text will look using various fonts, click one of the two "menu tabs" next to the font drop-down menu. Clicking one of these buttons changes the font in use to the next one on the font list, either up or down based on which button you hit. Set the Font Size to 130, and notice that there are an "increase" and a "decrease" button for quickly altering the font size. Hit the B for Bold and set Alignment to Center.

The second tab is the Alignment tab (see Figure D-14), and it allows you to organize the text and constrain it to a narrow or wide column. You generally should set this tab for Wrap, with a page width of 500 pixels. This will force the text you enter to have a line break when it reaches the screen width entered into the Page Width field. The value 500 is a good one for the page width field, because this is just a bit narrower than the Title Safe zone.

The next tab, the Fill tab (see Figure D-15), allows you to choose the text color. An interesting option is the ability to use gradient fills for your text, meaning that you can have the color change within the text itself. Choose the Text Fill tab and switch to Gradient to enable this. When you do, a Click to Edit Gradient" box becomes available,

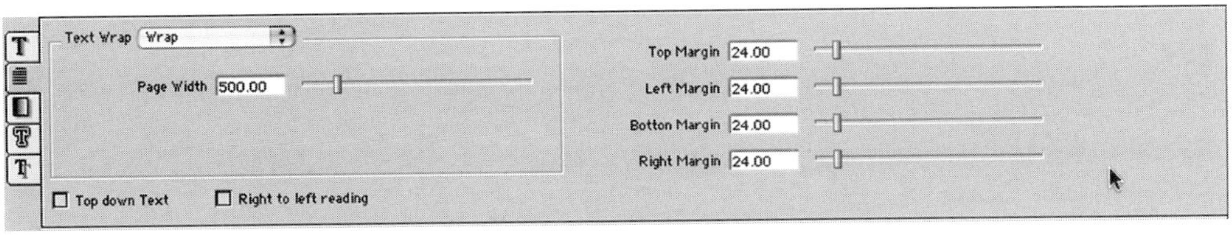

Figure D-14   The Alignment tab

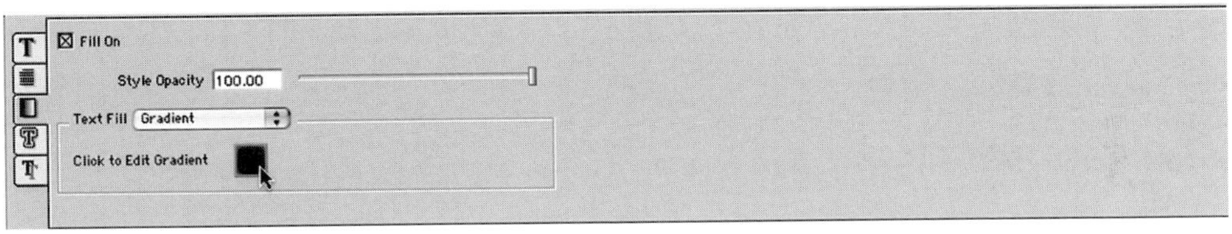

Figure D-15   The Fill tab

allowing you to choose the type and shape of the gradient as well as the colors that the gradient shifts between.

On the Edge tab (see Figure D-16), we find probably the most beautiful and useful styles available in the Calligraphy toolset. In order to put Edge styles to work, you need to check at least one of the check boxes. These check boxes are for presets you keep on the corresponding tab. If you click the Edge2 tab and make adjustments there, the adjustments will stick to the Edge2 tab, even if you don't apply it to any text. To apply the Edge style to your selected text, you need to check the tab's check box.

To see how great and easy the results are, check the Edge1 check box, and then change the Edge Style to Bevel. Change the Position to Inside, meaning that the text beveling will be located inside the text. Because the Bevel effect is a three-dimensional effect, you can also specify which direction the light appears to come from that is illuminating it on the Highlight Angle. Experiment widely with the Edge styles, and you will find that creating complex, beautiful text is quite easy.

We want to add a nice, light drop shadow, so click the fifth tab (see Figure D-17), and, just like the method of enabling the Edge style, click the first check box to enable a preset.

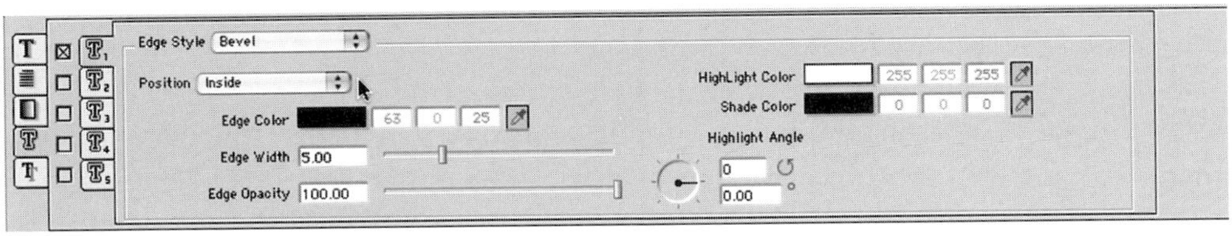

Figure D-16   The Edge tab

Figure D-17   The Drop Shadow tab

Set the Shadow Type of this preset to Drop Shadow, make the Shadow Color relatively dark, and set the Shadow Distance at 10. Keep the Shadow Opacity at 50, but increase the Shadow Softness to 5. Finally, manually drag the Shadow angle around to 45 degrees.

Click the Apply button in the bottom right corner again to apply your text settings. After you have applied them, you will be returned to the Viewer window. Now edit the Boris text clip into your sequence. It will carry alpha channel transparency just like the Final Cut Express Text Generator. If you need to change anything in the Boris Title 3D text clip after editing it into the sequence, simply double-click the text clip, choose the Controls tab, and select the "Click for Options" button to return to the text customization box.

Audio Production and GIGO: First Things First

A huge part of any video project is the audio. Although most people think of visual elements when we talk about video and movies, in reality, anyone in the business will tell you it's far more than 50% audio. Bad audio recording and mixing sticks out like a sore thumb and can ruin an otherwise fantastically shot and edited piece of work. New artists usually discover this sad fact of life after it's too late.

The key to success in video work is understanding and applying an old production term: GIGO—Garbage In, Garbage Out. If you don't start with a suitable recording, chances are that you won't have much luck when the time comes to edit. There's another line to go along with this that many editors use sarcastically: "We'll fix it in postproduction." They are being sarcastic because in most cases, and particularly with audio, you just *can't* fix it in post. The fact is that if you want good clean audio for your productions, you have to start by recording good audio. Although this is not a production book, there are a few tips about things to look out for as you shoot video and record audio. Although some of these suggestions require a little investment in time and money, they will pay for themselves in the long run with quality results and lack of frustration.

Use Professional Microphones

One thing that you can do to instantly improve the quality of your work is to use a professional-quality microphone. Using the onboard mike on a camera is almost a guarantee of recordings full of noise, crackling, and the whirring of camera motors. Within the $100 to $300 range there are quite a few great-sounding mikes you can plug into your camera for a phenomenal increase in quality. Depending on the work you intend to perform, you will be interested in one of two types of microphones.

The first is the lapel, or "lavalier," microphone (see Figure D-18). These are very small microphones that can be pinned to the cast members' clothing. They are great for recording interview and "talking head"—type videos. Because their pickup range is very small, they get very clear, strong recordings of things close to the mike, while "rejecting," or not picking up, annoying noises like environmental noise and ventilation systems such as air conditioners and heaters. If your subjects are going to be mostly stationary and don't mind having a microphone cable threaded through their clothing, the lavalier microphone is usually your best bet.

The second common microphone in video production is the "short shotgun" microphone (see Figure D-19). This microphone is very directional, which means it records sound better from certain directions than others. Shotgun mikes tend to reject sound (and unwanted noise) behind the mike very effectively, allowing you to isolate your subject from the noise generated by the rest of the world. Shotguns generally are so sensitive that they cannot be handheld and require special microphone mounts to be used effectively. But the ability to record clean audio from a distance (up to 15 feet in some circumstances) and get strong, clear audio recordings free of environmental noise makes them the workhorse of the industry.

Figure D-18 Lavalier microphone

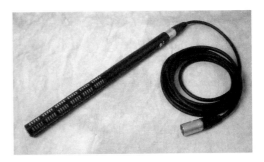

Figure D-19 Short shotgun microphone

You might have access to the inexpensive and more common "dynamic" mike, the mike that your favorite rock star can be seen singing into onstage. But these microphones are rarely suitable for film and video work, with the possible exception of news gathering and documentary work, where the convenience, ruggedness and lack of batteries of the dynamic mike is worth more than the unsightly image of a giant mike head sticking up in front of the camera subject.

Use Decent Headphones

Get a pair of quality headphones that actually cover your ears (Walkman-type light head-phones won't do), and use them to monitor the sound from your camera while you record. Audio recording devices aren't like your ears. We tend to tune out the things that aren't important to us, such as ventilation and other environmental noise. But audio recording devices listen to *everything*, picking up hisses, hums, and everything else in the room. The only way you will hear that these things are intruding on your clean audio tracks is if you listen closely to what is being recorded. Never take this for granted.

Always Record Room Tone

Whenever you record audio in a location, make sure you record a minute or two of just pure silence in the space. Although the idea in recording is to minimize the noise in a loca-tion, a complete lack of sound is just as bad. Every room has a different "tone" or sound characteristic that is based on its size, what the walls are made of, etc. You can tell a lot about a room even with your eyes closed, simply because once you are trained to hear it, your ears can easily detect the size and shape of a space just by the "sound of silence." This "room tone" is critical in cleaning up noisy tracks, since it allows you to chop out sections of an audio clip that may have big noises, such as an airplane or a cough, without leaving an empty vacuum of sound. When you replace the background coughing noises with a little bit of quiet room sound that you intelligently recorded as a backup resource, you will feel very smart indeed!

Plan Ahead

Do a little research and scout the location you are going to record in. Are there things like air conditioner and heater vents, and can they be shut down for the duration of the record-ing? Are there refrigerators or other big, noisy appliances, and can you get permission to turn them off? Are there windows that you can close? How close is the location to streets with loud traffic and, believe it or not, the worst enemy, the random airplane? You can solve 99% of location audio problems by showing up 10 minutes early with a couple of thick blankets and some gaffers tape!

Index